Center for Basque Studies
Occasional Papers Series, No. 20

Basque Pelota

A Ritual, an Aesthetic

Olatz González Abrisketa

Translated by Mariann Vaczi

With a foreword by Joseba Zulaika

Center for Basque Studies
University of Nevada, Reno
Reno, Nevada

This book was published with generous financial support from the Basque government.

Center for Basque Studies
Occasional Papers Series, No. 20
Series Editor: Joseba Zulaika and Cameron J. Watson

Center for Basque Studies
University of Nevada, Reno
Reno, Nevada 89557
http://basque.unr.edu

Copyright © 2012 by the Center for Basque Studies
All rights reserved. Printed in the United States of America.

Cover and Series design © 2012 Jose Luis Agote.
Cover photograph: "Pelota a mano (3)," courtesy of Xosé Ignacio Miguel García (Acasadovento)

Library of Congress Cataloging-in-Publication Data

González Abrisketa, Olatz.
Basque Pelota : a ritual, an aesthetic / Olatz González Abrisketa ; translated by Mariann Vaczi ; with a foreword by Joseba Zulaika.
   p. cm. -- (Occasional papers series ; no. 20.)
Includes bibliographical references and index.
Summary: "This anthropological study considers the sport of Basque pelota and its relationship with Basque history, culture, society, and life"--Provided by publisher.
ISBN 978-1-935709-31-2 (pbk. : alk. paper)
1. Jai alai--History. 2. Basques--Sports. 3. Basques--Rites and ceremonies. 4. Basques--Social life and customs. 5. Sports--Anthropological aspects. I. Title.

GV1017.P4A26 2013
796.33'48--dc23

2012041742

CONTENTS

Foreword by Joseba Zulaika 7

Preface to the English Edition 9

Introduction 15

Part 1
Banka

Basque Pelota: The Most Beautiful of All Games 25

1. The Basques of Pelota 35
2. The Pelota of Basques 51

Part 2
Larzabale

A Ritual That May Lend Unity to a People 73

3. The Control of *Indarra* 79
4. The Fiesta of Pelota 127
5. From *Joko* to *Jolas* 169
6. *Harrizko Herria*: The Village of Stone 185

Part 3
Aldude

An Aesthetic: Play Honestly, the Plaza Is Always Judge 211

7. *Esku*: The Hand as Depository of the Person 213
8. The Ball: Culture Objectified 227
9. The Plaza: The Embodiment of Society 243

Epilogue	281
Glossary	291
Bibliography	301
Index	317

Foreword

Painters, writers, and filmmakers (from Orson Welles to Julio Medem) have turned Basque pelota into a powerful source of images and metaphors. But this vibrant and communitarian game had to wait for Olatz González Abrisketa for a much needed ethnography that would reveal its social and symbolic dimensions. She not only provides historical background and a typology of the various modalities of pelota, but re-creates for us the full cultural context of the traditional fronton games. Her thesis is that pelota constitutes a ritualized action that both stages and repairs social antagonisms by offering a "deep play" that prevents violent conflict. She argues that the game of pelota is an event that implies a paramount cultural transformation for the Basques. By digging into the historic, symbolic, and even mythological roots of the sport, and by describing interconnected webs of meaning in the various domains of social, juridical, bodily, and imaginative experience, this anthropological study shows that the *joko* or "agon" of pelota has a foundational role in culture. The metaphoric extensions of "hand," "pelota," "body," and their relations to activities such as hunting and art are most revealing.

The pelota court or fronton is, in Basque traditional society, the public space par excellence. Hand pelota is the primary pelota game but there are other modalities—including the one with a basket attached to the player's hand and which is internationally known as jai alai ("happy fiesta" in Basque). It refers both to the open-walled fronton arena where the game is played (consisting of the front, back, and left walls, plus the floor), and the game itself. In the United States jai alai became a gaming operation. The goal of the game is to force the opponent to *miss* a return, which in Basque is said to create an *huts* "void" or "error"—*huts* being a pivotal concept in the aesthetics of the void for Basque artists such as Jorge Oteiza and Eduardo Chillida, as well as for traditional folk curers for whom being "empty" was equivalent to being "cured." Scoring is forcing a void. The fan, whose eyes, imagination, strategy, and wishes move with the ball, provides order and intentionality to the ball's erratic trajectory. The viewer replicates the moves in the "empty" field where the fans are trapped with the ball in a game that will deliver failure or success. The fronton becomes a quality space in which imagination and subjectivity can move and project with the ball.

The spectator's desire is constituted in such *play* of "voids." The subject is the throw of the dice that will not eliminate chance. Each point—the event—is evanescent, the result of chance, traceless, its future temporality and existence depending on its happening. The subject of the pelota court is the one that perseveres in the distance between what he wants and the "void" that is offered to him/her in the empty field of the yet-to-come *huts*. It is the fan's function to close this infinite progression, to contain the endless potentialities, and to give shelter to the excess generated by the game. This fronton is the traditional *topos* (field of play) that implicitly teaches citizens their primary categories of action and subjectivity.

Stéphane Mallarmé knew it best: a throw of the dice, a play of cards, a pelota serve will never eliminate chance. That capricious and undefeated goddess will always be there for those who, even in a shipwreck, dare take risks and wager and endure a jai alai. The cosmos is renewed again and again by chance while the subject confronts the dice and is, once again, constituted in a timeless game. Knowing with Plato that man is a puppet in the hands of gods, the player dismisses the links between cause and effect, mocks questions of why and for what, while conspiring against the laws of the universe with all the tricks at his disposal—roulettes, lotteries, cards, rituals, games. And, if he is lucky, he might even discover with Sophocles that the dice of Zeus fall ever luckily. For every pelota serve is new, every throw of dice impartial, everything probability and grace.

Joseba Zulaika

Reno, Nevada, May 2012

Preface to the English Edition

This book was published in Spanish in December 2005. A small publishing house took care of the publication; its owner, Ignacio Uribarri, was one of my most enthusiastic informants during my fieldwork. Ina and his friends took me to all the important games of the hand modality during the five years of my fieldwork (1998–2002). Much of this book was written in his house in Gueñes, where I stayed on various occasions. The publishing house had never published similar texts before, and they have not ever since; its owners, educated entrepreneurs from Bilbao, had waited thirty years for someone to investigate the cultural significance of pelota, a game they adored since their childhood. Although I was neither by gender nor by age the researcher they had in mind, Ina accepted me immediately when his niece Arantxa took me to her house to introduce me to her uncle.

During the past fourteen years, hand pelota has undergone important transformations, mostly provoked by television broadcasting. With a viewership rate of 47 percent at the hand modality finals of 2006 and 2011, the game is living some of its best moments. Pelota remains most popular in small localities; in villages of a population less than two thousand average viewership reaches 75 percent (2006). Nevertheless, the popularity of the recently (March 2011) inaugurated Bizkaia fronton in Bilbao shows that hand pelota has also conquered the cities despite the fact that they were traditionally home to instrument modalities, and that pelota has been a marginal sport in the past few years. The fame of *pelotaris*, the substantial contracts which in some cases reach three thousand euros per game, have significantly regenerated interest in the game among the younger generations. Public policies have also set as their objective the recuperation of the cultural value that pelota enjoyed during most of the twentieth century.

As the hand modality has grown, however, the rest of the modalities have declined; their professional practice has significantly diminished in the last few years. At the end of 2011, the last fronton of professional pala, the Deportivo of Bilbao, closed; the jai alai fronton has been consecutively opened and closed, without being able to consolidate itself. The last open remonte modality fronton, the Galarreta in Hernani, was saved from closure in 2010 due to the intervention of various players who took charge of its management.

As I return to this book eight years later and prepare it for a reader that has no firsthand knowledge of the world of pelota, I see it necessary to explain why I treat these transformations only marginally, and why I neglect the enormous conflicts that the game suffered during the years of my fieldwork (1998–2002). Although I am describing present events, pelota gives an impression of harmony, timelessness, and homogeneity through these pages. I believe that reflecting on this question will help prepare the reader for what this book has to offer.

When I first visited a professional fronton under the guidance of Ina, I saw one of the most memorable games of the recent history of hand pelota: the four-and-a-half championship final between Retegi II and Titín III on December 13, 1997, at the Ogeta fronton of Vitoria-Gasteiz. It is there and then that I decided that the world of pelota would be my object of research. The Geertzian concept of "deep play" made me think of pelota as an object of research, and that particular game convinced me there was something important behind its passions. What makes all these men enjoy this game? What attracts them to the fronton time and time again to watch two or four young men alternatively hit a solid leather ball against a stone wall? The practice of a sport stimulates gathering for the spectacle, and the majority of the men who were applauding had had many balls in their hands during their youth. But why is it precisely this game that conquered the centers of urban spaces in the Basque Country and the neighboring provinces? Why do Basques play this game and not another? What is its specificity? What does it tell us about the Basques? Why do they consider it their "national sport"?

During my fieldwork I encountered a great discrepancy between the ideological and cultural importance of the game on the one hand, and its modest social presence on the other. Pelota did not have the same vibrancy that it seemed to have had years before; nor were the majority of people I met pelota fans. In the Baztan Valley, where I lived between May and October 1999, almost no youngster discussed pelota regularly. In a scarcely populated area where there are at least two frontons in each village center, where a great many different modalities including direct games have survived like nowhere else in the country, the majority of the young people preferred to play soccer or basketball as an organized sport. Almost all had played hand pelota during their childhood; they had even belonged to some pelota club, only to lose interest as adolescents. People would later rediscover pelota, play it informally and almost always with a racquet; but they would not follow professional pelota and they could not be considered *pelotazales*. Despite the fact that it was difficult to find an empty fronton on the weekends, almost all the people who were interested in talking about pelota were either pelotaris, or over the age of fifty.

The appearance of a young man, Mikel Goñi from Baztan, in the professional world of hand pelota did have a positive impact on fandom. Goñi II was at this moment the man who attracted most people to the fronton. They had never seen a pelotari of such strong hits; his presence guaranteed public success in any corner of the Basque Country. Everybody wanted to see Goñi II; in Baztan a televised pelota game did not eclipse a soccer game unless it was a final and the hand modality. The same happened in Gernika (Guernica), home of the jai alai, where I resided from March to May, 2000, and in Iparralde (the northern Basque Country), where *pelotazale* activity is so minor that the hundreds of well-kept frontons have become authentic monuments of an increasingly distant past. Between September and December 2000 I lived in Angelu (Anglet),[1] from where I visited places, and where pelota is ordinarily present only in souvenir shops and in two key areas: the Euskal-Jai fronton where at times they played jai alai, and the trinquet Plaza Berri, where they played hand pelota. These frontons made me reflect on the imaginary of pelota, which became a central theme of reflection during my stays in Buenos Aires, Argentina (March–May, 2001); Havana, Cuba (July–September 2001); and San Francisco and Nevada, United States (July–August 2002).

Despite the discrepancy between the imaginary of pelota and its practice, the professional game was remarkably active in 1998. Generating smaller or greater turnout, you could see hand pelota in Tolosa and

---

1. Editorial note: Many localities in the greater Basque Country are known by—at least—two names, a Basque language name and a Spanish or French name. The Center for Basque Studies prefers Basque place names, with the Spanish or French variants provided in parenthesis at first use. This is the case unless the Spanish or French place name is an actual topic of discussion, in which case the Basque name is given in parenthesis.

jai alai in Gernika on Mondays, and in Bergara on Wednesdays; hand pelota in Eibar, pala in Bilbao and remonte in Hernani on Thursdays; pala in Bilbao and remonte in Iruñea-Pamplona on Saturdays; hand ball in Eibar on Sundays. Almost always organized around the weekly market, the pelota festivals were still numerous (three games of distinctive categories). Nevertheless, the average age of the spectators was sixty. One could count on at least two televised fiesta encounters on Fridays and Saturdays, which may have been played at various other frontons: Ogeta in Vitoria-Gasteiz, Adarraga in Logroño, Atano III in Donostia-San Sebastián, or any other village where they celebrated fiestas. Television broadcasting at these weekend games attracted a more heterogeneous crowd to the fronton, including women and young people.

It was the Asegarce company founded in 1992 that changed the colors of the fronton and the clothing of the pelotaris—which used to be white—to tailor the appearance of the players and the frontons to the demands of televising. Asegarce started out managing all the modalities, but within six years it exclusively dedicated itself to hand pelota. The rest of the modalities did not look good on television because of their velocity, and their audience was geographically more local than that of hand pelota. Hand pelota, however, had a following in all of the Basque provinces including Navarre and even neighboring regions such as La Rioja or parts of Castile. In a few years Asegarce turned the hand pelota into a profitable sports spectacle, which caused another company to emerge and break its monopoly in 1998, just as I started my fieldwork for this book.

Only a month after the famous finals of December 1997, Titín III signed a million-peseta deal with the new company, Aspe. Aspe was financed by the Basque public television network ETB; years later it lost a law suit against Asegarce for unfair competition. Because of irreconcilable disagreements between the two companies, the 1999 hand pelota singles championship split in two: one axis was the Asegarce-Tele 5-Basque Federation, and the other the Aspe-ETB-Spanish Federation. The ETB, which was controlled by the governing Basque Nationalist Party, resuscitated the Spanish Federation, which was officially in charge of organizing the championships—a function Asegarce had appropriated from it years before. There were two champions: Beloki and Eugi, the two best players of the moment, both from Navarre. That year they did not try their skills against each other. They did so the following years and both won a *txapela*. But we will never know who would have won the third one. The relationship between the professional pelota and the Basque Federation has not been smooth, either; the latter was left out of play in 2004 by an association of companies that had previously confronted each other, the LEPM (*Liga de Empresas de Pelota Mano*, League of Hand Pelota Companies). Relations also aggravated between *pelotaris*, referees, and the public. Power games and conflicts continued. Despite all these occurrences, this book describes the unity and nobleness of pelota. Everything unruly that pelota has struggled with since the beginning of this century is reduced to an epilogue. Why?

I was asked this question by the anthropologist Francisco Ferrándiz. In response, I argued that the objective of my research was to understand the imaginary of pelota and the common consciousness that it reveals rather than its historic practice bound by contemporary events. Practice is evident in the descriptions of the game, the narrated events and testimonies; interpretations, however, are articulated not through what pelota is, but how it is thought about, and what role it has in the imaginary construction, hegemonic if you will, of Basque identity. As the anthropologist Lidia Montesinos rightly pointed out to me, it is an imaginary that the book itself reproduces. Her exact words were the following: "Are you aware of the mythopoeic effect of the text?"

I am not quite sure if any anthropological text is free from generating myths; what I would nevertheless like to add is that these types of interpretations fit well with the epistemological apparatus of anthropology. After all, anthropology learns what it does based on two perspectives: *emic* and *etic*, which perhaps we should call intentions. I say intention because I think that they are the strongest of wills in anthropological production, especially if we are talking about the product of a young anthropologist. The author's style, the historical process, and even the observed events remain subordinated to what the natives want to relate, and to what the theoretic tradition framing the work wants to argue.

I have already talked about Ina, one of the key informants of this work. Ina was for me what Muchona was for Victor Turner or Boesoou Erijisi for Maurice Leenhardt. It would be difficult to discern which interpretations in this book are a product of my mind, and which ones are his. Or maybe the mind, as Gregory Bateson says, is extended beyond us.[2] After reading passages of this book, several players told me: "That is

---

2. Bateson, G. *Mind and Nature: A Necessary Unity*.

true, although I have never thought of it like that." The book appears to harmonize well with the spirit of pelota, a spirit that is nevertheless materialized in bodies, spaces, and specific objects. The bodies that pelota moves are those of men: Basques, Navarrese, and Riojans, of all ages in rural areas and above fifty in cities. It is their testimonies that constitute the *emic* intentions of this book.

The *etic* intention arises from two principal sources. First, from what Josetxu Martínez Montoya taught me to love in his classes of symbolic anthropology: Emile Durkheim, Victor Turner, Mary Douglas, Clifford Geertz, and so on. Second, the fascination with the books written by Joseba Zulaika, especially his *Tratado estético-ritual vasco* and *Basque Violence: Metaphor and Sacrament*. A mixture of both titles composes that of this book. I am grateful for their inspiration.

The book is now presented to an entirely new audience, one that is very different from that for which it written for at the beginning. This is a revised and updated version that includes new bibliographical references, and offers complementing descriptions that situate the reader in a world that may be completely foreign. Various parts of the first edition have been deleted, especially the more theoretical passages; at the end of the book we added a small glossary with the native terminology that has no translation, and which are left in their original form. During the work of adapting the text I relied on my translator Mariann Vaczi, editors Cameron J. Watson and Daniel Montero, and editorial assistant Kimberly Daggett. Many thanks to them for their help.

Olatz González Abrisketa
February 19, 2012, Gamiz, Bizkaia

Introduction

Haurrak ikas ezazue   Learn, children,
euskaraz mintzatzen   To speak Basque,
ikas-pilota eta   Play pelota,
oneski dantzatzen   And dance correctly

— *Basque popular song*

Pelota is one of the most significant cultural manifestations for the Basques. Pío Baroja described it as "the Basque game par excellence."[1] While it was already present in some places in Europe in the early Middle Ages, pelota was first documented in the Basque Country in the sixteenth and seventeenth centuries, at the advent of the modern era. It spread through the social fabric during this time and imbued it to such a degree that, by the eighteenth and nineteenth centuries and by then with its own etiquette, it had become—in the words of Wilhelm von Humboldt—"the principal festival of the Basques."[2] By then the game had well-established spatial and temporal boundaries and ignited much male enthusiasm. Men played pelota for both ludic and ceremonial reasons at the very center of towns and villages.

By the end of the nineteenth and the beginning of the twentieth century, when most of its modalities were formalized, pelota was so closely associated with the Basques that when it got exported to foreign countries, it emerged officially institutionalized as "Basque Pelota."[3] As of 2012, it is a sport that embraces a professional elite supported by an

---

1. Baroja, *Guía del País Vasco Español-Francés*, 61
2. Humboldt, *Los vascos*, 84.
3. The International Federation of Basque Pelota was founded in Buenos Aires in 1926.

extensive business organization, as well as a network of amateur players coordinated through clubs and federations. There are national federations in twenty-three countries and infrastructure in many more.

The game is played on the fronton. It consists of a rectangular court and a wall—the *rebote* or rebound wall. During the nineteenth century, courts consisting of two walls—the front wall (*frontis*) and a left wall—were also created, with specific elevations, based on preexisting models using ramparts and various other architectural features.

More than simply the site of a game, the fronton is the place of celebration par excellence; it is generally the main square of the village, and serves as the communal hearth for community events: other competitions, neighborhood feasts and dances, *bertsolaritza* (improvised oral poetry) performances, and politicians' speeches all take place on it. It was often the first paved open space in a village, as it grew away from being merely ground situated by the foot of the church, or empty space near other monumental buildings or other constructions whose walls were suitable for the game. In fact, the most common term to refer to the outdoor fronton of the village is "plaza" (square).

The centrality of pelota in public space demands of it an interpretation that transcends the mere sportive. The game's liturgical form and the reflections on it made by its own practitioners clearly make it a foundation ritual and a fundamental representation of community. Although it took the shape of a sport, pelota is not merely a sport. And while it is spectacular, it is not just a spectacle.

In *The Elementary Forms of the Religious Life*, Durkheim emphasizes the recreational component of rituals. In his view, the autonomous sphere of the ritual—which transfers the participants into a world of representation—provokes cults to acquire an "outward appearance of recreation: the assistants may be seen laughing and amusing themselves openly."[4] This ludic factor of the ritual, which as we will see becomes primordial, does not contradict but rather supports the fact that the above mentioned representations respond to a concept of the world in which the agents involved participate actively. In *Desde el espectáculo a la trivialización*, Enrique Tierno Galván argues that social events are "the fulfillment of a conception of the world through spectacle"[5] and, despite the tendency

---

4. Durkheim, *The Elementary Forms of Religious Life*, 380.

5. Tierno Galván, *Desde el espectáculo a la trivialización*, 47. Unless otherwise noted, all quote translations are by the translator.

of Western societies to reduce the expressive power of these events to spectacle alone, they maintain their value as "a testimony to how a community *is* because of participating in *this* fundamental conception and not in any other."[6] In the same vein, in his 1973 study of the ritual of cockfighting in Bali, anthropologist Clifford Geertz interprets cockfights as a text that reveals who the Balinese really are. While not considering them the "key" to life in Bali—after all, "there are a great many cultural texts"[7]—cockfights are in his view a meta-social commentary: A story that the Balinese create about themselves and tell to themselves, a means of expression that "brings to imaginative realization a dimension of Balinese experience normally well-obscured from view,"[8] and allows us to approach their subjectivity.[9] In a similar way I hope in this book to illustrate through the game of pelota a culturally original way of being in the world and to explore the imaginary of the Basques through one of their most significant manifestations.

The book is divided into three parts, whose titles refer to three legends of the frontons of Banka (Banca), Larzabale (Larceveau), and Aldude (Les Aldudes), respectively. These legends condense the central idea of what each part is about, and they each constitute a fundamental pillar of the imaginary that I wish to explore. The first legend highlights the beauty of the game, and urges the youth to take responsibility for the game; I use it as a frame for the first two chapters, which contextualize the object of study both historically and culturally. The second part analyzes the ritual of the pelota game, interpreting it in a Turnerian sense as a "redressive action," as a public act that reconstructs unity. The legend of Larzabale points to the game's capacity to affect cohesion, describing pelota as a game that unites people. Finally, the third part is framed by a moral mandate that we find at the plaza of Aldude: "Play honestly, the plaza is always judge." This section analyzes the cultural message pelota transmits through the interpretation of its fundamental ritual symbols: the hand, the ball, and the fronton or plaza.

---

6. Ibid., 49. Emphasis added.
7. Geertz, *The Interpretation of Cultures*, 451.
8. Ibid., 44.
9. Ibid., 412–55.

Chapter 1, "The Basques of Pelota," introduces the game and its principal space, and through this explores the cultural imaginary that has nourished the idea of what *Basque* is. For scholars Juan Aranzadi and Alfonso Otazu y Llena, this imaginary started to take shape in the sixteenth century, at the beginning of the modern era. It was also this moment when the game started gaining relevance for Basque society as a whole. Chapter 2, "The Pelota of Basques" explores the historic evolution of the game, and focuses on the central importance pelota acquired in the physical and moral education of man during modernity.

Pelota is a male game, very much like other cultural manifestations of public importance such as *bertsolaritza*, *txokos* or gastronomic societies, and certain *fiestas* such as the Alardes (military-style parades) of Irun and Hondarribia – all three of which have been transformed in recent years—sometimes controversially, sometimes not—by greater female participation.[10] Despite the fact that women have always played informally at the plaza, they have little presence in the "world" of pelota; it is quite unthinkable that a woman should occupy a leading role in the professional sport, which shows the highest degree of formalization and enjoys greatest popularity. This is the primary subject of chapter 3, "The Control of *Indarra*," which argues that pelota favors the establishment of male relationships through a jocose rivalry that incites participants to take a *position*, to become involved in the event; at the same time, it neutralizes fanatic behavior by passing the responsibility of the fight over to those who are consecrated to do it: the *pelotaris* (pelota players). This chapter starts with the life history of one of them, and reviews the customs and procedures that play an essential role in the cohesion of the male population.

Considering ritual as lenitive of violence is an approach theoretically postulated in Victor Turner's thesis on social dramas, and René Girard's ideas on the confluence of the violent and the sacred. Following these approaches I argue that, in terms of structure (the Spanish *partido* means both "game" and "split" or "divided") and function (forger of relations) pelota affects the overcoming of latent conflicts in the community's political make-up. It is understood as a sacrifice because it *renders sacred*, as it consecrates those elements that are considered essential for the cohesion of the community. The ritual structure itself is analyzed in chapter 4,

---

10. On some of these issues, see Esteban and Amurrio, eds., *Feminist Challenges in the Social Sciences*; and Bullen, *Basque Gender Studies*.

"The Fiesta of Pelota," which depicts this sacrificial disposition. Taking place in determined space and time, the fiesta of pelota proceeds through three phases that coincide with the phases of any positive cult: preliminary, liminal, and postliminal.

A game of pelota, as its name in Spanish (*partido*) indicates, creates a primordial scission in a totality (split), which is resolved exemplarily through an act of collective catharsis. Chapter 5, "From *Joko* to *Jolas*," aims to understand precisely the tension that originates in the split and that is boosted by, among other things, gambling on the outcome. Due to the extreme emotions that the game generates, moments of genuine communal feeling emerge in which the individual heart absorbs cultural meanings. A scheme of struggle is reproduced (*joko*) to be resolved in an act of suture (*jolas*).[11] As Durkheim writes, there are "a whole group of ceremonies whose sole purpose is to awaken certain ideas and sentiments, to attach the present to the past or the individual to the group."[12] Belonging and permanence are the grand purposes of ritual action, purposes that manage to strengthen precisely these two sutures: emotion and memory.

Memory as an instrument of permanence plays a major role in chapter 6, "*Harrizko Herria*: The Village of Stone." The chapter shares the conviction that memory is a process of reconstruction of the past upon which the community is based; as such, it is contingent on present developments and oriented toward the future. From the premise of the perpetual reinterpretation of the pillars that constitute the community, it is postulated that the community's permanence is only possible through the medium of monuments, through elements of the symbolic

---

11. Editorial note: There is no grammatical gender or noun class in Basque and all nouns are marked by declension cases or postpositions. Suffixes are added to Basque nouns to form the equivalent of the definite article in English: -a for singular nouns and -ak to form the plural. Thus, depending on the context of the phrase, the word *joko* ("game," implying some degree of competitiveness) might be rendered *jokoa*, with the addition of an "a" marking the absolutive case of the definite article. In plural, this would be rendered *jokoak* ("games"). In this book, Basque nouns are given in their most common form in English-language texts, regardless of this distinction. For example, the word *bertsolari* (Basque oral improviser or poet) is used instead of *bertsolaria* (literally, "the" or "a" Basque oral improviser or poet). Moreover, the English plural form is used (*bertsolaris*) rather than its Basque equivalent (*bertsolariak*). However, when it comes to the word *indarra*, the stem word is *indar*, but in this case -ra is added to make the definite article (if a noun ends in -r an extra "r" is added, -ra). The form *indarra* will be used here following other treatments of the concept in English.

12. Durkheim, *The Elementary Forms of the Religious Life*, 378.

suppression of time. The fronton is without a doubt one of them. For its special, privileged position, the fronton is the home of all the communal events, whether spontaneous or planned. It possibly came from a field where the community gathered in its free time, or to do business, to represent or to govern; the fronton, the plaza, is born from the very bodies of the crowd gathered there, bodies that were its first boundaries. With time, flesh was replaced by stone, and the fronton became the community turned into place. This is why its very image recalls the constitutive beginnings of the group, a conception of the world, religious convictions and a bonding which all those who gather there share, and which will be analyzed in part 3.

Chapter 7, "*Esku*: The Hand as Depository of the Person," explores the importance the hand has in the Basque language when it comes to expressing personal competence. This chapter also discusses the disposition of the hand in the ritual and explores its mode of contact with the ball, a theme that emerges in chapter 8, "The Ball: Culture Objectified." The ball is conceived as a fundamental element of mediation that enables the game and, by extension, an understanding of the self through it. This chapter focuses on the socialization of the pelotari, the shaping of his personality, of his style; it penetrates the symbolic proximity between the manner of hitting the ball, the technique, and the character of the player. The game thus becomes a paradigm of moral knowledge. The elements that compose that knowledge reveal fundamental cultural values like the acclaimed "nobleness," an adjective used to refer to balls just as much as to frontons ideal for the game.

The fronton, the plaza is the protagonist of chapter 9, "The Plaza: The Embodiment of Society." Inasmuch as it has rules and it offers a possibility for action, the fronton is closely linked to society; it complies with a kind of supra-individual judgment that those involved in the game share, with a common consciousness that presumes a coparticipative understanding of reality. By interpreting the basic elements of the game, its fundamental symbols, part 3 procures to understand a cultural ideal behind the practice of pelota, as well as how that ideal is incorporated by players and other actors.

Ritual and aesthetics, practice and belief, pelota is one of the most revealing frameworks of meaning for the understanding of the Basque imaginary. Men pursue it with great passion, and find in its practice every possible range of expressing their moral being. As the song that opens the introduction demonstrates, pelota is seen as a powerful tool for teaching children, along with other pillars of Basqueness, and as such its effectiveness for cultural identification is beyond doubt. It is a montage of powerful images of identity. It is them—and the people and culture that they represent—that this book is about.

Emazue gasteak ardura pilotan zeren den ederrena joko guztietan.

Devote time, youngsters,
To pelota, it is the most
Beautiful of all games.

Part 1
Banka

Basque Pelota:
The Most Beautiful of All Games

The game of pelota ... is the principle fiesta of the Basques. Not only does each town have its own fronton, erected with greater or lesser splendor, but also everyone participates in the game.... Regardless of social class differences, much of the town, men and women, and even the mayor and the priest show up on Sundays to watch the players; they follow them with visible interest through their approval and criticism. Entire villages challenge each other to formal games. In these challenges the muse of the fatherland does not fall silent. Poets of the national language appear. A song that I came across by accident starts with the following verse on occasion of a challenge between Markina [Marquina] and Mutriku [Motrico]:

> 'You have bet
> And on what? Oh, what presumptuousness!
> On the noble game of pelota
> Against all of Markina here.
> Through these challenges your pride
> Ah, people of Mutriku, show me!
> Have you not always lost to Markina?'

—Wilhelm von Humboldt

Basque pelota is a group of games in which a varying number of players (*pelotaris*) are positioned in front of each other or facing a wall (*frontis*), and exchange a solid ball wrapped in leather by hitting it with their hand or an instrument. The ball must always bounce within established boundaries (*eskas* or fault lines), and the players try to make it as difficult as possible for their opponent to return it; the objective is to win by earning points and by being first to reach the stipulated final score.

Within the typology of Basque pelota games it is necessary to make a primary distinction between games where the opponents face each other on opposing sides, and games where they are positioned next to each other, side by side. The first category is that of direct style games in which one player hits a ball, the opponent receives it directly, and then returns it. Such games are less common and are only played in very specific areas of the country. Indeed, most Basque people are unfamiliar with them.[1] The second category is made up of indirect style games, or games of *blé*, where the ball reaches the opposing player through the mediation of a front wall or *frontis*. Games where a wall is involved significantly change the disposition of the players in the court: in short, direct confrontation shifts to contest in front of a wall and sharing the same arena of play.

Most indirect games, the games of *blé*, are played individually (singles) or in pairs (doubles). The game begins when one of the players executes the serve.[2] The serve consists of bouncing the ball in front of a line marked for this purpose; the player propels the ball against the *frontis* in such a way that it bounces back between the lines of *falta* ("fault" or low off-area) and *pasa* ("pass," or high off-area), lines that divide the court into three parts. If the serve bounces before the low off-area line, the receiver wins a point. If it bounces beyond the high off-area line, the server has another opportunity; in the event of failing again (hitting the ball too short or too long), the point goes to the opponent, who also wins the right to serve. From this moment on the player who earns a point serves.

Once the serve has been made, the individual players or doubles alternate in hitting the ball—mediated by a wall—and the game stops the moment the ball: (a) first bounces on or outside of the lines that mark out the court; (b) flies on top of the fronton walls or bounces against the ceiling or beyond the upper off area lines (if it is a covered fronton); (c) bounces in the lower zone, in other words, on or below the *chapa*, a 1 meter (approximately 3 feet) high iron panel on the *frontis*; (d) is not reached by the pelotari before it bounces the second time; (e) hits a player's body;

---

1. There is a detailed discussion of these in chapter 2 under "The Establishment of Pelota."

2. The election of the singles or doubles player who takes the first serve depends on chance by flipping a coin. The two faces of the coin are the two colors—red and blue—of the players' sashes. See chapter 4, the part titled "Flipping the Coin."

or (f) there is a violation of the rules of how a player may hit the ball.[3] Scoring in the games of *blé* is by accumulating points until the final score is reached. Historically, the final score depended on a prior agreement; in modern play, each modality has its own final score: twenty-two in hand pelota, forty-five in pala, thirty-five in jai alai, remonte, hand trinquet, and xare (see glossary for descriptions of these).

The games of *blé* played in the open plaza, trinquet, or left-walled fronton principally differ according to the instrument used to play. *Pala, short pala, paleta, xistera, remonte, cesta-punta, xare,* and *racket* are the instruments that, together with the hand, mark the different modalities of *blé*. Today, only four of these are professional sports with a concomitant business organization: hand pelota, pala, remonte, and jai alai. In these modalities the length of the fronton, the weight of the ball, and the rules of the game vary. The liturgy of the game, however, is similar in all cases, as I discuss in chapter 4.

The game of pelota is played on a fronton, a space that varies considerably depending on the modality and the locality where it is situated. It can range from a court delimited by minimal architectural elements, like the fronton of Arraioz in the Baztan Valley (Navarre), to a stagelike box, where the public is seated beyond the fourth wall, as in the now defunct fronton of Tianjin, China.

Despite its extensive typology, professional pelota is played in what is known as an industrial fronton. It is a closed space whose interior is divided into three fundamental areas: the court, where the game is played; the counter-court, a space of mediation; and the terraces, a space that seats the public. These areas are only separated by the position of their actors, who are the principal agents of the game: the pelotaris occupy the court; the intermediaries, referees, and bookmakers, who are charged with officiating and overseeing the betting, respectively, are in the counter-court; and the public is seated on the terraces.

The court is the game's space, it contains the players' movements of the players; as an extension, it is the area of the fronton where the pelota (ball) can bounce freely without resulting in a point. A definition of the court in relation to the ball is more accurate than a definition in relation to the pelotari: the player may occupy other spaces; he can for example step outside onto the counter-court without stopping the game; if the

---

3. It is considered a fault to grab the ball, to hold it longer than allowed, to hit the ball more than once, or (if applicable) if it bounces on the particular instrument being used.

ball bounces off-court, however, play is finished. Therefore, the court is that area of the fronton where the ball can bounce and rebound[4] without terminating the game, without finishing the point.

Geometrically, the court is a rectangular cube that is open on the right side, the "fourth wall," beyond which the crowd is situated. In hand pelota, the court is 10 meters (approximately 33 feet) high, 10 meters wide and 36 meters (approximately 118 feet) long; it is composed of the *frontis*, the court (floor), the left wall and the rebound (rear) wall. The *frontis* is the front wall that, historically, would typically be the wall of some other building annexed to the terrain of the game, and which was given a specific elevation. Originally marking the boundaries of the game, the frontis acquired relevance when the direct style modalities were abandoned for the *blé*. The front wall imposes a supreme power on the rules: the ball must rebound off it with each strike. If it does not do so, the point is finished. At a height of one meter' on the frontis there is a long metal panel (*chapa*) that marks the minimum height where the ball must rebounce above. If the ball rebounces on or below it, it is a fault, and the point is added to the opponent's count (*cartón*) or score.

Since the second half of the twentieth century, the frontis has shared importance with the left wall, an element that has significantly influenced the game. Beyond imposing a new spatial configuration, the incorporation of the left wall provoked an authentic revolution in the game of pelota, which was increasingly turned into a spectacle following changing societal demands. The 36 meters of the left wall, which served as an authentic background curtain, were divided into ten squares (*cuadros*), each being 3.5 meters (approximately 11 feet) long. The squares are marked by a vertical line painted on the left wall, which usually has a number on top of it. The square closest to the frontis is number 1, and that closest to the rear wall is number 10. The squares substantially increase the spectator's understanding of the game, and make up a fundamental point of reference to appreciate the contest between the pelotaris. In hand pelota they often say that a player keeps his opponent "two squares behind:" this happens when he manages to force his opponent back a few meters behind him, and thus keep him farther away from the frontis. The closer the ball to the frontis, the greater velocity and force it has, giving the player a greater chance to surprise his opponent. The

---

4. The ball *bounces* on the floor, on the court, and *rebounds* off the walls of the fronton.

squares help calibrate questions as primordial and complex as the players' strength or the liveliness of the ball.

Two quarters stand apart from the rest. They are the *fault* (*falta*) and the *pass* (*pasa*) lines. In Euskara, these are termed *motz* ("short") and *luze* ("long"), respectively, adjectives that refer to the serve. They are indicated with a line painted higher than the rest, and they are extended on the floor up to the counter-court. These squares converted into lines divide the floor of the court into three zones, whose use as noted is reduced to the serve. When serving, the pelotari has to bounce the ball in front of the fail line, which is in square 4, at 14 meters (just under 46 feet) from the frontis. Once it rebounds off the frontis the ball has to bounce between the two lines (the fail and pass lines) or square 7, at 24.5 meters (80 feet) from the frontis. After rebounding off the frontis, if the ball bounces before reaching the fail line, the point (and, for that matter, the next serve) goes directly to the opponent, while if it bounces beyond the pass line, the server has another opportunity to execute the serve; this time, however, it has to be between the two lines, or else he loses the point.[5]

The floor of the court is reduced to these divisions; depending on the modality of the game, however, there might be additional lines to give advantage with the serve and thus balance the game. Besides, there is a form of competition in hand pelota that expands the number of lines in the court. It is called *jaula* or "four-and-a-half;" precisely at this point of the court, between squares 4 and 5, there is a line that the players cannot pass (bouncing the ball, that is) once the serve has been taken. The space of the game is reduced in order to enliven the game, and to favor strength and imaginative play on the front squares.

With respect to the last element that makes up the court of the industrial fronton, the rear wall or rebound wall, its importance varies enormously from one modality to another. In jai alai and remonte it is an element that determines the game; there are plays like the *txula* or the *txik-txak*[6] that are defined with reference to the rebound wall. In these

---

5. In recent years, in the singles hand pelota modality the serve is limited to one opportunity. The pass line violation is therefore considered a fault.

6. Both are definitive plays; the ball bounces very close to the angle that the floor and the rebound wall form, and does not, therefore, have the necessary trajectory to be returned. In one of the cases the ball bounces first on the floor and then on the rebound wall—*txik-txak*; in the other case the ball impacts first on the rebound ball, and then dies by crashing into the floor—*txula*.

modalities, the players are accustomed to *rebounding*;[7] this is indeed a fundamental move in the game. In hand pelota and pala, however, it is practically impossible to return a ball that has reached the rebound wall. In hand pelota, if a ball reaches the rear wall before its second bounce, it is effusively celebrated. Even if the opponent intercepts the ball just before it might reach the rear wall, it is still considered a "rebound," and is applauded; it is entered in the accounts of postgame statistics as a ball that reached the rear end of the court.

By "court" I mean the space between the *eskas* or fault lines. These are the lines that mark the exterior contours—limits of height and contact with the rest of the spaces; counter-court and terraces—of all the elements that I have described; frontis, left wall, floor, and the rebound wall. They are white lines, boundaries that do not belong to either of the spaces they separate and that, within the game of pelota, constitute a fault. They are excluded from the valid routes of the ball and as such, they are outside the court.[8] They are the boundaries of the play area.

The counter-court is situated beyond the fault lines. It is a space of mediation at the fronton; it is traditionally covered with wood, and separates the two primordial spaces: the court and the terraces. It is the counter-court where the intermediaries execute their functions: the referees, *epaileak*, and bookmakers, *artekariak*, which literally means "intermediaries."

At the frontons of modalities with instruments, like those of the pala, remonte, or jai alai, a metal net protects the spectators from extremely hard balls that reach great speeds when in play. The net divides the counter-court into two areas: the area right by the court (the counter-court proper) with its own physical characteristics—determined space and wooden surface—and the small area by the terraces for the bookmakers, these intermediary counter-court agents who serve people wanting to bet on the game. For reasons of security, the net separates the two types of intermediaries at the fronton—referees and bookmakers—and limits the direct contact between the court and the terraces. The referees are

---

7. "Rebounding" is used to refer to the action of returning the ball once it has rebounded against the rebound wall.

8. Unlike in all other modern ball games like tennis or paddle tennis, where such contact is *valid*. While at some frontons like the Konsejupe of San Nicolás in Algorta they are counted as valid, the bounce or rebound on the *eskas* is normally a fault.

positioned, naturally, alongside the players on the counter-court, while the bookmakers serve the requests of bettors by the terraces.

When a game is broadcast, the television crew also occupies this area of the fronton. Two fixed and a mobile camera assist the technical team: the fixed cameras are located at each end of the counter-court—by the frontis and by the rebound wall; the mobile camera moves from one end to the other, incurring sometimes on the space of the terraces to focus on a well-known face in the crowd. The commentators, a prestigious journalist and a retired player, narrate the events of the game from a table set in the same area, more specifically by the rebound wall. This new element of the fronton, the television, is another intermediary—a medium of communication, a channel of information—between the fronton and private homes, bars, or any place where there is a television. This mediator did not choose a spot on the terraces, nor did it carve itself out a specific space to exercise its function; rather, it is positioned on the counter-court, in the area of mediation of the fronton.

The terraces are the fronton's final area; they are the space occupied by the public. In open plazas the terraces surround the court, seating the public on both of its sides and at its rear end. With the appearance of the left wall, however, the view becomes unidirectional. Now there exists a paradigmatic place from where to watch the game, and the spectator occupies it. It is the *fourth wall*, the area parallel to the left wall.

When pelota became more commercialized and the big frontons were built, the terraces were divided in terms of different entrance fees. In the majority of modern games prices are fixed; entrance prices only differ during the latter stages of championships. Regular bettors, whom the bookmakers themselves supply with entrance tickets before the games, always sit in seats close to the court, where they have direct contact with the bookmakers. Former players, well-known people in the world of pelota, and those with the funds to do so also sit in this area. The average age of people in this zone is about sixty. People of more modest financial means, which usually means younger people, have to make do with areas of the terraces that are farther away.

Another key space of the fronton is located on the terraces: the bar. Its position depends considerably on the arrangement of the fronton. While its paradigmatic location is above the courtside seats, as in the case of the Astelena fronton in Eibar or in the Jai-alai in Gernika, it is also often located on the first floor of the terraces, as in the Beotibar fronton in Tolosa or Galarreta in Hernani, where many bettors sit. Being an open area (a counter) and above the courtside seats, the bar gives a perfect view over the court.

The bar is the meeting point of the fronton. Former players (who are asked to give their opinion on the game), board members, and recruiters from companies that employ professional pelotaris gather around it. It is also normal to see currently active players whom fans and acquaintances greet, but who do not normally occupy the courtside seats because contact with spectators in this way is usually frowned upon. Therefore, in instrument modality frontons (pala, remonte, and cesta-punta), where most of the public participates in betting, the pelotaris normally occupy a designated area of the fronton. They can almost always be seen in groups in one of the corners of the terraces—in Gernika and Galarreta, by the rebound wall; in the Deportivo, by the frontis—keeping a prudent distance from the spectators. They are not permitted to maintain a close relationship with the public so as not to jeopardize the betting system.

Without counting the interior spaces (locker rooms, press conference rooms, and so on), the fronton is therefore composed of three basic spaces: the court, the counter-court, and the terraces. These spaces are occupied by the pelotaris, the referees and the bookmakers, and the crowd, respectively. The layout of these areas does not only reveal the functions of their agents, but also emphasizes the fronton's status as public space. Historically, it was the village plaza, an open plaza where people could freely congregate. Despite being subsequently formalized as a closed space, the fronton maintains its open disposition without fixed boundaries. Participating agents move around the distinct spaces with absolute liberty, always respecting the game's temporal boundaries.

The annual schedule of professional pelota is divided into periods of fiesta games—summertime encounters that coincide with the feast days of different towns' patron saints—and championships. In hand pelota there are three principal championships: the singles, doubles, and "four-and-a-half" competitions. The doubles championship starts in January and ends in March, a moment when the singles championship resumes, which is the most anticipated event of the season. Once it is over, tournaments and fiesta games start: that of San Fermín (Iruñea-Pamplona) and La Blanca (Vitoria-Gasteiz), together with the fiestas of Donostia-San Sebastián, Bilbao, and finally, the San Mateo fiesta tournament in Logroño, which closes the great summer contests. The "four-and-a-half" championship starts in the summer and ends in late December.

Besides these official championships and fiesta games, special festivals are organized throughout the year: afternoons of pelota that feature three or four games organized by the promoting companies. They are mostly doubles, which is the paradigmatic mode of playing *blé*, playing against a wall. The schedule is normally made up of a second division game, followed by a *stellar* (first division) contest, and then a third division game to finish. The third and the second division games may rotate depending on the time slots, but the *stellar* game always takes place in between them.

With the professionalization of pelota, the different frontons settled on one or various days of the week for the organization of their festival games. Until recently, the weekly schedule of professional hand pelota was: Monday, Tolosa, coinciding with the weekly market day; Tuesday, a rest day; Wednesday, Bergara; Thursday, Eibar; Friday, Vitoria-Gasteiz; Saturday, Bergara; and Sunday, Eibar. Nowadays, arranging games depends on the companies involved, and they do not maintain a set cycle but instead schedule games in different localities depending on logistical considerations.[9]

For a significant part of the male population pelota is indispensable. Until the 1960s the great majority of Basques were socialized in frontons. Village, town, and city centers were configured into spaces in which the population came together in its free time and for communal celebration. Urban and rural people alike played pelota from a very early age. The squeamish were channeled toward pala, and the rest toward hand pelota. Meanwhile, xistera or guante were only played in very specific areas of the country.

In contrast, pelota has not been so important in the lives of Basque women. Generally, they did not follow the game and had no access to professional careers in it. One exception to this was the racket game, a modality that existed between the beginning of the twentieth century

---

9. The rest of the modalities maintain a traditional system, convoking the players on specific days and in different frontons. As of 2012, because of a crisis they are experiencing, each modality has been restricted to a single fronton; remonte is played on Wednesdays, Saturdays, and Sundays in the Galarreta fronton in Hernani, and pala on Thursdays and Sundays in the Deportivo in Bilbao. Jai alai, which used to be played on Mondays (market day) in Gernika and on Sundays at the "University of Pelota" in Markina, is now featured together with the pala festivals, because they share the same business organization. This modality has started to program games for Tuesdays and Saturdays in Biarritz, and Sundays in Berriatua.

and the 1960s, almost always in industrial frontons outside the Basque Country.

Beyond its heterogeneity, pelota has been a key symbolic referent in the construction of Basque identity. During the five centuries of its documented existence, and due to its idealized origins,[10] pelota has acquired specific ritual and aesthetic forms that constitute a prism through which many Basques think about themselves, and through which others think about Basques. Its reiterated (albeit debatable) rural character has made the game a model of Basque representations of difference, forming an essential part of the Basque nationalist imaginary. Nevertheless, its practice has transcended political ascriptions because it is played by Basques of different ideologies (as well as non-Basques). Due to the various and diverse experiences it offers, pelota has been a popular practice among Basques,[11] despite the fact that since the 1970s its influence on Basque social life has declined significantly. It is not my purpose to analyze the possible causes or factors that have contributed to the current situation: for example, the adoption of new sports, transformations in urban configurations, or a growing range of alternative free-time activities. Rather, I wish to offer an interpretation that helps understand pelota's significance: a phenomenon that is still an essential source of meaning despite—or rather, because of—the changes and innovations it has undergone.

---

10. In the world pelota championship organized in Iruñea-Pamplona in 1962, in the trinquet of the Tennis Club it read: on top of the frontis "Pelota was born Basque;" on the rebound wall "Pelota has become worldwide" and on the right wall "Pelota is a racial symbol, the most complete sport, where challenge mixes with traditional prayer." Galbete, "Miscelánea de datos para una historia del juego de pelota."

11. There are more than five thousand frontons in a territory of about 3 million inhabitants; they are used daily to practice one of the fifteen games that compose the category of "Basque Pelota."

1

The Basques of Pelota

> *Euskaldun jatorra izateko*   To be an authentic Basque
> *behar diran sei gauza:*   Six things are needed;
> *pilotan jakin,*   To know how to play pelota,
> *sagardozalea,*   To be fond of cider,
> *ibiltaria izan,*   To be a keen walker
> *anka aundia*   Long-legged
> *bizkar zabala*   Wide-shouldered
> *ta sudurluzea*   And long-nosed.
>
> — Basque proverb

While I am well aware of the fact that, as Manuel Delgado argues, "we may not aspire to find clearly delineable cultures, ones that are able to significantly organize human experience around an all-embracing vision of the world,"[1] and that the Basque case is not an unproblematic example, it is the case that pelota has been an object of study in a culture that has been systematically marked as "Basque culture." Furthermore, pelota displays many of the properties that literature on the Basques has qualified as specific features of this culture. Therefore, this chapter attempts to contextualize pelota with the marker of Basque culture.

Assuming that it is impossible to discuss the Basques as a homogenous group, as opposed to a multiplicity of desires, affects, manners, and reasoning, the following pages attempt to approach the cultural complex that has been historically viewed as Basque, a complex that we may consider almost in its entirety as "modern."

---

1. Delgado, *El animal público*, 9.

Instead of an in-depth analysis, this chapter aims to configure a different frame of understanding for the object studied: Basque pelota as a celebratory ritual of collectivity, as a cultural expression of the values Basques praise, and as a symbolic complex upon which communal understanding rests.

Etxea eta Herria: Independence and Communitarianism

> *Herrik bere lege, etxek bere aztura.*
> Each village has its laws, and each house its customs.
>
> — Basque proverb

The traditional, essentially modern Basque world is sustained by two basic institutions: the *etxe* ("house" or "home"), the basic unit of reproduction and provider of essential values, and the *herri* ("village" or "town"), image and nucleus of the collectivity, shelter for all who were born within its borders. *Herri* is an ideological complement to *etxe*: the latter offers the traditional values of independence and permanence, while the village is associated with the ideals of community and belonging.

The inseparable coexistence of the rural (characterized by the *baserri*, or farmstead) and the urban (symbolized by the street, the *kale*[2]) has been perhaps the fundamental driving force of modern life in the Basque Country. And yet, we now consider as rural certain contexts (physically concentrated in the plaza) in which much of popular culture, like pelota itself, was born. It is certainly the agrarian world that fills the Basque cultural imagery with meaning, and which represents the prototype of the "golden age" of Basque culture. Despite the diverse landscape of Euskal Herria,[3] the environment that characterizes this agrarian world has become the country's prototypical image: green humid mountains enveloping tight valleys where small population nuclei reside around a central church building and scattered stone *baserris*. It is this environment

---

2. The *etxe* is the house, the sphere of the private; the *herri* is the village, the community; the *baserri* is the farmstead, but in its totality it implies a wider system of rural organization; and the *kale* is the street, the urban space par excellence. See Arpal, *Processus sociaux, idéologies et pratiques culturelles dans la société basque* and Fdez. De Larrinoa, *Hitzak, denbora eta espazioa*.

3. The Basque territory (Euskal Herria) is composed of diverse landscapes that are grouped in three fringes: the Atlantic, Pyrenean, and Mediterranean. Each one of them has its own bio-climactic, economic, social, and cultural diversity. See Martínez Montoya, *Pueblos, ritos, y montañas*.

in which Euskara (the Basque language) is principally spoken, and where production has revolved around agriculture and livestock managed by the *baserri*, a supposedly self-sufficient or at least autonomous unit. The landmarks separating the farmsteads have to be well determined even between brothers: *Haurride bien artean ongi dago zedarria* ("Between two brothers, it's good to have a milestone").

The *baserri* did not only consist of the main building (the *etxe*), but also of the land around it, as well as a sepulture. Since the sixteenth century, the sepulture has been situated in the church building, but has maintained its vital link to the *baserri*. Among other tasks, it was the job of the *etxekoandre* ("woman or mistress of the house") to look after the *baserri*'s ancestors, whether or not they shared blood relations. It was her task to keep alive the fire of the hearth as well as that of the sepulture, on which she would be seated while Mass was celebrated. The *etxe* granted subjects juridical and social status: individuals took their last names from the *baserri* they occupied. If for whatever reason a new family moved into the *baserri*, they would take on the name used by the previous occupants: the name of the house. Even if desirable, primordial belonging did not necessarily stem from the consanguineous continuity of the family, but rather from the house, *etxe*. Every social pattern conspired to ensure that continuity: for example, an undivided single inheritance following the main family branch, and marriage between an heir and the second child of another family, if possible. Inheritance patterns ensured that the house would remain in the same family, and that no new ones would be formed. Under these conditions, most of the children of the house had to either stay in the *etxe* as (unmarried) servants of the farmstead, pursue a life in the church, or emigrate. Socioeconomic stability thus depended on maintaining only a strict number of houses, because representation on the council was granted by the *etxe*.

The modern legal system that focuses on the individual and promotes an equal division of an inheritance among children, as well as new industrial modes of production that concentrate people in urban centers, have tremendously damaged traditional life worlds based on the reproduction of the *baserri* as an economic, social, and political axis.

These changes, however, have not lead to a symbolic estrangement from the *baserri*. While stripped of its primary productive importance, the *etxe* continues to nourish the Basque cultural imaginary, especially from the second part of the nineteenth century on. Gabriel Aresti's poem "*Nire aitaren etxea*" ("My Father's House") is a clear example. In the words of its final verse: *Ni hilen naiz / nire arima galduko da / nire askazia galduko da / baina nire aitaren etxeak / iraunen du / zutik* (I will die / My soul shall be lost / My descendants will be lost / But my father's house / Will remain / Standing). This poem describes a son's vigorous defense of his father's house against a hypothetical attack, and became the anthem of a generation in the 1960s and beyond. It came to symbolize the struggle of Basque youth to maintain upright a homeland that is considered systematically attacked: Euskal Herria. The house embodies the homeland and the *baserri* becomes the "reservoir of that which most genuinely makes up Basque culture—its language, customs, worldview."[4]

The *etxe* as such, as the anthropologist Joseba Zulaika argues, is "an image of the idea of closure."[5] It implies closure not only at the level of architecture, with its walls and fences, but also at a social level. The house marks a clear boundary between neighbors, owners, and tenants; a logic that sustains the functioning of the *herri*, of the village. Only by owning a house with *fuego vecinal*, or "neighborhood fire,"[6] did one have a voice in the council. Communal rights and obligations rested in the *etxe*, not in the individual.

The clearest example of this was communal work or *auzolan*. When a household needed help with threshing or any renovation, when roads and public property had to be repaired, each household had contribute one person to do the given work. When the bells rang in the morning, neighbors met to undertake the work. This type of communal work still exists in certain parts of the Basque Country. I myself saw an example of *auzolan* in the village of Eratsun (Erasun, Navarre) for the cleaning and upgrading of the new fronton, which was going to be inaugurated the next day, June 6, 1999. I was told that any household that did not send a member to work had to pay a fine to the city council.

Solidarity among neighbors in a territory in which each house is in principle independent of the rest became crucial, and constituted one of the main pillars by which the council was formed. The council was a medieval institution that divided the area into *feligresías* (parishes), valleys,

---

4. Zulaika, *Basque Violence*, 132.

5. Zulaika, *Tratado estético-ritual vasco*, 28.

6. The houses of the neighborhood, with a right to vote in the council, had to keep the fire alive permanently; they were thus prepared to be alerted any moment in case a pilgrim arrived, or for any other urgent necessity. This is why they were called houses with "neighborhood fire."

and *villas* (boroughs or towns with foundational charters), almost always along the lines of geographical divisions preceding its constitution.

Socioeconomic matters and rituals were centralized in a nucleus, normally the church, that gave shape to villages as a whole; precarious "urban" developments of homes and services. Many of the houses in these villages were named after the trade of their occupants: *Apextegia* (house of the priest), *Arotzena* (house of the carpenter), *Sastrerena* (house of the tailor), and so on, and surnames such as these (and their variations) exist to this day.[7]

The village, *herri*, as administrative, social, and ritual center, became the image of the community. It sustained a national concept of identity: the connection between all the subjects that participated in a specific perception of the world (nourished by the *baserri*), that shared a language (Euskara), and that occupied a determined territory (Euskal Herria). As in the Spanish *pueblo*, *herri* means both "village" and "people," and the two referents are concentrated in the same word: the physical, spatial structure where the social life of the community takes place; and the group that inhabits it, or the community itself. *Euskal Herria* designates the Basque territories as well as the population that lives there and that displays a series of distinctive features.

While it had preserved elements from previous eras and its actual institutionalization took place centuries later, this ideological configuration centered in space had a precise historical beginning: the overthrow of feudal lords and the strengthening of the *villas* or boroughs in the fifteenth and sixteenth centuries. I will now explore this era that preceded the abovementioned group awakening; an era that gives us many clues as to just how that Basque imaginary was shaped, and at the same time clarifies important questions about Basque pelota. This was the epoch that preceded the first documentation of the game: the Late Middle Ages.

The Early Middle Ages: *Gorriak ala Urdinak*

The Basque rural world in the Late Middle Ages was characterized by a perpetual series of blood feuds among antagonistic clans or factions, kinship lines grouped around a central lineage, a family, which lent the entire group its name. The most well-known factions were the Martínez

---

7. Caro Baroja, *The Basques*, 109–117.

de Oñaz family and the Gamboas: with them and their followers being termed Oñacinos and Gamboínos.[8]

These clans or factions were made up of lineages around which land, the means of production, and farmworkers were organized. The lineages were formed by noblemen linked by blood relations. "When a nobleman possessed greater property and lived a superior level of life than the rest, when his leadership was recognized in the affairs of the lineage, that is, the extended family united by the bond of agnatic solidarity, they thus became 'feudal lord' over the group of nobility."[9] The group of nobles, or the particular lineage then ascribed to one or other of these groups, led by their "feudal lord."

Apparently, the fundamental origin of disputes among these factions was neither territorial invasion nor ideological conflict over the management of social affairs. The functioning of both factions was similar and there were no qualitative differences between them. Conflict was always regarded as a life-or-death struggle, motivated by the desire to measure up forces and to maintain the integrity of honor. The factions were fighting, at times viciously, with one apparent motivation: to decide "who was worth more in the region."[10]

This impulse might seem trivial, but it was nevertheless sustained by one basic desire: to differentiate oneself. Shifting allegiances between the two factions cannot have been so unusual, especially for members who did not share obvious kinship ties. Subjected to a feudal organizational hierarchy, the families of farmworkers had no difficulty passing from one lineage to the other, depending on the incentives and advantages offered. These medieval struggles, therefore, must have been motivated by an excessive equality between the factions, which seems to support the theory of René Girard, who argues that tragic confrontation is always produced as a result of symmetries between the antagonists: "when this difference has been effaced . . . violence spreads throughout the community."[11]

---

8. For English-language treatment of the war of the factions, see Collins, *The Basques*, 248–54; and Monreal Zia, *The Old Law of Bizkaia (1452): Introductory Study and Critical Edition*, 36–37.

9. Bazán, *De Túbal a Aitor*, 263.

10. Ibid., 294.

11. Girard, *Violence and the Sacred*, 51.

In order to survive, the factions needed to differentiate themselves; the source of conflicts must have been excessive connivance, especially at the base of the social pyramid. Periods of peace when products catering for basic needs were exchanged between laborers, amorous adventures in the style of Romeo and Juliet, as well as the traffic of goods and individuals between the territories were no doubt threatening the survival of factions.

The principal motivation behind these blood feuds was most probably the establishment of boundaries between the factions at the territorial as well as the symbolic level. The groups had to maintain their own consciousness of identity, a sense of belonging among their members in order to survive; and to achieve that, there is nothing better than confrontation. Perpetuating conflict in order to safeguard authority is one of the most recurrent phenomena in the political history of humanity.

In fact, the decline of the factions began the moment they could no longer keep the loyalty of the laborers who made up their followers, when these farmworkers abandoned their lands under the pressures of landlords and organized themselves outside of the factions, especially in the newly established chartered towns or boroughs. Indeed, the determining factor that led to the final disappearance of the factions was the emergence of the *hermandades* ("brotherhoods" or "confraternities"), judicial-political institutions formed by "peasants, small rural land owners, and townspeople,"[12] who counteracted the power of feudal lords. While their origins go back to the end of the thirteenth century, they were most prominent during the mid-fifteenth century, at a moment when the hegemony of the rural nobility declined, and when the general assemblies (*juntas generales*) and provincial governments (*diputaciones*) were established.

A system of collective nobility, although some essayists (for ideological reasons) subsequently dated it to the sixteenth century,[13] would not be established until the nineteenth century. This system of collective nobility came to form the basis of what might be termed the "prehistory" of what subsequently became identified as the ideology surrounding

---

12. Bazán, *De Túbal a Aitor*, 296.

13. For an English-language discussion of these essayists and their debates on the question of Basque collective nobility, see Madariaga Orbea, *Anthology of Apologists and Detractors of the Basque Language*, esp. pt. 1, chaps. 1–3.

Basque culture. Politically, it was based on two basic pillars: territorial configuration and the *fueros*, or traditional customary laws.

The anthropologist Juan Aranzadi contends that ancien régime Basque society rested upon these foundations;[14] it was a society whose local solidarity was no longer determined by blood relations but by residence, by the *etxe*, or "house." Aranzadi terms this the "transition from kindred relations to territoriality," and believes it to have been perhaps the most radical transformation ever of the Basque social-political system.

The moment when the house became the fundamental reference at both the socially reproductive and the symbolic level, when blood relations were relegated to secondary importance, marked a point at which late medieval social structures were rapidly deleted from Basque collective memory. The "egalitarianism" promulgated by the concept of universal nobility[15] and land as magma of identification were suddenly conceptualized as elements that had already been present during the Neolithic; a Neolithic that, as Aranzadi remarks with irony, "did not arrive to the Basque Country until the twelfth, thirteenth centuries."[16]

The shift from descent to residence as a basis of identification provoked an ideological configuration that prioritized space as a basic fundamental of cultural representation: the *etxe*, or unit of reproduction; the *herri*, or communal center; the *legezaharrak (fueros)*, or customary laws; the tree of Gernika, a sacred oak that insufflated deictic power to Basque territory; and Mari, principal muse of Basque mythology, all came to form part of a symbolic complex based on the ideological reference of land as primordial source of identity, of *being*.

So much so, that Basque surnames that predated this territorial conception of the world came to be considered to be Castilian.[17] Consequently, in many parts of the Basque Country during the seventeenth and eighteenth centuries medieval patronymics were substituted by place names, abandoning paternal nomination and adopting the names of the

---

14. Aranzadi, *Milenarismo Vasco*, 288–317.

15. On the origins of "egalitarianism," see Otazu y Llana, *El "igualitarismo" vasco*, 101–32. Universal or collective nobility referred to a status of nobility that all Basques and a large part of the Navarrese acquired in the fourteenth century as a result of an agreement with the Castilian monarch. This original agreement served to maintain the particular political and juridical status of the Basque Country and Navarre down to the present day.

16. Aranzadi, *Milenarismo Vasco*, 302–3.

17. Ibid.

houses.[18] Any change of residence thus implied taking on the name of the house occupied, being obliged to preserve it through undivided inheritance, and of worshiping an ancestor cult, whether the ancestors were blood relatives or not.

The survival of the house, not the lineage, constituted the essential factor in a shift from agnatic to territorial solidarity, which was a necessary change for the maintenance of a rural world beset by deficit, and which was maintained only due to family lineages, tax exemption, and a free trade agreement that ensured the *foral* system (the system based on the *fueros*). It was precisely the defense of this *foral* system that led to one of the central conflicts in the history of the Basque Country: the nineteenth-century Carlist Wars.

Acknowledging the obvious reductionism implied, there was at the core of the Basque conflict until comparatively recently a confrontation: on the one side were adherents of a traditionalism who advocated maintaining the *fueros*, the customary laws that granted Basques a degree of autonomy through the formula "one obeys, but does not fulfill, as it is something outside the land," and which became a chief cause of Carlism and a later proverbial reference for Basque nationalism;[19] and on the other, proponents of a liberalism with civic aspirations rooted in political coexistence with the Castilian crown. Curiously, all these conflicts wore the colors used by the medieval factions—the Oñacinos and Gamboínos—to differentiate themselves: *gorriak ala urdiñak* (red or blue).

The Sons of Mari

There was nevertheless one factor that transcended all antagonism and that Basques of all factions shared: religiosity. One might argue that Basques have been a profoundly religious people for much of their history, especially with respect to liturgical practices, which no doubt contributed to the diffusion and maintenance of Christianity in the Basque Country. Julio Caro Baroja affirms that "the religious activity of the

---

18. Araba was an exception to this in that there it remained typical to form surnames by combining patronymics and place names.

19. Despite the fact that the Carlists and Basque nationalists fought under opposing banners in the Spanish Civil War (1936–39). Of course, the very emergence and development of Basque nationalism (in a large part out of Carlism) in the late nineteenth century and beyond forced a reconfiguration of Carlism to the point that the latter was ideologically very different by this time compared to its nineteenth-century counterpart.

Basque town (like that of many others) shows two tendencies that seem contradictory but that are intimately linked and tied to very strong needs of the human spirit. One is the tendency to always try to fit the facts of life to the doctrine of final causes. In the face of this teleological position, typically Christian, we find the complementary position of mechanizing religious activities to different degrees, adjusting them to the phases of the same life, to the periods that constitute it, seen from both the individual and community positions."[20]

With respect to the first of these features, the accommodation of facts to the doctrine of final causes, Basques—although the generalization is as questionable as any other—have historically displayed a strong sense of traditionalism that accepts without much dissension that which is already given. "What was good enough for my father is good enough for me" is a profoundly Basque statement. The fact of responding to customs and practices with an "It has always been like that" escaped any philosophical reflection whatsoever, which was for most people a waste of time: As one saying goes, "*filosofia baino hobea da oilo-zopa*" (chicken soup is better than any philosophy). Indeed, Rodney Gallop emphasizes this feature as one of the most evident characteristics of the Basque psychology: "he unquestionably accepts his ancestors' views of the essential problems of life and death and wastes no more time in idle speculation."[21]

Nor would it appear that dogmatic questions were particularly central to the development of the Catholic Church, which was more concerned with "issues of morality, liturgy, discipline and organization."[22] Aranzadi follows Charles Guignebert in arguing that there existed in Western Christianity a high pagan component: "the doctrinal body lost its importance in the face of compiling legends and the *sacred*; the essence of religion orientated toward a *practical* finality channeled through a ritual full of *magical actions*."[23] This would explain the perseverance of cults considered heretic elsewhere, which led to many observers thinking about and ideologizing on the late appearance of Christianity in Euskal Herria. Tardy or not, the fact remains that the undisputable religion of

---

20. Caro Baroja, *The Basques*, 255.
21. Gallop, *A Book of the Basques*, 53.
22. Aranzadi, *Milenarismo Vasco*, 237.
23. Ibid., 238.

the Basque population has been, exclusively, Christianity. This was a Catholic Christianity imbued with a mythical world rich in narrations that guaranteed the transmission of religious knowledge, and in rituals that energized communal relations.

The figure of the mother has been charged with circulating a perception of the world that is alive, in constant movement, in which one must actively participate, and in which one has to invest a trajectory, an interchange. This is a world to which one talks, but that above all responds. It is manifested in thistles that protect the house; laurels that purify when burned; dogs that warn of the presence of death; lady bees that people must ask to shed light on their journeys with their wax and prolong the memory of the deceased; legends of curative exorcisms; and endless other forms of meaning.

It was a belief in a world populated with nonhuman forces, a world that required people to make allowances for its cycles but that could be channeled by human action; a world that nicely dovetailed with the moral of Christian retribution and the belief in an omnipotent and omnipresent God. The concept that perhaps most approximates this signification in Euskara is that of *indarra*:[24] a force that is likely to grant a qualitatively different status to those with whom it comes into contact.

The contact with *indarra*, the Basque equivalent of the Melanesian concept of *mana*, the notion of the sacred, is regulated by a series of fixed practices which the mother transmits through mythical narration by the fire of the hearth. This profoundly religious teaching strengthens a shared vision of the world, which in turn structures individual behavior.

Jesús Arpal argues that the prototypical structure of Basque behavior is based on a binominal alternation between security and liberty, one that "could be interpreted as integration in the group 'versus' individual self-realization."[25] I contend that this binominal dynamics results from the conjugation between the two primordial landscapes of meaning: the *etxe* and the *herri*. One might speculate that it was precisely this combination of a religious teaching replete with magical patterns that invited individuals to actively partake in the world and a vast ritual complex that taught them to adapt their behavior to the rhythms of the other that contributed to the development of a diligent socializing attitude within

---

24. For a discussion of the various meanings of *indarra*, see Ott, *The Circle of Mountains*.

25. Arpal, *La sociedad tradicional en el País Vasco*, 205.

Basque society. Together with a pronounced sense of naturalism, this attitude made individual subjects integrate the inevitable with great existential composure.

Hermeneutics expert Andrés Ortiz-Osés postulates that both naturalism and communalism are a reflection of a "psychosocial structure centered around and focusing on the symbol of the Mother/Woman, which finds in the archetype of the Great Basque Mother 'Mari' its precipitate as projection of the divinized Mother Land/Nature."[26] He suggests that this structure dominates traditional Basque culture, and terms it "matriarchalism," a theory that has been widely attacked by feminist anthropology.[27] Without going too deeply into this debate that confronts two different epistemological realms, it is certainly true that the figure of the mother is key to iconic representations of Basques.[28] She is the living image of protection, compassion, and understanding—unlike the image of the wife who, after all, "is not even a relative."[29]

Outside of the realm of the *baserri*, women have not played a preponderant role as active agents in social space, and they have been systematically excluded from communal rituals.[30] A few important factors, however, have led to the idea that, even if there was no matriarchy per se in Basque culture, then there was a marked equality between the sexes. These include women's importance in the maintenance and religious representation of the *etxe*, where they enjoy prominent roles as workers, administrators, transmitters of language and traditional customs; being in charge of the cults of protection and death; and their right to inherit and to own the goods they bring into marriage.

The anthropologist Teresa del Valle refutes this thesis by pointing out the profound inequality that underscores gender relations in Basque society, just as Otazu y Llana deconstruct the similarly problematic concept of Basque "egalitarianism."[31] Both social and gender egalitarianism

---

26. Ortiz-Osés, *El Matriarcalismo vasco*, 105.

27. For more on this debate, see Del Valle, *Mujer vasca*.

28. Zulaika, *Basque Violence*, 273–75; 372n5.

29. There is a popular joke that involves a conversation between two farmers: "If your farmstead was burning with your mother and wife inside it," asks the one "who would you save?" "First the mother." Says the other. "The wife is not even a relative."

30. Del Valle, *Mujer vasca*, 126. See also Esteban and Amurrio, eds., *Feminist Challenges in the Social Sciences*.

31. Otazu y Llana, *El "igualitarismo" vasco*. In English, see Hess, *Reluctant Modernization: Plebeian Culture and Moral Economy in the Basque Country*.

are great inventions that have sustained an ideal of traditional Basque justice; deep down, however, they are nothing but the products of a modern mentality. As Girard says, equality as justice is foreign to premodern thinking: "human justice ... is ... defined in terms of 'differences' among individuals."[32]

Like all inventions, these too have a trace of truth,[33] which perhaps lies in the fact that the traditional Basque culture that constitutes our imaginary is part of the modern in us. Proclamations of egalitarianism are part of the *shift from kinship relations to territoriality*, which marked the boundary between the Middle Ages and the Modern Period, as Aranzadi contends.[34]

Following this same author, the supremacy of the mother in the Basque symbolic complex led to an identification between the figure of the woman and that of the mother; this identification linked the essence of womanhood to maternity, and established the position of the son as an ideal, paradigmatic position.[35] Joseba Zulaika emphasizes the predominance of the Marian pattern, a scheme of mediation where "God is conceptualized basically as a son."[36] The *aberri eguna* or "day of the Basque fatherland" is celebrated on Resurrection Sunday: at the culmination of communal salvation through sacrifice, and through the posterior resurrection of Christ, the son of God, God himself.

The Plaza: Encounter and Challenge

Enrique Gil Calvo argues that adult confraternity, whose principal characteristic feature is fellowship, has been practically eliminated by mass culture. He highlights the fact, nevertheless, that this has happened "outside of some atavistic corners of the world, like the Basque Country."[37]

In Euskal Herria the confraternity that was traditionally maintained by brotherhoods and associations is certainly still present in the form of

---

32. Girard, *Violence and the Sacred*, 54.

33. In any monograph on the Basque rural world we find an explicit or implicit recognition of the other as equal, even if inequality is patent in customs and practices. See Ott, *The Circle of Mountains* and Douglass, *Death in Murelaga*.

34. Aranzadi, *Milenarismo Vasco*, 393.

35. Ibid., 523–533.

36. Zulaika, *Basque Violence*, 281.

37. Gil Calvo, *Estado de fiesta*, 118.

cuadrillas: "groups of persons similar in age and gender, persons whose solidarity—with typical functions as an agent of socialization—is often strengthened through childhood neighbor relations, common schooling, experiences, and memories, as well as certain initiation rituals and rites of passage."[38] Confraternity is also expressed through associations: groups of men gathering in one locale, at the *txoko*, which they organize and maintain in an egalitarian manner, and where they meet and celebrate their belonging in the fellowship of dining.[39]

These fraternal organizations are nevertheless not atavistic. Rather, as Arpal argues, they are a modern phenomenon based on "codifying insertion into society in terms of the community."[40] The marked overlap of the rural and the urban—a context that was not especially prevalent in the Basque Country until well into the nineteenth century when an urban bourgeoisie emerged as a result of industrial exploitation and financial activities—led to a relative similarity between the two lifestyles: "Transmission between one and the other [has favored]—for their immediacy—the development of a small town lifestyle, the emergence of urban communities, of 'urban villagers.'"[41]

The *cuadrillas*, a widespread phenomenon in most of the Basque Country, derive from "the construction of a community that surpasses the domestic community. One leaves home but does not accept what the street implies in the modern city: the reduction to individuality, to the 'solitary crowd.'"[42] In no Basque city does Manuel Delgado's "public animal" enjoy a majority presence; these "beings of indefinition" that swarm through a public urban space plagued with "spontaneous protocols."[43] The street in the Basque Country has been occupied by the community, which is not as much a liminal *communitas* as a codified community with regular patterns of sociability. Walk the streets of the old quarters in Basque cities, towns, and villages any day of the year, and you will find groups of people singing in front of the bars, with a glass of wine in hand, doing what they popularly call the *poteo* or *txikiteo*: a daily round

---

38. Arpal, *Processus sociaux, idéologies et pratiques culturelles dans la société basque*, 136.
39. See Andreas Hess, "The Social Bonds of Cooking."
40. Ibid., 131.
41. Ibid., 135.
42. Ibid., 139.
43. Delgado, *El animal público*, 119.

of bar hopping which may be repeated in the morning or afternoon, and which convokes the local *cuadrillas*.[44]

This attitude of camaraderie and joviality in the public space stands in contrast to individual behavior, which is normally described as serious and closed. In her study of Basque immigrants in southern California, Sonia Jacqueline Eagle emphasizes the great differences between individual and collective behavior.[45] The author claims that Basques are individualistic and aggressive at work, but spontaneous at social events; they are timid and modest in everyday life, but exhibitionists in games; conservative in their everyday clothing, but exaggerated in the ornamentation and the colors of their best Sunday suits. Eagle argues that outside of the group, Basques are dignified and reserved; inside, they are loud, gregarious, and affective.

According to Eagle, this double behavior is manifest in the ideals and values transmitted and expressed through play, the most relevant activity in maintaining Basque identity in the United States. Games periodically reunite men at the fronton, and encourage them to challenge one another, to compete, which allows them to release accumulated tension and to interact with others.

In the Basque Country, any physical work is likely to be converted into a challenge, an agonic competition. The majority of traditional rural sports derive from chores around the *baserri*: *sega* (grass-cutting), *idi-probak* (ox-drawn stone dragging contests), *harrijasotzea* (stone lifting), *aizkolaritza* (woodchopping), and so on. The public exhibition of the everyday chores of the *etxe* in the village plaza, as well as this demonstration of the idea that "I am better than you," have configured the sporting consciousness of Basque men.

The display of the *etxe*'s individualized power in the shape of agonic contests among young athletic men and the strengthening of relationships through celebrations characterized by jokes and jocosity are the typical images of the Basque plazas, which were traditionally "spaces for the insertion of the rural and the urban."[46] The plaza is the place for representing popular culture, the center where the population gathers in its free time and to celebrate. On the one hand, it is home to ceremonies

---

44. For a discussion in English of the importance of *cuadrillas*, *poteo*, and so on, see Pérez-Agote, *The Social Roots of Basque Nationalism*, 167–73.

45. See Eagle, "Work and Play among the Basques of Southern California."

46. Arpal, *Processus sociaux, idéologies et pratiques culturelles dans la société basque*, 133.

of communal encounters, of fiestas, neighborhood meals and dances; on the other, the plaza features displays of skill, which in many cases are exhibitions of power and tasks related to maintaining the *etxe*.

The plaza is home to the body of the community because, as we will see, it represents the community in its own physicality. Any performance or cultural expression is likely to take place in the space of the plaza. While this may be generally true in other communities as well, the Basque Country has a peculiarity that is relevant for my purposes: the irrevocable relationship between the plaza and pelota. The latter has contributed to the configuration of the central public space. In fact, at first the place and the practice shared the same name. On the cartographer Francisco Coello's maps drawn up in the mid-nineteenth century, the fronton is indicated as "game of pelota;" this suggests that the configuration of the place was later than the game itself, which was played in streets, plazas, and against walls before occupying a definite space; a space that, as I have said, has become the communal place par excellence.

2

The Pelota of Basques

There are documents dating back to the beginning of the sixteenth century that show the presence of pelota in Euskal Herria. As early as 1509 a municipal ordinance was promulgated in Bilbao prohibiting young people from entering the atrium of the church of Santiago to play pelota and other games:

> The boys, playing with balls and / spinning tops and other games in the cemetery of Santiago, disturb and impede the divine hours of the / church with the noises they make; they even climb on top of the cemetery building to fetch their balls.[1]

The church of Santiago was the most famous building in the city; "for being the good and honest plaza,"[2] its atrium—the cemetery—was the busiest place, the nerve center of the city. It was also here that the game was first documented.

The historian Manuel Basas argues that "we find people who love playing the game of pelota—so rooted among the Basques—in the very origins of the city of Bilbao. Just like in other localities of the community, this following was cultivated by using the wall of the most famous building, the church of Santiago, and one its sideways."[3] He argues that at

---

1. Enríquez, *Ordenanzas municipales de Bilbao (1477–1520)*, 178.
2. Ibid., 42.
3. Basas, *Bilbao*, 30. Bilbao was founded in 1300. There is no documented evidence of the game existing in what we today call Euskal Herria until the beginning of the sixteenth century. However, the game cannot have been so strange to Basques because its variants had been played in several areas of France and Castile, although apparently in the main only by the upper classes. Basque families with important positions in the Spanish court must have had close contact with the game; it is probable that the Basque nobility closest to royal power, and which normally settled in cities, played the game. See a similar view in Caro Baroja, *The Basques*, 351–52.

the end of the sixteenth century the game was moved to the rear end of the wall, where a new street was built; the street was named Calle de la Pelota, "Street of Pelota," and it retains the name to this day.

At that time pelota seems to have been a favorite practice in other areas of Euskal Herria. In 1526 the physician Johannes Lange traveled through Navarre and wrote the following:

> The Basque Country is situated in the abovementioned mountains, which home a rough people: they have their own language, which has nothing in common with Gallic, Latin, French, German, and Spanish; where the girls have their heads completely shaven [the custom for maidens and marriageable women] and play the tambourine at dances; the priests jump and show all their skills when dancing; they are even allowed to play pelota.[4]

Priests were decisive agents in developing the game, to which several ecclesiastic prohibitions and regulations attest. As in many other parts of Europe, pelota was probably played in monasteries, around which many medieval Basque towns were built.

The economic and demographic growth of towns (*villas*) with royal power stemming from the royal charters granted them, the nobility and rural gentries' loss of social importance, as well as the emergence of new employment in maritime and commercial companies "produced a radical change in lifestyle in both the city and the country."[5] It appears that in this context pelota gained communal importance, with the game developing in the (still precarious) urban nuclei, despite the fact that oral tradition traces it back to the mountains and rural areas of the country.

There are several legends that feature pelota games between *jentilak*, pre-Christian mythical personae who guarded the most valued secrets of civilization. These forest people—from whom the heroes of civilization stole the formulae of agriculture and other mysteries that divorce humans from their animal nature—left abundant evidence of their Herculean amusements. Big crags and rocks are considered balls abandoned by these titans, who disappeared with the birth of *kixmi*, Jesus Christ.

Moreover, shepherds' games in the mountains, in clearings, and spaces cleared in forests, have led claims that pelota has an agrarian prehistory. Added to this belief is the fact that, since the mid-twentieth

---

4. Urquijo, "Cosas de antaño," 339–40.
5. Caro Baroja, *The Basques*, 83.

century, the rural Basque Country has been the primordial reservoir of the game. The majority of famous pelotaris come from mountain villages and small towns where the fronton is still the communal center par excellence, and where pelota is practically the only recreational option.

Nevertheless, it seems that the evolution of pelota and its expansion as a communal representation had something to do with the development of major population nuclei as well as the changing relationship between classes in the sixteenth century. From an anthropological point of view, this hypothesis would not contradict mythological narratives that place the origins of the game in Basque prehistory. The *jentilak* were fundamental agents in the birth of culture. Mythology provides us with a cultural foundation, although it does not date it historically. Basque culture as we know it today, with land being a primordial source of identification, was born precisely out of the overthrow of the *parientes mayores* (senior lineage heads that evolved into the Basque nobility), and the massive development of chartered towns (*villas*) between the sixteenth and seventeenth centuries. Pelota may have been one of the cultural manifestations that was part of this epoch and that, with obvious transformations, was maintained during this time.

The Establishment of Pelota

As we may infer from historical documents, the first communal ball game in Euskal Herria was similar to that which is still played in the Baztan and Malerreka valleys in Navarre: the *laxoa* or "glove." It also resembled the *rebote*, the game widely played in Iparralde; it has also survived in Hegoalde in the Gipuzkoan villages of Villabona and Zubieta.[6] Both *laxoa* and *rebote* are direct style games in which the ball is exchanged directly between players, without the mediation of a wall. Similar direct games are found across Europe and the Americas.[7]

Long style games occupy open rectangular plazas that are between 80 and 100 meters (approximately 260–330 feet) long and 15 meters

---

6. As regards all the Basque provinces at one or the other side of the French-Spanish border I use their denomination in Euskara: Iparralde (literally "the northern side," the Northern Basque Country) and Hegoalde ("the southern side," the Southern Basque Country).

7. By pelota games I mean games where the ball is directly passed back and forth between two or more players. This alternating exchange of the ball in pelota makes it similar to tennis, but qualitatively distances it from basketball, handball, or any game where there is simultaneous competition for the possession of the ball.

(approximately 50 feet) wide. These plazas may have one or two walls (rebound walls) at their ends; the walls of buildings like a church, or a rampart.

The *Bote luzea*, *laxoa*, and *rebote* are long style games. The principal differences between them derive from the size of the court, the instrument they use, the number of players that make up the team, and the distance from which the serve is executed. For this serve they use the *botillo* or *botarri*, literally "bouncing stone;" historically, it was a stone but nowadays it is a wooden tripod with a stone or metal plate on top, on which the ball is bounced prior to serving.

Bote luzea players use their bare hands rather than any instrument. As it is a modality that has practically disappeared, there is no strict rule to determine the number of players that make up each team, which thus varies depending on the contest.[8] It is believed that this was the game that mostly sheepherders played in the *pilota-soros*, the fields that were created in the clearings or spaces made from forests for pasture.

Laxoa and *rebote* are very similar and both are extremely complex. The structure of both consists of two teams—four players in *laxoa* and five in *rebote*—situated in front of each other. They are composed of two frontcourt players or *quarters* with short leather gloves, and two backcourt players with long leather gloves in *laxoa* (server and number), and three with a wicker basket or *xistera* in rebote (first, second, and third *xistera*). In *laxoa*, the serve is executed by the server and with a long glove, from the end of the serving area, a field that the ball must surpass and which is half of the entire field of play (80 meters or just over 260 feet long). In *rebote*, it is a *quarter* who executes the serve with his bare hands from the line that divides the field of play. Here the court is 90 meters (approximately 295 feet) long and divided into the serving field (58 meters or 190 feet), and the remaining part of the court (32 meters or 105 feet long). The teams attempt to keep within this area, as the shorter the length, the smaller the court they have to defend.

The procedure of both games is the following: once the serve is executed, the teams hit the ball alternately until one of them scores a point or a *raya* (line). Points are scored when one team cannot return the ball

---

8. I am not aware of this modality being played in recent years. It is portrayed in the film *Pilotasorotik Madalensorora: Oiartzungo pilotaren historia* (From *Pilotasoro* to Madalensoro: A History of Pelota in Oiartzun, Lehize ekoizpenak, 2004). Madalensoro is the name of the Oiartzun fronton.

or, while returning it, it flies off-court without touching the ground. The score is counted in the same way as tennis: fifteen, thirty, forty, and game. The *line* is won when, after being served, the ball exits one of the sides of the court or if it stays inside on its own trajectory or through an opposing player's intervention, for the second serve.[9] The place where the ball exits or is stopped is marked with an object—which varies according to the locality—that is also termed a "line." This marks an imaginary line that divides the field of play when the teams change fields. Changing fields takes place when both lines are established, or when just one line is established and the game reaches forty. In these cases the fields of play are changed, and the lines are contested in the order they were arranged.[10]

The imaginary line that coincides with the place where the line is set, in other words where the ball exited or was stopped before the change of fields, now divides the field of play. The team that has the smaller field—the team that won the line before the change—will have a greater chance to score, given that it will defend its field better and will have more space (the opposing field) to return the ball.[11]

In summary, if during the game one of the teams manages to cover the entire field and to keep the ball within the side lines without it being intercepted by the opposing team, it wins the entire field and a score of fifteen is added to the scoreboard. If it has only won part of the field of play, it will have to play in the smaller area once fields are changed.

The game therefore consists of hitting the ball to a place in the opponent's field where no one can return it and thus gain terrain or field through use of the ball. Either the entire court is won by hitting, in which case one scores fifteen, or the team needs to defend the part that is not won yet, playing the line. Reducing the area that one needs to defend goes hand-in-hand with more control over this area. The game is over when one of the teams reaches nine games in *laxoa* and thirteen in *rebote*.[12]

---

9. In *rebote*, a quarter or frontcourt player on the same team who hits the ball may detain the ball and mark a line, a strategic line, aimed at making a change in the playing field and maintaining the smaller area.

10. Normally each line is of a different color. First they place the red one and then the blue one.

11. See more descriptions in Abril, *Dos siglos de pelota vasca*, 191; Bombín and Bouzas, *El gran libro de la pelota*, 1236–67. The difficult nature of this game makes it very difficult to understand. It is best to see it in person together with an expert.

12. Traditionally, *laxoa* also ended in thirteen games, but a decision was made to cut it to nine in order to reduce the duration of the game.

Laxoa is played in the Baztan and Malerreka valleys; and *rebote* in Lapurdi, Lower Navarre, and the villages of Zubieta and Villabona in Hegoalde. As regards *laxoa*, there is an annual championship between April and August comprised of twelve teams. Simultaneously, there is a youth championship as well. *Rebote* is in better shape; it is played at championship level in four different categories and it attracts greater crowds. The finals are held on the first and second Sunday in August, respectively.

Laxoa and *rebote* are Basque long style modalities, but similar variants exist around the world: *pelotamano* (handpelota) in the Canary Islands, Tuscan *pallone,* Frisian *keatsen,* Valencian *llargues,* and Colombian and Ecuadorian ball games. None of them has undergone the same kind of modernization as well-known short style modality games like tennis, badminton, and paddle tennis. The Valencian *scala i corda* also belongs to the same branch, as well as the *paxaka.*

The short game modality *paxaka* is played in covered spaces like the *arkupes* and *konsejupes*,[13] and closed spaces like the *trinquet,* where a net divides the court. The lines of the game are fixed, while it is scored once again in *quinzes*, fifteens. Each team consists of three players, and they play with bare hands or short gloves; the ball they use is bigger yet not as hard as that of the other modalities.

Most direct games, with the exception of tennis, paddle tennis, and badminton, have been exclusively maintained in a specific geographical area and linked to a particular culture. In spite of this, all of them share similar features, and one may say that they belong to the same family of games that captivated Europe during the Middle Ages.

Probably present on the continent from the period of the Pax Romana in the first and second centuries, the game of pelota is referenced in the early seventh-century *Etymologies* of San Isidro of Seville.[14] Known as the palm game (*juego de palma* in Spain and *jeu de paume* in France), pelota was played in both territories throughout the Middle Ages.

From the construction of covered halls in the fourteenth century to the regulation of ball manufacturing in the fifteenth century and the

---

13. *Arkupes* (literally "under the arches") are the atriums of church buildings, and the *konsejupes* ("under the city council") are those of the municipality. Typical of this kind of court is the one in Elizondo (Navarre), where *paxaka* was played until access to it was closed in the 1980s.

14. For background information, see Gillet, *Historia del deporte.*

confirmation of 250 playing courts in Paris in the sixteenth century, almost all monarchs, whether Spanish or French, promulgated some kind of a decree regarding one of the most widely played games of the Middle Ages. Apparently, the two royal courts developed both short and long style modalities: the first category occupied open spaces and the second one closed spaces. These were known as trinquets or *tripots*.[15]

The Navarrese court cultivated pelota in the same manner. As early as 1331 the king of Navarre, Philip III "The Noble," charged a carpenter—Pedro de Olaiz—with the construction of a tribune in the cloister of the preachers of Iruñea-Pamplona from where to watch the game. However, pelota was probably not a very socially widespread game and was most frequently played among the upper classes.

As I mentioned before, it was only in the sixteenth century that the game began to appear in Basque plazas and streets. The following testimonies from Navarre date from the beginning of the seventeenth century:

> Mr. Prosecutor versus the priests and the beneficiaries of Olite whom, with much indecency, *play the coarse game of pelota in the streets and in the palace*; they also play cards for great sums of money, generating a lot of gossip in the town.

> Mr. Prosecutor and Martín de Ororbia, a resident of Artajona [Artaxoa], versus D. Miguel Goyena, beneficiary of the parish. As they were playing pelota in the plaza of the town, they were arguing over a *fifteen* by Goyena *that they mistakenly annulled for having touched the ball twice*. During the argument the beneficiary *hit* the plaintiff on the head, causing him a great wound and leaving him in a grave condition.[16]

Inferring from descriptions in these and similar disputes, the game barely differed from the modalities described above. Perhaps only the instruments changed, with the paddle representing the most important modification. This tells us that this game was related to the one played in Castile—the game that Goya paints with great clarity in what was to

---

15. For a discussion of "palm games" see De Luze *Le magnifique histoire du jeu de paumme*; and Arramendy, *Le Jeu, La Balle et Nous*, 139–45.

16. Sales and Ursua, *Catálogo del archivo diocesano de Pamplona*. The documents are from 1612 to 1605, respectively. My italics. The "palace" (*palacio*) referred to in the first testimony may mean undeveloped land of the nobility outside of the borders of the town, as Zaldibia makes reference to that usage in Otazu y Llana, *El "igualitarismo" vasco*, 103–4.

become the bedroom tapestry of the Prince of Asturias in the El Pardo Palace: "El juego de pelota" (The game of pelota), painted in 1778 and 1779.

The paddle probably existed simultaneously with the glove as means, most likely, of protecting players' hands, and no doubt also with the racket, or rather what we know today as *xare*. The *xistera* derived from the glove in its two basic variations: *joko-garbi*, from where jai alai comes; and remonte. This transformation, however, did not occur until the nineteenth century.

The great variety of modalities that pelota exhibits today derives from the different ways of hitting the ball in contemporary France and Castile: the typical wrist play of the French, which prevails in the majority of the games of Iparralde, and the clean strike of the Castilians, which is very distinct from the game in Hegoalde.

The search for accessible materials, the location of the game area in social and urban centers of the community, and the passion with which the people played pelota in Euskal Herria stimulated its popularity there; just at the moment when other communities, especially those nations that became states, witnessed its disappearance. The decline of the French and Castilian games coincided with the end of the early modern era,[17] as defined by the French Revolution of 1789, which took physical shape in the new National Assembly—convoked at a trinquet court.

The Basques were at this time already playing games similar to those played in the rest of Europe, with the difference that in the Basque provinces these games were not restricted to the upper classes.

The Basque Plaza: The Fronton

Contrary to what would happen in other areas of Europe, the modern era appears to have been a fundamental moment for the emergence of pelota in Euskal Herria. From the sixteenth to the eighteenth centuries, the game permeated the social fabric to such an extent that it became crystallized in the very morphology of the villages and their people, as the Spanish Enlightenment figure and statesman Gaspar Melchor de Jovellanos observed:

---

17. Following generally accepted historiographical timelines, the Early Modern era corresponds roughly to the period between the 1500s and the 1800s. Sociology defines Modernity as dating from the French Revolution, the single historical event that marked the shift from the modern to the contemporary era.

The Basque Country is also different in this respect. There is practically no village where they do not play the game of pelota—a great, convenient, free, well-established and frequent practice. And if we argue that public dances affect moral character, we also find in them and in these games the reason for the robustness, strength and agility with which those natives are endowed.[18]

Jovellanos observes the widespread presence of "the game of pelota" in the Basque public space, yet he does not describe these spaces in any detail. They probably did not differ much from the open spaces, some of them still in use, that had traditionally been used to play the long style games. Normally they were open fields situated by the church buildings or ramparts or other constructions of relevance in the urban architecture, whose walls served as the frontal boundary of the game.

As noted, the atriums (*arkupes*) of church buildings were also used to play pelota, as is still the case today. Discussing medieval cities, Robert Fossier emphasizes that the place chosen for the organization of meetings and decision-making was the atrium, cemetery, or ossuary, where quarreling was considered sacrilegious.[19] In Lizartza (Gipuzkoa), the old fronton located precisely at this place is still called *zimitorio*, a name that Emiliano de Arriage includes as "simintorio" in his Bilbao lexicon with reference to "the atrium and portico of Santiago where the youngsters played pelota."[20]

When the city council, which had previously gathered in the atrium of the church or other important place, constructed its own building (the city hall), the fronton was located on its ground floor and came to be known as the *konsejupe*. Azkoitia and Elgoibar (Gipuzkoa), Algorta and Leioa (Bizkaia), and Elizondo (Navarre), among others are examples of this typology.

Plazas are also commonly framed by fronton walls, whether single as in the case of Iparralde or double perpendicular as in the case of Hegoalde. The latter is the prototypical model of the fronton: with an open, paved court, framed by two stone walls at a right angle to one another, which may simply be boundaries, or may resolve other urban planning considerations like the slope (as in Ondarra and Gueñes, both

---

18. Jovellanos, "Los partidos de pelota," 275.
19. Fossier, *The Axe and the Oath*, 141.
20. Arriaga, *Lexicón etimológico*, 122–23.

in Bizkaia), the effect of the dominating north wind (Gorliz, Bizkaia), or the river bank (Elgoibar).[21]

The plazas are sober constructions ornamented with coats of arms and plaques—either at the highest point or spread over the side wall—that normally take advantage of the walls of other major buildings such as churches (Mundaka, Bizkaia) or city halls (Elorrio, Bizkaia). Increasingly, however, they have their own status, which is marked with a specific elevation, a wall exclusively reserved for ludic purposes.

In the twentieth century many of these frontons were covered and closed in, and these form the majority of those in use today. They are closed frontons (termed "industrial" frontons) in which the pelotaris are not exposed to weather conditions. This type of fronton has spread all over the world with the name *jai alai* (literally "happy fiesta" in Euskara), a term that Serafín Baroja invented in order to designate the fronton in Donostia-San Sebastián constructed on Astigarraga Avenue in 1887;[22] today it principally refers to the game of *cesta-punta*.

Despite the tendency to transform the fronton into the nucleus of Basque towns and villages, a lot of them remained attached to the church building; in certain places the use of the church wall followed the construction of the fronton, and there were even free-standing frontons in the eighteenth century, like those of Markina (Bizkaia) and Irurita (Navarre). What remains clear is that the evolution of the plaza in Euskal Herria has been intimately linked to the practice of pelota.

The Nineteenth Century: Expansion

In the late eighteenth and early nineteenth centuries pelota experienced a profound transformation: the emergence of the iconic image of the pelotari, which is embodied by the figure of Perkain (Juan Martin Inda). For the official record collected in the compendiums on pelota, the figure of Perkain separates the prehistory of the game from its historical era.[23]

Christian d'Elbeé argues that before Perkain there were no Basque pelotaris.[24] He is partly right. There were many pelota players, as docu-

---

21. For a more discussion of this type of fronton see Uribarri, *El moderno juego de la pelota vasca* or González Abrisketa, *Frontones de Bizkaia*.
22. Bombín and Bouzas, *El gran libro de la pelota*, vol. 1, 1164.
23. Ibid., 580–91.
24. D'Elbée, "L'epoque de Perkain," *Gure-Herria*, 714–25.

ments, steles, and other previous references confirm. They might have even been as good as Perkain, but they were not as famous perhaps because what mattered was not the person who played the game, but the community that he represented. Perkain was a faithful reflection of a time that captured the community to which he belonged; in short, his figure concentrated the imaginary of an era that was becoming increasingly individualistic.

The French Revolution "produced heightened cultural anxiety in certain social classes, in the upper classes—an anxiety that later partly infected the people."[25] It was during the same era that *bertsolaritza* (improvised oral poetry), which hitherto had been performed and left to listeners to recall, was first transcribed and thereby recorded for posterity, and when stories in general began to circulate not only by word of mouth but also on paper.[26] Clearly, such new tendencies would have contributed to a growing interest in recovering and exalting the great events and characters of the era, including Perkain.

For his precision in the game and a notably rebellious spirit, Perkain became one of the great legendary figures of the game. Because he opposed the French Revolution, he went into exile, leaving Iparralde and settling in the Baztan Valley in Navarre. While there, he was challenged to a game in his home village, Aldude (Les Aldudes) in Lower Navarre. He crossed the border and, as he was playing the game, a policeman tried to arrest him. Perkain hit the ball so hard that it killed the policeman, allowing him to escape. There are several versions of this story but most importantly, Perkain became, without realizing it or wanting to, a faithful representation of many principles associated with the French Revolution. He was the first *individual* to rise above the institution to which he belonged. With Perkain, pelota was no longer just a game with which to demonstrate the glory of a people; the people wanted heroes, and their names were circulated from one end to the other of the Basque Country.

A major change in the way pelotaris were conceived took place during this same era. Most representative of this change was one of

---

25. Bombín and Bouzas, *El gran libro de la pelota*, vol. 1, 579.

26. This transformation has much to do with the previously oral nature of Basque culture. On orality and *bertsolaritza* in English, see Armistead and Zulaika, eds., *Voicing the Moment: Improvised Oral Poetry and Basque Tradition*; Aulestia, *Improvisational Poetry from the Basque Country*; and Garzia, Sarasua, and Egaña, *The Art of Bertsolaritza: Improvised Basque Verse Singing*.

Perkain's fellow-players: Azantza (Jean-Pierre Sorhainde). Azantza was from a noble family from Kanbo (Cambo-les-Bains) in Lapurdi. One day, a person who loved the game and who was of the same social status as Azantza reproached him for playing in the plaza with people below his rank. Azantza replied that he only played with gentlemen.

Bombín and Rodolfo Bouzas comment that this anecdote shows how the plaza was the most suitable place for an egalitarian encounter between classes.[27] The story also reflects modernity's profound transformational effects on people's mentalities in the most peripheral localities. Azantza was not considering the rank of his opponent but his worth as a player. Pelota thus came to rival one's birth as a source of social status, and the plaza strengthened the game's character as an equalizer.

In a similar interpretation of bullfighting,[28] Enrique Gil Calvo argues against the idea that this ritual must by necessity be associated with ancien régime traditionalism. According to him, there are three ideal figures in bullfighting, all related to the "thirds" or three stages of a bullfight: the "*feudal-purist*" who identifies with that part of the bullfight that takes place on horseback; the collectivist "*rural-ethnologist*" who prefers the San Fermines of Iruñea-Pamplona, and identifies with the *banderillas*, the stage when the barbed sticks are thrust into the bull's back; and the "*urban-bourgeois*" who identifies with the bullfight on foot, which became popular in the late eighteenth century. The bullfighter's skill in bringing the best out of the bull is identified with this type; he tranquilizes the bull and makes him yield to the sacrifice. The bullfighter appropriates the nobleness and ferocity of the bull, exalting his glory and gaining the honor of lineage thanks to his own merit. According to this interpretation, the bullfight on foot is a reflection of the modernization of Mediterranean society in a sense that it enables people from lower social classes to acquire a status that had been limited previously to persons of noble birth. Moreover, the marked social hierarchization symbolized by the bulls' nobility is broken in the ritual through a leader who participates in a "natural" situation of disadvantage but that, owing to his skill and tenacity, manages to direct and win over the potential force of his enemy. A more just ideal scene emerges, which eases social tensions.

---

27. Bombín and Bouzas, *El gran libro de la pelota*, vol. 1, 592.
28. Gil Calvo, *Función de toros*.

In a similar way, in the world of pelota during the late eighteenth century, individual exploits were exalted, recorded for posterity, and celebrated in song and verse. As a consequence, individual personalities emerged from their previous communal anonymity, and sources of social status no longer derived exclusively from family descent.

Key transformations in pelota throughout the nineteeth century were crucial in shaping the game we know it today. In the mid-nineteenth century the long style game was more popular; it procured most prestige for the player and attracted the largest crowds. But the game played against a wall, also called *blé*, had much fewer technical and instrumental requirements, and it started to spread quickly in the plazas. The introduction of elastic rubber in the making of balls had something to do with the boom of this game type, which had probably been played informally for centuries before.

The first precisely dated *blé* game in the records of pelota was held in Urruña (Urrugne, Lapurdi) on September 10, 1851, and pitted two players from Lapurdi against two from Bera (Vera de Bidasoa, Navarre). Already present in the plazas in the eighteenth century,[29] the *blé* style became gradually more popular than the long style modality. In most of Euskal Herria it was, however, typical to find signs that prohibited the new game in plazas: *Debeku da pleka haritzea* (Playing *blé* is prohibited). Despite trying by all possible means to control the invasion of the new game, the momentum of the new modality, which became increasingly attractive for both players and the public, ended up replacing long style modalities.

Pelota's new forms endangered the very recognition, the cultural patterns, and behaviors that the old game expressed. In the opinion of many critical voices, the change was too brusque, and it was not easy to adjust it within the traditional consciousness. The critics emerged from many different walks of life, and remained until into the twentieth century. In 1889, the physician Alejandro San Martín gave a talk in Madrid, contrasting the health benefits of long style modalities with the harmfulness of the new game of *blé*. The same year and following up on this lecture, the writer Inocencio de Soraluce declared that he considered the

---

29. The first reference that we know of dates back to 1771. It is found in a penal document from the municipality of Ordizia (Gipuzkoa), which mentions the disturbances that followed the prohibition of the game in its "Ple" modality because it disturbed the religious worship taking place in the neighboring church building.

game extremely violent and lacking any aesthetic element whatsoever. He also referred to the atmosphere that enveloped the game at the end of the nineteenth century: "what remains seductive is the sumptuousness and splendor of the motley frontons where they play; the affection and the caress that fashion confers the game; the theatrical and furiously aristocratic look, staunchly mixed and confounded with the popular; and the presence of presumptuous ladies, of wealthy bankers and noble titles."[30]

Making pelota more of a spectacle—evidenced by this mass behavior—was reflected in the very structure of the fronton. In the second half of the nineteenth century the left wall was added; it was now not merely a boundary but a fundamental element of the new game.

The left wall offers a much clearer vision of the game as the action is not blurred by what may be happening beyond the court. The fronton took on the appearance of a theater, and the game played there acquired its most dramatic form. Later, in the visual era of mass entertainment and of spectacle, the incorporation of the left wall accelerated the financial progress of the game as well as its geographic expansion.

By the end of the nineteenth century, pelota outside of Euskal Herria was no longer a mere recreational outlet for Basque immigrants professionally dedicated to other careers. Rather, some people emigrated specifically to play pelota, contracted by companies in the target country. Most were Basque and came during established periods—normally the spring and summer months, which alternate in the two hemispheres. The pelotaris, now professionals, crossed borders with their instruments on their shoulders.

> Some found a gold mine in their throats, others in their arms. These professionals were in possession of a skill that the companies rewarded splendidly; they were suddenly applauded, celebrated, adored, and exalted to a social level of which they had never dreamed. In short, they entered the category of those who exhibit to the public a value that draws attention.
>
> The pelotari, therefore, like the singer or the bullfighter, is an *artist* that makes a living by showing off his talent, who makes blunders and errors just as singers may sing out of tune or hit a false note, or just as the bullfighter may miss the heart of the bull and hit the neck instead, fail-

---

30. Soraluce, "Sobre la pelota," 533.

ing to kill the animal; and like them, the modern pelotari receives grand ovations and endures noisy whistling.[31]

In 1892, the year these words were written, there were frontons for Basque pelota not only in the Basque Country, but also in Madrid, Barcelona, Buenos Aires, Montevideo, among many other places. They were industrial frontons, spaces constructed exclusively for pelota, some with capacities to seat more than five thousand spectators.[32] In these frontons, the dominant game was mostly xistera, a precursor of jai alai, as well as the glove and pala modalities. Hand pelota was reduced to plaza frontons, those open frontons that occupied the center of the Basque towns and villages. There, pelotaris trained with the instrument in order to emigrate, but they continued to play the hand modality for fun.

The enthusiasm for pelota was so great in Bilbao that, between August 1886 and August 1887, three specialized journals appeared: *Pelotari*, *La Chistera*, and *La Pelota*.[33] Within a few years demand for such publications extended to Madrid, where in 1893 a weekly magazine, *El Pelotari*, was published with a circulation of five hundred copies. Such was its success that, ten months later, a subsidiary edition, *Frontón*, appeared in Barcelona. These journals published articles about pelotaris, frontons, championships, bets, vocabulary, literature, and similar topics that constituted the golden age of the game.

The Twentieth Century: Institutionalization

In the following years, the construction of frontons continued and extended to the United States, Brazil, Mexico, Southeast Asia, and North Africa. Women also started to partake in the pelota boom that, in 1917—the year when the first fronton of the racket modality (the Cedeceros fronton in Madrid) was inaugurated—included three hundred professional pelotaris all over the world. Indeed, during the twentieth century,

---

31. Peña y Goñi, *La pelota y los pelotaris*, 133.

32. Some eight thousand spectators were reported to have shown up for the game Paysandú-Chiquito of Eibar in the Plaza Euskera in Buenos Aires on April 19, 1885. To compare this with the game's standing today, the recently (2011) inaugurated hand pelota fronton of Bilbao seats three thousand people.

33. Uribarri, *El moderno juego de la pelota vasca*, 22.

the emigration of young Basques to play pelota became one of the major sources of foreign currency for Euskal Herria.[34]

In 1945 there were seventeen frontons worldwide with permanent teams,[35] with an average of forty players per fronton: seven in Barcelona, three in Madrid, and the rest in Donostia-San Sebastián, Iruñea-Pamplona, Bilbao, Zaragoza (Aragon), Lleida (Lérida) and Sabadell (both in Catalonia), and Seville (Andalusia). The teams that played in these frontons were about 95 percent Basque[36] and were divided up between the men's modalities of remonte, pala, and jai alai, as well as the women's racket modality. The latter was played in six of the seventeen frontons, although none in the Basque Country,[37] where, with the exception of industrial frontons in which instruments were used in some towns, hand pelota predominated.

In hand pelota, the professional contests that had been organized since the end of the nineteenth century[38] were completed with official annual championships in 1940, alternating between a singles and doubles championship. The first singles hand pelota champion was Atano III (Mariano Juaristi), who had already been a recognized champion for some years.

Professional hand pelota players from Hegoalde crossed the border to challenge their counterparts in Iparralde, trying their skills in places that are no longer used in Euskal Herria: the free plaza and the trinquet. In Iparralde, the industrialization of the game remained minimal, which left its mark on pelota. The frontons did not incorporate the left wall and the games maintained their traditional character that appealed to French, British, and American tourists, including film

---

34. A pelota player in the 1940s earned about four thousand dollars per month. See Bombín, *Historia, ciencia y código del juego de pelota*, 228.

35. The term *cuadro* or "team" referred to a group of pelotaris who were contracted to play for a specific fronton.

36. Possibly with the sole exception of female racket modality players, whose teams eventually included players from Catalonia and Madrid, despite the fact that there were also a considerable number of Basques among their ranks.

37. The Esperanza fronton in Bilbao was used as a "ladies' fronton;" the term used to describe frontons where women played the racket modality. Nevertheless, it is impossible to confirm if it was a fronton within the abovementioned categories, despite the fact that it was used for training and that women played racket games there.

38. Public contests where a fixed bet was made between the opponents, and with multiple other bets on the outcome among the public; in other words, bets made throughout the entire game and involving odds.

stars like Charlie Chaplin and Orson Welles, the latter of whom made a documentary about pelota in 1955.[39]

Both in its traditional and spectacle form Basque pelota became fashionable during the mid twentieth century. Hollywood stars held photo opportunities with pelota players, diplomats maintained private boxes in the world's most luxurious frontons, and writers were attracted to the game by the mixture of ostentation and permissiveness the frontons emanated. Al Capone, the Greek poet Constantine P. Cavafy, Ava Gardner, and Ernest Hemingway, amongst others, were all regulars at some point on the terraces of the Rambo fronton in Chicago, the fronton in Alexandria, the fronton Palace in Tijuana or the *Palacio de los gritos* in La Habana.

This atmosphere was interrupted as a consequence of political changes in many countries. In China, the Tianjin Forum, one of the most profitable frontons during the first half of the twentieth century, closed its doors as a result of the Japanese invasion of 1937 and would never reopen. The communist system considered betting a capitalist activity; and frontons shut down in all the countries where leftist absolutist regimes were established. The Palacio de los Gritos ("The Palace of Yelling") in Havana was one of the most emblematic frontons in the Americas, and it met the same fate three years after the Cuban Revolution of 1959.

The 1970s witnessed the beginning of the game's decline outside the Basque Country. Spanish society started developing habits that were common elsewhere in Europe; the range of free time activities grew substantially, and pelota was merely one of many options. Most industrial frontons in the Spanish state remained in use and some—like the Principal Palacio in Barcelona (1969)—were even inaugurated, but the practice of pelota decreased significantly: by the 1980s, no frontons remained active outside the Basque Country and La Rioja. In these areas, there was still a passion for pelota. In the hand modality in the 1960s, Atano X (Luciano Juaristi) and Azkarate (Hilario Azkarate), the David and Goliath of pelota, enjoyed for many years a leading role in the most anticipated contests. This proto-agonic scheme, which I will analyze in chapter 3, was reproduced in the pala modality between Iturri (Juan Manuel Martínez Iturri) and Saralegi (Miguel Goldarazena), and

---

39. *Pays Basque II (La Pelote basque)* (Basque Country II, Basque Pelota), the second part of the documentary series *Around the World with Orson Welles*. BBC, 1955.

in the jai alai with Orbea (Fernando Orbea) and Chucho Larrañaga (Jesús Larrañaga).

Jai alai, the only game that retained frontons abroad (in Indonesia, Mexico, and the United States), suffered two players' strikes in the United States, hurting the game considerably. The first of these ended in 1968 when American entrepreneurs traveled to Gernika and Markina and contracted the sons and nephews of the great players on strike. This led to major conflict in these areas at a moment when the quality of the game far surpassed that of both previous and successive generations. Twenty years later, in 1988, just as the game was enjoying another peak, a second strike took place. The jai alai players wanted to improve their working conditions, while the companies that employed them would not yield to their demands. Each of these strikes resulted in the closure of various frontons, and the public looked for other spectacles on which to bet. Since then, there has been a gradual decline. The fronton of Milford, Connecticut, one of the most important frontons in the United States, closed in 2003, leaving only four pelota courts in this country, all in the state of Florida: Fort Pierce, Miami, Dania, and Orlando. There were plans to build a fronton in Texas by 2006, but they never came to fruition.

Jai alai was also unable to recover the splendor it used to have in the Basque Country. In 2002, for the first time since it opened in 1963, the Gernika fronton did not open its doors every Monday of the year, as had been its custom. Yet after being closed for various years, it reopened in 2008. Its decline has not been universal, however, in Iparralde, the Biarritz fronton has grown in popularity and hosts professional games on Tuesdays and Saturdays. Eusko Basque, the company that for years has had monopoly in professional jai alai in Hegoalde, also organizes the pala modality. Its nerve center is the Club Deportivo in Bilbao, where every Thursday and on weekends there are festivals of four games that, on occasion, feature both jai alai and pala. This fronton has a regular public, like remonte, a modality that with the 2003 closure of the Euskal-Jai fronton in Iruñea-Pamplona, maintains only one open fronton: the Galarreta fronton in Hernani. With an extremely loyal public, yet one that is a little staid when it comes to risking its money, the Beti-Jai company is considering the (increasingly remote) possibility of reopening a fronton in Madrid.

The modality that currently enjoys the best situation is hand pelota. It has two principal companies: Asegarce and Aspe. They have been challenging each other for years, and have been confederated since 2002 in the LEPM. Hand pelota survives financially due to substantial television contracts, with at least four games being broadcast every week.

Pelota is also organized on an amateur basis, with thousands of affiliated federations all over the world. Distributed in twenty-three national federations, male and female players play one of the eleven modalities that make up this sport.[40] Their public or private clubs play against one another in championships at different levels and categories. These clubs send their best players to provincial or national selections, which in turn compete at annual national championships and world championships every four years.

The amateur modalities differ from their professional counterparts in four principal questions: (1) the ball with which they play is not always made of leather, and weighs less than professional balls; (2) women also play; (3) a simultaneous bet has no match, that is, there are no public-bets; and (4) games are organized by clubs and federations instead of private companies.

The game is nevertheless similar to the professional game. It consists of accumulating points, preventing the opponent from returning the ball, and following some basic rules: (1) alternative hitting of the ball between two singles or doubles players, where both hands may be used as long as the contact with the ball is according to rules; (2) the obligation that each ball should rebound on the front wall or *frontis*; and (3) a maximum of one bounce within predetermined fixed boundaries that mark the play area or court. The modalities differ in the number of points that one must score to win, the measurements of the fronton, the diameter and weight of the ball, and the specific rules that result from the characteristics of the instrument of the modality in question.

Beyond these differences, hand pelota is most closely linked to the Basque cultural imaginary. Although one might question this perceived primogenial nature, hand pelota is currently the modality that generates greatest popular enthusiasm. This is why this work principally concentrates on hand pelota, with occasional reference made to other modalities.

---

40. Women only play in one modality: Trinkete Paleta Rubber.

Huna zer emaiten ahal duen herrian batasunak.
Here is what may lend unity to a people.
— Larzabale Fronton

Part 2
Larzabale

A Ritual That May Lend Unity to a People

> The vestiges of ritual are like traces of chrysalis clinging to an insect; they are soon discarded.
>
> — René Girard

The game of pelota emerged in the Basque Country and first became a socially important communal event during the sixteenth century. Its popularization coincided with the end of the late medieval crisis and the strengthening of villas or chartered towns. Evidence of the game being played at this time is found in documents made up of its rules and regulations. These documents point to the fact that pelota was occasionally a source of social tension in urban areas;[1] yet they also show that Basque players were recognized at international competitions.[2]

At the beginning of the Modern Era the cultural system that has sustained the Basque imaginary up to the present emerged, revolving around the concept of an egalitarianism based on a supposed universal nobility.

At the close of the late Middle Ages an identitarian consciousness that transcended the clan or factional divisions prevalent at the time began to take shape. José de Aralar, in an act of historicized myth-making, dates the emergence of that consciousness back to the period between 1471 and 1476: the five years between the legendary victory at the Battle of Mungia (Munguía)[3] in which rival Basque armies united in order to fight against Pedro de Velasco, the Count of Haro, whose plan was to abolish the traditional laws and seize power in Bizkaia with

---

1. Examples in Huarte, *Euskalerriaren alde*, 183.
2. Blazy, *La Pelote Basque*, 3.
3. See Aralar, *La victoria de Munguía y la reconciliación de oñazinos y ganboinos*.

the approbation of Henry IV of Castile, and the invasion of Louis XI of France, against whom the Basques fought under different banners. "In this struggle we already see the emergence of a category that featured Euskadi [a term meaning the Basque Country conceived by Sabino Arana, founder of the Basque Nationalist Party, at the end of the nineteenth century] as an international political entity, pointing to the progressive consistency that the concept and the esteem of its own worth was obtaining."[4] The victory at Mungia is for Aralar "the first time. . . that Basques fought together, as a people, for their national liberty;" and the victory "generated a consciousness in the country of its own personality."[5]

It is certainly true that the *foral* system emerged in the period between the late fifteenth and sixteenth centuries. Likewise, a socioeconomic system emerged during this period that, by the nineteenth century, was firmly established in the Basque Country, together with the symbolic complex that we today properly call "Basque." The *hermandades* were also created during this time: these came to form a true policing force made up of priests and people outside the agnatic medieval system of solidarity. They established their authority over the use of violence and configured institutions like the general assemblies and the provincial councils. This embryonic notion of a state, of which there was some inkling in the new political order, might be construed as the beginning of a consciousness that saw beyond the factional alliances of the age and was based on an identity rooted in a territorial logic of belonging.

In his study on Western societies at the end of the Middle Ages, Jacques Heers argues that sporting celebrations represented the transference of armed conflicts, a compensation for the absence of wars. "In the life of the city," he observes, "peace among factions revived competitions of a different order."[6] While I consider pelota to be a ritual that dissipates conflicts, forges relations, and transmits cultural narratives, we may not assert here the historical authenticity of pelota as "redressive action" in the social drama of late Medieval life—which Caro Baroja describes as "the terrible split into two factions, which on the whole consumed the

---

4. Aralar, *La victoria de Munguía y la reconciliación de oñazinos y ganboinos*, 206.
5. Ibid., 192.
6. Heers, *"Fêtes, jeux, et joutes dans les sociétés d'occidente à la fin du moyen-âge,"* 79.

energies of the country during the fourteenth and fifteenth centuries."[7] However, there is one coincidence that, even if it lacks historical verification, points to the mythical origins of the ritual: the colors that served to distinguish between medieval societal factions were the same as those used today in the domain of sports, something that also happens in other European cultures.

According to Heers, as late as 1926 in Tuscany cities were still divided into black and white: a division originating in the rivalry of medieval societal factions, and one that was still strongly emulated during festivals. Relying on an article by Marecq on Byzantine Constantinople, Heers provides a similar example of transferring political schemes onto sports. In this case, the factions that held administrative as well as military power transformed at the end of the Middle Ages into major organizational bodies of equine sports, challenging each other to horse races. These factions, which later became competing teams, were also identified by color: in this case, green and blue.

In the Basque Country, the colors that pelotaris wear to differentiate themselves on the fronton (red and blue) are also those that historically marked the major Basque factions. The Oñacino and Gamboino clans identified with these colors and displayed them primarily on their shields. In Iparralde, where competing medieval factions evolved around the lineages of Urtubia (white) and Saint Pée (red), it is these colors (not red and blue) that are used today to distinguish pelota players. As in pelota today, these factions defined themselves by the *gerrikoak* (sashes) they wore around their waists and were thus known as *sabeltxuriak* (white bellies) and *sabelgorriak* (red bellies), depending on the color of the sash.[8]

Jean Giraudoux interprets the concept of game as an imitation of something that society obliges us to abandon, postulating that games are something like "misunderstood survivals of a past era."[9] With time, they lose all archeological content, and the origins become unrecognizable in their present form, as Girard's words at the beginning of this chapter demonstrate.

---

7. Caro Baroja, *Introducción a la historia social y económica del pueblo vasco*, 31.

8. There is some discussion of the importance of these colors in the political and social life of Iparralde in Gurrutxaga, *The Transformation of National Identity in the Basque Country of France, 1789–2006*, 98–102

9. Caillois, *Man and the Sacred*, 58.

Anthropological work has also confirmed the similarity between war and games. According to Kendall Blanchard and Alyce Taylor Cheska, the racket game (*toli*) of the southeastern Native American Choctaws evolved at formal communal encounters organized by ringleaders or local chiefs as a regular means of preventing other forms of conflict.[10] Although they readily entered into warfare if it was necessary, many conflicts were resolved on the *hetoka* (*toli* field of play),[11] a place where entire communities congregated. The players followed a strict diet and observed numerous taboos and penitence. The size of the bets on the outcome, which were always made in favor of one's own team, revealed the importance of the event. The encounters coincided with various ceremonies, festivities, and social gatherings.[12]

In the West, sports games are usually canceled during periods of bloodshed and political upheaval (as the Olympic Games were in 1916, 1940, and 1944), especially agonic contests and sports that reproduce a scheme of confrontation that is satisfied by war. For example, until quite recently, the greatest baseball playing nations—Cuba and the United States—avoided confrontation on the playing field.

Although many sociological studies see the function of sports as tempering the use of violence,[13] René Girard is the most vociferous proponent of ritual as a mitigator of conflicts: whenever violence is not ritualized, it inevitably flourishes at the heart of the community, producing what he calls a "sacrificial crisis."

According to Girard, the two primordial channels of controlling violence are religion and law. The former is a positive cult par excellence: sacrifice and guarantor of social harmony. The legal system fulfills the same function: both orders ensure that they are a "prevention or cure of violence. . . . Only by opting for a sanctified, legitimate form of violence and preventing it from becoming an object of disputes and recriminations can the system save itself from the vicious circle of revenge."[14] Turner also remarks that redressive actions are almost always "ritualized and may be undertaken in the name of law or religion."[15] In the face of

---

10. Blanchard and Cheska, *The Anthropology of Sport*, 170.
11. Cushman, *History of the Choctaw, Chickasaw and Natchez Indians*, 184.
12. Blanchard and Cheska, *The Anthropology of Sport*, 169–71.
13. See Elias, *Deporte y ocio en el proceso de civilización*.
14. Girard, *Violence and the Sacred*, 24.
15. Turner, *The Anthropology of Experience*, 39.

social dramas or "public episodes of tensional irruption,"[16] the underlying fear of disintegration or of chaos makes people embrace deep-rooted moral imperatives, often against their own interests: "choice is overborne by duty."[17] Nevertheless, redressive actions "may fail . . . if law and/or religious values have lost their efficacy."[18]

When social norms and values lose their rigor and the community looks for new exits and redressive actions, they are usually accompanied by a change in the ideological order that sustains the community. It is thus that "institution" takes place, which Hans Georg Gadamer defines as "the originating act by which [a sign] is established";[19] it is the consecration of a new meaning that may provoke transformations in cosmology, in the set and articulation of cultural symbols.

This is perhaps why the control of violence is a central argument in practically every cultural foundation. Almost every foundational myth revolves around a situation of primogenial violence, whose resolution implies the instauration of a new cultural order. Furthermore, in this initial state of crisis violence erupts between equals:

> Restorative violence, which is at the same time a destructive force and occasion for creative reform, is not inter social violence, intertribal war. . . . Violence, symbolized as violence between kindred, between brothers and twins, is part of the intra social, in other words, domestic violence: it is a specter that circulates within endogamic society, in the closed space of the township. Violence between equals inscribes on the collective memory of the city the recognition of a primordial danger that damages the sociality of the city on the one hand; on the other, it confirms its ritual exorcism by the mediation of the new order that the community adopts.[20]

Myths reproduce the latent danger in society as well as overcoming such danger because their function is precisely that of "maintaining and preserving a culture against disintegration and destruction."[21] The function of cultural preservation attributed to myth is likewise attributable

---

16. Turner, *Dramas, Fields and Metaphors*, 33.
17. Turner, *Secular Ritual*, 35.
18. Turner, *The Anthropology of Experience*, 39.
19. Gadamer, *Truth and Method*, 148.
20. Wunenburger, *La fundación de la ciudad*, 23.
21. García Pelayo, *Los mitos políticos*, 19.

to ritual, which fulfills it even more efficiently: "the part of myth which belongs to the world of theoretical representation, which is mere record or accredited narrative, must be understood as a mediate interpretation of the part which resides immediately in the activity of man and in his feelings and will."[22] This premise constitutes one of the most widespread certainties in anthropology: "it is rather the cult which forms the preliminary stage and objective foundation of myth,"[23] a premise that supports Durkheim when he says that believers "feel, in fact, that the true function of religion is not to make us think, to enrich our knowledge . . . but to *make us act*, to help us live."[24] This means the rite precedes the myth that, in many cases, will thrive in the form of history.[25]

For this reason, whether or not a specific social drama or sacrificial crisis exists de facto, it seems evident that conflict is latent in the social perception of reality. What ritual representation does is sublimate instabilities and disequilibrium, let them be personal or social. It serves as a "control over instability, as a safeguard against anxiety, as mediation with the divine or with certain occult and ideal forms and values, as communication and regulation, as the reinforcement of social bonds."[26] Rituals are means of strengthening the bonds within the community and thus avoid the outbreak of violence. They strive for confluence, for the dissolution of the self in something greater and sacred, in the communal force of "us."

---

22. Cassirer, *The Philosophy of Symbolic Forms*, 39.
23. Ibid., 220.
24. Durkheim, *The Elementary Forms of Religious Life*, 311. Emphasis added.
25. As was the case in Roman mythology, for example. See Dumézil, *El destino del guerrero*, 16.
26. Maisonneuve, *Ritos religiosos y civiles*, 20.

3

The Control of *Indarra*

Indarra in Euskara means "strength" and is a polysemic term that can also concurrently mean "power," "value," "energy," "capacity," and "violence." Sandra Ott likens the concept of *indarra* to the Melanesian *mana*, a vital root that occupies the center of the notion of the sacred;[1] a root that Durkheim would define as the essential principle that "gives rise to ... collective life."[2] It is a force likely to be embodied in objects, animals, plants, and people without any of them being able to possess it entirely.

He who possesses *indarra* is *indartsua* or strong, the strong man. He is courageous, sharp, and powerful. Without *indarra*, the body is debilitated and sick, and *indarberritu* (literally "to renew strength"), means to recuperate or recover; while *indarbide* or "the pathway of strength" is a remedy for health. The dependence of the body on *indarra*, a dependence that is physical as much as it is social, contrasts with another meaning of the term: that of "violence." In this case, however, the root is normally accompanied by a suffix that has a pejorative connotation: "-keria," *indarkeria*.

Girard notes that the Greek term *hieros* ("sacred") bears an ambivalent application to instruments of violence and war.[3] As opposed to Émile Benveniste, who attributes the coincidence to a simple accident by which two words share the same vocable, Girard finds another argument for his central thesis in the term *hieros*: "violence is the heart and secret soul of the sacred,"[4] a thesis that the concept of *indarra* also supports.

---

1. Ott, *The Circle of Mountains*, 87.
2. Durkheim, *The Elementary Forms of Religious Life*, 15.
3. Girard, *Violence and the Sacred*, 277.
4. Ibid., 32.

While it is problematic to compare meanings of terms from distant cultures, and it is the context that ultimately fixes the range of meanings of *indarra*, the concept itself implies a vital force that is necessary, contagious, and, if not controlled properly, may constitute an inexhaustible source of danger. For this reason, anything that is capable of channeling this force becomes sacred, thus establishing one of the most effective bases of power.

The connivance between power, violence, and the sacred has emerged as a key binding element when constituting the political. Georges Balandier attributes the emergence of the political sphere to the projection of sacred qualities on those who hold power:[5] on the one hand, it concentrates the legitimate use of violence; on the other, it consecrates every order that allows it to control and exercise violence.

In his discussion of Basque aesthetic-ritual, Joseba Zulaika reveals the implicit masculinity of the term *indarra*, emphasizing the suffix "ar" "which in general means 'macho,' . . . as a component to other terms like *senar* (husband), *oilar* (rooster),"[6] and so on.

The world of pelota is integrally masculine. There are no female *pelotaris*, no female referees, bookmakers, quartermasters, managers, directors, or federation officials. Even the specators are almost entirely male. Only when a game's appeal as a spectacle grows does the number of female spectators increase. In the sumptuous frontons of the early twentieth century it was quite common for "presumptuous ladies" to be present; according to writers of the period, they lent the spectacle a fashionable air. Recently, the presence of women on fronton terraces has increased notably, although only in the hand modality and at major games.

One could argue that women do not participate in the world of pelota. They could always play with brothers and friends in the plaza, and there may be a rare exception of a female coach or referee, but it remains unthinkable that a woman should occupy a central role in professional pelota, let alone as a protagonist of a game on the court: "Women being *burrukalaris* [fighters] and *jokalaris* [players] does not fit with the cultural premise of their character."[7]

---

5. Balandier, *Political Anthropology*, 99–122.

6. Zulaika, *Tratado estético-ritual vasco*, 101.

7. Zulaika, *Basque Violence*, 182.

The equality of the sexes, which translates into political activism in other realms of life, does not penetrate the sphere of ritual. Women's participation in the most important communal representations provokes seemingly irresolvable conflicts. One such example is the *alarde*, the military-style parades in Hondarribia and Irun.[8] The greatest resistance to gender equality is produced at the representational level, something that might result from the symbolic confluence of the different meanings of *indarra*, and the central place the notion of force occupies in the origins of the political community.

Born to Be Pelotari: A Life Story

> The pelota player is basically born, even if he later has to make himself great through devotion, sacrifice, and perseverance. Slumps, crises, and injuries are blows that he needs to overcome with great moral vision and thinking about the future. The sport is a fight to death.
>
> — Retegi II, pelotari

To be born a pelotari implies, above all, being born male. This first mandate is then followed by others. A glance at the life story of Retegi II, a player who for many was the greatest champion of all times, may reveal the attributes a player needs to have in order to achieve fame, and be a worthy representative of his people.

Julián Retegi was born on October 10, 1954, in Eratsun (Erasun), a rural village with a population of four hundred in the Navarrese mountains. It was poorly connected to the outside world by public transport and most people made their living from agriculture and livestock.

At the time, Navarre had no professional players in hand pelota; Gipuzkoa was the dominant province, with eight of the nine winners of official title games to that point coming from there. Besides Barberito I (Abel San Martín) from La Rioja, only Bizkaia equaled Gipuzkoa as a fertile quarry of professional hand pelota players. Even so, the two great champions of that era were both Gipuzkoan: Atano III, *azkoitiarra* ("from Azkoitia"), and Gallastegi (Miguel Gallastegi), from Eibar.

In 1954, despite being fifty and thirty-six years of age, respectively, Atano III (champion for twenty years, winning four official titles), and

---

8. For an anthropological approach to the conflict see Bullen and Egido, *Tristes espectáculos*; and Bullen, "Gender and Identity in the *Alardes* of Two Basque Towns," 149–77.

his successor Gallastegi (winner of three titles), played doubles on both sides of the border; they were the last remnants of the traditional dueling system. They were two legends of pelota whose stories spread from the old to the young of Eratsun by word of mouth. Everyone dreamed of becoming like them one day, a painfully distant dream considering the fact that until then no one from Navarre had even debuted as professional hand ball player.

And yet, pelota was the preferred entertainment for the youth of the village who headed for the fronton every day after school or work to play *a punto*,[9] a ball game where the best player wins by the gradual elimination of the rest from the game. Even today, the nucleus of the village has barely changed; it features a few houses, the church, the school, and the fronton, which dates back to 1932. It has an ashlar front wall with the village coat of arms at the top. The fronton is attached to the priest's residence, whose wall forms the left wall. The priest, a great fan of pelota, "taught the essentials and the technique of this game to the children"[10]

At about the age of six, girls and boys would start hitting the ball; at an even earlier age they would be throwing it *harrika*[11] against the walls of the fronton. Julián Retegi started to take a greater interest in pelota in 1962, by which time two Navarrese players had emerged in the professional field: Ezkurra (José Ezkurra) and the recently debuted Bergara I (Marcelino Bergara). He spent most of his time at the fronton, from where he and his peer group would be at times expelled when they wanted to play the game. On such occasions, he and his friend would either return to the school, where there was a *kaiola*[12] in the basement, or stay around to watch older people play. They would sit at the right side of the fronton on the wall that bracketed the terraces, or stand at the rear end of the wall.

One of the young men of the village who excelled at the game was one of Julián Retegi's fourteen paternal uncles, Juan Ignacio Retegi, who

---

9. *Punto* is synonimous with *primi*. For a description of the game *a primis* see chapter 5.

10. In the words of Retegi I (Juan Ignacio Retegi), Julián Retegi's uncle, in Garcés, *Campeones manomanistas, 1940–1990*, 159.

11. *Harrika*—literally "by stoning." It means grabbing the ball and throwing it as opposed to hitting it.

12. *Kaiola*—literally "cage." This is a small fronton, closed on all sides, where the ball can bounce against every wall.

was eleven years his senior. Juan Ignacio Retegi had been at a seminary boarding school since he was ten, and would return home to Eratsun only occasionally, especially during summer vacations. On one such visit, Juan Ignacio recognized that he could beat youngsters who had the opportunity to play the game the whole year round—something that was impossible for him as he spent his later seminary years in Córdoba (Andalusia), far away from any fronton. He became aware of his "natural disposition" for the game and, on seeing a photo of the great Azkarate, he promised himself to reach the highest level, thereafter practicing enthusiastically against the walls of the seminary building. He returned to Navarre a year later, and settled in Iruñea-Pamplona to earn his teaching certificate. Every day as he left the university, Juan Ignacio met up with his friend Martín Ezkurra, the owner of the boarding house in which he was staying: the Hostel Mendi. And on Sundays he would play games in other Navarrese places.

The enormous potential of the player spread by word of mouth, and he quickly became a well-known figure in the amateur field as he won the singles title for three consecutive years. As a result, recruiters from Empresas Unidas ("United Companies)—which since its inception in 1953 had enjoyed a monopoly over hand pelota—recognized in Juan Ignacio the mysterious quality that a great pelota player needs to possess. They thus signed him up and he made his professional debut on May 20, 1965, under the name Retegi I.

Retegi I was characterized by his spectacular game of great strength and powerful shots, something that made him a frontcourt player among the *cuadros alegres*[13] of the fronton. Juan Ignacio revolutionized the game with his signature *volley*, a play in the air that moves from being a defensive hit to becoming a great weapon of attack. The frontcourt player from Eratsun used to destabilize his opponents with this shot. Even when he would appear beaten, Retegi I hit this volley and he was back in the game, exhausting his opponents. This was possible, above all, due to the power the pelotari possessed, the power of a backcourt player that plays at the front because, as a genuine left-handed pelotari, he had tremendous talent and an ability to surprise his opponents. On the right-hand

---

13. The *cuadros alegres* or "happy squares" of the fronton are the front part of the court typically occupied by frontcourt players. This area of the court is characterized by more intensive play and faster movements, and this is where scores are typically made—hence the name "happy squares."

side, however, he was rather hopeless. Apart from this weakness, Retegi I was a well-rounded player of strength and cunning.

In 1967, Retegi I won the *txapela* (literally "beret," the Basque beret awarded a champion) for the second division singles championship title with the assistance of his inseparable friend and now also his *botillero* (adviser), Martín Ezkurra. As a result, he was promoted to the first division. At this time Azkarate was the great champion, a Hercules of a backcourt player from the Bizkaian village of Elorrio, who had just won his sixth *txapela*. He played out great duels in the hand modality with the other great champion, Atano X, a lucid and skillful frontcourt player from Azkoitia (Gipuzkoa), a member of the famous Atano pelota clan, who had weak hands but great cunning. Atano X was accompanied by his uncle who was also his trainer, and who for many was the greatest champion of all times, Atano III: "the revolutionary pelota player [who] excelled not for his power and aggressiveness, but for his rapid and intuitive movements, his rigor and spirit"[14]

The last great pelota player of this family, Atano X, coincided with the first members of another dynasty that would in future make an enormous mark on the world of pelota: the García Ariños from Axpe-Marzana (Bizkaia). Jesús, champion in 1957 and 1963, together with his twin brother Ángel, the second character in this particular family saga, formed one of the most resolute doubles formations in the *cuadro*, the team that plays in a specific championship or for a particular company.

The 1960s brimmed with great figures. Besides the archetypical battles between the David and Goliath pairing, between the ingenuity of Atano X and the right-handed powers of Azkarate, perhaps most complete, well-rounded player ever in terms of physicality and intelligence also emerged at this time: Jose Mari Palacios, Ogueta, the "cyclone" from Araba.

Champion in 1958 and 1959, Ogueta suffered a back injury that ultimately kept him out of the *manomanista* (hand pelota singles championship); he nevertheless remained the pelota player who, according to fans, exhibited the most beautiful postures in the court. He was tremendously spectacular, and by virtue of his unparalleled intent, this robust pelotari played at the front quarters of the fronton. With outstretched

---

14. Beristain, *Azkoitia: Cuna de pelotaris*, 46.

arms in *besagain*[15] and an unpredictable wrist action, Ogueta drove his rivals crazy. He literally "nailed" them on the court. Julián Retegi admired Ogueta. Each time he accompanied his uncle to the fronton, he would become transfixed by the rigor and power of the "cyclone." The force that he transmitted was unforgettable: "in my childhood, we never stopped talking about Ogueta,"[16] he said.

In 1969 Retegi I won the first division hand pelota championship, becoming the first Navarrese to win a *txapela* in the singles division. The delirium throughout Navarre, and especially in Eratsun, was indescribable. The final was held on Sunday, November 30, having been postponed for six months because of an injury to Atano X, Retegi I's opponent, and despite the extreme cold—(Retegi I and his *botillero* Martín Ezkurra were trapped by snow and arrived just in time to start the final). The impact of Retegi I's victory was felt immediately, with an unprecedented growth in popularity for the hand modality in Navarre. Now young players there had someone to look up to and Retegi I demonstrated that it was possible to be from Navarre and become a hand pelota singles champion. In fact, since 1969, out of a total of forty-four first division singles hand pelota championships, only three have been won by players from outside Navarre: Gorostiza (Iñaki Gorostiza) from Atxondo, Bizkaia, in 1977; Tolosa (Joxean Tolosa) from Amezketa, Gipuzkoa, in 1989; and Xala (Yves Salaberri) from Lekuine (Bonloc), Lapurdi, in 2011—the first player from Iparralde to win the *txapela*. In sum, then, Retegi I's victory did indeed prove to be a productive game!

Martín Ezkurra and Retegi I detected a pelotari *e nature* in Julián Retegi, who seemed to have inherited from his uncle an absolute control of the court space. However, his somewhat skinny frame and little apparent strength did not initially appear to mark him out for greatness. Even Julián Retegi himself had little faith in his future as player. Without any other options, and at the age of just fourteen, he started to work in the quarries around his village, and later in the paper mill of Leitza. At the age of sixteen, he was selected to compete for the Federation of Navarre in an amateur provincial tournament, and, despite not possessing the muscular stature of his opponents, he beat them easily.

---

15. Literally "arm in the air." The capacity to hit with open arms is a great advantage as it multiplies the possibilities of managing the ball and deceiving the opponent.

16. Julián Retegi (hand pelota player), interview by the author, Atxondo (Bizkaia), November 20, 2000.

At the same time, Retegi I was becoming a legend of the game. Followers saw in him a serious player who enjoyed playing with the harder balls, something that had been quite forgotten in the previous era; besides, he was winning games through spectacular play and by lending the game a noble air. In 1970 he won the *txapela* again only to be beaten the following year by the backcourt player Lajos (Julián Lajos), whom many would say was not born a pelota player but compensated for it with great passion and devotion. Retegi I recovered the championship title in 1972, and successfully defended it until 1975.

Retegi I was also fighting another, more personal battle to talk his nephew into becoming a pelotari. Julián Retegi was at the difficult age of eighteen when most players abandon the game because of family pressure or a lack of commitment. He took a job logging in the Alps and on his return found out that, without his knowledge, he had been signed up to play in an amateur doubles championship together with Martirikorena. They won it.

Martín Ezkurra, was likewise convinced that Julián Retegi was "very much a pelota player": "the ball fit his hand very well, which, even if he is not strong, helps any pelotari with his game."[17] But Julián still hesitated. He had decided that he would keep logging, and had already received the necessary papers to go to France. Despite these arrangements, Ezkurra and Retegi I did not waver until they convinced him. They advised him to sign up for his obligatory military service voluntarily (before being automatically drafted) so that he could stay in Iruñea-Pamplona and keep playing. They told him that if he did not make his debut within a year, he could always go back to France to take up the logging job.

Volunteering for Spanish military service was not a straightforward affair. However, Retegi I enjoyed widespread acclaim in many walks of life and he was able to help his nephew. Through personal connections, the governor of Jaca (Aragon) interceded on behalf of Julián. While doing his military service, Julián Retegi made his professional debut on July 11, 1974, in Zarautz (Gipuzkoa) under the name Retegi II. Due to his enormous disposition for the game, he was soon assigned rivals of the highest category. He even got to play against his idol, Ogueta, thus fulfilling one of his greatest dreams.

---

17. Martín Ezkurra (botillero to Retegi II), interview by the author, Iruña-Pamplona (Navarre), June 18, 1999.

The following year, 1975, was the year of Eratsun, the small village in Navarre that was home to Retegi I and Retegi II. That year, uncle and nephew became *manomanista* champions in the first and second categories, respectively. It was the first time that both titles had been won by players from the same town and the same family, although family sagas were and are a recurring phenomenon in the world of pelota.

The most distinguished families in the hand modality have been the Atanos, the García Ariños, and the Berasaluzes. It is also common for brothers to form doubles pairings: Atano II (Luciano Juaristi) and Atano III, Arriaran II (Joxe Arriaran) and Arriaran I (Félix Arriaran) Tapia I (Fernando Tapia) and Tapia II (Juan Ramón Tapia), García Ariño I (Jesús García Ariño) and García Ariño II (Ángel García Ariño), among others. The same families would also produce people with different functions in the world of pelota: ball-makers, bookmakers, trainers, managers of material, or any other roles assisting the game. While fandom permeated the entire Basque Country, the circle of pelota was relatively small inasmuch as it relied heavily on the—moral as well as logistic—support of the family so that a young person could dedicate himself to the sport.

The pelotari is born, most of those involved claim. It is enormously difficult to get to the top. In the Basque Country of the 1970s there were few children who did not play pelota and one had to be among the ten best players to be able to make a living from the game. There is a cutthroat selection process that usually takes place when players are around seventeen or eighteen years of age, the same age at which both Retegi I and Retegi II had doubts about whether to continue with the game or try another career. It is precisely at this moment when those who were "born" for the game stay on track. In order to decide to play professionally, something that is more likely if there are role models in the family, pelotaris need to be aware of the great sacrifice and devotion that the path to the top requires. Besides skill, becoming a *pelotari* requires a lot of passion.

Retegi II had a passion for the game. He enjoyed it and, in contrast to his cousin Retegi IV (José María Retegi), who was endowed with greater physical qualities but lesser discipline, did not find training so hard. He was a born winner and he proved it as he gained more and more confidence; so much so, in fact, that in one game against his uncle (who by then hardly played hand pelota singles matches) Retegi II dominated Retegi I to such an extent that he was keeping his opponent's score to zero. Then with one right-handed—his weaker hand—bad-but-lucky shot, Retegi I scored a point and, although it was the only point he made in the whole game, Retegi II disputed it ardently, claiming he had heard the sound of the iron sheet, indicating that the ball was off court. The spectators reproached his excessively competitive attitude and scorned him for being disrespectful. Martín Ezkurra, claimed nevertheless that "pelota is like that"; that "one has to fight for each point like it was the winning one";[18] he argued that the game did not create any conflict between uncle and nephew who, upon leaving the fronton, had lunch together amicably.

The contest in the plaza, no matter how intense it may become, does not necessarily have consequences for life outside the game. On the court one plays "to the death," but after the game pelota players often have lunch or dinner together, or go out for drinks. A pelotari is normally good friends with his main rivals, even if sometimes spectators believe they have played unfairly against one another. Many claim that Gallastegi was treated unfairly in favor of Atano III. Nevertheless, they were good friends. In fact, they played a lot of doubles, games they arranged for themselves. Atano III showed up for the celebration in Gallastegi's honor when he became champion by beating him, and Gallastegi speaks fondly of the player from Azkoitia. The rivalry between Retegi I and Lajos is another common example. Of the five finals they were supposed to play, two never took place. In the first case Lajos withdrew on account of an alleged injury; in the second, petitions by the injured Retegi I to postpone the game went unheard. Lajos was the first pelota player signed to the books of Eskulari, a company that broke the monopoly of Empresas Unidas and whose star player was Retegi I. Indeed, the struggle between the two companies undermined the 1976 singles final. Yet despite all this, Retegi and Lajos had been training together for years before.

The pelota player knows that rivalry exalts him; this is why star players often come from the same village or family. The pelotari is judged by the quality of his rivals, just like his salary: "he [Gallastegi] received fifteen pesetas for his first game as professional in Eibar in 1937. But the 'mini salary' soon increased in proportion to the quality of the rivals the robust young man from Eibar played."[19] Besides ensuring the right

---

18. Martín Ezkurra (botillero for Retegi II), interview by the author, Iruña-Pamplona (Navarre), June 18, 1999.

19. Bombín and Bouzas, *El gran libro de la pelota*, vol. 2, 1406.

emotions on the terraces and generating passion for the game, a worthy rival makes the pelota player grow. This is why a pelotari truly holds his opponents in high esteem. If he is unhindered by injuries and spends long enough time on the court—the kind of fortune Ogueta did not enjoy, for example—every great hand pelota player will have his great adversary, his rival par excellence. It is normally a prototype, an exemplary, ideal type embodied by a specific player.

In 1979, a nineteen-year-old youngster from Baraibar, Navarre, debuted in the professional league: Galarza III (Ladis Galarza). He was an archetypical pelotari: strong, elegant, with an ideal posture for the game and with a very special, magic touch. His innate talent for the game allowed him to advance through its ranks swiftly and, since he had not played in the second division hand pelota singles championship, he went directly into the first division of the game. Here he joined Tolosa, another pelota player of great strength, who had been playing in the division for years. Subsequently, both of them would become Retegi II's major rivals during the next ten years. In 1980, however, Retegi II won the *txapela* from another giant, Maiz II (Antxon Maiz). And he would repeat the championship victory in 1981 and 1982 against Garcia Ariño IV (Roberto Garcia Ariño), the eternal finalist who, despite playing five finals, never secured a championship title.

Aware of his physical deficiencies, Retegi II developed all kinds of tricks to neutralize the strength of his opponents. Moving and wearing out the opponent to the maximum before finishing off the point characterized his game. He would make his opponents run to all corners of the fronton; he set out to exhaust their rigor, to neutralize them. As the game proceeded and his opponent's power was waning, Retegi II played increasingly comfortably. With very fast legs and exceptional hands— "in which," as Ezkurra remarked, "the ball fitted as well as if he were a backcourt player"[20]—he managed and placed the ball with mathematical accuracy. Because of all this, he was undisputed champion for nine straight years between (and including) 1980 and 1988.

In a world of players much stronger than him, Retegi II resorted for a while to the *atxiki*[21] technique, a shot traditionally considered a

---

20. Martín Ezkurra (botillero for Retegi II), interview by the author, Iruña-Pamplona (Navarre), June 18, 1999.

21. Literally "sticking," it refers to grabbing the ball with the hand to pass it back instead of hitting it. According to the rules of the game, it is a fault.

foul because the pelotari retains the ball in his hand, because it facilitates control and converts any shot into an offensive weapon. First played by Arroyo II in the 1970s, the *atxiki* was used by players who possessed lesser power. Retegi I fought his own battles to eradicate "such a harmful strike;"[22] it was also frequent in the game of his greatest rival, Lajos, who reportedly perfected the *atxiki* in a quarry training with a lead ball.

Martín Ezkurra, the inseparable companion and *botillero* of both Retegi I and later Retegi II, considered the *atxiki* the great ailment of pelota. However, because the technique was widely used and because of Retegi II's relatively weak hands, he encouraged him to use it. Within a few days of training, Retegi II incorporated it into his game as a tool that he himself would have found unaccpetable in the plaza of Eratsun, but which at that time was not penalized and was used by many players, especially by those who suffered from the dreaded *mal de manos* (injury to the player's palm).[23]

Until it was prohibited and penalized in 1984, Retegi II used the *atxiki* especially when his opponents were gaining an advantage over him; when they would make "an errand boy" out of him by sending him all over the court. In such cases he resorted to the volley, neutralized his rival's strength, and even managed to dominate him. Something similar happened in the first final in 1983 between Retegi II and the player who was to become his greatest rival: Galarza III. That year, the then three-time champion was having a difficult time at the finals. Despite an initial disadvantage of 16–6, the young backcourt player from Baraibar remained undaunted and decided to let loose with his powers. Magnificant games obliged Retegi II to employ the volley, some of which went unnoticed by the referees. Retegi II, despite the complaints of the crowd, who jeered these shots, persisted in his strategy and won 22–16.

The following year the potent twenty-four-year-old backcourt player and the astute, thirty-year-old, four-time champion frontcourt player faced each other again. This time the referees did not overlook Retegi II's volleys and sanctioned him with two faults. Galarza III played him as an equal, but because of a lack of maturity, he made the mistake of abandoning various balls at key moments of the game. Despite the defending champion leading 21–18, the contender's pride and a few

---

22. Martín Ezkerra (botillero for Retegi II), interview by the author, Iruña-Pamplona (Navarre), June 18, 1999.

23. See Gámez and others, *Measurement of Hand Palm Pressures in "La Pelota Vasca" Game*.

mistakes on the part of Retegi II lead the game to sudden death, a 21–21 tie. Experience, or rather ingenuity, would decide the game: "The defining score was played according to the expectations of logic, a ball from the right side which Retegi volleyed back; Galarza turned to the referees and claimed a 'fault,' but had to rectify his position on seeing that he had not been not heard. He arrived late, and Retegi shot beyond him."[24] It was the fifth consecutive title for the champion.

Julián Retegi, that skinny boy who never saw himself a champion, was now making history. He was the first player to win five consecutive titles since the championship had been an official annual event, and in 1985 he would have the chance to equal the record of Azkarate and his own uncle, Retegi I: six *txapelas*. Retegi II did not forget that he was the boy who lacked a pelotari's prototypical physique. He trained hard. Without renouncing classic training methods in the mountains and the fronton, he revolutionized the pelotari's physical preparation. He incorporated the gymnasium into his program: lifting weights produced the muscles that nature denied him. He also changed his diet: the traditional T-bone steak was substituted for white meat. Vitamin pills and glucose also became part of the player's diet. For his part, Galarza III possessed an ideal body and unsurpassable skills; he however did not deprive himself of the pleasures of life and, although he did enjoy the fronton, he had trouble making the necessary sacrifices to reach the very top of the game.

The 1985 final, remembered for the extreme humidity in the Atano fronton in Donostia-San Sebastián, reflected this reality. Despite the age difference that favored the contender, he did not manage to better his game. On the contrary, the champion, who was by then in his thirties, was improving each day. Galarza III disappeared from the next two finals. He was beaten in the semifinals by Tolosa, a pelotari from Gipuzkoa who was cruder but possessed similar skills. Yet not even Tolosa managed to break Retegi II, who was now going for his eighth consecutive *txapela*.

Through Galarza III's lesson in humility, which caused him to miss the 1986 and 1987, he returned stronger and more ambitious. The defending champion was now thirty-four years old, but Galarza III was still in his prime at the age of twenty-eight: "now I have gone through the worst. I played against Tolosa [the semifinals] with a lot of inner pressure,

---

24. Garcés, *Campeones manomanistas, 1940–1990*, 87.

an enormous responsibility. Now it will be different, and I still think this is going to be my year."[25] But Retegi II, who could withstand so much, grew in the face of this adversity; with an emphatic game he undermined the confidence of the contender—who both agreed afterward was on the way to becoming the new Garcia Ariño IV—for a fourth time.

Galarza III returned in the shadow of Tolosa, another colossus who was setting his forces against the ingenuity of the champion. In 1989 Tolosa snatched the title from Retegi II, preventing him from winning his tenth consecutive *txapela*. Yet this came just a year later, in 1990, when Retegi II beat Tolosa by eight points.

But now it was not the same. Retegi was thirty-six years old and Galarza III confirmed during the game between Retegi II and Tolosa that his arms were good enough to beat the champion of the decade. In 1991, Galarza III beat Retegi II comfortably. The following year he repeated the victory, keeping Retegi II to only twelve points.

Without a doubt, it was Retegi II's pride and self-confidence that forged the greatest champion in the history of the championship. He possessed qualities that serve as the best resources for a pelota player: "an ethic that revolved around the desire to win"[26] made him win the last great duel against the player who had always been his greatest rival: Galarza III. In 1993, for the eleventh time and at the age of thirty-eight, Retegi II once again successfully won the *manomanista* title.

Martín Ezkurra, the person who most tried to convince Retegi II of his capabilities, thought that he would be able to win yet another *txapela*, but the recently founded Asegarce company did not want to support him any longer. Retegi II's contract offered him the same amount of money for playing singles hand pelota as for playing doubles, yet the former required a lot more effort and dedication. During the final years of his career Retegi II preferred playing more games and earning more money over giving his all for a title, something that would have implied a great deal of dedication throughout the year. Even so, Retegi II had the opportunity to feel the heat of a final as a protagonist. It was in 1997, in the four-and-a-half modality,[27] and a championship that he had already

---

25. Galarza III (hand pelota player), interview by Fernando Castro, *Deia*, Monday, April 18, 1988. The final was played the following Sunday, April 24.

26. Ogueta, as told to Garcés, *Campeones manomanistas, 1940–1990*, 155.

27. The four-and-a-half modality is played in singles championship. The players cannot pass the 4.5 mark line, a line that is located between the fourth and fifth square of the court. They have to play within the area marked by this line.

won three times. His rival: Titín III (Augusto Ibáñez Sacristán), from La Rioja.

The first final I witnessed as a part of this research was played at the Ogueta fronton in Vitoria-Gasteiz on December 13, 1997. The game produced great shots and exhibited real quality on the part of both players, but it was nothing exceptional until Titín III reached twenty-one points and was on the verge of victory. Everything indicated that the game was over. The terraces began to applaud the end of the game; the spectators were mostly from La Rioja and thus vigorous supporters of the player from Tricio, who was now enjoying his greatest moments. At 17–21 Titín III executed his last serve amid applause. Retegi II, now over forty and aware that this was to be his last final, pulled out the self-confidence that had always characterized him as a pelotari. He scored the point and got to serve; 18–21, inquietude in the terraces; 18–21, nervousness in the *cátedra*.[28] The more cautious ones started covering their wagers by making counter-bets. At 20–21, emotion was running high. Shouting, uncontrolled laughing, *aupas* (let's go!) everywhere, hands in the air asking for bets. The bookmakers were running around from one side to the other at the opposite end of the court, red in the face and breathing heavily, overwhelmed with work. Retegi II, that old fox, aware of the shock, walked around patiently on the court. Titín III was tense, increasingly nervous; 21–21, an outburst. Vertigo was overtaking the terraces; people were shouting in their bets from all over the place. Yet bookmakers were discriminating and playing dumb to the calls of the crowd, pampering to the *puntos*, the strong bettors. Some brave spectators were holding on to the bet without covering their eyes, sitting down and without wanting to look, at the edge of the precipice. The rest were on foot, ready to applaud the champion. Retegi II, intent on his final comeback, with the ball in his hand, bouncing it tum, tum . . . tum, tum . . . tum, tum . . . to the beat of the heart of the terraces, and allowing the bookmakers to finish their job. Finally, he crossed himself, took the ball, threw it up lightly and, once in the air, ran down the court amidst the general clamor. Ogueta commented on television that this was a game that made people pelota fans. "There was definitely no lack of emotion," he said. Retegi II served, Titín III returned it, Retegi II jumped and hit a drop-shot in the *txoko*: 22–21. He had won. Retegi II and his *botillero* Martín Ezkurra were

---

28. *Cátedra* (cathedra) refers to spectators who regularly wager, and who are seated in the first rows, close to the bookmakers.

carried around the court by the crowd on their shoulders. Today Ezkurra is retired after winning three more hand singles titles with Eugi (Patxi Eugi), making twenty in total; meanwhile, Retegi II is technical director of the Asegarce Company.

The story of Retegi II highlights the qualities and conditions a pelotari needs in order to become great. As he himself claimed, to become a noted player "you need to be born of a certain quality; in the end pelota is a mystery, it has a special touch."[29] Discovering "the chosen one," the one that has *indarra*, power, the one that has all the necessary qualities to win over the crowd and bring them collective glory is not an easy task. Retegi II himself, as technical director of Asegarce, could not detect them in today's best active player, Juan Martínez de Irujo, who ended up being contracted by the rival company Aspe; in fact, Retegi II disregarded the trainers' recommendations. All the important qualities are markedly inexplicable, quasi-religious: devotion, self-confidence, the capacity to suffer, and the desire to win. In and of themselves, attributes like strength, skill, astuteness, and velocity do not make a good pelotari. There is an extra element that is beyond all of these qualities, one that makes the spectator say "this is a pelotari."

Retegi II says it is a "mystery" that only those see who are profoundly affected by pelota: those who make the game a fundamental aesthetic criterion for their lives. Martín Ezkurra discovered it in Retegi II: "the ball fit his hand very well." Like Cinderella's shoe or Arthur's sword, the ball fits the hand of the person who is meant to be a pelota player perfectly.

This natural disposition for the encounter with the ball must be accompanied by something that has a lot to do with youth: the *nervio*, or "vigor." Vigor is the power of the arm, a natural ability. Losing vigor is losing the grace of *indarra*, something that may happen during a game or with age. While it may come and go, it is believed that vigor ultimately wears away with time and practice. The seven-time remonte champion Koteto Ezkurra claims that "if you start your career too early, you might lose your vigor early."[30] Nevertheless, experience that comes with age may certainly compensate for the loss of vigor through good positioning

---

29. Julián Retegi II (hand pelota champion), interview by Ana Baiges, in *Euzkadi* 225, January 16, 1986.

30. Koteto Ezkurra (remonte champion), interview by author, Doneztebe (Navarre), September 1, 1999.

on the court, something that is achieved "with the fronton:" by putting many hours and a lot of devotion into the game.

Devotion to pelota implies a great capacity to suffer and make enormous sacrifices. The mere hitting of the 105-gram (approximately 3.5 ounces) ball requires great physical strength and consequently an effort that is difficult to explain to someone who has never tried the game. The swelling of a pelotari's hand may make it twice its natural size. The game itself, the short but explosive moves and the body's overall disposition to catch the ball that needs to be hit with the maximum effort each time exhausts the pelotari. Retegi II lost two kilograms (approximately five pounds) each game in the singles category, and players of Gallastegi's build may end up urinating blood after a game.

Suffering is compensated by a passion for and the call of the fronton: by doing one's best on the court. Great dedication is required to overcome the crisis typically experienced at the age of seventeen, to resist family pressures prompted by work and financial necessities, and to finally decide to dedicate one's life to a tremendously uncertain future. This is why great players normally emerge from the dynasties and nests[31] of pelotaris; they stimulate dedication and, in that context, young players may find the necessary rivalry to develop their skills. As the champion himself comments: "since I was little, I played against older men and learned to suffer. What mattered was this wisdom."[32]

Rivalry makes the pelota player grow, and every great player needs an antagonist by whose power he may measure himself. After all, pelota is a "fight to death" between two proto-*agon*ists.

Proto-Agonists: Foxes and Lions

> Cunning like a fox,
> And strong like a lion.
> —José María Salaverría

Despite the fact that the pelotari establishes his ultimate renown at singles games, the indirect game par excellence is doubles. Indeed, most of the games in pelota are doubles. It is in doubles that the pelotari learns

---

31. Villages with a great tradition of pelota.

32. Julián Retegi II (hand pelota champion), interview by author, Bilbao (Bizkaia), October 16, 2002.

and understands his place on the court. Place conditions his character as a pelota player and the way he confronts his opponent in singles. In doubles, each player occupies a determined position on the court, a position that defines the action he needs to execute, and which officially divides the set of players into frontcourt players and backcourt players.

The backcourt player occupies the rear squares of the fronton. He is the guardian of the back of the court His responsibility is to cope with the onus of the rally. His objective is to hit the ball farther than the opposing backcourt player, to make it difficult for him to reach the ball, and make sure that the opposing frontcourt player cannot intercept it. The backcourt player must *hit the ball as far back as possible*, and play it high in order to take it away from the frontcourt player so that he cannot finish it off or, if he does, that the rebounding ball should favor the same backcourt player or his partner's position. Besides, as he has a better view of the court, the backcourt player tries to organize the game by giving instructions to his partner and trying to *bring the ball down*[33] if the strategy so requires. It is also the backcourt player's task to *guard the back* of the frontcourt player by staying within the radius of the ball's range in case his partner misses it. To this end, the backcourt player synchronizes his movements with those of the frontcourt player at a distance of two squares, or 7 meters (about 23 feet). That way, if the frontcourt player is tricked and moves toward the opposing side of the ball, the defender can take care of it, and stop it from bouncing another time and gaining a point for the opposing doubles.

The principal task of the frontcourt player is to intercept balls that the defenders exchange. After serving, which in hand pelota is his responsibility, the frontcourt player must try to position himself optimally to finish off the play. Drop-shots, hooks, two-wall hits, and shortcuts to the side form part of his repertoire, a repertoire that is principally designed to score points. The frontcourt player must be able to finish off the point, prevent his opponent from taking the initiative, and hit the ball into an area from where the opposing player cannot return it. He has to anticipate the fatigue of his partner and move his position farther back to incorporate himself in the game. He needs to help the backcourt player to deploy his powers to maximum effect. He yields the ball if it is in a better position for his partner, and he knows at which spot of the

---

33. Bringing the ball down means hitting it into the front squares and moving it farther back to the back side by hitting it strong, looking to strike it high on the frontis.

court his partner is most dangerous. He thus devises the game so that the backcourt player can take the ball under the most optimal conditions and can hit the ball farther back than the rival players.

A good doubles pairing is therefore defined by their particular specialized and complementary skills: each player needs to know his objectives and must focus on them. However, in case of a destabilizing attack by the opponent, both need to be able to *assume the position of the other*. Just as the backcourt player sometimes moves forward to retrieve a ball unattainable by the frontcourt player, the frontcourt player must occasionally move back to help out his partner. The good doubles pelotari is generous and able to assume responsibilities when the situation requires. He brings the best out of his partner's abilities, does not sell him out in search of personal glory, and is able to regain control of the game in weaker moments.

Generally speaking, the great singles hand pelota players have not reaped important victories in doubles. The search for equality, which is essential for the game, normally pairs them up with partners of a lesser category. As Retegi II said "they always match me up with partners of less experience, and I have to take the weight of the responsibility. I lack a bit of concentration when I play doubles."[34] An equally matched pair is more efficient than one of unequal ability, even if the latter includes the best player. Both functions are equally important: a frontcourt player who does not deliver or a backcourt player who does not finish off a play create irrecoverable gaps.

The best attribute that the backcourt player may have in order to handle the heavy responsibility of the rally is strength; a force of vigor, of a spectacular energy called power in pelota. For the frontcourt player, whose mission is to finish off the point by deceiving his rival, it is essential to be cunning and to have the necessary degree of agility to carry out the desired objectives.

The conjunction of these three qualities, or rather reduced to two—because cunning without agility or agility without cunning does not last long in the fronton—is what defines the ideal pelota player: ideally, he should be "cunning as a fox and strong as a lion."[35] Yet these two attributes are rarely present to an equal degree in any pelotari; instead, players

---

34. Retegi II to Garcés, *Campeones manomanistas, 1940–1990*, 192.
35. Salaverría, *La gran enciclopedia vasca*, 120.

usually excel in one or the other. Although backcourt players are normally the *lions* and frontcourt players are the *foxes*, there are exceptions like Retegi I, Ogueta, and Goñi II (Mikel Goñi) who, despite strength being their best attribute, possessed the infallible talent of fathoming the game a second before their opponent. For this reason they played the frontcourt.

These two terms—"foxes" and "lions"—are used to describe the ideal type of pelotari in the competition or the *agon*; they are thus proto-agonists. They are foundational models of the contest, and paradigmatically coincide with the two positions a pelotari can occupy: the frontcourt or the backcourt.

The pelotari, as noted, has had an assigned position in the court since the beginning of his career as a player. Strict positioning only applies in doubles, but it is something that indefectibly determines the player's manner of playing. The backcourt player who occupies the rear squares of the court is usually taller and has a stronger build than his frontcourt counterpart; he is responsible for attending to the opposing backcourt player. These characteristics translate into powerfully struck long balls, as his basic quality is strength. The frontcourt player, who is more accustomed to finishing off the point, to "hiding" the ball in difficult-to-reach positions, and deceiving his opponent, must develop the virtue of astuteness. And finally, there is the manner of approaching pelota, something linked to the style of the game, and which I will discuss in part 3.

The greatest players excel in one of the qualities that define the prototypical agonic genius. Mondragonés (Juan Bautista Azcárate), Gallastegi, Azkarate, Galarza, Beloki (Rubén Beloki), and Barriola (Abel Barriola) would, with all their differences, fit in the first group of strong (backcourt) players. Atano III, Atano X, Retegi II, and Olaizola II (Aimar Olaizola) fit in the second group of astute (frontcourt) players.

A diachronic revision of singles championships shows that both prototypes alternate when it comes to winning titles. Pelotaris of one of these two models usually snatch the championship title from players who excel in the other model: in other words, the strength of the lion beats the cunning of the fox, or the cunning of the fox beats the force of the lion. Vilfredo Pareto's thesis on the alternation of power between conservative, stable persons (whom he terms "lions") and astute, innovative people ("foxes") serves as a curious parallel.[36] Weapons unlike his own, weapons that he lacks, dethrone the champion; beating strength with cunning and cunning with strength; hitting where it hurts most, searching for flaws and holes.

Fans tend to prefer one type of pelotari over another. Miguel de Unamuno described such predilections like no one else. In an 1889 article the Basque philosopher wrote about a game in Abando (Bilbao) between Chiquito de Eibar (Indalecio Sarasqueta) and Elicegui (Vicente Elicegui) against Baltasar (Francisco Alberdi) and Mardura (Juan José Eceiza). Unamuno's account refers to the agonic contest of powers—of strength and cunning—and its effect on the spectators:

> "There are *mardusristas* [fans of Mardura] and *eliceguistas* [fans of Elizegui], slaves to their blood and temperament; there are those who follow the force of cunning, of calculus and rapidity, and those who adore and believe in blatant and solid strength, open and without deceit.... There are hardly any *Chiquitistas* [fans of Chiquito] while secretly they all are: they adore the player from Eibar like Homer without having read him, by hearsay and as a matter of course. Some talk about his better days, others believe he is among the best; some say he has sunk, others say the ground has risen; he is a legend already.
>
> "Shut up, big mouth, shut up! Elicegui just keeps hittin' and hittin'!"
>
> "You've screwed us! And Marduras... dirtier than who knows what..."
>
> "Dirty or not, he's winning... and the other guy, what? What matters is winning."
>
> "No sir! What matters is playing clean!"
>
> The substance is always the same, it's only the garnish that changes. Elicegui and Mardura are two symbols, two flags.[37]

Chiquito de Eibar was the best, the player who combined all the qualities necessary; but it was Mardura and Elicegui who ignited passions. They represented the two poles, the two types of power: cunning, at times linked with playing dirty, with the desire to win at all costs on the one hand; noble strength on the other. Cases like this invigorate the great history of the game. During the same era there was a famous rivalry between Vega (Roberto Vega) and Irigoyen (José Irigoyen). After a game that Vega won, he approached Irigoyen and asked him: "But

---

36. See Pareto, *The Mind and Society*.

37. Unamuno, "Un partido de pelota," 305.

you, what do you think? That all you need is strength? Brute force? No, man, you must remember the essence of the game, which is fine play." Later, after another contest between the two this time won by Irigoyen, he went over to Vega after decimating him with his powerful strikes, and affectionately put his arm around his opponent's shoulder: "And now, where are your essentials now?"[38]

Fans are affectively attached to one of these pelotari prototypes: to those who turn strength, or power, into their fundamental weapon, or those who rely on cunning and rapidity to beat their rival. They, too, have played pelota, and have had their role in the fronton. The confrontation the game implies taught them about their own qualities, their fundamental weapons. They understand the game as something that belongs to them because they, too, have actively participated in it and devoted considerable time to it. They admire qualities that they lack but, most of all, they are fascinated to see the qualities they possess chiseled to perfection by a star player.

What the spectator desires to see on the fronton is, among other things, the representation of himself. He praises the virtues that he as a pelotari never had; what he enjoys most, however, is discovering the sublimity of his own powers through their extraordinary execution by a player. He identifies with the virtues he has, and seeks to recognize them in the pelota player he is watching. The fan is inclined toward the player who reproduces his own genius and style in an exemplary manner, while this preference is linked not to a model of play, but rather to a specific representative of the model. Fans are attracted to the fronton by specific players, while they recognize in them idealized moves and manners that transcend any particular pelotari.

Olaizola II masters the proto-agonic model of the "fox" inasmuch as he embodies the archetype; what captivates fans is the power that the pelotari personifies and which in him is reinvented, represented. The model is fulfilled by incarnation, and constitutes an ideal unity, a meaningful whole. "Proto-*agon*ism" becomes the paradigm of a particular rivalry that exists behind its general verbal manifestations and that sustains a certain expression of personal autonomy. Characteristic of the whole people and implied by private rivalry—be it among farmsteads or individuals—this archetypical rivalry serves to psychologically

---

38. Bombín and Bouzas, *El gran libro de la pelota*, vol. 2, 923.

sustain a certain ideal of independence within the context of strong group solidarity.

The Dialectics of Pelota Fandom: The Urge to Challenge

In the feature film *Vacas* (Cows), director Julio Medem portrays the grand rivalry between two farmsteads or household units that spans generations and is dramatized through the agonic contests of *aizkolaris* (woodchoppers).[39] One of the principle reasons why these competitive relationships are maintained is without doubt the importance of the household's (*etxe*) independence and reputation in the Basque cultural imaginary.

In the summer of 1999, I was conducting fieldwork in the Baztan Valley, Navarre. At that time, the frontcourt player Eugi from the Agoitz (Aoiz), Navarre, and a powerful backcourt player Beloki, from Burlata (Burlada), also in Navarre, were engaged in the greatest hand modality duels of the era. During a conversation with a young person from Amaiur (Maya) I asked who he was, if at all, supporting. He said he was pro-Eugi. I thought I knew his reasons: Eugi was from the prototypically Basque "humid Navarre," while Beloki belonged to the "dry," supposedly more Castilian, Navarre. Presuming political reasons I asked why he supported Eugi. The response was categorical: "We have always supported Retegi, and now Eugi. The neighbors supported Galarza." "And now?" I insisted. "I'm not sure. But I guess they support Beloki." I inquired if they had opposing ideologies or any other friction that might skew their answer. Nothing. The only rationale behind player choice was apparently this: positioning oneself against the neighboring household. Theirs was an antagonism in its purest state, with no apparent motivation beyond the representative sphere.

The fight with the other, acting to the contrary, and adopting an opposing stance to demarcate one's own personality have probably contributed to the emphasis in the Basque ethos on a marked awareness of independence. This sense of independence leads to paroxysm in the Basque rural figure whom Caro Baroja calls "*xelebre*," the rustic "villager fond of paradox."[40] He is the person who above all "is particularly distinguished for his witticisms, his comments, in which he generally

---

39. *Aizkolaritza* or woodchopping (see above) is a traditional Basque sport.
40. Caro Baroja, *The Basques*, 233.

defends the opposition (inverse) opinion from that externalized by the majority."[41]

The display of autonomy through an antagonistic positioning against friend, neighbor, colleague, or even brother nevertheless dovetails with a behavior that ties one to the community, symbolically enveloped by the image of the territory: the *herri* or "country." Beyond particular preferences, fans share ascription to a group by the locality of their birth; these places are often represented by a pelotari, whether active or retired.

When the fan communities meet in a village or town to see a game, they make comments related to the locality where the rival fans come from or the player they support—a pelotari with whom they normally share the same birthplace and maybe even age-group. One frequently hears comments like "here they are, those from Ondarroa," "seems like the fans of García Ariño [sixty year olds from Bilbao] have arrived," "have you seen Titín's lot [supporters from La Rioja]?"; "they say that those from Baraibar have arrived with their pockets full." Individually or collectively, the fans identify with players through birthplace; they follow players who share the same origins, even if they are retired from playing. They might prefer a certain playing style over another; the natal village or province, however, creates a bond that is recognized within and outside the group.

A penetrating look at the rows at the fronton aims to check if one group or another is present. If not about the game per se, conversations on the terraces revolve around the "who is who:" the village, profession, family, and life of the person under scrutiny, who is normally introduced at the end of the game. Exchange of information and introductions follow; besides a high degree of familiarity, they create a social network among those coming to the fronton. These encounters and reencounters contribute to the consolidation of friendships that will resound for the person as well as the community in other facets of life. Pelota thus becomes a solid reinforcement of relationships among men who fraternize around a common passion that goes beyond the physical space of the fronton. It is a social resource of great importance and a recurring theme that fuels a major part of sociality in the Basque Country.

Fans talk a lot about pelota. Most of all, they talk about the players. The conversations begin with some statement like "Have you read

---

41. Ibid.

the paper, what it says about the game on Saturday?"; "They have no idea. I think *X* is not prepared for the *manomanista*;" "I don't know what is going on lately, he is just not taking the ball well." An assessment of the player who will be the favorite's rival follows: "Nevertheless, have you noticed how *Y* has been enjoying his game lately?"; "I haven't seen such strength in a frontcourt player since Ogueta." And such judgments lead to hypotheses: "At any rate, if *X* gets to hit the ball, *Y* won't even score 12"; "Of course he will, a little pressure will do it. He will eat *X* for breakfast;" "In Labrit [a fronton in Iruñea-Pamplona] he will not even catch a cold, let alone the ball;" "I'd like to see him against *Z* one day." Fans work up an appetite for the event. They want to see contests of great quality. They want to take sides, to create polemics. They are excited by games between recurring rivals. They recognize the style of the pelota players and have seen them play each other before. They each have their favorites and they eagerly await how and in whose favor the contest will end this time. They predict the outcome and bet against one another. They get submerged in a dialectic duel that boils down to a display of one's own knowledge about the game. To do so, they blend an analysis of play, a historical overview, playful personal comments, and allusions to destabilize the rival and, as a climax, references to the fan community itself.

The degree to which the *pelotazale* or pelota fan is immersed within the world of pelota is measured by his capacity to refer to/talk about the amateur field: "They say there is a young player in Burlata who can beat anyone in hand pelota;" "The other day in Logroño a young player played a devastating hook. His opponents didn't even see the ball;" "it seems like in Eibar they are training a backcourt player with a prodigious right hand, and his left hand is also phenomenal." Until quite recently, the popular desire to see the protagonists of these rumors and speculations on the court was crucial when it came to organizing the vast majority of the contests.

The growth in regulations and of organized structures—schools, clubs, and companies—has without a doubt left the amateur field rather segregated from the professional world of pelota. This happens despite the horizontal disposition of the game in which most fans know one another, and eventually get to know many of its actors: the pelotaris, the company representatives, and the bookmakers. The effect of the crowd in influencing the organization of contests is decreasing; a certain way of settling games has disappeared.

Traditionally a public challenge was made by the pelotaris themselves, or the "societies" that supported them and that usually included people from the pelotari's hometown. The challenging party directly posited the conditions, which would be open to negotiation, through the media. If the couple in question accepted the challenge, which was almost a moral obligation, the parties would meet to negotiate and establish the conditions. They prepared a voucher that detailed the moneys bet, the date and place of the contest, as well as its basic rules. The amount proposed, which depended on the financial situation of the interested parties, friends, relatives, and fans, was deposited with a competent authority—in Basque towns and villages it was normally the mayor. The particulars of the duel were then announced in the press, thus convening the public. Anticipation would depend on the level of the players, the quantity of the moneys proposed, and the peculiarities of the contest itself; the more *chirene* (unusual),[42] the better, especially if the players were still of little renown.

Generally, the crowd was accustomed to this type of contests; they coexisted with games organized at frontons with permanent teams, which normally played instrument modalities. In these duels no money was exchanged between the players; it was the crowd that bet depending on the moneys stipulated and during the whole game, very much as it is done today.

If games were organized by the fronton, the pelota player earned the stipulated amount from the owner or leaseholder of the fronton; if the pelotari was not a permanent member of the fronton's team, they added a certain percentage of the box office to this. The entrepreneurial structure, which emerged in the second half of the nineteenth century in Argentina, remained in place until the 1950s and exploited one or several frontons. The business or the businessperson in question was responsible for managing the fronton, which normally had its own team of players.

During summer vacations pelota players were hired by the villages for fiestas, fairs, and other events. They would agree on a fixed amount of money as a price for the winning pair, as well as an additional price for the best player of the game. In the Basque fiestas of Elizondo, Navarre, which coincided with the *santiagos* (the feast days of Saint James) in 1879,

---

42. Many of these contests had meta-rules; for example, X would play with his left hand tied and would not be able to hit the ball between specific squares.

rebote games with *xistera* were organized, with the winning pair awarded four hundred pesetas and the best player one hundred pesetas.[43]

Because there were no professional pelotari teams associated with specific frontons, which was typical in the instrument modalities, at this time, hand pelota owes its existence to such festive contracts and challenges, a system that was also applied to the singles championship. After beating the most prominent players in the game, a title aspirant would have to publically challenge the champion, who reserved the right to consider the challenge. If it was accepted, a game was organized in which the champion would play with one hand only, to see if the aspirant was worthy of playing the final. If the aspirant won, a three-game final was agreed on, two of which had to be won in order to take the championship title. This is how, for example, in 1926, Atano III snatched the title from Mondragonés, who had held it between 1917 and 1925. The games were played in Donostia-San Sebastián, Eibar, and Bilbao during the fall and winter of 1926.

From 1940 on, the structure of the official championship organized by the Spanish Federation (set up the same year) changed the system and established an elimination tournament and a laddered structure of the round of sixteen through which the champion enters the final directly. This system that was used in hand pelota until the 1990s and is still maintained in remonte, jai alai, and pala. For the rest of the year, games were organized either through challenges or by fronton managers, who organized festivals and paid the players according to their usual fee.

This situation changed in 1953 with the founding of Empresas Unidas by the different companies that had used various frontons to that point. As opposed to the business organization of the rest of the modalities, which worked with specific frontons and had teams of renewable players, Empresas Unidas started to keep a full-time team who were summoned to various frontons over which it exercised monopoly. The pelota players signed a contract that stipulated that they could only play under the name of the company. No challenges, no fiestas—they were in theory unavailable for nonprofessional fans' games, unless the company accepted their organization.

---

43. *Laurak bat*, Year II, no. 19.

Some of the best pelotaris—for example, Gallastegi, the champion who did not play the final one year for financial reasons and who, rumor had it, was one of the reasons why Empresas Unidas was founded—did not want to be part of the new company and remained loyal to the traditional system of challenging. Empresas Unidas's eventual monopoly, however, meant that all those who wanted to play the hand modality professionally would have to sign a contract with this company. The contract consisted of an annual fixed payment in exchange for a set number of games that, if exceeded, meant the company had to further recompense the pelotari.

The fans noticed a decline in the pelota players' motivation, and complained that the cartels made do with inconsequential games to fill the program, disregarding the emotive component of the game. Through their alliance, the companies managed to neutralize the financial demands of the most celebrated pelota players, especially those of Gallastegi, but they failed to stimulate the fronton as the wager did. In order to offset players' financial demands, they allowed the pelotari, who was accustomed to betting a fixed amount in contests, to participate in the betting like any other member of the public, always betting on himself of course, and without being able to cover his losses by betting on the other player. This ensured that the player would do his best on the court, which calmed the public and especially the bettors.[44]

Once contests are agreed upon, whether through the traditional system of agreeing on the conditions and a fixed financial amount beforehand, or through the company's arrangements as is the case nowadays, news of the games spreads through the fan community, prompting several predictions: "Everything depends on what kind of balls they are, I suppose, but I don't think he has much chance these days. X is very strong;" "Yes, but Y is an old fox. With his long serves he can do a lot of damage;" "I don't think so." Having sized each other up, then comes the bet: "I bet thirty euros that he doesn't allow him fifteen points." "Thirty that he does." "Deal."

Bets are made even before the selection of the material: the balls that are used in the game. They may be the result of individual initiative, verbally or through mediators, normally in bars whose counters serve to make the bets. Posters displayed on the wall announce the bid: "500

---

44. Nowadays, pelotaris do not bet on games in industrial frontons.

to 400 euros in favor of *X*," "1,000 euros that *Y* will not get to 10." Both challenge-bettor and challenged-bettor pay the quantities wagered in the bar, with the eventual winner taking everything.

In the late nineteenth century, this was the typical method employed by pelota bookmakers in the old quarters of cities. In Bilbao's Arenal section, for example, bookmakers set up their stalls and put up posters featuring the bets of all the games played all over the world. In fact, when the Bilbao Stock Market was founded on private initiative, the pioneering founding families approached the bookmakers in the Arenal in order to get their help in the buying and selling of stocks. Bilbainos (inhabitants of Bilbao) could therefore aquire stocks in Altos Hornos (a major iron and steel works in Greater Bilbao that would subsequently become the largest manufacturing company in Spain) as well as bet on a game between Chiquito de Eibar and Paysandú (Pedro Zabaleta) in Buenos Aires.

As the game approaches, so news and rumors mount about the condition of the players: "*X* has something wrong with the left hand. . ." "Well, yesterday the papers said that he was optimistic, that he liked Astelena [a fronton in Eibar] and if he gets a *pelota de toque,* a ball that strikes hard, he will do some damage." "What is he going to say? When the only thing he has is condition! Beyond that he is done, that is obvious. He won't even score 10." "With only the right hand he already has it all." "Yeah, whatever." The comments of each denote the fans' positions and their favorites.

The fan takes one side or the other in the contest so that he can play against a colleague, a friend, a neighbor, or anyone with whom he can amicably compete. He thus satisfies a desire for autonomy by taking up a position against the other, yet also establishes great networks of fraternity. One invitation to bet calls for another, and wagering for a cup or a quarterfinals against someone implies entering into a series of exchanges similar to a potlatch. There is always an obligation to accept the challenge, especially for the person who won the wager before.

The Wager with Bookmakers: Turning the Coat

In the early twentieth century wagering followed patterns of identification by birthplace or province. The spectators who attended a game divided into two groups, and supported one or the other player or pair. The pelotaris deposited a fixed amount of money with a competent authority in order to seal the contest. In the following game described by Unamuno, the players wagered five thousand pesetas,[45] a quantity offered by the people closest to the player—family, friends, neighbors, and so on.

This type of bet, similar to what Geertz calls "even money" in his analysis of wagering at Balinese cockfights,[46] demonstrated rivalry between families and communities; more than anything else, it had to do with honor and prestige. As early as 1889 Unamuno affirmed that the fronton brought together "people of the wars of the factions."[47]

Today, the even bet is only relevant in certain modalities of the game; earlier, it was accompanied by another, informal type of bet made before the start of the game or during the first few shots.

> Back in the day, during the patriarchal period of pelota when there were no *Bosses* in this world, nor were there fixed games or cartels, nor did pelotaris say "Why not!" one could hear every now and then a voice that yelled:
>
> *"Sei ontzurre sakien alde"* (Six ounces in favor of the serve).
>
> Another voice would respond:
>
> *"Errestuen alde; eguiña dago"* (In favor the return, go!).
>
> And one needed to say no more. From their sashes they pulled up the green or blue, knitted purse, which guarded the ounces; they deposited the money in honorable hands and it was done.
>
> How times have *changed*! Yesterday people were their own bookmakers, and the vast majority of the betting took place before the pelota game.[48]

This type of informal betting was probably practiced by people who were not especially close to either of the players; they were spectators who were not directly represented in the main bet. Free of the obligations associated with being identified with the players, these bettors leaned one way or the other purely on competitive grounds: they wagered in favor of style or power, or just on predicting the game's possible outcome.

This type of crowd normally concentrated in cities, and here growing numbers prompted the introduction of *momio* ("odds ratio)" or the weighing of odds. It emerged in tandem with the industrialization of the game in the mid-nineteenth century.

---

45. Unamuno, "Un partido de pelota," 305.
46. Geertz, *The Interpretation of Cultures*, 425.
47. Unamuno, "Un partido de pelota," 303.
48. Peña y Goñi, "Los corredores," 227.

The *momio* is basically financial compensation against the pelotaris' supposedly unequal possibilities of winning the game. The introduction of weighted odds as opposed to the more simplistic even money wager points toward changes in the perception of the game, and to shifting cultural conceptualizations: "Contemplating these fundamental changes in the *joko* context, such as from dual to multiple participation, from binary to plural arrangements, from direct to mediated polarity, one begins to understand why the traditional *joko* in its pure form is becoming marginal. This progression of *joko* frames into more complex forms can be taken as a major indicator of cultural change."[49] Put simply, through this new betting system the game itself acquires importance, and downplays external identificational allegiances, resulting in a lesser degree of rivalry among the spectators.

The betting public therefore is divided on the basis of other considerations such as the very capacities of the bettor or the total sum of the bet made, which determines the direction of the bet. When the players are of a very similar level and spectators have no obvious favorites, the odds ratio is *a la par*, at par. Betting on one or the other costs the same, and the spectators are divided according to the preferences of each bettor. The situation is different when one of the players is clearly the favorite. In such a case, it is the bet itself that links the bettor to one or the other player. Spectators are thus divided between *puntos* (odds-givers, backers of the favorite) and *momistas* (odds-takers, backers of the underdog); the category that differentiates them is not the pelotari's style, but rather that of the bettor.

The difference between bettors is not visible to the naked eye as they do not wear distinguishing signs, nor are they divided spatially; the *puntos*, however, are those who bet large sums of money and form what is called the *cátedra*. They usually play *upbound*, in favor of the potential winner, and determine the *momio*, the odds ratio. In other words, they fix the odds for those who play *lowbound*, for the *momistas*. The *puntos* decide on whom they are going to bet, who is the favorite of the game, and determine the odds they need to give so that other gamblers would want to bet on the player they do not consider the favorite. The *momio*, or deliberation, is then established.

---

49. Zulaika, *Basque Violence*, 175.

If the odds are at par, it means that the *cátedra* is divided and it is unsure in whose favor it should bet. If this is the case, personal inclinations and the game itself tip the balance. If on the other hand the odds are uneven, it is because there is a certain agreement over who the favorite is; the agreement is certain when the *momios* result in odds of two-to-one, or even more skewed. In this case the *cátedra* is certain about the winner despite the fact that "the ball is round," and any outcome is possible. The strategies of *momistas*, the bettors who play *under* are contingent on this process. If the *cátedra* is mistaken and the prognoses turn around, they win double by risking little.[50]

The *momio* has led to a softening of allegiances to the pelotari. It is the bettor's very own ways of wagering that determines his choice of color instead of affective predilections stemming from common origins, or affinity for the power represented by a given pelotari. In this sense, the odds ratio reduces the fanatism of the terraces; it no longer evokes considerations that transcend the game, but is confined to the game itself. The bettor will lean toward one or the other color depending on the game's proceedings.

The most obvious example of this transformation are the bookmakers or *artekariak*, literally "intermediaries." It has been said of this figure that:

> Among the many *ingredients* that lend the pelota game its ambiance of passion one of the most important and substantial is, without a doubt, the bookmaker.
>
> Absolute lords of the space that stretches from the first rows of the terraces to the boundaries of the court, bookmakers maneuver as though on a battlefield; they announce the bets of the *puntos* in raucous yells, deafen the space through discordant details, and mix it all with every possible vocal register.[51]

Besides their position as an authentic retaining wall of the terraces, bookmakers are recognizable for various features. They normally wear light- or dark-colored jackets (depending on the season of the year) with a breast pocket in which they keep a pen. In one hand they hold a pile of blue and red betting tickets. They also have a tennis ball with a big

---

50. On the style of the bettor see the section "Postures at the Fronton" in chapter 9.

51. Peña y Goñi, "El pelotarismo moderno," 26. The following texts are from the same article.

hole in it, which they use to throw the tickets to the bettors. Meanwhile, they use their other hand to write or stir up the crowd. All the while, they shout at the terraces, announcing the *momio*. They also announce the quantity and color they defend: the closed part of the bet that normally belongs to the *puntos* or strong bettors.

> They sing in a high pitch, middle pitch, and then a falsetto; they lend the melody solemn, excited, or supremely anxious accents, depending on the specificities of the game; they drag out sentences, or yawn them; other times they blow them forcefully into the air where they vibrate, battle-hardened, like a trumpet; and many are the times when the situation is desperate and there emerges an urgent need to fend off a dooming defeat, when the synagogue explodes in all its splendor and the bookmakers, out of their minds, cornered and deranged, *lost* madmen, yell, howl, bellow, run up and down in a state of alarm like rivers that have stepped out of their beds and threaten to flood the court.

When the tide of the game turns, the bookmakers have to find matching bets from the other side to compensate for the *puntos* (odds-givers) bet on the one side, since their predictions have not been ascertained and the *puntos* run the risk of losing great sums of money. Bookmakers mostly handle the money of the *puntos*, the strong bettors. Each bookmaker relies on a few bettors who play with him right from the beginning, although later he may accept any bet he wishes. Most importantly, he needs to be able to find sufficient money to accommodate the bets of his best bettors and, in case their predictions are wrong, he needs to find opposing bets so that he can cover them against damaging loss.

> The bookmaker is the phonograph of the *punto*; in his shouts are locked, we might say, the heartbeats of all those who bet:
> To be a good bookmaker is far more difficult than it looks at first sight. Besides a great voice, he needs to have great eyesight, a great sense of smell and touch, agile legs, a special sense to sniff out the hunt and hang out the net for "gullible little birds."
> The secret of it lies in speed. A moment lost means falling into the abyss; from point to point they may mediate the victory or the loss; and an inflection of the voice, an expressive gesture, may cause a naive one to fall, and allow the bookmaker to fill a hole.[52]

---

52. Translator's note: "to fill a hole" refers to finding a matching bet. Because the bookmaker is a mediator between two bettors, he needs to find matching bets; his loyalty lies with the strong bettors, the *puntos*; if they are not covered by another bet for the other player, it

The bookmaker must above all maximize the profit of the strong bettor, since it is he who contributes the greatest sum and the greatest percentage of the bet; it is definitely the *punto*'s energetic stakes that sustain the wager. It is obvious when a *punto* launches a powerful offer. Despite the fact that the bet is made discreetly, through direct contact between bookmaker and bettor, the exaltation of the bookmaker's shout—who is now looking for swift closure—gives it away (the existence of the offer, not the bettor). Because the odds ratio is so temporary, it is necessary to close the bet as soon as possible. For this reason, the bookmaker, helped by the rest of colleagues, need to find a counterweight for the increased amount staked by the *punto*, which provokes a real commotion of shouts.

These *hordagos*[53] constitute the moments of greatest tension in the court. They parallel the game and it is very difficult, if not impossible, to have them when a game is a forgone conclusion, when the result is predictable, and when the score gap on the board is growing instead of shrinking. An equal game, or by default a surprise, is normally the ideal context for wagering. This natural and evident parallel between the court and the terraces shows that the bookmaker's importance transcends the merely economic sphere. As Unamuno observes,

> The bookmakers were coming and going, they bent over every now and then, took notes in their notebook. They were yelling "10 to 8 for Elicegui," and later again "10 to 8 for Elicegui!" Betting tickets rushing from hand to hand, and bookmakers from chair to chair. Their shouting was the *barometer of the game*; first at par, and then . . . until two to one, it rose, fluctuated, and fell again. It was a place throbbing with people.[54]

Through the constant reiteration of the *momio* and his obsessive hunt for the bet, the bookmaker becomes a fundamental stimulant of the fiesta. He clearly invigorates the interactive emotional channels that run between the court and the terraces. For his shouts, gestures, movements, comments to the spectators, and his access to the betting frenzy that he proportions, the *artekari* is the ultimate agitator of the fronton, the

---

means the bookmakers "have a hole to fill in," they have to find a bettor who wagers for the other player.

53. *Hordago* is a typical feature of the Basque card game, *mus*: it means betting everything, challenging an opponent by calling their bluff. It comes from the Basque *hordago* (there it is, there you are). Here it refers to a very strong bet.

54. Unamuno, "Un partido de pelota," 305. Emphasis added.

revitalizing tonic of the ritual. He is a cheerleader subordinated to the court; for it is the court, in the end, that is responsible for creating the right atmosphere so that the bookmaker can carry out his task.

In the event of games being decided before reaching score of twenty-two, it is common to see bookmakers turned around, facing the court. This happens when the game has practically lost interest, when the outcome is so predictable that the tension is minimal, when the result is obvious and as such, the game is "over."

In moments of intensive effervescence, the bookmaker never watches the court. His position is that of total obedience to the crowd, deploying all his persuasive powers: yelling, warnings, bartering, gestures, balls flying all over the terraces, fingers encouraging compulsive gambling, betting tickets, scribbles, accurate shots, rushes, gimmicks; sometimes he would even accept bets himself, "into the pocket."[55]

While fully concentrated on the terraces, the bookmaker is nevertheless perfectly aware of what is happening on the court. His commentaries on the proceedings of the game are surprisingly accurate. He is capable of following a play without seeing it directly, by the mere sound of the ball and by the play's reflection in the crowd. At a pala game, I heard a bookmaker say "*chapa*" (the iron sheet that indicates the ball is off court) as the player hit it with the paddle; a second later, I heard the sound of the iron sheet itself.

An experienced bookmaker is capable of following all the bets that are made at the fronton; not only his bets, but also other bookmaker's. Wagering at the fronton is done by verbal agreement. Although a betting ticket in the color and the amount on the part of the bettor seals the bet, no moneys are given in advance. Under these conditions the bookmaker has to be able to remember all the bets made with him and, because they routinely interchange tickets with other bookmakers, he needs to remember his colleagues' bets as well.

The bookmaker is an intermediary between two bettors who want to place their bets on different players. To make sure that both bets are guaranteed and he will not have to be responsible for either one, he needs to recognize to whom he is giving the bet. There has to be mutual recognition and confidence between the bettor and the bookmaker as the entire betting process is verbal and the bookmaker is its guarantor.

---

55. Translator's note: He takes bets himself, "into the pocket," in case he finds no matching bets, in order not to have to turn down a bet.

The bookmaker is a sort of notary who countersigns a deal between two persons; in this case between two bettors (who may very easily not know each another). He charges a certain percentage for this verification, which the winner pays.

The mission of the bookmaker is that of a mediator (*artekari*) between bettors. His basic task is to find in the terraces a bet on the opposite color of what *his* bettor has made, although his activities often go beyond this duty. Depending on the excitement offered by the game, his search will be more or less urgent, his movements more or less agile, and his voice more or less prominent. In the event of an ideal situation—equality between the pelotaris—his gestures and shouting will turn the bookmaker into a stimulating force at the fronton, and will definitely encourage the necessary public emotion for a satisfactory outcome to the fiesta. In cases when emotions overcome the fronton, the presence of the bookmaker may even prove decisive, especially in the hand modality.

The line of bookmakers in the counter-court constitutes a wall against an open space that has no physical boundary between the court and the terraces; it is a wall that restrains unbound passions, that soothes grave annoyances and irrepressible desires to rush at the referees and the players. Bookmakers become a boundary that does not otherwise exist and is tremendously porous between the crowd and the court.

Before the emergence of bookmakers, bets were made along lines defined by neighborhood and provincial allegiances. Today, however, they depend on the bettor—if he is *punto* or *momista*—the prediction (which is clearly affected by the previously mentioned affects), and above all the standing of the game itself. The possibility to cover oneself and change the direction of the bet neutralizes its purely agonic, bipolar tendency.

Odds betting mitigates fanaticism. The fixed allegiance to one or the other player is diluted by a system that urges the bettor to change the colors of his bet if that is opportune. Depending on the proceedings of the game, if the bettor did not make the right choice at the opening bet, he may ask for a betting ticket in favor of the player he did not consider the favorite at the beginning of the game. He may, as Antonio Peña y Goñi says, "volver la casaca,"[56] or "turn his coat."

---

56. Peña y Goñi, "El pelotarismo moderno."

Betting in pelota—at times considered a perversion of the game—has contributed to the emergence of the educated spectator who prefers a discerning take on the game to blind fanaticism. This type of spectator is now considered traditional and very characteristic in pelota. As early as 1896, Emiliano Arriaga was aware of this transformation when he claimed: "Ah, if only today's *pelotarismo* [the world of pelota] elevated to the *cátedra* had known that permanent faction!"[57]

The *Cátedra*: Do You Think It's Raining?

The *cátedra* of pelota consists of a group of *puntos* or strong bettors. It is they who make the predictions about the game that are laid down in the *momio*, the odds ratio; they are considered to be expert *pelotazales* or aficionados. However, if it is experience that characterizes the *cátedra*, this denomination may be extended to almost the entire terraces.

Most of the people who go to the fronton have played pelota at one point in their lives. They have been actively immersed in the game: they know what it feels like to volley a leather ball and hit it against a stone wall; they are familiar with the pelotari's movements; they have incorporated difficulty, satisfaction, and suffering into their knowledge of the game. They may be called experts: "The experiencer has become aware of his experience, he is 'experienced.' He has acquired a new horizon within which something can become an experience."[58]

The spectator perfectly understands the player's behavior on the court. He knows what it takes him to execute a given hit. He remembers his own incapacity to carry out a certain move, and marvels when it is successfully executed by the pelotari. He likes to speak from experience, to discuss the game with those around him: he evaluates the game, scrutinizes the player, and analyzes every detail. He compares the experience with the pelota of his time, of his youth, with his own style or that of his contemporaries; he remembers all the formal games and knows their anecdotes.

The *pelotazale* prefers to demonstrate his knowledge of the game rather than his fondness of or loyalty to it. This is why a traditional crowd applauds only the execution of a point, never an error or failure. They also applaud him when the pelotari *connects well with the ball*,

---

57. Arriaga, *La pastelería y otras narraciones bilbaínas*, 22.
58. Gadamer, *Truth and Method*, 348.

when he plays with efficacy and vigor; when he executes a complex hit; or when he takes risks at the right moment; or when he surprises his opponent(s). But above all, they applaud when he makes an effort.

The traditional follower does not display unconditional allegiance to a player, although he does have preferences for one over the other. On the terraces he tends to be critical and applauds the performance of the player on the court instead of his initial preferences. A fan may have a fondness for a player due to his power, his force. He enjoys honest and devastating play, he likes the sumptuous style of the calm player who looks for the ball with strong arms, and who plays cleanly. On the court, one of the players will represent and exalt that prototype, and the fan will be inclined toward him at the beginning. He may even wager one thousand euros in his favor.

As the game procedes, however, the ingenuity of the rival, his light movements and rapid resolutions, prevent the pelotari from improving his game. He does not take the ball confidently, he tramples on it and he finds himself playing *a pie quieto* (heavy-footed), unable to position himself well toward the ball. The spectator begins to enjoy the repertoire of the pelotari whom he at first did not consider a potential winner. He will attempt to cover himself by betting on the other player so that his loss would not be so grave; meanwhile, he celebrates the superiority of the rival without reservation. Fanatism as the unconditional adoration of the pelotari does not characterize the traditional fandom of the *pelotazale*. He considers himself level-headed and scrupulous about the proceedings of the game.

The tremendously critical attitude of the crowd refutes any accusation of being a passive spectator. Pelota is not merely a spectacle that produces unidirectional communication; it is not mass information fed to people sitting in rows and uncritically consuming sensations that the court gives them. The fronton crowd is not a "motley, gray, dense crowd palpitating like a bunch of maggots," as Unamuno puts it.[59] Nor is it a mass in the Spinozian sense of *multitude*, which is "not being anything [that] would constitute them in pure potential, permanently activated disposition to become whatever thing;"[60] nor is it Ortega y Gasset's mass

---

59. Unamuno, "Un partido de pelota," 303.
60. Delgado, *El animal público*, 15.

man, a term the author uses "not so much because this man is myriad, but because he is *inert*."[61]

The spectator is not a passive recipient. He is looking for what he considers valuable in a player and lets him know it. By applauding, he supports certain modes of play, certain images that for him have a narrative, a meaning. The gaze of the crowd is filled with passion, but it is not easy to please. The spectator is active, knows what he likes, and wants to see it at the fronton, no matter which pelotari executes it.

The almost ceremonial impartiality exhibited by the crowd in pelota has largely disappeared from the grand duels of the hand modality. It has, however, survived in the close link that the spectators traditionally has maintained with the main authority at the fronton: the referee.

Traditionally, posters advertising games would read: "The customary norms will govern." These norms were learned by everyone in the most efficient way possible: by playing pelota. The norms were deeply rooted in common sense and an awareness of all those who observed them; the referee was no more than a person popularly known for his exemplary way of respecting the rules, for his celebrated impartiality. This is why referees were persons of accredited prestige either for their civic activity in the case of mayors or other officials, or for their charisma and popularity.

> The tribunal was born like the game itself, in the heart of the people, from the most intimate sources of their being; today, pure and immaculate, glorified by prestige and a clean record that not even the twists and turns of the game itself could contaminate, circumstances so far from the game's original being. . . . Of the three judges in this "tribunal," two are appointed by each competing party, although it is not an obligation to be representative in the Jury. The third judge and referee, the third voice in case of discord, is elected from among persons of credit and prestige.[62]

This method of choosing the referees, one by each team and the third by the *cátedra* of the fronton, stems from the necessity that the public's interests, and especially the bettor's, should be protected.

The recognition of the crowd's authority intensified when the referees were unable to make a decision. In case of any ambiguity, the referees were obliged to consult credible persons in the crowd; it was an obliga-

---

61. Ortega y Gasset, *The Revolt of the Masses*, 54.
62. Irigoyen, *El juego de pelota a mano (1900–1925)*, 183–84.

tion determined by the rules. The following excerpt is from the Juego Nuevo (New Game) fronton of Pamplona, 1847:

> It is the players' duty to nominate judges for each game.
>
> Once the judges are named for the game, only they will have the capacity to voice their opinion *with validity*: whatever the spectators say accounts to nothing.
>
> When the judges are unable to make a decision, they will consult the right persons in the crowd.
>
> In the event of no judges being appointed for a game, the players are submitted to the verdict of the public or of one of the spectators.
>
> Decision-making will not be possible by persons who have been known to show impartiality.[63]

The referee is placed there by the crowd not as a restriction of the liberties of *their* pelotari, but rather as an appendix to the public itself. Located in the same direction (facing the court), the referee received his authority from the crowd. Much remembered is the case when, as it started to rain, the referee turned to the crowd with a question that is most illuminating of his role. Uncovered and obviously wet, the referee asked out loud: "Do you think it's raining?" Depending on the atmosphere of the game and the monies bet, the crowd would answer yes or no. The referee would make a decision accordingly.

There are also documented cases of the crowd extending or suspending games: for example, the game on January 1, 1886 in Buenos Aires between pairs formed by Chiquito de Eibar and Brau Menor (Brau the Younger, Eustaquio Brau) on the one hand and the trio Vega (Roberto Vega), Brau Mayor (Brau the Older, Juanito Brau), and Manco de Villabona (Pedro Yarza) on the other. The game was a tie at 54, and they decided to play another 20 points. When they tied at 14, the crowd, *el respetable*, asked for 30 points; at a 25 tie, they agreed on 35 as the maximum. The game was a tie at 26, 27, and then 28 points when the spectators called for its suspension due to the players' exhaustion. This game was played again on the January 6 with a new scoreboard; the trio won 50–40.[64]

The pelota spectator is tremendously critical of the pelotari's performance. An undeserved applause provokes malicious smiles and

---

63. Galbete, "Miscelánea de datos para una historia del juego de pelota," 304.
64. *Laurak Bat*, Year VII, no. 156.

condescending looks that make it clear that the devout admirer has been in the wrong—even if ignorance is increasingly hidden by a devotion that applauds just about any performance. I will further discuss this transformation of public attitudes in the epilogue.

Txapelas onto the Court: The Consecration of the Pelotari

> The pelota player is primarily born. Then comes the forging of his trade. Hard and without concessions, he will need ten years of effort and dedication for his virtual consecration.
>
> — Ogueta

Traditionally, it was not just a part but the whole fronton crowd that acted as referee; similarly, it is the entire crowd, not only *his* supporters, that consecrate the pelota player. The case of Barberito I, the only player from La Rioja to ever become the hand pelota singles champion (in 1953), is an obvious example. Besides this achievement, he was the last pelotari to see the *txapelas* or berets of the crowd thrown onto the court to honor him. This took place at the Astelena fronton in Eibar, at a time when Gipuzkoans maintained an obvious hegemony over the game.

The throwing of *txapelas* onto the court is a tangible expression of homage to the player, an homage that is the only sure sign of consecration. Many times the player is consecrated upon his winning the singles title. After all, by winning the champion's *txapela*, the pelotari directly enters the annals of the game; consecration is not partial but implies permanence in collective memory.

There are pelotaris, however, that won championship titles under various circumstances and who cannot be said to have been consecrated. This is the case of Patxi Ruiz in 2003, who followers claim still has a long way to go to demonstrate his worth. There are also those who were consecrated without any *txapela*, including Titín III, Errandonea (Inaxio Errandonea), Alustiza (Martin Alustiza), or Unanue (Mikel Unanue). There are those who won the *txapela* once they had already been consecrated, like Galarza III (1991, 1992), and for whom the title was mere confirmation. Finally, there are those to whom, having already been consecrated, the champion's title implied no glamor inasmuch as the circumstances of their victory were not appropriate, such as in the case of Barberito I (1953) or Lajos (1971).

Clearly, consecration and triumph normally go hand in hand; it is, however, unconditional recognition by the crowd that consecrates the pelota player. Recognition is unconditional because it is not gained by affections external to the game court but by the player's performance at the fronton. This unconditional recognition is unlike that of the fanatic supporter; rather, it is that of an enthusiastic admirer of pelota who is convinced that the pelotari is an ideal being for struggle who does his best in order to win under any condition.

The first part of this chapter emphasized the widespread belief that the pelotari is born, and that his mysterious essence surfaces in the encounter between the player and the ball, in the way he positions his body and connects with the ball: "the pelotari is born with his postures."[65] However, the fact of possessing a natural talent that enables the ball to fit in his hands like Cinderella's slipper does not ensure the player's consecration. Other circumstances are also necessary for a pelotari to carve a place in collective memory that, as we will see, resonate with the fairy tales of Charles Perrault.

It is his capacity to make sacrifices and endure suffering that distinguishes the pelota player. For this reason, it is head-to-head clashes that reveal his class. Through such encounters the player proves his capacity to suffer, which is strongly associated with his will to win. Frequently in the hand pelota singles championship, when faced with a major attack on part of his rival, the pelotari breaks down psychologically. The tremendous physical effort makes a dent in the mind of the player who feels he is unable to overcome it. He loses ground and loses his nerve. He keeps saying to himself that his rival is no better than him, but he does not really believe it. He is broken, *haustuta*, dead beat.

The crowd therefore wants to see the pelotari making an effort and trying to rectify the situation even when he is losing the game. If he fails to do so; if he starts hitting the ball around wishing the game was over; if he takes risks precipitately, "waiting for the Holy Spirit to descend," the crowd reproaches him by shouting and whistling. If, on the other hand, the player makes a real effort by changing his strategy and he keeps doing the best he can; if he plays clean and with all his soul in the game, even when in pain, he will be effusively applauded despite an unfavorable result in the end. What exasperates the crowd most is slovenliness, giving up. An apathetic player provokes indifference and

---

65. Two-time hand pelota singles champion Galarza III's opinion.

it is very difficult for him to get consecrated consecrated. Physical and mental force is considered to be the major guarantor of success in the court and consecration by the crowd. It is force, *indarra*.

Pelotazales believe that a player's capacity to fight basically depends on his character; that character, in turn, is forged by certain circumstances of life. Many classic descriptions of pelotaris' lives highlight their humble beginnings: that he would play without stopping at any corner, barefoot so as not to wear his *alpargatas* (or espadrilles, shoes made of hemp) out, during impossible hours, putting money aside to buy a *xistera* (the racket used in the jai alai modality), or a ball. The decision to become a pelotari is a debate between wasting one's life away, "falling into vagrancy and roguery,"[66] or achieving popular glory.

Even if it is not entirely true or biographically verifiable, the life of the pelotari tends to be dramatized; such dramatizations feature a life of trials and tribulations or a struggle against an attraction to the void. As mentioned earlier, before he became hand pelota singles champion Retegi II had been working in the Alps felling trees. Although this job lasted less than three months, it became one of the most quoted anecdotes of his life. Thirty years later, interviews with him still highlight the moment when the player was vacillating between becoming the greatest figure in the game, or just another worker.

A state of scarcity seems to be the ideal circumstance to transcend mediocrity, to assume *indarra*, and to attract the interest of the crowd. Reflecting on why it is Navarrese, not Bizkaian or Gipuzkoan players who win titles nowadays, the three-time hand pelota singles champion Gallastegi argued that it is because people live very well in the latter two provinces. Retegi II himself claimed that "the quintessence comes from a certain place and especially from suffering; it is in the absence of comfort when quality emerges."[67] They believe that one has to start out with a background of deprivation in order to become a good pelotari. When there is shortage, the path is rockier, and sacrifice is fundamental in order to achieve objectives that life denied at the beginning.

It is believed that a state of deprivation helps the player forge a desire to win, a will that is the most determining feature of the *plaza-gizon*, the "man of the plaza;" he is a man who does not wilt in public, who

---

66. Salaverría, *La gran enciclopedia vasca*, 645.

67. Julián Retegi II (hand pelota champion), interview by author, Bilbao (Bizkaia), October 16, 2002.

grows in adversity, and who has a capacity to suffer that never loses sight of victory. The *plaza-gizon* possesses *indarra*, the "spiritual electricity" that Clifford Geertz captures through the Moroccan notion of *baraka*; "a gift of power more than natural . . . that enable[s] some men to prevail over others."[68] Geertz identifies this power with charisma, a quality implying that a person maintains a privileged relationship with the sources of being; it is a quality resembling hypnotic powers that certain individuals have in order to unleash passions and dominate spirits. Meanwhile, it remains unclear whether charisma is a state, an emotion, or an ambiguous fusion of both.

In pelota, *indarra* is the power that the pelotari deploys in the plaza.[69] "To have power" is to give force to the ball, to hit it with strength, which is something absolutely celebrated at the fronton. A player captivates the crowd when he shows his strength on the court, whether through an energetic strike, a proud posture, or a masterly play. They find in him something sublime, a force of which they think they are a part.

Jordi Pujol, former president of the autonomous government of Catalonia, once said in a television interview that when he hears the song "Al vent" (To the Wind) by the singer Raimon he feels part of it: "I feel that I am part of this force," he said. Pelota spectators experience the same; a feeling of communion, of sharing something that is beyond the individual, but that he or she has profoundly internalized.

The conjunction between what the pelotari does and how the crowd feels is often described with an illuminating phrase: "the crowd has been carried away." This is a surrender, but unlike that of the pelotari. Saying that "the player has surrendered" means that he has lost all hope to win, that he has renounced the contest, something that is absolutely despised by the crowd. A player may never yield to his rival—he may only give himself over to the struggle. He must maintain the capacity to fight, the will to win.

Once this is accepted, it is not always the best pelota players who have the greatest number of followers. Closeness, contact with the public, and an ability to share the pleasures of victory with the fans is just

---

68. Geertz, *Local Knowledge*, 136.

69. There is another way if designating power, the word *ahala*. As opposed to the direct power of the hit, *ahala* refers to the power of play, of a trick, to the power of the fox, to the capacity of execution. *Hori da ahala, hori!* "this is power!" Is the expression used for magical, unexpected turns in the game.

as important as victory itself. Players who manage to combine triumph with celebration are the ones who most effectively capture the crowd, which is necessary for the game to survive.

The pelota player owes his existence to his public and, besides exploiting the talent that made him excel, he must let his fans participate in it. The pelotari has to share his enjoyment with the crowd; he must know how to celebrate his successes together with his followers. Otherwise, he might end up like Polonio Urrestarazu: "Guernica [Gernika in Basque] also had its hero, but he never connected with the people, nor could he ever respond to popular fervor toward him through his public performance. The people started out calling him 'Coral' for his finesse; disillusioned, they ended up calling him 'Satza' (garbage)."[70]

The pelotari has been historically associated with being a *bon viveur*, including living licentiously. Although today the pelota player is a professional athlete bound by contract to take care of his body, the game has not managed to shed this reputation. Every now and then rumors emerge in the fronton about the parties or amorous adventures of players; rumors that, while often unfounded, lend the player a certain attraction. Any type of excess that jeopardizes the player's performance is absolutely prohibited; there is, however, a certain attraction to the player who knows how to party, to enjoy himself.

The case of Goñi II is a recent example. He was a frontcourt player of inexhaustible energies and with a special talent for the game; even though he never won an important title, he was the player most capable of filling frontons until he was finally sanctioned. The terraces were boiling in his presence. The crowd felt it was part of the extraordinary powers the player emanated. Besides, his private life was a breeding ground for gossip: drugs, alcohol, women of all ages and backgrounds, fights, car crashes, and all-nighters before games. If the reality of his lifestyle was indeed full of excesses, the fans imagined three times as much; they were convinced that this *indarra*, this infinite force, must also find outlets beyond the court.

The sociologist Pierre Bourdieu claims that "one of the privileges of consecration resides in the fact that it confers on the consecrated an indisputable and indelible essence, an essence that authorizes trans-

---

70. Irigoyen, "En los juegos de pelota," 10.

gressions otherwise prohibited."[71] Without a doubt, the moment these transgressions affect the player's performance on the court, or if celebrations are not in keeping with successes, or if the player's partying makes him stop caring about winning and playing well, the fronton will demand explanations. This is reason enough to lose the grace conferred. *Indarra* is an active force and, while it lasts, it is effective and real. This is why they say in Euskara that something is valid when it has *indarra*, when "it is in force," *indarrean*. All the while, consecration does not imply perpetual grace; indeed, "falling from grace" is proverbial evidence to the fact.

Without triumphs on the court, the crowd becomes alienated. Without money bet on him, the player cannot sustain himself. The pelotari cannot let himself go, cannot get carried away by his success and forget what he owes. He needs to attract the crowd to the fronton, get under the skin of the spectators, and stimulate the terraces. The spectator must see the player's total surrender to the contest, his desire to win, which is the only way for the pelotari to stay in grace and to maintain the framework of pelota.

Pelota is a struggle; it is a fight between two proto-agonists who are believed to possess a special talent for relating to the ball. They have a special power, the vigor of force or the ingeniousness of cunning, which allows them to overcome the other. The player owes himself to the fight because it is precisely what the crowd renounces that is given to him.

The fans assume their positions before the game. They act out a certain ceremony of rivalry. "I bet you six hundred euros that Aguirre will not score ten." "What are you going to bet, you, when you never guess right?" "You go to the fronton all your life, and know less than my little girl." Anything counts in order to incite the challenge; boastful mockery ensues, always in an informal, jocular manner. The roosters show off the colors of their plumage and, several days before the game, they invite everyone to appreciate it. If others are of the same standing, they chat a bit more about the game and that is it. If the interlocutor prefers the opponent, they get entangled in a dialectic warfare where each party would slyly deconstruct the opinion of the other, poking each other until they end up betting. They will make references to the bet each time they meet before the game. It does not really matter if one loses a few feath-

---

71. Bourdieu, *¿Qué significa hablar?*, 85.

ers when arranging the bet; what matters is to position oneself, to show one's own criteria, to "*tomar postura*" (take a posture).[72]

This positioning always takes place before the game. Once at the fronton, it is rare for the *pelotazale* to ostentatiously show his preferences. He might talk about his favorite with those sitting around him, but he would not praise a priori the game of *his* chosen one, nor would he underrate that of *his* rival. The game is the sole criterion that will determine his judgments. If he wins, after the game he will rejoice in the loss of the other, ridiculing his adversaries without mercy. He might not even claim his gains, but he will never forego ironic and sarcastic remarks each time he meets his opponent. If he loses, he will stoically bear the same on the part of his adversary, and will even attribute the outcome to sheer luck; he will hold onto whatever pretext to ignite another dialectic challenge and another bet.

At the fronton the fan is not devoted to the player, he is devoted to the game. He enjoys the struggle from outside, although he is also involved in it; he deposited responsibility in the player, who has to give himself over to what the crowd has renounced.

Pelota is a ritual manifestation whose practice creates strong bonds among the male population. It congregates men around a passion that they share, one that is part of them and that confines rivalry to a context of representation, of sportsmanship. Pelota keeps *indarra* under control, this force as creative as it is destructive; the game concentrates *indarra* in those spaces or bodies that embody certain values of communal cohesion. Consecration happens when an object, a space, or a person is considered important enough to represent interests or to embody values that the community believes to be its own. Thus, realities that serve as a medium or link for the cohesion of the group, and that strengthen the image the community has of itself, become imbued with grace and are converted into icons. The search for the ideal pelotari, therefore, is one of the most relevant endeavors, inasmuch as "great figures are essential for the boom and popularity of hand pelota; if there aren't any around, everything becomes simplistic and plain boring;"[73] mobilizing passions is the only way for ritual to be efficient.

---

72. Translator's note: in Spanish, in addition to the normal meanings of behavior, composure, and taking a position, *tomar postura* also means to bet, wager.

73. The words of the pelotari Ogueta to Garcés, *Campeones manomanistas, 1940–1990*, 154.

4

The Fiesta of Pelota

> The sacrificial service is fixed by very definite objective rules, a set sequence of words and acts which must be carefully observed if the sacrifice is not to fail in its purpose.
> — Ernst Cassirer

The game of pelota begins the moment the challenge is made: a challenge that determines who will play, who will face each other at the fronton. This challenge is not conceptualized in terms of outcomes like those at the level of amateur competitions, where the result of the game implies the glory or failure of the village or country that the player represents. Rather, the election of players concerns the beginnings of the game: a search for an equality of departure is indispensable.

The professor Allen Guttmann argues that the search for equality is an important factor in the evolution of sports.[1] By the term "a search for equality" he is referring to the compartmentalization of championships according to age and categories, something that is undeniably relevant in modern sports. Nevertheless, Guttmann forgets that this feature is implicit in any game of confrontation, especially when betting is involved. To achieve equality, it has been customary in pelota to impose on the game what Rivka Eifermann calls meta-rules, which aimed to level off the abilities of the players.[2] They allowed "doubles" of three players (something that still happens in the remonte modality, and an example of which we have already seen in the description of the Buenos Aires game in the previous chapter), and organized games where one of the players

---

1. Guttmann, *From Ritual to Record*.
2. Blanchard and Cheska, *The Anthropology of Sport*, 210–11.

could only play with the left hand, jumping on one leg, or turning around before each hit; an infinite variation of similar formulae was invented so that players of unequal ability could play on an equal footing.

An equal starting point is so important for the ritual to be efficient that it becomes the only nonnegotiable premise when organizing professional games. In the case of doubles, the pairs usually compensate for the shortcomings of each other. Therefore, the backcourt player of exceptional strength will cover a less efficient frontcourt player; a shrewder frontcourt player will be accompanied by a weaker backcourt player. In singles games the arrangement is different because there is no possibility for compensation. For this reason, contests are reduced to very specific players or championships. In the case of championships, the greater the level of the player, the later he enters the competition.

Traditionally, and today in modalities that employ instruments, the reigning champion enters directly into the finals; the contender has to seize the *txapela* from him, after all. It is different in the hand modality, where a pyramid competition system has been substituted by mini leagues of semifinals. This way it is more difficult for players to get to the finals in their best form, but the companies guarantee six semifinals instead of two, with all the box-office and television rights revenue that this implies.

The moment the players' names is announced, *pelotazales* start preparing the event. The media begins to publish interviews with the protagonists; people start making predictions, and betting opens. If it is an important game, like a final for example, fans do not hesitate to mobilize their contacts in order to get entrance tickets, and *cuadrillas* (peer groups) carefully devise plans: they have to establish the time and place for meeting, reserve the restaurant, buy cigars, fetch the entrance tickets, and so on. There is usually no variation either in the proceedings or the execution of each mission, but plans have to be confirmed so that everything goes smoothly without any hitches.

The anticipation of an important game is much more intensive than its repercussions. The expectation of the event, according to Vicente de Monzón (writing in 1894), implies "not being able to sleep . . . dreaming with a thousand moves of the game . . . getting up early; roaming the streets in search of some player to shake hands with; forgetting to have breakfast; losing one's mind, really."[3] Hours before the game, more

---

3. Monzón, "Zazpiak bat."

and more people gather outside of the fronton. Circles are formed in the center of the space, and individuals stand around their peripheries, looking at them and waiting. Twenty-some individuals stick out from the crowd with their navy or garnet-colored jackets, depending on the companies they represent. They are the bookmakers; they move around from group to group, greeting them and connecting groups and individuals. They comment on the possible incidents in the game, exchange money, provide entrance tickets, and chat informally. This is the moment of unexpected encounters and reencounters, of introductions, of jocularity, which will not be over until the following day. Some people head toward the box office to fetch the tickets they had reserved, or to see what is left. Not much. The day of the final tickets are almost always sold out. The price—some cost about a hundred euros—does not deter the crowd, which wants to participate in the event, which wants to *be present*.

When a player arrives at the fronton and makes his way in the crowd, some of them pat him on the back, others grab his arm and ask how he is doing. He, nervous but smiling, says he is doing fine. He does not want to stop and never turns his strong body entirely toward the people who stop him. Always tilted and with a big sports bag on his left shoulder, he does not establish any contact that goes beyond a cordial greeting. "Good," "we'll see," "it will be a struggle," "ready to go," is the most he would say to the fans, most of whom are bettors. When he finally passes by the last group, he heads toward a side door. He prefers to avoid the main entrance as he would need to greet even more fans, those who are having a drink and discussing the latest news at the bar of the fronton.

The side door is directly linked to the locker rooms and the court; it is also here where the television crew is stationed. Hundreds of cables run from the truck from which the broadcast is emitted toward the fronton; they are linked to the commentators' tables as well as the cameras that shoot just about every incident that happens inside. Authentic umbilical cords of communication, these cables enable the transmission of images to an audience of half a million people, who are waiting for the game to start at home or in bars. Some other personnel of the game also have access through the side door: organizers, quartermasters, trainers, and managers, among others.

The referees are already inside, making sure the fronton is in optimal conditions for the game: that the air is not excessively humid, that there are no puddles, no *eskas* or lines missing, nor there are too many of them. The keeper of the pelotas is also around. From Thursday, the day the balls were selected,[4] until they are handed over to the players he has custody over the balls that will be used in the game. He needs to make sure they suffer no changes. The heat of the crowd that gathers at the fronton to watch the game moistens the atmosphere a bit, which may cause the balls to change their behavior. If the ball keeper finds interior conditions inadequate, he has to take the balls outside.

In the locker room there are four players who are playing the doubles' game prior to the final. They are wearing white pants; two of them have red jerseys on, the other two are wearing blue ones. Several strips of band aid are stuck to their pants; they are putting on the *tacos* to protect their hands.[5] The atmosphere is quite relaxed, the players are chatting about the latest news, mostly sports news. The language may switch back and forth between Euskara and Spanish, depending on the nature of the conversation and the interlocutors.

Outside, the crowd is growing. The comments, jokes, exchanges, greetings, laughs, and glances continue and only abate when some pelotari appears: old glory or active player. The former one, contrary to the player who has to carry the responsibility of playing that day, stops to talk with acquaintances. He receives enthusiastic greetings and introductions, and continues to listen to any comment that comes his way.

The bookmakers have already entered the fronton, and are at the terraces fixing bets before the first game, the doubles game, begins. Part of the public gathering outside starts entering the court; the game prior to the final will start soon. The gatekeepers greet them at the main entrance and, like everyone else, talk about the players' chances, the features of the balls chosen, entrance ticket prices, or any other order of the day. The companies' public relations representatives are seated in one corner; they check accreditations and accommodate the press, which has been following the event for days.

The people find their assigned seats, the regulars always at the same location.

---

4. The ball fabrication and selection process is described in the section "The Box of Weapons" in this chapter.

5. See description in following section, page 135.

The Transformation of Actors

> The finals are a source of inexplicable tension for the *pelotari* who is about to play. Not only the day of the game, but also those leading up to it. You have to isolate yourself, and concentrate to the maximum.
>
> — Tolosa

From the moment he arrives, the pelotari goes through different states, each of them requiring a different predisposition and behavior on his part.

When the player appears in the vicinity of the fronton, people recognize him as a person of a specific trajectory in the pelota world. He has played an infinite number of games with various results, which has earned him a position in the hypothetical ranking of *pelotaris*;[6] this creates certain expectation in the terraces. The player may be considered a contender for the title, seeking to dethrone the former champion; he may be a contender with no real possibilities as the incumbent champion is clearly superior; or, he may represent a great mystery. All these predictions will no doubt affect the player's spirit, who knows before he arrives at the fronton the odds ratio or the percentage of the bets, which is a great reflection of expectations.

The encounter with the public at the fronton's entrance is the final moment of extreme pressure on the player. Cheering and supportive comments and voices make him release his tension and face the game as if it was his sole responsibility, as if nothing else existed, as if he had been born to play it and die afterward.

For the player who is defending the *txapela*, if either of them are,[7] as much as for the contender who aspires to win it, the game starts

---

6. This is a hypothetical ranking given that it is not a habitual element in pelota. However, besides the positions that are established through the championships, rankings have been drawn up at different times and places to determine who the best player is at that particular moment. Based on the quantity of the sports lottery or the number of victories, rankings have been and are very common in the jai alai modalities, given their popularity for betting. Recently, in the hand modality, the web page www.manista.com (in Spanish, last accessed June 25, 2012, at which time rankings were listed that up to June 25) has established a ranking of pelota players in the first division.

7. Traditionally, the *txapela* was played against the player who possessed it at the time. Nowadays the champion enters the championship before the final, which may mean that he does not ultimately get to play it. However, to really crown himself, a player must ideally beat the incumbent champion. In the 2003 hand pelota singles championship, a fan remarked it was strange that Olaizola II had won against three champions, including the reigning title

with an omission of statuses. Both players, the champion as well as the contender, begin from scratch: with a total absence of any reference to previous defeats or victories.

In order to completely erase the past, for this abrogation to be possible, the pelotari distances himself from spaces that assign him a category. He segregates himself from the group. Reclusive in the locker room, his cabin of initiation, the player tries to forget everything that takes place at the fronton. He tries not worry about the odds ratio, nor the comments made about him on the terraces, nor think about this article that praised him as favorite or that criticism that considered a title for him premature.

The locker room and the corridors become for him spaces where he interiorizes a single notion: that he, just as his rival, will start out from scratch. Retegi II often comments that, had he thought like many others did that Galarza III did not take care of himself and was not self-confident, then he would have always lost. "If someone gets to the finals, it happens for a reason,"[8] he said to himself. The pelotari avoids thinking about who his rival is and what he does beyond the pelota court; he keeps in mind that he is in the finals. The categories that define him and his rival disappear completely as a way of confronting the game. He respects his rival, but neither does he make him out so great in his mind that his opponent controls his strategies.

The pelota player knows his own attributes, but he does not want to close himself up in them; rather, he wants to use them whenever he needs to invent new weapons. The rest is superfluous. He detaches himself from some of his own codes as only this way can he face unexpected situations without becoming blind to them, without recourse to old solutions also considered by his opponent. One knows his weapons but seeks to abandon them, too, or to adjust them before a destabilizing attack on the part of his rival: "the ball is round and it allows for no a priori layout . . . the game produces all the tricks one may think of."[9]

Each encounter with the other is different, and a fixed repertoire of strategies can turn out to be a double-edged sword. On the one hand, it may ensure control over a few hits; on the other, it may lead to a block-

---

holder Barriola, and he had still two games to go to crown himself—something that, in the end, did not happen.

8. Julián Retegi II (hand pelota champion), Bilbao (Bizkaia), October 16, 2002.

9. Garcia Ariño I to Garcés, *Campeones manomanistas, 1940–1990*, 143.

age that will not be broken until the end of the game. The best pregame strategy therefore is emptying oneself of categories. Knowing one's own qualities as well as those of the other is important; one accepts, however, that each encounter is unique; that both pelotaris start out from scratch; that the less strategizing, the more capacity to change and surprise.

The period of segregation that the player undergoes in the locker room, this voidlike situation, is similar if not analogous to the same one must endure before initiation. The three characteristics Turner attributes to the liminal period of ritual are ambiguity, invisibility, and lack: "The attributes of liminality or of liminal *personae* ('threshold people') are necessarily ambiguous, since this condition and these persons elude a slip through the network of classifications that normally locate states and positions in cultural space."[10]

Andrés Ortiz-Osés confirms that the culminating moment of ritual is the liminal. He considers it a "confrontation with otherness" and one's own limits, "in which the dramatic fight with the other takes place."[11] This is exactly what happens at the game: an encounter with the other. It is not the other who poses the problem, though. The other is known by now. Normally one has already played several games against him. What is unknown is the encounter, this unique encounter that the game implies, and which Turner calls "pure possibility."

In order to shut himself away in his cabin of initiation—in the locker room—the pelota player empties himself. He internalizes the fact that, as much as he might know his rival, as many times as he might have won or lost before, as much as he might have trained or fought before, now he starts out from zero. At the 2002 four-and-a-half mark final, the incumbent champion Barriola was asked if he was going to repeat the triumph. He answered: "I don't want to think about last year. Everything was very nice, but this is another thing now. I have to forget about it and leave it on the side."[12]

This preliminary period of segregation does not only take place internally, in the mind of the pelota player. The preliminary status implies an emptied person, an abandonment of identity that has to be indicated by clear signs of transformation. "Their structural 'invisibility,'" Turner

---

10. Turner, *The Ritual Process*, 95.
11. Ortiz-Osés, "Mitología del héroe moderno," 387.
12. Statement to the press at the time, at which the author was present.

says, "may be marked not only by their seclusion 'from men's eyes' but also by the loss of their preliminal names, by the removal of clothes, insignia and other indicators of the preliminal status."[13]

When a *pelotari* makes his debut in the professional league, he adopts a name that often has nothing to do with his real name but with other things—for example, a farmstead (Atano), a village (Eibarrés), or a profession (Panaderito, the Little Baker). Although it is increasingly common for players to use their paternal last names,[14] an ordinal number is added to it to distinguish the player from those who played with the same name before, whether he is related to these predecessors or not. For example, Atano X (Luciano Juaristi) was indeed the tenth player from a family of *pelotaris*, while Goñi II (Mikel Goñi) is not related to Goñi I (Oscar Goñi). The ordinal serves to single out the player who will not play with a name that has been used before.

The only things the player really possesses is his nickname and his style of play. The principle of equal initial conditions that the game requires demands that the player wear a specific kind of outfit shared by all. In this outfit are inscribed the liturgical precepts that protagonize the ritual: purity and disjunction in equality.

Like the propitiatory victim, the pelota player is submitted to *bos creatus*: "he must be dressed in clean clothes or special garments that lend him the element of sanctity."[15] Traditionally, the clothing of the pelotari was, with the exception of the *gerriko* or sash, completely white. Long pants of tergal, a jersey or shirt, and *alpargatas*, white espadrilles, or tennis shoes, depending on the era. Nowadays, the demands of television broadcasting have extended the color of the *gerriko*, either colored (red) or blue, to the jersey as well.

The anthropologist Edmund Leach argues that when clothing is very similar and it is only distinguished by one feature, the binary quality becomes explicit as it transmits a substantial amount of socially significant information by very economical means.[16] The importance of counterposing colors does not lie in the use of a specific color, but in the disjunction that characterizes the game.

---

13. Turner, "Variations on a Theme of Liminality," 37.

14. In Spanish and Basque culture, it is the custom for people to take both parents' last names.

15. Hubert and Mauss, *Magia y sacrificio en la historia de las religiones*, 82.

16. Leach, *Culture and Communication*, 55–57.

Despite the cultural reference that both colors possess and which I have outlined before, the distinctive mark of color between the players gains meaning in agonic play, in competition, which is accompanied by simultaneous betting.[17] The colors characterize the game, the *partido* which also means "split" or "divided" in Spanish; they imply the division of totality, a totality expressed among other things by the similarity of both pelotaris' attire.

The transformation that takes place in the locker room is not only graphic as indicated by the clothing; it also implies a process of emptying oneself and internalizing the other before the game. The routine that the pelotari executes in the locker room contributes to his preparation for the game.

Once the player is dressed in white, he starts the slow process of covering his hands to protect them. He puts a few small pads of polyurethane—the *tacos* or "wedges"—at strategic spots on the hand (making a hollow at the weak parts) and covers them with strips of band aid that he heats on a portable stove so that they stick better.[18] Although this process is done in the presence of one's opponent, the players barely talk. "The fact that you change in the same locker room as your opponent makes you relaxed in a way. You barely talk with him, but there is tacit communication emanating companionship and affect; it's like we wish each other good luck, and we know that either of us may win the game."[19]

Besides the presence of the opponent, the pelotari also has to face the comments of those who are around the locker room, a space increasingly restricted: "On the day of the final, in the locker room you say banal things of little sense, hiding the nervousness and the hope that overtakes us contenders. Sometimes someone enters and asks: 'are you nervous?' which is trivial. You suffer for the obligation because you know that there are people behind you who appreciate and adore you."

Once they are done with the preparation of the protective bandage, the players start to activate their body. Pre–warm up consists of

---

17. Bettors allude to them, pointing to the arm, with reference to *kaiku*, a traditional jacket of marine blue color, and to the head, with reference to the *txapela* or red beret, respectively.

18. The use of *tacos* is something recent. They have been around for less than thirty years on the court. Before, players did not protect the palms of their hands at all.

19. Bengoetxea III (Juan Mari Bengoetxea), to Garcés, *Campeones manomanistas, 1940–1990*, 184.

short sprints, jumps, and stretching. As the time of entering the court approaches, so the rivals distance themselves from each other. They seek out separate spaces that enable isolation, an internalization of the rival, an analysis of one's own possibilities, and the visualization of strategies.

In the case of hand pelota, mental concentration is normally accompanied by bouncing the ball against a wall with alternating hands, which affects their warm up. They usually choose the corridors for these moments before the game. Places of transit and enclosed from the general public are emptied by the centripetal force of the court.

Television channels directly connect with the fronton. Hundreds of thousands of spectators anxiously await the beginning of the game; many of them are placing a bet over the phone. Although the doubles game is not yet over, the commentators are disputing predictions about the final with each point. They mostly feature expert opinions, almost always of pelota players, who are interviewed by a "mobile" journalist moving around with a camera. They inform the TV audience about the standing of the *momio*, the odds ratio, and contrast the predictions of experts with what the *cátedra* says, the ultimate concretion of the public.

The applause rising from the terraces signals the end of the game previous to the final; the four players proceed to the locker rooms and give the floor over to the protagonists of the day. The terraces break out in applause, shouting and, lately, repeating steady cries of acclamation. Totally disregarding the commotion among the public, the pelotaris start warming up their hands. They do so by hitting the ball against the frontis or the left wall, gradually distancing themselves from it as they are warming up.

The bookmakers quickly change the betting tickets[20] and they start throwing balls again to certify bets that have been sealed by gestures before. Most of the accounts of the first game are settled after the final. The first game is usually a test for the bettors to see how their luck is doing that day. Great bets are reserved for the final; this is now the moment to make important offers. The *momio* is satisfying expectations

---

20. The quartermaster of each company is responsible for collecting the wads of the tickets the bookmakers have used the game before. They give them new tickets of a different color. This allows the company to know the quantity of bets made and to do the calculations with the bookmakers.

paying up lowbound just as much as upbound, and the bookmakers cannot handle the amount of bets. They are constantly throwing balls at the terraces and go up the stairs to hand over tickets as it is now almost impossible to take care of the excessive number of bets. There are about twenty bookmakers, and none of them idle around. Yelling, signaling, closing, writing, throwing, signaling, catching, throwing, catching. The bet is matched and the process is repeated again and again.

The referees are seated in a corner; they are checking the players' accreditation before calling them on to start the game.

Strictly speaking, warming up is over when the pelotari starts exhibiting the skills of his game. This is the moment of presenting his repertoire. The pelotari shows the power of his arms, the velocity of his legs, and the precision of his hits. His performance attracts much attention on the part of the crowd, which normally comments on his dexterity with a suspicious "let's see if you can repeat that later." The real game has not yet started; both the player, who takes pleasure in the choreography and the more elaborate use of his body, and the public, which is enjoying this visual appetizer, are aware of it.

The television cameras do not pay attention to this pregame performance. Channels opt for commercials or offer the viewer quantitative information, something that is not available to the fan on the terraces. The commentators review the trajectory of both players in the championship: their age, height and measurements, the year of their debut, and the course of their professional career. They make references to all those who have won the *txapela* since the start of the championship, spicing up the information with historical knowledge that the commentator provides once he has finished reading what the fan may read on the screen. The bombardment of information stops when the court offers some news to discuss.

The Box of Weapons

About ten minutes into warm up, the other protagonists of the day emerge, the weapons that will mediate the duel between two adversaries: the pelotas (pelota balls).

As each ball is different, the pelotas are a determining factor in the game; the choice of one over the other may substantially change the proceedings of the game. Here it is worth examining in more detail the fabrication and selection of the balls; they have enormous relevance for the ritual, and they form part of the preliminary phase.

A small ball of miter wood covered with strips of elastic rubber constitutes the heart of the pelota. The ballmaker artisan, or *pelotero*, melts the rubber and stretches it on a plate; he then puts a sheet of newspaper over it. That way the rubber solidifies evenly and remains thin. Later he cuts it into strips and, after separating them from the sheet of newspaper, he wraps the miter ball with the strips until it reaches the desired size. This is called the *potro* or *kiski*; the bounce of the ball, its vigor, its way of connecting with the players' hands, and the pain it causes will depend on its weight and solidity. The pelota may be dead or alive, of "knock," of greater or lesser exit and route, basically depending on the bulk of the rubber. Later, however, one may apply specific care to sooth or stimulate its natural features.[21]

The *pelotero* wraps this nucleus with wool to soften it and with thread or cotton wool to compact it until it reaches a diameter of about 60 to 65 millimeters (approximately 2.5 inches). This process is known as *devanado*, or "winding." He then cuts two pieces of goat leather in the shape of an eight, which he puts in water to soften, and which he now nails on the wool to be able to sew them. Once the stitching is done, he takes out the nails and hits the ball against a mold with a hammer, or pressurizes it by putting it in a molding plate. After this process, which lasts about an hour, the pelotero lets the ball rest. A few hours later, one may start discovering its character.[22]

The *pelotero* is an artisan. He does not mass produce but elaborates each one of the balls from beginning to end. When he is done with one, he starts another. They cannot be repeated. Each one is original and the *pelotero* always attempts to perfect them.

Depending on the style of the pelotari who will use them, the *pelotero* will make the balls in one way or another: with more or less *potro*; with the wool more or less pressed and even wet so that the ball gains weight; with the leather upside or turned inside out. The combination of material allows for as many types of balls as one could wish for. In fact, it is quite impossible for two balls to be identical.

---

21. If it is dead and one wants to enliven it, one needs to heat it up. If it is alive and bouncy, it needs cold to settle down. On the treatment of pelotas, see Muntión, *50 años de pelota en La Rioja*.

22. The fabrication of the balls is beautifully filmed in Leth, *Pelota*.

After resting the ball it needs to be broken in. The father of Cipri[23] used to give brand new balls to the children who were playing on the fronton where his workshop was located. The extreme hardness and weight did not allow the children to play well, but by hitting them against the walls, the balls were "tamed." Nowadays a machine does this job. The ball is inserted into the machine and bounced around so that its entire surface is broken in; it is thus prepared for the game.

After making sure the balls are ready, the *pelotero* sends them to the company that ordered them. The company has a person responsible for the choice of material; after checking the balls—by touching, bouncing, and hitting them around lightly—he selects those he considers most fitting for the game between the players who are going to confront each other.

The material selector knows the game of the pelotaris and he knows which balls suit their style best. If both players are from the same company, the selector will prepare a set of balls that equally accommodates both players. If it is a mixed game in which not only players but also companies confront each other, the selectors of each company will choose balls that most fit their own player and least fit the style of their opponent.[24] In this case, each selector chooses five balls, which makes the set a total of ten for the day on which the material is selected. This day is announced in the media, and entrance to the fronton is free; the pelotaris test the balls and pick four that will be used for the duel.

The fronton where ball selection happens is the same fronton where the game will take place within three days. The type of balls chosen also depend on the fronton, because there are courts more rugged than others, frontons that are more or less humid, with stone or concrete flooring, to mention only a few of the factors that may influence the behavior of the ball.

---

23. The preparation of the balls has been a complete artisan's job that has been passed on from father to son. Until 2010, the person who prepared the balls for professional hand pelota was Cipri, a *pelotero* from Sestao (Bizkaia), whose father and grandfather of the same name also dedicated their lives to preparing pelotas. Currently (2011), most of the balls used at games are provided by Punpa, a company situated in Donibane Lohizune (Saint-Jean-de-Luz) in Lapurdi, which was established in 2004 with the objective of modernizing ball production. Its owner, Ander Ugarte, took over the business from a *pelotero* in Senpere (Saint-Pée-sur-Nivelle), who had no successor in the family. They use machines for making the *potro* and the winding, but the stitching is still done by hand.

24. The league of professional hand pelota companies, founded in 2002, agreed that there should be only one selector: Atano XIII (Juan Mari Juaristi).

The first people to arrive on the day of material selection are usually the selectors, who come at a specific hour to do the preselection of balls right there. The pelotaris arrive with their entourage—trainers and colleagues with whom they can hit the balls around—and go directly to the locker room to change and fix the *tacos* to protect their hands.

When they come out on the court in their tracksuits, this time not dressed in white, the doors are already open to the public. There are already numerous fans on the terraces, many of whom are bettors who want to know what balls will be used in the contest, since they are important factors when it comes to making predictions.

The pelotaris try the balls by bouncing and hitting them against the frontis; they play a bit against the player who has accompanied them for this reason. They play one-on-one. The player who will play in red in the game gets to choose first, and then the player who will wear blue.

Each player seeks out the balls that best suit his game, a game designed to counteract that of the opponent, which is also considered in the choice of the ball.

Journalists and individuals related to the pelotaris and the game remain in the rows, waiting for the decision concerning the material: they want to know whether the players have found balls to their liking, what the quality of the balls is, and what type of balls will constitute the *cestaño*,[25] or basket. The material makes news in its own right through the selection process, but will be rarely mentioned until the day of the game; almost certainly, postgame remarks on the balls will abound.

When the players finally finish the selection of the balls, the selector takes them for weighing under the strict supervision of a federated delegate, or the keeper of the pelotas. The weight of the balls must be between 101.5 and 107.5 grams (approximately 3.5 ounces). Once they are weighed, the selector marks them and puts them in a wooden box with compartments; it will be immediately sealed with wax. The date of the game and the name of the players who will play are written on the box. The players sign it and the box is handed over to the keeper of the pelotas, who keeps vigil over it until the day of the game. He will need to make sure that the box is not affected by any kind of change in climate; he must keep it away from humidity, and always at about 15 degrees Celcius (59 Fahrenheit). On the day of the game he will be the first one

---

25. The *cestaño* or basket consists of the four selected balls with which the game will be played. They are placed in the basket that the referee carries.

to arrive at the fronton; once he is there, he seeks out the most suitable place (which is usually assigned) to keep the pelotas. If the fronton is very humid, he will go outside with the box so that the balls will not be affected. Every moment until the box is opened he will be guard them.

On game day, after the ten minutes the players have for warming up, the keeper heads toward the middle of the line of the terraces with the wooden, wax-sealed box. The players also proceed there.

With the entire fronton watching, the keeper opens the box with the four selected balls inside. The pelotaris reach for them (each player his ball), and as they touch them they make sure that they are the chosen ones: they check their marks, they press them, they bounce them and start hitting them against the frontis.

The characteristics of the balls dominate the terrace conversations. That this player's balls are bouncy; that it will be a nice ball for a good game; that this one will be hard to return; that the fronton is more humid than the day of the selection because the balls do not bounce off the frontis in the same way; that the player who gets to serve will choose this ball because it flies like lightning; that this ball does not look like the same selected on Thursday, and look how it bounces at square six and flies all over to nine. The pelotas also form the central topic of television commentaries at that moment.

Although it seems like mere formalism, the moment the pelotas are selected by the players, there emerges a notorious communion among all the agents of the fronton: a communion concentrating on the ball's sound. The pelota's sound reveals its soul: if it is of mediocre bounce, if it is dead or alive. The knock of the balls implies a fundamental flow of communication between distinctive spaces, and it is essential to recognize its quality in order to fully participate in the ritual, in order to understand it.

Still today in Adarraga, in Logroño, we see a lot of people leave their seats after the first game is over and go to the front part of the terraces and, if there is no room, even onto the court. While this could be seen as a mere encounter between the matchmakers and the bettors, it is more than that; it is the desire of those knowledgeable about the material of the pelota to hear the ball's sound up close. I was told by one spectator (who was, incidentally, a bettor) that he always went down to the court hoping that one of the balls would escape the hands of the pelotari and that he could catch it, touch it, and even bounce it. Knowing what the ball feels like, how it enters the hand, is discovering the pelota's *indarra*.

Although they look the same and even measure and weigh the same, the way they nail the hand, the way they hurt it, reveals their true nature, inasmuch as the real difference between the balls lies in their core, in the *potro*, which is invisible.

The public's ignorance of the ball makes it difficult to evaluate a game, something that the spectators do not always realize. The ball may unbalance a game in favor of a lesser category pelotari who, with a serious ball, would not even score twice. This happens frequently in the summer when there are a lot of scheduled games. The pelotaris of greater power do not usually find balls to their liking; because if balls more suited to their more powerful style of play were used, then most pelotaris would not be able to play. This way, the pelota itself may become a fundamental weapon of control for the companies.

Aware of this, some players reject the balls before the game. Six-time champion Retegi I, they say, would show the balls to the public, since the lighter ones gave him a lot of trouble on the court. When he found the balls inadequate, he moved in front of the crowd and started to hit the ball in such a way that it would go all the way up to the ceiling. In effect, he was trying to warn the crowd that with these balls he would not be able to win and they had better not bet on him.

The act of delegitimizing the ball and showing the public—by an exaggerated hit or an excessively worn ball—that under these conditions the player will not be able to guarantee a favorable outcome is the gravest incident that can happen. Namely, if the element of mediation between the agents is rejected, the game becomes totally devalued. "Not finding ball" is like being paralyzed, disabled, which means that equal opportunity is slightly upset. Aware of this, pelotaris often complain ardently about the *cestaño* in case they lose—something which, if done after the game, is considered a mere excuse.

The Greeting

Once the balls are checked, the referee calls on the players to hand them over to him and to stand in line for the parade of honor. The referees stand in between the players in a way that the line judge leads them, followed by a player or a couple. Then comes the head referee, the other player or couple and, to close the line, the assistant referee. They all walk up to the side line of the court, from the back wall until the middle of the court. Once they arrive there they turn toward the public and all five, the referees and the players, raise their hands with an open hand to greet the spectators. The crowd breaks out in applause; the shouting calls to the court those stragglers who are still in the bathrooms, the corridors, or the bar.

This act is relatively recent in pelota, and it condenses various meanings that were formerly expressed through other acts such as leaving the jacket under the frontis, or swearing loyalty and nobleness in front of the referee.

With the first one of these actions, that is leaving the jacket by the frontis when coming out onto the court, the pelotari symbolically promised to *dejarse la piel*, "leave his skin," that is do his best in the game. This is reinforced by the fact that inside the jacket was the amount of money the player offered for the game. It has been often interpreted as an act to protect the jacket from "foreign hands" by leaving it at a place where it is visible for all and which doesn't disturb the game. Nevertheless, when the player comes out onto the plaza, a plaza replete with referees, quartermasters, and trainers who could take care of the jacket, the player leaves it under the frontis in a ceremonial manner. It is not a utilitarian act, though it could have derived from one; rather, it is symbolic. The player parts with his jacket and places it, like an offering, by the frontis as a patent sign of what he came there to do: to give his all in order to win.

The players express the same by showing their open hands or their instruments to the spectators. They will give all they have to win, and they will do it by the instrument they have and which symbolically condenses their power: the hand or its extension, the tool. A hand that disguises nothing, that shows itself as it is.

The second action, swearing loyalty and nobleness in front of the referee, has also disappeared; or rather, it has been incorporated into the symbolism of the greeting. The No-Do (official Spanish state newsreel) documentary directed by Joaquín Hualde in 1950, *Frontones y pelotaris*, features how the players swear loyalty and nobleness before the referee, in this case a priest. This act and its significance is also condensed into the lifting of the arm with open hands or with the instrument. Showing the weapons to those whom one is going to fight emanates an image of cleanness, an honesty that is required from the player. Through greeting, the pelotari promises that he will fight to win, that he will suffer if needed, and he will play fairly.

The referee, in his turn, also shows by this act the attributes that legitimize his judgment. By showing his open palm to the crowd he displays his impartiality, an oath that was formerly done verbally like the player's oath.

As they lower their hands after the greeting, both the referees and the players shake hands: "they gave each other the hand, as a token that they wanted once more to recognize each other."[26] Each recognize the others' display of attributes: the referee recognizes the fairness of the player, which is also recognized by the other player, and both players accept the impartiality of the referee. By the shake of the hand they recognize the *other*; he is acknowledged as the rival as much as the magistrate of the contest.

The head referee's act of legitimating, however, is not over yet. Although the players have recognized the impartiality of he who raises his hand like them—a command baton that will enforce the norms of the game—he must completely assume the faculty of power, a power that is given to him by the entity that he addresses: the public. The referee, who has showed his impartiality through the greeting and by shaking hands, must now use that impartiality to fully legitimize his second attribute: authority.

Flipping the Coin

After shaking hands, the referees and the players step back, distance themselves slightly, and form a semicircle in the middle of the court. It is then that flipping the coin takes place, which decides who will get to serve first.

Historically, the coin was a valuable piece of money, even a gold doubloon, which the referee brought with him. This is why many called flipping the coin "lion, castle," in reference to the two sides of the coin. Today the coin is just that, a round coin with an obverse and reverse colored in red and blue.

The head referee takes the coin from his pocket and, with his right hand, which he has showed to the public, shows it to both players, who have just recognized his impartiality. He throws it vertically about one meter (three feet) above their heads. The intensity of chaotic noise that normally overtakes the fronton drops substantially, and all eyes are fixed on this round, flat object that flips around in the air. The fronton succumbs completely to the designs of chance. The tension is patent, and

---

26. Nietzsche, *Thus Spoke Zarathustra*, 269.

the metallic noise the coin makes as it lands on the ground only exacerbates it. Blue, red, red, blue, the coin stops at last. "I don't know why, but it almost always turns out red" says a spectator. One of the players bends down to pick up the coin and hands it over to the referee.

A moment of maximum tension, the flipping of the coin is the most uncertain attribute of the game; this act will greatly affect the game because it will not be compensated a posteriori. The first serve has no counterpart: unlike in the majority of ball games, the serve does not alternate in pelota. With the exception of the first serve, which is decided by chance, the player needs to score to be able to serve and choose the game ball, because the server picks the ball. Of the four balls in the basket that the referee guards and of which each player has contributed two, the player who won the right to serve must choose one to start the game. From this moment on, whoever scores gets to serve and choose the ball. Johan Huizinga emphasizes the relationship between the words "right" and "shoot" in Hebrew, where "*thorah* (right, justice, law) has unmistakable affinities with a root that means casting lots, shooting, and the pronouncement of an oracle."[27] The contact with hazard, with "casting lots" implies for Leviticus (16, 8–10) the divine intervention,[28] something that transcends human control.

The referee becomes the intermediary of chance, a form of justice that does not stem from human design like norms do; it comes from someplace else. In this contact with *alea*, with designs of another kind, the referee becomes imbued with the necessary authority to enforce the fulfillment of norms. With reference to the maximum authority, the state, Jesús Ibáñez says that it "reserves chance for itself and assumes the norms for itself."[29] The referee does the same. On the court, a consecrated space par excellence, the referee assumes authority through direct contact with chance. He transcends the counter-court, his natural space, in order to consecrate himself and consecrate at the same time the boundaries, norms, and precepts that from this moment on will govern the game. The contact with pure (sacred) chance sacralizes the norm, a norm that is physically concretized in the *eskas*, or fault lines, and which is represented by the referee. His principal responsibility is adjudicating if the ball has bounced within the bounds of the court or not.

---

27. Huizinga, *Homo Ludens*, 80.
28. Leach, *Culture and Communication*, 91–92.
29. Ibáñez, *Nuevos avances en la investigación social II*, 194.

The coin introduces the third fundamental element that enables the game to take place: the boundary, the *eskas*, or the material representation of the norm. The way of establishing the norm at the fronton, the institution of boundaries happens precisely through chance. It is as though by flying, the coin illuminated all the *eskas* of the fronton, as though it gave them life and consecrated them again, since it is only from this moment on that the boundaries have absolute validity. During warm up, they were mere signs of reference for practice; now they are indisputable limits that will decide if a hit is valid or a fault.

The coin establishes the norm, a norm that is based on an alternating interchange of the ball with the intermediation of the frontis within established boundaries. It also establishes order. It plants the first bud of difference between the players, placing them in a determined position vis-à-vis the other: one serves and the other returns. From this moment on the player uses every medium at his disposal—strength, resistance, imagination, and dexterity—in order to hunt down his rival and avoid being hunted down by him within the established boundaries. From this moment on they will put to the test different strategies and each player will configure his game in relation to the other within the established boundaries that are enforced by authority and chance.

The throwing of the coin determines some cardinal precepts of the game, as well as its basic requisites: the acceptance of a set of rules and the incertitude of an unforeseeable outcome. The game is principally order, inasmuch as it structures the relations of members who participate in it; it is also tension, given that it tends toward an uncertain outcome.[30] The vertical contact with the sacred, with chance, establishes the necessary elements of play: The boundaries: it establishes what the boundaries represent; the norm: it imbues with authority he who distributes it (the referee); and it determines how the first positions are established at the fronton: who serves (and picks the ball) and who receives.

Coin flipping is the action that marks the passage from the preliminal to the liminal phase of the ritual, to this "realm of pure possibility whence novel configurations of ideas and relations may arise," to quote Turner.[31] Everything is ready for the game to start. The pelotaris have been transformed, the balls presented, and the boundaries established. *Alea iacta est*, "the die has been cast."

---

30. Huizinga, *Homo Ludens*, 10.
31. Turner, *The Ritual Process*, 97.

Liminal Phase: The Game

Here I initially intended to describe the 2003 singles finals. However, fans themselves criticized the course of this championship, because it was "conceived on the bases of entrepreneurial interests and against the *pelotazale* logic."[32] Instead of the final, therefore, I decided to describe what many considered to be the real final: the game played between the winners of the first semifinals round that in normal circumstances would have been the final that year. The two opponents were Beloki, a powerful backcourt player from Burlata and three-time hand pelota singles champion who had beaten Patxi Ruiz in the first round of qualifiers; and Olaizola II, a sagacious frontcourt player from Goizueta, who had beaten the incumbent champion Barriola in the first round of the semifinals. The game was played on May 18, 2003, at the Astelena fronton of Eibar.

Under the attentive watch of the pelotari in the blue jersey and *gerriko*, in this case Olaizola II, Beloki, in red and with the right to serve, takes the balls and tests them one more time.[33] He picks the ball with which he will execute the first serve, and hands it over to Olaizola II to try out. Olaizola II hits it against the frontis a few times, inspects it again and again, hits it as he approaches the back wall, rubs it with both hands and grabs it with his right hand as he throws it in the air. When Beloki looks at him, he hits the ball back to him and assumes his position to receive the serve.

The *momio* is a hundred to forty euros in favor of Olaizola II, who has showed himself superior to the rest of the players during the championship. The bookmakers are inciting the usual bettors by waiving their hands and running from one side of the terraces to the other. The referees have taken up their positions by the line assigned to them.

Beloki makes the sign of the cross twice, shakes hands with his rival, and prepares to serve. Olaiza II is waiting by the back wall bending his

---

32. Personal communication to the author from a pelota fan.

33. Traditionally, if the incumbent champion did not play the final, the red sash was worn by the player whom the *cátedra* considered the potential winner. Nowadays, it depends on neither favoritism nor predictions. With the exception of the hand pelota singles champion, who plays in red all year through, red is worn by the player who debuted in the professional championship earlier than his opponent. In the case of doubles, the pair with the longest professionally serving frontcourt player gets to wear red. Whoever has been playing for the longest time in the professional court will wear red, and his rival blue.

knees slightly and his torso leaning a tad forward, ready to sprint. He swings where his arms lead him and exerts the utmost effort. Grabbing the ball with the right hand and raising it by his face, Beloki starts the shot, bounces the ball before the fault line, steps forward while extending his arm, and hits it brusquely against the frontis.

The public is palpitating, the referee sharpens his vision, and the commentator announces in Euskara: "The second round of the semifinals of the 2003 first division hand pelota singles championship has started."

Most answers to the question "*what* is a game?" allude to a struggle under equal conditions between two players or pairs who are subject to certain rules and share the same objective: winning. A desire shared by both, but which only one of them can enjoy. In agonic struggles, the antagonism is fixed by the other proto-agonist who longs for the same object of desire, but which both cannot ultimately possess. The scheme of struggle is planted, and the players need to negotiate it. Besides, the game itself has one condition: equality between the contesters, the equilibrium of departure, something that lends the contest a substantially tragic character.

Girard emphasizes the conflicting symmetry of the tragic inspiration. In Greek tragedies, "what matters is the confrontation between two protagonists" who resolve power between them under an equality of conditions: "The symmetry of the tragic dialogue is perfectly mirrored by the stichomythia, in which the two protagonists address one another in alternating lines."[34] Similarly, the players resolve the question of power between each other through the alternating exchange of a ball in an ideal situation of equal conditions.

A game therefore (*partido*, as we have already seen, also means "split," or "divided" in Spanish) consists of splitting a whole into equal parts. As Javier Echevarría notes in his take on the concept of play from the perspective of Hegelian phenomenology: "The contesters are two living self-consciousnesses that emerge from the splitting of equality."[35] This is why the players share the same garments. Both parties fight to win, to assert themselves, and reconstruct in themselves that unity.

Nevertheless, the process of construction that is implied here begs the question of *how* the game proceeds, a how that for Patxi Lanceros

---

34. Girard, *Violence and the Sacred*, 47.
35. Echeverría, *Sobre el juego*, 58.

"introduces an index of variability, of possible transformation and diversity."[36] It is obvious that the struggle between two subjects is a sublime layout for conflict. Nevertheless, it is not the resolution of this conflict that draws the public to the fronton. As Huizinga notes, "the contest is largely devoid of purpose.... The action begins and ends in itself, and the outcome does not contribute to the necessary life-processes of the group.... Objectively speaking, the result of the game is unimportant and a matter of indifference."[37] What the crowd wants to see is how the player faces a dilemma; how he handles pressure; what solutions he finds, solutions that will define his qualities to a great degree. During a game the end is implicit in the layout: each and every time one will prevail over the other. It is the process of the game that makes it unique. The result alone says little about the game, because the layout and the outcome are always the same. What makes a game unique is its core, the way the pelotaris fight, suffer, and come up with formulas to resolve the game positively: to win and save themselves. In fact, the pelotari's formation itself depends on this, on the search for exits from pressures that the crack itself, in the case the encounter with the other, imposes.

The layout of the game obliges the pelota player to make a series of decisions that will contribute to forging his character. The pelotari is formed as he accommodates his actions to the answers that his actions provoke in the other player, as he presupposes them. The extension of interactions to other social spheres is nothing but the game taking place.

The pelotari emerges in the court with a *background*, with sediment of knowledge that he has incorporated through interaction with others. This familiarity makes him opt for a specific strategy, a strategy that has worked on previous occasions. The pelotari has configured a particular style on the bases of previous encounters, and this experience will now prompt tactics that will determine the beginning of the game. The same way, his opponent knows about the strategies of his rival, given that he knows his and his own style as well. Both know the weapons of the other, their attributes; by choosing particular balls it already becomes clear what type of strategies the players will use to beat their opponent.

---

36. Lanceros, *Diccionario de hermenéutica*, 169.

37. Huizinga, *Homo Ludens*, 49.

The blue pelotari appears before his red opponent like prey to a hunter. He must know his movements, his inclinations, his preferences. Just as the motor system of the antelope and the leopard have evolved in relation to one another, so do the strategies of the players unfold during the game. On the pelota court, however, there are two hunters who are also potential preys; thus, the player may easily become a hunter who is ultimately hunted down.

José Ortega y Gasset's appropriate assessment of the hunt is as follows: "If the hunted is also, on the same occasion, a hunter, this is not hunting"; rather, we are faced with a reciprocal action that we would call fight.[38] The hunt is a valuable analogy that helps us understand the game of pelota, especially if we consider that game terminology has various references to venatic art such as "he hunted him down," and the use of "trap." Curiously, hunting is not only the most widely used metaphor to understand the game, but one of the most favorite pasttime activities of players as well.

The game is set forth as a fight, "in which both parties have the same intention and similar behavior."[39] But as it proceeds, the dissolution of equality between the players configures a hunt scheme in which one tries to dominate and exploit, while trying to avoid being trapped by the other. Besides, the chances the dominated has to escape domination and, in the case of pelota, to dominate—to "turn around" the vicious circle—maintains the tension of the game. The longer equality and the fight scheme is maintained, the greater the tension; it will be sooner or later be substituted by another hunt scheme, where one will acquire the status of hunter and other that of the beast; one will become he who offers the sacrifice, the other the sacrificial victim.

The Basque sculptor and thinker Jorge Oteiza recognized that Basques "play as hunters and to hunt each other; some emerge as hunter and man, others as prey and hunted animal. Some escape the labyrinth, and others stay in it, they play our Minotaurs and Theseus. And the style they play, revealed at the fronton, is that of traps, periphrastic of holes."[40]

---

38. Ortega y Gasset, *Meditations on Hunting*, 60.
39. Ibid.
40. Pelay Orozco, *Pelota, pelotari y frontón*, 24.

Sizing up (*Tanteo*), or How to *Hunt Down* the Other

The search for a hole where he can hit the ball is the player's ultimate task. There are hundreds of strategies to reach this goal, although they can be generally reduced to two kinds: hitting the ball farther than the opponent, or displacing the opponent. The first strategy means hitting the ball so far or with such force that the other player may not be able to return it or, if he does, his strike is so weak that it "surrenders," and it may be finished off easily. This is the lion's game plan: whoever is forceful enough to launch long balls or hit them with such strength that the opponent's arms fail before them. Rising to a volley by Retegi I, or returning the right-hand strike of Azkarate was a complicated affair for the opponent, so superior was their power.

The other great strategy, which may be able to counteract power, is preventing the opponent from hitting the ball comfortably and probing for spots that are for him unattainable. The best way to achieve this is moving him around until he loses position and, at the perfect moment, hitting the ball where he cannot reach it. This is the tactic of the fox, who compensates his lack of strength with a lot of astuteness and agility. In the game described here Beloki embodies the first type, the lion, while Olaizola II is more redolent of the second type, the fox.

Both are prototypes of the pelotari: the strong and the cunning, the lion and the fox. They seek to overcome the other, and each of them does so in their peculiar way: the lion through the power of strength, while the fox prefers tricks. There are as many variations of these archetypes as pelotaris, whose strategy, while it may fit categories, is defined in the end on the basis of a fundamental variable: the encounter itself.

The always unforeseeable encounter determines the players' style of play as well as the balls that they will use. It is not the same when two lions confront each other at the rough Labrit fronton in Iruñea-Pamplona, for example, as a fox and a lion at the fast Atitzbatalde court of Zarautz, just to mention two of the innumerable possibilities of combinations. One must also remember that there are no two identical lions or foxes, and each player leans toward a different ball: lively, of medium bounce, dry, languid, more or less worn, one that flies the court low or high, one that bounces off the frontis forcefully or stays on it, a ball that "knocks," that has smaller or greater diameter, or weight, and so on. The encounter is unique and it will determine the construction of game plans. From this perspective, any description of a game is just one of the infinite possibilities it may produce, which in turn reveals what exactly an encounter means.

Following Beloki's serve, the first score between Beloki and Olaizola II is a tremendous struggle of power. Neither of the players wants to lose his position, and Beloki resorts to the volley five times so that Olaizola II may not dominate him. Olaizola II has chosen to dispense with his usual game—fighting at the front squares of the fronton—and is attacking Beloki with his weapons: by hitting the ball hard. Olaizola II controls the game by playing off the bounce, and Beloki has to resort to the volley in order not to lose court. The roles seem to have turned around. After twenty-one exchanges of hits, Olaizola executes a dropshot from square 5, which Beloki fails to reach; 0–1, and Olaizola's serve.

The players have chosen balls of great quality: "a man's balls," some say. Olaizola II prefers weighty balls of medium bounce tending toward the languid, so that they stay on the frontis and do not bounce on the court. Beloki prefers balls that fly low and rise little. A pelota *zakarra*, some call it: slow, rough, able-bodied, and one that hurts the hand.

Enormously difficult points follow. The players cannot seem to find open spots whereby they might dominate the game, and the scores alternate on the scoreboard. Beloki manages to slightly overcome Olaizola and, after a surprising point that is quite imaginative for a lion, he loses his head: "*bere burua saldu du*," ("he betrayed himself") comments Eguskitze, the ETB1 reporter. He loses a very difficult point: 5–5. Equality persists and the players are playing at a great level.

The crowd is enjoying the game, which is now favoring Olaizola II because of a mistake by Beloki. The latter feels dominated and pulls out the volley to fend off his rival's hits. Olaizola II raises his hands to claim a fault against Beloki for a delayed volley, an *atxiki*. The game continues and ends 5–7 in favor of Olaizola II. Beloki recriminates his *pido*, his opponent's request for a fault.[41]

The next score causes great suffering for both players: "*leher eginda daude*" Eguskitze comments. The players are worn out. Besides, after the clash between the players over the *pido*, the "request" by Olaizola II, the crowd whistles at several of Beloki's attempts to hit the volley. The atmosphere has soured: *gaiztotu egin da giroa*.

---

41. "Pido" refers to the request for a fault by a player during the game.

This intensity can be barely maintained by the pelotaris and, after two especially tough series it seems like it has to break down at one point. Beloki takes the serve and scores two against Olaizola II, which is followed by a few prompt resolutions by both players: 10–10. The equality is maintained. The game is reaching its maximum tension and, despite the rapid sequence of the last two scores, the crowd is witnessing one of the best games of the season.

Various mistakes by Olaizola II, one of which is overlooked in his favor, determine the game, which now totals 180 correctly exchanged shots.

At 12–12 there is a change in the game. Beloki answers a fair return by Olaizola II with a two-wall hit. Olaizola II runs and surpasses his rival in the air: *buruz gain* (over the head), a humiliating strike for his opponent. *Hori da ahala, hori!* This is power!

Two more scores by Olaizola II on the scoreboard makes the game 12–14. Through the last point, however, the player grabs his right arm and complains about his triceps. He goes to the locker room and the possibility of suspending the game is looming. In that event, Beloki would win the point for the championship, and the bets would be settled by apportionment.[42]

But Olaizola II seems like he is ready to continue. He emerges from the locker room with a bandage on his arm, and launches a strategy of *saque y remate* (serve and return) that is designed to finish off the game and end the struggle as soon as possible.

Some bettors think he should retire if he is not in conditions to play, but it looks like his tactics are paying off; Beloki has trouble liberating himself from the ominous number, one of the superstitions that revolve around scoring: 13–17.[43]

Clearly, Beloki has the most potent arm in the championship and, positioned to the far right, he strikes four tremendous balls that touch the left wall. Olaizola II returns them with a left-hand hook but fails the fourth volley. *Egurrean Beloki*, "Beloki is beating up his opponent." He

---

42. The difference in the score between the two sides is multiplied by a hundred, and this is then divided by the difference of the player that is further from finishing the game. The result would be a percentage score to satisfy the winner. Bombín and Bouzas, *El gran libro de la pelota*, vol. 2, 613.

43. Other scores that are considered predictive of outcome are 16–19 or the other way round, which indicate a turn around in the game's proceedings. There is also a widespread belief that the player who exits first from a 13–13 tie will eventually win the game.

is gaining vigor, determined to destroy his rival. But Olaizola II is very much of a fox, and Beloki is only advancing by sharing out the scores.

Olaizola II cannot keep up the rythm and eventually his dropshot ends up below the *chapa*, the iron sheet. *Nekearen mina*, the pain of fatigue sets in. Beloki takes advantage of it to strike from the side, toward the injured right side of Olaizola II. He manages to overtake him: 19–18, but ambition plays him a dirty trick and the next serve ends up off court. He prefers the easy point to the tedious one; in the *manomanista* this strategy, however, is rarely successful. Olaizola II, *goizuetako aztia*, the wizard of Goizueta, is taking over again with a return dropshot at the *txoko*, the corner: 19–20. They draw again after Beloki's cross-shot that Olaizola II cannot volley back. The next score comes from Beloki's serve: 21–20.

Andrés Ortiz-Osés argues that the key to dramatic fight with the other is "the assimilation of one's opponent for his co-integration: this is why the fight symbolically appears to be a lover's dispute, in which the *mixis,* or sacred union, between the hero and his destiny takes place. . . . The authentic heroic action is about the re-mediation of contraries."[44] The hunt is exactly this: discovering the other, assimilating him, and appropriating him.

When the pelotari talks about hunting for the other, he means cornering him, moving him around in order to win the score. Nevertheless, to the question of how to hunt for the other, another meaning of "hunting," implicit in the term itself, emerges: discovering him. In common parlance, when someone hunts for the other he either discovers his intentions or simply understands them. In order for the player to win, to appropriate for himself this split reality, he needs to understand his rival, needs to know his intentions, and discover his weaknesses; hence the word *tanteo*, or "sizing up."

Synonyms of sizing up include examining, testing, spying, recognizing, probing, and measuring, among many others. Every open process is about sizing up. A game is a succession of *tantos*, of points, twenty-two in the hand modality. This is the interval the pelota player has at his disposal to explore, understand, and thus overcome his rival. The player uses the time of the game to size up the other and acknowledge his abilities. He starts to examine how he responds to the right, then to the left, low and high, how he moves, and how he recovers; he keeps looking for

---

44. Ortiz-Osés, "Mitología del héroe moderno," 387.

weaknesses and lapses. The player who first discovers his rival's weaknesses has greater possibilities to hunt him down in the second meaning of the word. As Unanue said after a game against Arretxe: "I was trying very hard, but I couldn't get a handle on him."[45]

In order to hunt for the other, the pelotari must possess two prototypical features: strength and astuteness. The lion tries to push his opponent back toward the backward quarters, or force him to play in the air; in short, he attempts to wear him out. Once the distance is sufficient or the fatigue apparent, he hits the ball to an unattainable spot, thus nailing his opponent. On his part, the fox does not get entangled in games of power; rather, he attempts to divorce his opponent from his vigor, he attempts to exhaust him. In order to achieve that, he plays the paradigmatic vacuums of the fronton, those spaces that Oteiza has been able to read masterfully: below the *chapa* or the iron belt, in the *txoko* (corner), on the left wall, on the rear wall, in the air (*buruz gain*), and the sides.[46] He executes dropshots, two-wall shots, hooks, and lateral shots. He attempts to move his opponent around brusquely until he surrenders, followed by a prompt finish-off.

In any case, the main objective is that the opponent should not reach the ball or if he does, that he should not be able to return it. The most perfect and terminal way of doing this is by nailing the opponent, paralyzing him either by forcing him to play "quiet foot" or by making him trample over the ball. Forcing him to lose his position is hunting him down. Preventing the opponent from feeling comfortable at the fronton, forcing him in the air in defense, is breaking him, killing him little by little, smashing him.

In the game described above, once Olaizola II has hurt his right hand Beloki feels he has found the obvious weakness that will help him win the game. He attempts to shoot every ball to the right because he has been unable to discover more shortcomings, more hollow spots in his rival's game. The great fox that he is, Olaizola II now feels Beloki's pulse. He knows that he is nervous, that he is obliged to win because Olaizola II is injured. He focuses on patiently playing his own game: abrupt stops, hooks toward the terraces, dropshots at the *txoko*. In turn, Beloki subordinates himself to his rival's game and forgets that he has

---

45. Statement to the press after the match.
46. Oteiza, "Revelación en frontón vasco de nuestra cultura original," 24.

the strongest arm in the whole competition. Instead of striking like a lion, he faces the fox on his own territory, falls into his trap, and fails to control him.

For the Bride

The game score is 21–20. Beloki prepares to serve again for the last time; if he wins the point, he wins the game.

In modalities in which the points are still announced, the *kontatzaile* or scorekeeper repeats the score out loud as the game's standing changes. The moment a player is about to make the last point, he yells "For the bride" as I have heard it on various occasions, or "Here comes the bride, *jaunak* [gentlemen]," as Pío Baroja relates it.[47]

In professional games where there is an electronic scoreboard and the custom of shouting the points out loud has disappeared, the crowd applauds his run-up to serve when the player is about to execute the last serve that may very well be the last point of the game. Moreover, if the crowd thinks the player deserves it, there is a standing ovation on the terraces.

Before serving, the player waits until the bettors cover themselves and match the bets on the terraces.[48] While waiting, Beloki takes the ball and, before hitting it, he makes the sign of the cross. This is a typical act before the last strike; a conscious request for the game to turn out favorably and for the player to win. Unconsciously, perhaps, it is an act of expiating guilt for devouring the other, for the integration of the other, and for the hunt that crowns the game. The pelotari now plays the role of a person offering up a sacrifice and, as Henri Hubert and Marcel Mauss affirm in their analysis of sacrifice, he makes the sign of the cross: "its pardon was asked before it was struck down."[49]

The crowd starts applauding Beloki. The player runs toward the frontis and strikes. Olazoila II's return is a straight drive, and Beloki shoots it off court: 21–21. Maximum tension on the court. This time it is the last serve, Olaizola II's bride; it is also the last hit of the game because

---

47. Baroja, *Guía del País Vasco Español-Francés*, 63.

48. This custom is not regulated but based on a tacit agreement among all agents in the fronton; recently, it conflicted with the time slots calculated by the needs of television—time slots that do not coincide with the unforeseeable time of the pelota game.

49. Hubert and Mauss, *Magia y sacrificio en la historia de las religiones*, 33.

the players are now facing a tiebreak, sudden death: he who wins the point wins the game.

The dizziness of the game stuns everyone at the fronton. The excitement makes the crowd rise from their seats and applaud the last serve. Olaizola II makes the sign of the cross.

The fight as such is about to terminate, it is about to be resolved for one of the parties. The next game starts out from scratch once again: "One must keep playing. Even if you lose, you don't lose anything"[50] Retegi II says. In fact, when the moment of the bride arrives, the game is normally resolved; as partition, as duality it is over. This is why the bride is announced, this is why the crowd applauds. Normally, at this point of the game the objectives are fulfilled, the roles are clear, there is a victim and a sacrificer, even if the final touch is still missing. Not in this case, however: both players have 21 points. The tragic rivalry has persisted until the last moment, and both players are facing sudden death.

Olaizola II strikes the ball amid the excited applause of the crowd, and returns Beloki's hit with a left hook. Beloki barely reaches it and Olaizola II finishes off with a drop shot: 21–22. Olaizola II wins.

The game lasted an hour and a half, of which twenty minutes and twenty seconds were real time, with the ball in the game. The players have exchanged 316 correct shots. The crowd is content, happy, except for a preoccupation with Olaizola II's injury. The following day the press emphasizes that "until the injury we saw play in its purest form in the 'cathedral.'"[51] The game was elevated to the highest levels of spectacle because of Beloki's fierce lashes and Olaizola II's elegant creativity. The shots were executed at breakneck speed, with an extraordinary level of play, and titanic effort. "'It's been years since we've seen a game of such quality' Retegi said."[52]

The game, this initial split of an equilibrium, is finally resolved through *sizing up* between the players, in the recognition of one another in new situations. He who is better able to understand the other and the circumstances they find themselves in usually hunts the other down,

---

50. Julián Retegi II (hand pelota champion), interview by author, Atxondo (Bizkaia), November 20, 2000.

51. Qualifier for the Astelena fronton of Eibar, where they played the game.

52. Tino Rey, *El Correo Español*, Monday, May 9, 2003.

overcomes him. "Catching the prey requires holding it... the chased object has to be grasped with one's own hands."[53]

Once the game is over, the loser walks over to the winner and offers to shakes his hand. The winner accepts it and gives the loser a big hug; the greater the tension, the more effusive the gesture. The winner devours the loser through this gesture, a symbolic ingestion after which he walks over to the crowd with his fists in the air, showing a sign of victory.

With his hands open and clean, without grasping the ball, and in an equality of conditions, he has hunted his rival down. Now, once he has captured the prey, he raises his fists toward the crowd and offers up the victim to it, as though he had him inside. *"Eskuratu dut,"* the player says; "I did it." Literally he says "I grasped it in my hand."

The player who lost also walks over to the crowd. Although also with open hands, he greets the spectators without celebration; he thanks them for their support. If he played well, the spectators also applaud him. If not, he proceeds to the locker room amid absolute indifference.

Postliminal Phase: The Consecration

> Every ceremony well performed, every game or contest duly won, every act of sacrifice auspiciously concluded, fervently convinces archaic man that a boon and a blessing have thereby been procured for the community.
>
> —Johan Huizinga

With reference to noble and chivalrous wars, Huizinga observes that "there can be no talk of victory unless the prince's honour emerges with enhanced splendour from the field of battle."[54] The same is true of pelota: one may win a lot of games, but real victory happens when the figure of the player emerges strengthened from the fight, when the crowd expresses an explicit recognition of his skills.

Traditionally, when the crowd deemed that the pelotari deserved to be honored, they threw their *txapelas*, or berets, onto the court. In the 1950s Barberito I was honored several times this way in the Astelena fronton in Eibar, reputed as the most demanding fronton of all; it was called "The Cathedral of Pelota." He is said to be one of the last pelotaris

---

53. Zulaika, *Basque Violence*, 198.
54. Huizinga, *Homo Ludens*, 97.

to have been honored this way. Now, the crowd stands up and gives the pelotari an ovation when it wants to express its recognition. This means the player has been consecrated, that he has a place in the history of the game and in the memory of the *pelotazales*.

To achieve this confirmation, the pelotari has to prove himself superior to a player who is already consecrated, to a well-known figure. It is the greatness of his rivals that makes a pelotari great. If a player makes the game hard for an accredited opponent in good standing, if he sizes him up and seeks his weaknesses, he will emerge from the game greatly strengthened even if he loses it. The crowd appreciates the loss if the player has used his entire repertoire and has faced on an equal footing the player who is supposed to be his superior.

As we will see in part 3, the importance of how one plays acquires tremendous relevance in pelota. Although in most cases playing well goes hand-in-hand with triumph, the rankings in pelota, which were first conceived in the late nineteenth century to determine the profitability of a player for betting purposes, did not always correspond to the players the crowd deemed to be the best. In fact, the crowd values players who give their all on the court, who take risks: "Create spectacle, show off, be audacious and take risks. I managed these things and I was profusely applauded."[55]

The titles, the *txapelas* are the most coveted commodity for the pelotari. It is the singles championship that imply the greatest triumph one can wish: "it is in singles where the pelotari is consecrated."[56] The *txapela* proclaims the champion and grants the privilege of wearing red all through the year, something that has become a valuable extension of the victory; a sort of reign.

The Coronation

On a regular game day, when the contest is over the pelotaris congratulate one another, the loser walks away to the locker room, the winner greets the public and he leaves as well. In a final, however, the winner receives the *txapela*, a larger beret than normal and which is a sign of mastery: it has been the traditional way of crowning the winner. For the last half a century, the *txapela* has been accompanied by cups and medals,

---

55. Ogueta in Garcés, *Campeones manomanistas, 1940–1990*, 154.

56. Koteto Ezkurra, seven-time singles champion in the remonte modality.

which extends the moment of coronation, the moment that is fundamental in the transmission of *indarra*.

It is usually politicians who are charged with honoring the players: federation officers, councilmen, ministers, and even the president of the Autonomous Community of the Basque Country, the *lehendakari*. Like in any act of consecration, an exchange takes place. On the one hand, the victory is blessed: the legitimate representatives of the people crown the player, grant him the victory, and recognize his supremacy. On the other hand, through contact with the players politicians get imbued with grace and with *indarra*. The consecration of the player has already taken place on the court. The delivery of the laurel is nothing but the transmission of the pelotari's *indarra*, whom the crowd has already consecrated, to the politicians. The hand that swore honesty, that played fair, that suffered and that later became a fist of power by seizing the opponent, opens again to hand over its gifts to the politicians, who receive popularity from the hands of the hero. The crowd knows that and renounces this usurpation: politicians are routinely booed when they award a player, they receive whistles and dismissive insults. Once the pelotari lets go of the politician's hand and raises his fist or the cup toward the crowd, the public applaud and cheer the champion once more.

At the same time as this exchange of glory and popularity between the player and the politician takes place, the terraces settle up the debts of the game. The bettors take their betting tickets, leave the terraces, and go over the numbers with the bookmaker, who pays them and subtracts the handling fee, depending on the result of the bet.

These two exchanges conclude the ritual within the space of the fronton. What remains is the celebration of the game, normally a populous meal in some restaurant associated with the *pelotazale* tradition, and the dedication or consecration of the *txapela*.

The Celebration

The celebration includes a lunch or dinner in a restaurant typically frequented by *pelotazales*. Family members, friends, and various individuals from the world of pelota sit around the table to share with the winner a copious meal accompanied by great quantities of wine. The player is not left alone to eat in peace on these occasions. He constantly stands up to greet congregating fans who line up to shake hands with him and congratulate him.

Years ago it was typical for the player to announce where he was going to celebrate the postfinal meal. He informed his followers through the press where they could celebrate with him in the event that he won. The fans flooded the champion's table and, as is the case today, he greeted them one-by-one and invited them to drink champagne from his cup, inviting whoever wanted to partake of his victory.

The case of long instrument modalities, the final includes a meal where all the players who participate in the championship are invited along with those who want to come along with the champion. They gather to celebrate the end of the season and congratulate the champion team. Toasts and songs follow, and the meal turns into a drunken feast that ends in the bars of the village where the game takes place. Everyone is invited to drink a toast and have a sip from the cup of the champions, and the celebration goes on well into the night.

Not counting revenge on the part of defeated players and the privilege of playing in red the whole year through, the hangover of the celebration is, together with the reports and commentaries, the last glimmer of the final. Some forty years ago, however, the champion used to take his *txapela* to the Virgin to be blessed. Among others, Barberito I took it to the Virgin of Valvanera in Anguiano (La Rioja), and García Ariño I to the Virgin of Begoña in Bilbao. In 1957, then, Jesús García Ariño (García Ariño I) coincided with two of his sporting namesakes from Bizkaia in seeking the benediction of the Virgin of Begoña, protectress of the province: Jesús Garay, from the soccer team Athletic Bilbao, who brought the King's Cup the team won that year for a blessing; and the cyclist Jesús Loroño, who came with the King of the Mountains at the Tour de France. Three Jesuses for the Virgin. A noble representation for the devout people of Euskal Herria, who ritually sacrificed themselves for something greater: for the people.

The celebration of a pelota game is done in a ceremonial scheme of three phases that are comparable to any other positive cult or cult of consecration. The preliminary phase of the game establishes the necessary precepts in order to prepare for the encounter, the game: the liminal period of rescission and margin, where any outcome is possible. Dressed in white and bowing to the authority of the referee, the players represent the split of a totality, the *partido,* the game; they are two sides of the same coin, of the community. The liminal phase launches the *tanteo,* or "sizing up," and the hunt for the other. A tragic layout is established: the *agon* in which, through an alternative hitting of the ball under equal conditions, he who more quickly discovers the weaknesses of the other seizes the victory. In this tragic struggle, says Ortiz-Osés, "as mediating *polemos*, it is about devouring and being devoured, winning and enduring, overcoming and suppurating, transcending and implicating."[57] The pelotari sacrifices the other; he grabs him with his fists and devours him in order to offer him up for the crowd, for the community, which emerges refounded, renewed.

The three phases compose the diachronic time of the ritual, the succession of ceremonially accentuated images that are repeated each time the ritual takes place. Parallel to these interconnected intervals, one might speak of a pace that is unique to each of the modalities of the game. This pace is subordinated to the variety that the patterns emphasized before create, and configures the rhythm of pelota, that which makes each ritual a unique and unrepeatable event.

Postscript: The Rhythm of Pelota

"For there to be rhythm, strong times and weak times, which return in accordance with a rule of law—long and short times, recurring in a recognizable way, stops, silences, blanks, resumptions and intervals in accordance with regularity."[58] It is precisely the images in which ritual is decomposed that mark the rule to which Henri Lefebvre is referring to here. Actions that are repeated, or rather ones that return, in each ritual, actions that have an assigned place—spatially as well as temporally—and which imply its radical fractioning. The discontinuity that intervals introduce allows the game to gain importance and become a ritual. These are "con-centrated" periods where the fundamental symbols of ritual are presented or represented, and where core values are established and personified.

Nevertheless, if "rhythm brings with it a differentiated time, a qualified duration,"[59] the succession of these significant stages configure the rhythm per se. Rhythm necessitates an "overall movement that takes with it all these [accentuated] elements,"[60] it necessitates an intra-temporality; this is the cadence of the game that comes from the conjugation of its key

---

57. Ortiz-Osés, "Mitología del héroe moderno," 3.
58. Lefebvre, *Rhythmanalysis*, 78.
59. Ibid.
60. Ibid.

elements, from the contact between the player (with his instrument), the ball, and the fronton. This way, each modality would have its own, characteristic intra-temporality, in spite of the fact that the aforementioned patterns are analogous.

Jean Arramendy identifies the *atxiki* as the reason why the different modalities have different beats and tension.[61] The *atxiki* is the time of contact between the instrument and the ball. It spans a moment from the absence of *atxiki*, the prototypical dry and forceful hit by the pala, to the *atxikihaundia* (grand *atxiki*) of the cesta-punta or jai alai, which retains the ball for a couple of seconds with each hit. The instrument-ball contact determines the game in its entirety: the movement and postures of the player, the force of the hit, the velocity of the ball, the duration of a series of hits, the sound, and so on. From the aggressive, tough, and forceful movements, the necessary adhesion to the court floor, and the rapid resolutions of the pala, the remonte, or the *laxoa*, to the measured steps and dance forms repeated over and over again and the long hits and delayed finish offs of jai alai or great xistera, through the vividness of the *atxikitxikia* (small *atxiki*) characteristic of the games of Iparralde—*joko-garbi*, *rebote*, and *xare*—to the combination of impetus and measure in the hand modality.

The meter (or its absence) of each of these modalities differs qualitatively and marks without a doubt the particular rhythm of the game. A great fan of the pala modality chides his friends with a "what's up, are you going for the slow one?" when they prepare to see a game of hand pelota. Together with this intra-temporality that, as it were, constitutes an archetypical percussion for each modality, there exists another temporality that most of these modalities share, and which depends on the rhythm of the ritual: the voice of the bookmakers, the canticle of the bet. These voices animate and stimulate the ritual like a mantra. They are voices that are synchronized with the transformations of the game, transformations that gain priority if we want to really understand the nature of the ritual rhythm and not distort it with chronological or cyclical interpretations.

Neither the time dissected from the analysis of the ceremony nor the intra-temporality of the different modalities serve in and of themselves to explain the ritual rhythm of Basque pelota. They are both repetition, the return of the same, something that repeats itself all the time. And

---

61. Arramendy, *Le Jeu, La Balle et Nous*, 27.

While mechanical repetition works by reproducing the instant that precedes it, rhythm preserves both the measure that initiates the process and the re-commencement of this process with modifications, therefore with its multiplicity and plurality. Without repeating identically 'the same,' but by subordinating the same to alterity and even alteration, which is to say, to difference.[62]

In order to complete the rhythm, therefore, a transformation is necessary: the present and unrepeatable event that each game implies. As Amparo Lasén says, the rhythm "is a configuration of variation and repetition,"[63] and if we stick to the previous analysis, we would be distorting the real nature of the ritual and its principal attraction, which combines the representation of primordial time with the unpredictability of the present, rules with liberty, the created with creation. The ritual is not a simple song that we can repeat again and again; the ritual is a jam session. Within the limits of each instrument and the features that define them, an unrepeatable creation emerges. There are not only significant discontinuities that shatter the continuous to be able to digest it; there is also a present that causes this continuous to react differently to the imposition of the discontinuous.

There is thus a continuum—the constant percussion of the ball as determined by the propulsion of the instruments, and the bookmakers' voice—that is introduced, shot through and finalized by these significant intervals: the "box of weapons," the greetings of the crowd, the flipping of the coin, the bride, and so on. But since what these intervals bring is always different—the balls are never the same, and maybe the players are not the same either; the coin may be red or blue, and the fronton may be different—the present provokes the continuum to acquire a unique rhythm each time.

Within the rhythm of the modality, within its own limits, the velocity of the game depends on whether the ball is alive or dead; whether the players are front- or backcourt players; whether they like to take risks or prefer to play it safe; whether the fronton is paved with stone or concrete. Similarly, the bookmakers' voices change their intonation in concert with the tension that the rhythm of the game provokes; as Unamuno observed, the bookmakers' shouting is the "barometer" of the game. Their voice

---

62. Lefebvre, *Rhythmanalysis*, 79.
63. Lasén Díaz, "Ritmos sociales y arritmia de la modernidad," 185.

changes in keeping with the pressure of the game, and we could say the same of the voices, applause, and movements of the crowd.

I agree therefore with the sociologist Ignacio Mendiola when he argues that we must overcome dichotomies (change-permanence; lineal-cyclical; process-repetition) in the analysis of time.[64] In order to study time at the fronton we cannot confine ourselves either to the lineal, homogenous, and quantitative time of modernity, or to cyclical, mythical, and primordial time, mostly because they do not exist. They are useful ideas to explain the functioning of modern or traditional society, but they do not exist and have never existed as such. In time, as Leach argues in "Two Essays Concerning the Symbolic Representation of Time", it is *oscillations* that appear most generalized and whose alternations may be expected, but are not foreseeable or specifiable.[65]

This is precisely the rhythm of the fronton whose pauses, instruments, and arrangements we know, but whose transformations are unforeseeable. It may accelerate if the game is played in the frontcourt squares; it may be boring if the play never gets finished off and if it does, always by the same player; it may be frenetic if equilibrium is never broken. It may be a changing rhythm with critical and sleepy moments alternating. There are almost as many rhythms as games precisely because "the rhythm is opposed to measure, given that it is 'unequal and incommensurable,' the human way of voicing duration and intensity."[66]

Ritual time, therefore, cannot be studied from the perspective of Newtonian time that has a beginning and an end; nor can we apply the "eternal return of the Same. Rather, it is the periodic return of the similar, re-wrapped in the specific peculiarities of each present."[67] Ocean waves have been recurrent images for the explanation of rhythm. In a similar vein as above, Lefebvre argues that the "waves have a rhythm, which depends on the season, the water and the winds, but also on the sea that carries them, that brings them. Each sea [like each modality] has its rhythm: that of the Mediterranean is not that of the oceans. But look closely at each wave. It changes ceaselessly."[68]

---

64. Mendiola, *Movimientos sociales y trayectos sociológicos*, 202.
65. Leach, "Two Essays Concernt the Symbolic Representation of Time," 124–36.
66. Ibid. Quotation marks refer to Gilles Deleuze and Félix Guattari.
67. Mendiola, *Movimientos sociales y trayectos sociológicos*, 206.
68. Lefebvre, *Rhythmanalysis*, 79.

Oteiza's comments on the *bertsolari*'s improvisational poetry are therefore applicable in pelota, because performing *bertsolaritza* is for him similar if not identical with playing pelota: "this incoherent and continuous rhythm of the waves, apparently incoherent; its continuity, a tied and free style (which needs no reasoning), which reiterates itself without repeating itself, successive, long, plain, recited, slow and brief, multifaceted, elliptic, topologic (changing), insisting, flowing, astonished and antiphonal, automatic, reversible in its variability and irreparable natural direction."[69]

Each game is therefore an original creation in which patterned time envelopes a new combination, which varies and causes to vary the initially intra-historic pace of hits and voices. This is the sea, those are the seasons, the moon, and the wind. The outcome: this (ir)repeatable experience that captures you like fire, with this varying rhythm that tears you away from the world. Maximum concentration: something happens so that nothing happens. And that is something: Cronos cannot now devour his sons because he is devoured. Suppression of time, magical union of all times in the ritual. Catharsis. Inexhaustible monument of the community. "In our conventional way of thinking, every interval of time is marked by repetition; it has a beginning and an end which are 'the same thing.'"[70] *Hasiera da Amaia.*[71]

Time is overcome in the ritual by its disappearance. The circle is completed but does not shut down; the awareness of spiral time is manifested in a song of greeting that is often sung at the beginning and end of games. It is a symbol of fraternity for the Basques, and implicitly points to a new encounter: the "Agur Jaunak."

Agur Jaunak	Greetings/Goodbye sirs,
Jaunak Agur	Sirs, greetings/goodbye
agur t'erdi	warm greetings
denak jinkoak	we are all
inak gire	made by God
zuek eta	you and
bai gu ere	also us

---

69. Oteiza, *Quousque Tandem . . . !,* 22.

70. Leach, quoting F. Hoyle, in "Two Essays Concerning the Symbolic Representation of Time," 126.

71. "The beginning is the end." Basque proverb.

agur jaunak, agur	Greetings/Goodbye sirs, Greetings/Goodbye
agur t'erdi	warm greetings
emen gire	here we are
Agur Jaunak	Greetings/Goodbye sirs

5

From *Joko* to *Jolas*

> It is probably no accident that the very peoples who have a pronounced and multifarious play-"instinct" have several distinct expressions for the play activity.
>
> —Johan Huizinga

Joseba Zulaika distinguishes between the terms "*joko*" and "*jolas*"[1] with reference to two cultural markers that constitute Basque consciousness and behavior. These terms coincide with two types of ludic behavior that, except for their cultural peculiarities, express "game" and "play" in English and "ludus" and "paidia" in Latin. By adopting this approach to the diverse meanings of play in order to understand the cultural behavior of Basques, Zulaika agrees with Huizinga's thesis when he claims what matters is not identifying "the place of play among all other manifestations of culture, but rather to ascertain how far culture itself bears the character of play."[2]

Joko is a competitive game, one in which two or more opponents confront one another with a single objective: to win. Fundamentally disjunctive, *joko* may be extended to any activity that is done *seriously*: "Gaming, betting, playing, singing verses and working can all easily become *joko*."[3] On the other hand, *jolas* is noncompetitive, illusory play: it "is of a metaphoric kind, and there is no reduction of values to a win or lose alternative."[4] It is playing *as though*, it is joking and masquerading where the rules, if they exist, may be broken without serious consequences.

---

1. Zulaika, *Basque Violence*, 169–87.
2. Huizinga, *Homo Ludens*, Foreword.
3. Zulaika, *Basque Violence*, 172.
4. Zulaika, Ibid., 170.

Pelota at the fronton exhibits both behaviors, which correspond to two ways of playing: playing to keep a game going, and playing to win it.[5] Playing to keep a game going is playing in such a way that one's partner may receive the ball in optimal circumstances so that hitting and returning the ball may continue indefinitely. When playing to keep a game going, one does not intend to overcome the other, or make it hard for him to receive the ball, or hit the ball where he may not reach it, or seek his weak points. On the contrary, playing to last is about enhancing the skills of one's partner, facilitating his splendor, and trying to play a game together where its beauty and the relation between the players is the most important objective. In this type of play unity is maintained, not division, like in a competitive game. This is the purest concept of play as *jolas*.

An intermediary game between playing to keep a game going and playing a competitive game that is also considered *jolastu* ("playing" or "to play") is the game *a primis*. *A primis* is played in a group and without teams; each player is responsible for him or herself. They might collectively pick on a player, normally the best one, but the basic logic of the game is that of "save yourself if you can." It consists of hitting the ball against the wall; the ball is returned by the person who happens to be closest to it as it bounces back, or by the person in the most optimal position to return it. There is no alternating, no interchange. Those who have returned the ball may not hit the following one, but they may join the series thereafter, even if there are ten players on the court. The game proceeds by the elimination of those who fail to return the ball or those who, despite being closest to it, miss the ball.

When only two players are left on the court, they incorporate the scheme of a game and they hit the ball alternatively until one beats the other. The winner gains a *primi*, a life, which he or she will use to avoid expulsion from the court if he or she misses the ball in the next round. The *primis* may be accumulated, although according to the logic of the

---

5. The emic perspective of differentiating between *joko* and *jolas* at the fronton differs from what I give here. The former approach basically confines itself to *joko* as competitive, formal play, in which participants are normally, though not always, adults. In this reading *jolas* refers to play among children, normally called *a primis*, or *a punto*, depending on locality. Zulaika discusses this distinction, as I will show. Nevertheless, for a better understanding of the cultural implications that the concepts of *joko* and *jolas* have, age is cited here as a determining factor in distinguishing between the two.

game only one player may accumulate. Girls and boys play this game without any distinction; it is a paradigmatic childhood game.

"The cultural definition of becoming an adult is precisely the capacity to internalize the *joko* scheme and operate within it."[6] This is the outcome of not only the *primi* game, but also of the process of child development. The moment when only two are left on the court, the scheme becomes that of a game. The alternating exchange of the ball until winning the *primi* is framed by the same boundaries and has the same norms as a game. Because there are no restrictions on participation, it is normally older or more talented players who come to the level of *primi*, to antagonistic confrontation. Anyone may play on the court. When a boy or a girl excels in an evident way and he or she wins the *primi* without serious opposition, the game ceases to please him or her other challenges are sought. He or she has incorporated the *joko* model and rejects *primis* as child's play.[7]

The possibility of losing is an essential part of the *joko* scheme, because it includes the presence of "I" as a totality that assumes an absolute risk. Loss is as fundamental as victory; this is what it means to understand *joko* and be a player, a *jokalari*.[8] The game is about being open to this possibility, about walking on the verge of the abyss without security, without infallible weapons to defend oneself. Everything depends on the game itself, on this uncertain reality before which one suffers a transformation of any kind, even if nothing gets seriously changed otherwise.

A boy walking toward the plaza with a ball in his pocket is a recurrent image in the Basque Country. Some informants confessed that a pelota, *their* ball, which perhaps they themselves fabricated, always accompanied them everywhere in their pocket as though it was their "third ball" (*tercer cojón*).[9]

---

6. Zulaika, *Basque Violence*, 180.

7. I am talking in absolute terms. It is normal for both children and adults—pelotaris of all kinds—to play on frontons at the same time. To play under such conditions, the best player imposes on him or herself some metarules or limitations in order for the game to be possible.

8. It is revealing that there is no word *jolasari*. He who plays *jolas* is an *ume*, a child.

9. This is yet another example of the masculinity that is inherent in pelota. In this context, it also should be added that pelota has a clear linkage with "becoming a man." While boys and girls play together until about twelve or thirteen years of age, at this age girls, often the best players in this age group, have to stop playing due to family, "medical," or other kinds of

Always having the ball on him allows the child to play without requiring anything more than a wall against which he can hit it. At first, hitting is imprecise, the ball does not have a clear trajectory, and he has to abruptly adjust his body trying to reach it. Uncoordinated movements, varying strikes, and a lot of running after the ball characterize this phase. By hitting the ball so many times, he learns about the nature of the ball, and about the nature of his own body. He is growing. Coordinated, repetitive, and precise movements accompany a ball that has a measured trajectory, which allows the player to hit it at a certain distance from the wall and to execute learned postures. Now he plays with the rhythm of the body, with the enjoyment of precise and controlled movements; he uses both hands alternatively. The coordination between his body and the ball is now so close that he does not see the ball as an external, separate object, but rather as one that responds to his will like his arms or legs do. The ball has become part of him. The (con)centration is maximum. As his hands warm up, he gradually distances himself from the wall to hit the ball with greater strength. Distancing no longer means new readjustment; rather, it is part of equilibrium, of a mechanical control over the ball.

The constant repetition of the same movements produces such a conjunction between the body, the ball, and the wall that previous concentration becomes de-concentration. There is now no subjective will that dominates the action; rather, the body lives its own life, it is part of a whole that works by itself. The subject gets de-centered in this relation and feels a great relief, an unburdening of himself, a state of zero reflection. In this moment the subject does not think; he feels. He completely yields to the flow, the void of time, the void of space, the void of subject and object, to life, to play. We might intuitively sense that he succumbs to his animality, liberated from the parapet of his conscience. Even when the conscience becomes present, when the action is rationalized, when the subject thinks about it, as in Zarathustra's dream at midday, a certain eroticism takes over and the body keeps yielding to this exercise that procures so much satisfaction. We are at the most intimate sphere of play as *jolas*, as *paideia*. This is pleasurable play that does not involve any rivalry.

---

pressures. This is the subject of my forthcoming article "Bodies out of Place: Gender, Space and Community in the Basque Sport of Pelota."

Zulaika argues that the sphere of *jolas* "belongs to the children's domain" and "nothing is really serious in it . . . everything is acted out *gezurretan* (in a lie)."[10] He therefore locates the notion of truth in the center of the distinction between noncompetitive play, *jolas*, and competitive play, *joko*. Roger Caillois situates norm and order as a fundamental delimitation between the two concepts. There is on the one hand the unbridled fantasy of *paideia*, and on the other the normative functions of the *ludus*.[11]

There are remarkable pairs of opposition within this distinction between informal play (*jolas, paideia*) and formal game (*joko, ludus*): children's domain/adults' domain, lie/truth, trivial/serious, alone/with others, absence of norms/norms, chaos/order, and so on. Nevertheless, none of these manage to absolutely define both levels of play. Any of these categories may emerge at either levels, while all of them display what I wish to emphasize: that the essential difference between these two types of ludic behavior lies in the type of relation that one established with the other, who is not necessarily present, and thus with oneself.

In *jolas*, one dissolves into the other and contributes to the constitution of a pleasurable totality where there is no separation between the one and the other. Limiting ourselves to ball games, the abovementioned playing to maintain the game, or playing pala on the beach for example, is paradigmatic of this type of play. Both players construct the game and make it easy for the other to receive the ball. They produce a conjunction of forces to create enjoyment based on repetition, a pleasure analogous to what I described above; a play where the subject strikes the ball with rhythm against a wall, and provokes the de-centering of his body in the conjunction.

Alone or with partners, *jolas* in its most extreme sense causes us to dissolve in an all-embracing totality that brings us pleasure. It is pleasure produced by the continuous repetition of an action.

The pleasure that comes from repetition is complemented in the game with the search for chance, with tension, which provokes the emergence of the *joko* scheme. Once the body is warmed up, once it has entered into a conjunction with its environment, the player starts playing with possibility, with chance. He hits the ball in different ways, he hits it

---

10. Zulaika, *Basque Violence*, 178, 181.
11. Caillois, *Man, Play, and Games*.

right against the metal sheet or above it. He breaks the rhythmical strikes to challenge his body, to try new postures, and play with distance and velocity. This gives him the measure of his potential, of the ball and the fronton. He will hit the ball to the foot of the opponent, he will directly shoot it low, he will look for the *txoko*, he will hit it hard and run to reach it, he will strike it *sotamano* from below and with extended arms, half volley, *besagain* with arms moving laterally. He will do a dropshot and a double-wall shot. He plays against himself, he exercises his weak points, and perfects his virtues. There it is, the *joko*, the challenge.

Whether it involves an adult or a child, a group or an individual, *joko* incorporates the other as "other" or as an opponent and, as a consequence, the purest perception of the self as a delimited totality. *Joko* is not about dissolution but competence, fight, *agon*, split.

The boundary of the "I" and the "you" is what establishes the pattern of *joko*, of agonic competition; it is a boundary that is established within the framework of equality that makes the game possible. The game of pelota necessarily implies it; although, as I have suggested before, it is possible that *real* equality only exists in ideal conditions, in formalized ritual, at professional games—not in the plaza. In the plaza the game is played between people of different levels; they play to construct a game, even if it means that the stronger must play *as if he was not stronger*, suspending his power, and exploring new strategies. Against an equal, who requires him to use all his weapons, he perhaps would not be able to do so. This, although it involves the rejection of some skills, is also *joko*. There exists a game. The stronger player imposes limits on his own game and lessens the force of his strike in order for the conditions to be equal and to be able to play.

The precept of equality is an integral part of *joko*: the two ends of the rope must have the same resistance in order to keep its tension, and the two faces of the same coin must have the same weight for doubt to exist and for chance to impose its laws. It is because reality tends to reject the equality of forces that the *momio* exists in the bet.

Limiting ourselves to professional play in which both players must deploy the maximum of their capacity, equality between them is essential for the game: "I am, and was ever, your counterpart," says Zarathustra, "and I am also your best enemy."[12] Equality is an essential fountain of

---

12. Nietzsche, *Thus Spoke Zarathustra*, 46.

struggle since, as Girard remarks, it is the opposition of symmetric elements that plants conflict; the conflict of persons among who power is not dissolved. This symmetry is manifested in the stichomythia of classic tragedy, where each verse has a response.[13]

In his Basque concepts of play, Zulaika has introduced the notion of boundary. The first concept, *jolas*, "neutralizes the competitive elements or aggressive purpose."[14] This is the unregulated play of children, while *joko* is based on limitation established by competence and challenge. *Joko* "is geared to an end result."[15] The alternation that emerges between winning or losing implies imposing limits that affect ritualization, inasmuch as "both parties are within a framework of exclusive disjunction";[16] in pelota, either blue or red.

The imposition of a boundary is what really differentiates both levels of play. In *jolas* there are no boundaries, the conjunction is total, and the players belong within an undifferentiated set. In *joko*, it is quite the contrary; it is two differentiated sets that face each other: you and me. The boundary between the two is evident. They meet because they share the same objective: winning. It is a disjunctive objective that creates conflict. Since both of them cannot win, the players become antagonists, contraries, opponents. The tension that results from this conflict is fundamental in the *joko* scheme.

From Tension to Effervescence

> People do not understand how that which is at variance with itself, agrees with itself. There is a harmony in the bending back, as in the case of the bow and the lyre.
>
> — Heraclitus

Claude Lévi-Strauss argues that ritual is conjunctive, that its goal is to unite, while play is disjunctive because it differentiates a winner and a loser.[17] In its formalized aspect the game of pelota is a ritual that shares a competitive logic of the *joko* type, and achieves the community conjunc-

---

13. Girard, *Violence and the Sacred*, 47.
14. Zulaika, *Basque Violence*,169.
15. Ibid., 180.
16. Zulaika, *Tratado estético-ritual vasco*, 78.
17. Lévi-Strauss, *The Savage Mind*, 32.

tion of the *jolas* type. It poses a split (*joko*) that is resolved in an act of communion, of suture (*jolas*).

The tension that agonic, competitive, and disjunctive play provokes leads to excitement, and to the emotiveness of those present: to a collective catharsis and magical transformation. This is why ritual turns from *joko* into *jolas*, from disjunction into conjunction, and from tension into excitement.

Many authors have postulated the importance of ritual as giving access to this state of excitement that consolidates the group: "the communitas is born from liminality."[18] Nevertheless, many others mix up both concepts, making communitas out of liminality, of "pure possibility," which is a domain of action. This way, communitas is emptied of content: "that which unites us as a community . . . is less a content, which is the realm of faith, than a container, that is, a common matrix, a foundation of the 'being-together.'"[19]

This sociality of emphatic predominance sustained above all in proxemics as defined by Michel Maffesoli, is present in Rof Carballo's notion of "group hunger," which satisfies emotional necessities:[20] "the community is characterized less by a project (*pro-jectum*) oriented towards the future than by the execution *in actu* of the being-together."[21] Without denying the cohesive force and agglutinating effect of "being-together," what remains precarious is not the argument that contact is a primordial source of excitement, but rather the claim that it is only that "being-together" wherein lies the significance of ritual.

Without discussing emotiveness as a channel for the incorporation of relevant meanings for the communal project, meanings that doubtless stage and determine this "being together," it is worth considering as primordial the quality or the nature of the event as a source of emotions. One game is never the same as another even if both fill the fronton and have the same outcome, namely, that one player will always beat the other. How contact is established is more important than the contact itself, even if contact is obligatory in each case.

Being together is for the crowd what winning is for the player: an obligation. The "how" of winning and the "how" of being together

---

18. Turner, *Dramas, Fields and Metaphors*, 232.
19. Maffesoli, *The Time of the Tribes*, 38.
20. Rof Carballo, *Entre el silencio y la palabra*, 334.
21. Maffesoli, *The Time of the Tribes*, 16.

determine whether there is excitement or not, and what it implies. This is why the ritual must proceed according to certain fixed patterns that need be respected.

In pelota, like in any other agonic play, emotion starts with a tension that "unleashes the unforeseeable" and that is, "in effect, the sacred moment of the fiesta."[22] An exciting game is one that maintains tension, a tension that implies the equality of the players. In fact, tension is directly proportionate to equality. The greater the equality, the longer the tension lasts.

It is the uncertainty of the event, the pure, open possibility that produces strong emotions in the spectator who under these conditions surrenders himself integrally to the game, with all his passions and finances. The tension unleashes enthusiasm and, at the same time, the bet, which will heighten tension if it is at all possible.

Gadamer affirms that "the attraction that the game exercises on the player lies in risk,"[23] which is unfailingly linked to danger, with that possibility of losing, which every decision implies. The "pure possibility" that perfectly defines liminality has more to do with risk than with being together, even if proxemics is inherent to collective action.

Contributions to risk on the court are of many kinds. The game itself guarantees excitement if the split does not turn into domination and losing, but remains an equal fight between powers. The uncertainty of the result maintains the tension, whose maximum paradigm is the 21–21 tie; this is the moment when a verdict is inevitable and that causes the entire fronton to experience a shiver as though it was one body.

Even though this ideal situation might not happen, the court has sufficient resources to maintain the tension of the game. When a player enjoys a considerable advantage on the scoreboard, or when the initial equal footing does not exist, the excitement may be maintained on the basis of the beauty of the game, which is another way of fascinating the spectator. The player may also keep the public's interest by taking many risks. An example is the game between Alustiza and Beloki in the four-and-a-half mark championship in 1999. Alustiza, who was very inferior to Beloki in terms of strikes, took every risk possible and turned around a situation that had been very unfavorable to him. Opening oneself up to

---

22. Barrios, *Narrar el abismo*, 105.
23. Gadamer, *Truth and Method*, 106.

counterattacks and taking many risks and playing to the limit but never gratuitously or prematurely is highly valued by the crowd.

This risk has to do with the burden of chance that is incorporated in the game. Playing close to the limits is paradigmatic. Once again, it is interesting to note the closeness of boundaries, which are a specificity of the norm, to chance. In fact, both share the same principle: the equality of opportunity: "Agon and *alea* imply opposite and somewhat complementary attitudes, but *they both obey the same law: the creation for the players of conditions of pure equality denied them in real life.*"[24]

The *momio* is another way of maintaining tension in moments when the court has lost it. The *momio* is a way of compensating for the absence of an ideal situation of equality, which the rules guarantee but which in reality is denied. Equilibrium is fundamental for the game, whether the equilibrium of the court or of the terraces, considering the fact that, following Huizinga, the general characteristics of game are tension and uncertainty,[25] and that doubt over the outcome must be prolonged until the end: "an inescapable result is incompatible with the nature of play."[26] The same is implied by the image of the bookmakers turned around, looking at the court. Tension has disappeared, uncertainty has turned into certainty, and betting loses interest; the game dies.

What excitement is maintained when the scoreboard shows 9–19? Perhaps if the struggle is titanic, even if the points always go to the same side on the board; perhaps if one of the players is offering a recital of strikes that is making it difficult for his opponent who will not surrender and will do his best. Only the beauty of the game itself, which I will discuss in part 3, may save the emotiveness of such a game.

With a bet in the pocket, nevertheless, there is something that will always shake up the spectator until the score of twenty-two. A bet with an odds ratio of 200 to 5 (euros), for example, with which by risking a hundred you can win four thousand; or the other way round, for one hundred you risk four thousand; even if the risk is very low, such betting would unnerve anyone. With all that they have put to risk in the bet, the tension never gets relieved, no matter how flat the game gets. Besides, the greater the number of bettors, the more the bet excites the

---

24. Caillois, *Man and the Sacred*, 19. Emphasis added.
25. Huizinga, *Homo Ludens*.
26. Caillois, *Man and the Sacred*, 7.

crowd, bettors and nonbettors alike. And if one score on the board starts catching up with the other, it has an explosive and cathartic effect on the public.

This is exactly what happened at the fiestas of Mungia on June 28, 1998. Ariznabarreta-Lasa III (Karmelo Ariznabarreta-Oskar Lasa) were playing against Nagore-Errasti (Jorge Nagore-Jokin Errasti). The scoreboard was 9–19, and the *momio* 200 to 5; Ariznabarreta received a shot that cut his head open. After a few moments of doubt about whether the game would carry on, the player returned to the court and turned the game around.

As the score of the losing team was increasing, so was uncertainty. The court, which had been until then incapable of holding the attention of the terraces, now absorbed all eyes; the public applauded and was overjoyed; unlike the bettors who, unable to let go of the tension, remained paralyzed in their seats and moved their bodies as if they could telepathically drive the ball toward the frontis.

The crowd wants to receive a dose of uncertainty from the court that will make it vibrate and get excited. Spectators need to be affected by what happens on the court, the more, the better. Therefore, when reality denies the equality that the norms ensure under ideal conditions, the odds ratio becomes the best way to create the tension that the court fails to transmit. The imposition of economic inequality makes up for the natural inequality that the norms cannot ensure, the inequality of the participants and the inequality that derives from the game itself.

Excitement is unleashed in the tension, in the uncertainty of the result, in the risk in which the spectator is directly implicated through wagering. The bet generates emotions at the fronton; it also provokes the extension of uncertainty, of risk, and contributes to the diffusion of passions. Tension is essential for the emergence of collective effervescence that Durkheim discussed. The sociologists Elias Norbert and Eric Dunning argue that a Durkheimean analysis of collective excitement may extrapolate the passions and excitement of modern sports events.[27]

In pelota, tension ideally comes from the court, from the real equality between the powers represented in it, and its maintenance throughout the game. An open game ensures an emotional flow between the terraces and the court, spiced up by the shouting of the bookmakers, repeated

---

27. Norbert and Dunning, *The Quest for Excitement*, 3.

like mantras. The pelotari must give himself over to the game totally, and expose everything when necessary. So must the public, whose essence beyond the possibility of materializing this surrender through the bet, "consists," as Gadamer argues, "in giving oneself in self-forgetfulness to what one is watching."[28]

It is not only the fact of being together, but also the veritable surrender of all the fronton agents that creates a channel of excitement in the ritual: "It is not difficult to imagine," says Durkheim, "that a man in such a state of exaltation no longer knows himself. Feeling possessed and led by some external power that makes him think and act differently from normal times, he naturally feels he is no longer himself."[29]

The Tidal Wave of Dionysious

> What hath befallen me: Hark! Hath time flown away? Do I not fall? Have I not fallen—hark! Into the well of eternity?
>
> — Nietzsche (Zarathustra)

Eduard Subirats uses a story by Bertold Brecht to exemplify domestic rebellion against domination. Sir Egge, the protagonist of the story is asked by a nobleman if he wants to become his serf. From this moment on, Sir Egge accompanies the nobleman throughout his life, but executes his chores in the most absolute silence. At the deathbed of his lord, Egge makes sure nothing is missing. He dresses him and takes care of him aseptically until he dies. It is then when he blurts out: "No!" Sir Egge conserves the identity of his autonomy "in interior disobedience, in the negation of recognition and in resistance."[30]

It is in the same sense that Zulaika discusses the semantics of Basque negation: *ez* (no). Against the subordination that the affirmative *bai* (yes) implies, "the negative clearly expresses independence and personal autonomy." In fact, "a well-known Basque definition of the ideal person is 'he who says *no*.'"[31] The person is formed on the basis of constructing small spaces of autonomy, imposing certain boundaries between the self

---

28. Gadamer, *Truth and Method*, 122.
29. Durkheim, *The Elementary Forms of Religious Life*, 163.
30. Subirats, *El alma y la muerte*, 384.
31. Zulaika, *Tratado estético-ritual vasco*, 70–71.

and others: "Ever to say YE-A that hath only the ass learned, and those like it!"[32]

Nevertheless, the social configuration of the subject obliges him or her to say a few yeses, which suspend the "distance between oneself and others"[33] and that uncritically allows the community to penetrate him or her. This is what Maffesoli calls *entièreté*, or "wholeness," that "induces the dissolution of the small I into a greater 'Yes', that of otherness, natural or social."[34] Ritual action creates a journey, a journey that Friedrich Hölderlin would call eccentric, between the separate and the dissolution in one. It unleashes the tidal wave of Dionysus under which all *principium individuationis* disappears and gets suspended until "the subjective fades into complete forgetfulness of self."[35]

This submission, which generates a feeling of relief and an extreme conjunction with the other, has been called by many "ecstasy," Or, in a more literal sense, "othering." One might recall the child who gets decentered in the space created by the ball, the wall, and himself: "in the form and function of play, itself an independent entity which is senseless and irrational, man's consciousness that he is embedded in a sacred order of things finds its first, highest and holiest expression."[36]

Something similar happens in ritual, more specifically in those eternal moments that the beauty of hitting the ball, or the tension before the outcome, implies. They are moments of full conjunction between the agents of the fronton; they are moments of *jolas* when the subject is outside of himself, in contact with something that transcends him and of which he now feels a part. He touches upon eternity and feels transformed.

In the de-individualizing ecstasy that ritual creates, in this moment of communion that leads from "'pure possibility' to 'eternal actuality,'"[37] one sees "oneself transformed before one's eyes and ... act as if one really had entered another body, another character."[38] One ceases to feel the weight of one's smallness, of one's separate and finite being, since

---

32. Nietzsche, *Thus Spoke Zarathustra*, 220.
33. Maffesoli, *The Time of the Tribes*, 98.
34. Maffesoli *El instante eterno*, 10.
35. Nietzsche *On the Genealogy of Morality*, 18.
36. Huizinga, *Homo Ludens*, 17.
37. Maffesoli, *El instante eterno*, 53.
38. Nietzsche, *On the Genealogy of Morality*, 39.

one is getting in touch with something that preceded and will survive him or her.

This feature of self-forgetting, which for Gadamer doesn't mean the negation of being in oneself, is the "positive possibility of being wholly with something else,"[39] of surrendering to it. This allows the subject to participate in a reality that transcends him or her, but of which they feel a part; it is a totality by which one feels transformed while one participates in it. As Unamuno said: "I want to be myself, and yet without ceasing to be myself to be others as well, to merge myself into the totality of things visible and invisible, to extend myself into the illimitable of space and to prolong myself into the infinite of time."[40]

Ritual provokes this experience in the subject: it leads him or her into a tunnel where his or her sentence seems to be suspended, and affectively integrates him or her in a special and unforgettable totality. This is why Turner says that communitas—the eternal now—is born from the liminal, or pure possibility. Binding, the dissolution of subjects in the community, takes place in these moments when categories are absent, in moments of rescission and of the cancellation of everyday orders where any outcome is possible:

> Indeed, we have seen that when collective life reaches a certain degree of intensity it awakens religious thought, because it determines a state of effervescence that changes the conditions of psychic activity. Vital energies become over stimulated, passions more powerful, sensations stronger; there are even some that are produced only at this moment. Man does not recognize himself; he feels he is transformed, and so he transforms his surroundings.[41]

Disjunction, which Lévi-Strauss considered specific to games as opposed to ritual conjunction, becomes a phase of the ritual process rather than a trait of typological distinction. Very much like what happens in Arnold van Gennep's classification of ritual: there are rituals of separation, transition, and reincorporation, but each ritual incorporates all three phases.[42]

---

39. Gadamer, *Truth and Method*, 122.
40. Unamuno, *Del sentimiento trágico de la vida en los hombres y en los pueblos*, 122.
41. Durkheim, *The Elementary Forms of Religious Life*, 317.
42. See van Gennep, *The Rites of Passage*.

In a similar way, the fundamentally agonic positive cults share a scheme of *joko*, of conflict, only to converge into a scheme of *jolas*, of communion. If the tension that the rupture creates—the *partido*—and if the boundary between two equal subjects that share a common objective (to win) is maintained and executed aesthetically, an avalanche of emotions is unleashed. The tidal wave of Dionysus takes the "single small individual crests"[43] on its back in a way what Nietzsche calls magic transformation, the dissolution of each subject in a totality.

---

43. Nietzsche, *On the Genealogy of Morality*, 45.

6

Harrizko Herria: The Village of Stone

> Becoming with the character of Being—
> that is the supreme will to power.
>
> — Nietzsche (Zarathustra)

The suppression of time finds its greatest efficacy in the monument that manages to retain time in a specific, tangible space. Jacques Le Goff approaches the word "monument" etymologically, and finds that its root is "men," an Indo-European root that is directly associated with the word "memini," "memoria," derived from the verb "monere": to remember, instruct, illuminate.[1] In Basque, the relation is even more direct. "Oroigarri," monument, literally means "that which serves to remember."

The physical concretion of imperceptible transformation is fundamentally important for the preservation of institutions that allow the community to remain as it is. Seeking stability in what is taking place around them, human beings believe they transcend their peremptory mortality. Monuments, essential conductors of memory, manage to physically concretize the community inasmuch as they are immune to the erosive effects of time.

I have already mentioned that the fronton was originally called the "game of pelota." This implies that the configuration of the place came after the emergence of the game itself: it was situated in open spaces, streets, plazas, churches, and ramparts before it would occupy its own, autonomous space. The game occupied spaces that constituted a fundamental center of public relations; nuclei that attracted the population for political, commercial, ludic, festive, and religious purposes.

---

1. Le Goff, *El orden de la memoria*, 227.

Pelota was and still is part of community events. Market days featured several games, in which the goods that people had not managed to sell or the day's earnings were wagered. Also, Sundays after mass were favorite moments to play the game, a game that acquired growing protagonism to the point that it became a public event par excellence:

> Just like bullfighting days in the provinces, like opera seasons in Italian villages and national shooting contests in Switzerland, and the German *kermeses*, the pelota games of Gipuzkoa, Bizkaia, Navarre and [the] Baztán [Valley] caused a whole county to lose its mind; all congregated at a determined place and got carried away by the impulses of provincial passions.[2]

Pelota became a major reason for the convocation and gathering of people, who arrived in great numbers. On Sunday, August 9, 1846, Irun (the border town with Lapurdi in Gipuzkoa) hosted a long modality game[3] between a Basque team from the south, and another from the north, the latter including Gaskonia (Jean Erratxun), the greatest player of the day. According to the French newspaper *Journal du Havre*, twelve thousand people turned up for the game in Irun, and campsites had to be set up in the vicinity. People from all the Basque provinces converged on Irun; they left their homes two or three days earlier on horseback, by oxen, or other means, sufficiently supplied with money in order to wager on the game.

The centripetal force of pelota attracted thousands of people to a specific place, normally an open ground by the more representative areas of the village or villa. Grounds were leveled and slopes eliminated, and courts situated by churches or ramparts whose walls were used for the game.[4] At first these grounds were probably unfenced, and it was the crowd itself, its bodies, that marked the boundaries of the court. Even today, the Valencian game of *scala i corda* allows the ball to rebound off the crowd without interfering with play. At the Basque fronton, if the court is larger than what the modality requires, chairs are placed on the court area to accommodate the crowd. The pelotari can, therefore, liter-

---

2. Peña y Goñi, *La pelota y los pelotaris*, 61.

3. Descriptions of this game may be found in Baroja, *Guía del País Vasco Español-Francés*, and the *bertso* ("improvisational poetry") "Irungo pilota partidaren kantia" in Pilota Kantuz, 1993.

4. First as a boundary, then as the *frontis*.

ally hit the ball into the crowd. Put more accurately, it is the body of the community that hosts the game—that gives it a place—in the same way as when a fight breaks out suddenly.

As the use of the ground for the game was established and the event was repeated time and time again, the boundaries of the court got marked with lines, walls, hedges, or other permanent markers. In this moment the sociological fact, as Georg Simmel would say, acquires a spatial form, and the place where pelota is played becomes, strictly speaking, the "game of pelota." The performance of bodies in that space creates a place, a place that becomes a symbol, a monument to that which gave it its form: the community itself.

The plaza, the fronton, is therefore nothing but the community petrified, extended beyond its corporeality, and granted a place. The community has moved outside of itself in order to maintain itself; periodically, the community returns to the place that was borne by it in order to keep the bond alive, and to periodically re-create itself.

Field and Temple

Monuments rely on the mnemonic mechanism of periodic oblation. Some monuments only acquire leadership on important dates, or in relation to certain events: In France, the Bastille and all it signifies is revitalized each July 14; the Fuente de Cibeles (Cybele Fountain) is flooded each time the soccer team Real Madrid wins a title; the *Lehendakari* (President of the Basque Autonomous Government) takes the oath of his office in front of the sacred tree of Gernika whose roots extend over the whole Basque territory. These rituals serve to affect that the pillars of the group's constitution, pillars represented by the given monument, may not be forgotten. The offerings that the community deposits in them serve to prolong their memory.[5]

In contrast to these celebrations, the fronton is brought to life by a ritual that is its own: the game of pelota. It is a temple with its own rites. It was born by a public display that wraps around narratives of self-sacrifice; within the Basque community it is a place that generates grace, it is a principal purveyor of *indarra*.

---

5. Perhaps this is why the fans of the white team (Real Madrid) keep smashing off parts of the goddess Cybele each time there is a celebration. It might be an unconscious desire to prolong the memory of the victory through modifications in the physical state of the monument.

Nevertheless, while it maintains an aura of sacredness akin to that of a temple, the fronton cannot strictly be identified with what a temple represents. Generally speaking, the temple is characterized by exclusive use and restricted access to specific persons and times. The fronton, however, has retained the openness of the field from which it emerged. The pelota court is a space borne by the community, and it maintains this bond despite modifications in its physical structure. The fronton and the community belong together, inasmuch as the court is likely to be used for a variety of free-time activities or festive purposes, whether scheduled or improvised.

Despite the fact that industrial frontons have undergone a process of privatization that implies payment for their use, the fronton is fundamentally a public space of free access and free use. This is why it is likely to be used with a range of objectives, from processions to the practice of the *botellón* (a social practice whereby young people congregate in public spaces to consume alcohol).

The fronton accommodates ceremonies, fiestas, and rituals that have great importance for the community. Except for mass, it is the fronton where all the reuniting practices of the people (con)centrate: dances, neighborhood meals, fiestas, and so on. Moreover, various kinds of performances of skill are organized at the fronton, performances that endow skill with prestige: for example, the performances of *harrijasotzailes* (stone lifters), *bertsolaris* (oral poetry improvisers), and *aizkolaris* (wood choppers), among others. The pelota court is also used as a place of leadership: for rallies, commemorations, and so forth. And it may host agricultural and crafts fairs or other types of markets, as well as meetings, speeches and lectures, concerts, and late night dances.

The fronton opens itself to the community and thus returns to its state as a field. The interaction of bodies in its heart breaks the formal disposition that it adopts as a temple when it is used for pelota, for its own ritual. It thus maintains the genetics of the community. The village acts in its totality upon the space. People dance and eat at the fronton; they later become a crowd and form the space that allows the proto-agonists to represent again the much awaited drama, the game. The game, as I argued before, unites the community and consecrates the space through an outcome that is purely sacrificial; it creates a void that is likely to be inhabited again by other rituals of communal celebration.

Described here in its ideal state, this magic, transformative circle that affects communal space—transforming it from field to temple, from temple to field—does not necessarily manifest itself diachronically. While communal fiestas may reproduce this cycle, alternating in the same space the performances of skill and acts of collective communion, the fronton maintains its ambivalent character in most of the manifestations that it hosts; it thus becomes tremendously effective in the transmission of the narratives that it embodies.

Place of Narratives

> The space is theirs, even during the ebb, and in its emptiness it reminds them of the flood.
>
> — Elias Canetti

On October 24, 1999, the *aekeguna* was held in Sara (Sare), a village of a few thousand inhabitants in Lapurdi. The *aekeguna* is a fiesta that annually gathers tens of thousands of *euskaltzales* (pro-Basque culture sympathizers) with the objective of collecting funds for the dissemination and teaching of Euskara via AEK (Alfabetatze Euskalduntze Koordinakundea, the Coordinator of Education and Literacy in Basque, an organization dedicated to adult Basque-language learning). The events of the fiesta were organized around four special axes, all of which were frontons. The plaza of the village, a monumental open fronton, was the nerve center of the fiesta. It was there that the *bertsolaris* sung their improvised poetry, and where the people danced traditional dances. Meanwhile, various concerts of Basque rock music concerts were organized in the trinquet; the sports center, the covered fronton, hosted the typical *comensalidad*, or "fellowship of house and table:" it is a meal where the whole village typically unites and listens to the traditional songs of the area during dessert. All these rituals serve to affirm Basque culture, and their channel is the Basque language, Euskara; they take place at the communal area, the fronton.

One of the major events of the day was the rebote game: a typical modality of Iparralde, the northern Basque Country, where the contest was organized. The modality, however, was unknown to the great majority of those present. This lent an ancestral character to the gathering, and allowed for the incorporation of a figure that has disappeared from the industrialized, more widely known modalities of the game: the *kontatzaile*, or the person who counts the score by shouting it out loud. This figure granted the event historical consistency and, for that matter, a certain legitimacy to the protest that the game itself was attempting to register.

The game of rebote that took place that day at the fronton of Sara served to vindicate the officialdom of a Basque national team that is independent of Spanish and French national team. One of the teams emerged at the court wearing a T-shirt that was in favor of creating a Basque team: a white T-shirt with two strips of red and green on the sleeve, with the slogan "Euskal Selekzioa Bai," "Yes to Basque Team" on the back. After a difficult game, one that generated the right level of excitement, the Basque team—supported by most of those present—triumphed against its opponent dressed in anonymous white. The protest was complete. The *Euskal Selekzioa* triumphed. The *kontatzaile*, on his part, was conducting the pelotaris' present actions through the tradition that legitimized it. An elderly man, his role was to explain the customs and traditions of the game to the crowd, besides counting the points. He suspended the game at twelve to pray the Angelus, asking those present to stand up for a minute. It was a way of connecting present desires with the remote past that renders them familiar. The pelotari symbolized the protest activity, and the *kontatzaile* embodied the historical memory that sustains and legitimizes it.

Beyond the process of legitimization and protest, the event was an example of the incorporation of certain narratives by way of ritual action; of the reconstruction of the memory of those present; and of socialization within a specific space.

As the crowd rises to sing the Angelus, the primogenial position that gave form to the space is recovered. The communal construction of the fronton itself is recreated, and each subject incorporates its condition as a fundamental pillar of space and what it contains. The subject is actively integrated in the ritual and becomes part of what it represents. The ritual action thus establishes ideological points of reference, which are incorporated by the participating subjects and are imprinted for them on this space, which persists beyond the time of the ritual. Through this experience the subject is socialized in the space, which now has a specific symbolic charge for him. From this moment on he does not need a direct interpersonal relation in order for the narrative of the place to seize him. It connects with him in a way that it produces a communication, a transmission of narratives, without the necessity of the "other," the *alter*. He has experienced the place and, as Gadamer would say, has gained a horizon of possible future experiences.

Places possess their own significance. By interacting in them, the subject has incorporated them and, depending on the encounters and moments he or she experiences, people construct their own meanings around them. The communal character, however, penetrates all of them; a communal character that shaped them and that remains in their indelible essence. More than anything, the fronton evokes the community. The following words of a Basque emigrant, in reference to the fronton of Buenos Aires in the Euskara Plaza and published in the journal *Laurak Bat* in October, 1891, serve as a testimony to this:. "Especially for the Basque-speaking residents here, this plaza and its enchantments recall for us with mute eloquence the absent fatherland; by stepping on that land one experiences a sense of well-being that cannot be explained, but is strongly felt."[6]

Through its mere being, the fronton commemorates the community, which converts it into an essential source of affect. The evocative and at the same time emotive power that the fronton possesses has made it useful for the organization of protest actions like the example above. The fronton is home to all kinds of messages, legends, and symbols that have the purpose of becoming consecrated and, as an extension, of surviving in memory and moving the body of the community.

The Iconography of the Fronton

Those knowledgeable in photography understand why the following occurs: if we keep the shutter of the camera open for thirty minutes in front of a plaza replete with people coming and going, the eventual photograph of the plaza is empty. The space remains, the stone remains, yet the people are gone. The stillness of space persists in the film for thirty minutes, but the moving bodies do not. The perennity of the plaza is printed on the caducity of bodies. The movement of the bodies takes refuge in the infinity of space.

The experience of finitude has resulted in the conversion of space into a privileged framework where specific values are inscribed, knowing that in it they will persist beyond our inevitable transitoriness. This is why the fronton, which in principle is an aseptic space, displays numerous emblematic or simply propagandistic additions. Sometimes it does so in the form of legends and statues, other times through symbols or icons; still other times in more temporary and ephemeral paintings of political protest or advertising posters.

---

6. No author, in *Laurak Bat* 228, Year XIII, October, 1891.

From this point of view, we find very different behaviors on each side of the French-Spanish border—a border that divides Euskal Herria into two parts not only territorially, but sociologically and culturally as well. While there is a Basque culture that transcends this territorial division, historical circumstances have differed widely in Iparralde and Hegoalde. The differences are clearly reflected in the modalities of pelota as well as the structure of the fronton, something that influences the way it is treated.

I have already referred to the distinctive legacy of the modalities by discussing Iparralde in terms of the typical wrist play of the French pelotaris, and Hegoalde in terms of the Castilian dry hit. The typology of frontons also differs; most markedly, in Iparralde, they did not incorporate the left wall, which was a determining aspect of the modernization and expansion of the game in Hegoalde.

In Iparralde, there have been no industrial or demographic developments comparable to the southern Basque provinces, or the rest of France. Iparralde has become a repository of folklore and is an important destination for French tourism; it has conserved the traditional forms of the game and has treated the fronton as a relic of urban architecture. This is why villages have barely modified the plaza space; rather, they protect it as a jewel of the monumental patrimony of the village.

In Hegoalde, however, industrialization provoked a demographic explosion that resulted in a fundamental transformation of urban nuclei, and which also affected rural areas. Since the 1970s, villages have undergone radical transformations. Utilitarian considerations outweighed aesthetic ones; as blocks of houses were constructed on village beachfronts, for example, so covers that did not match their environment were added to exisiting frontons. Some of them were even just demolished straight away depending on the value of the ground they occupied, because the frontons were not considered a part of the patrimony and therefore protected.[7]

The different evolutionary processes of the fronton have also been largely influenced by the political circumstances that characterized the two sides of the border, circumstances that affected the fronton as a space of memory, and which are manifested in its iconography. One must bear in mind that in the last one hundred years the political histories of

---

7. As of 2012, there are still no frontons that enjoy the protective status of patrimony in Hegoalde.

France and Spain have had little in common. While France successfully emerged from two world wars, Spain was submerged in civil war and a forty-year-long dictatorship—a dictatorship that was especially repressive about anything to do with the Basques. The most radical opposition to the dictatorship was ETA (Euskadi ta Askatasuna, the Basque Country and Freedom), an armed organization that has until recently[8] remained active; it maintained it's violent activity—and concurrent violence on the part of "counterterrorist" groups—well after the democratic transition in Spain, which began in 1975. Meanwhile, while the Spanish democracy is officially less centralized than France, it maintains a dialectic of conflict between Basques and Spaniards. This dialectic has been more or less virulent, but has barely changed. This political as well as social conflict is staged on the fronton, which in many cases is the central square of the village.

At the frontons of Iparralde we often see find plates and reliefs that commemorate the soldiers who died in the world wars. The fronton of Sara is prototypical of this: it features a double relief in homage to a youth of the village, a soldier who died in combat; it features an image of a pelotari and a soldier of the French armed forces. France makes its presence in a prototypically Basque space and promotes patriotic emotions by linking two heroic actions: giving one's life—real and symbolic—for the consecration of the nation. The monument, which I discuss in chapter 9 (page 257), is located in the central plaza of the village, at an open fronton typical of Iparralde, in which in October 1999 the previously mentioned *Aekeguna* dances were held. It is also the same space in which commemorations are held for those who died in the world wars every year on July 14. In these two examples, then, one sees the fronton used as a space to confirm two potentially conflictive collective identities: those of the Basque and French nations, respectively.

What may seem contradictory and incomprehensible for Basques in Hegoalde is lived with relative normalcy in Iparralde. In the village of Larresoro (Larressore, Lapurdi), for example, we see a rooster, a typically French icon, displayed together with the *lauburu*, the Basque swastika at entrance of the public school. There are plazas like that of Lehuntze (Lahonce, Lapurdi) in which, right next to a frontis decorated with *lauburus*, there is a monument to honor soldiers of the village who

---

8. ETA appears to have definitvely laid down its arms following an October 2011 declaration.

died defending the French nation in the World Wars. Before the finals of the rebote modality at the fronton of Hazparne (Hasparren, Lapurdi), the *ikurrinas*, Basque flags and the French tricolor are jointly displayed on top of the frontis.

Despite the apparent normalcy of the integration of both identities, the greater part of the frontons in Iparralde that incorporate national symbols display *ikurrinas* or *lauburus*. This is also general in Hegoalde except perhaps for southern areas of Navarre, where it is possible to see Spanish flags officially painted at the fronton.

Despite the fact that there are many frontons in non-Basque areas such as La Rioja and much of Castile, some of which may be as old or even older than Basque frontons, the court is so significantly linked to the territory of Euskal Herria that it grew into its main symbol. In and of itself, the fronton is a fundamental icon of the Basque nation, which is why in the majority of the cases there is no need to vindicate the space through added national symbols. Normally, the fronton displays only the shield of the village in stone or paint; sometimes they also feature the year of construction or remodeling, if relevant.

Far more than the icons officially located at the fronton, the attitude of locals toward the space differs enormously from the north to the south. In Hegoalde, communal space has been the center par excellence of political protest and demands for years. The walls of the open frontons have been used and are still used as veritable banners calling for insurrection, revolutionary convocation, and support for the armed struggle. This typology, however, has diminished markedly lately. In Iparralde, on the other hand, the fronton remains immaculate. This attitude, which characterized the behavior of younger age groups in both territories, is nevertheless extended to covered frontons as well, in which professional games are played. The frontons no longer display messages of protest, but commercial signs that cover the left wall like the games broadcast on television. Similarly to the use of fronton for political purposes, this commercialization of the space of the fronton has profoundly displeased much of the crowd: they feel that this temple, where people congregate religiously, has been desecrated.

The fronton is the communal space par excellence; as such, it contains and irradiates everything that happens within Basque society. It was used by both parties in the Spanish Civil War as a place for disseminating propaganda; it saw the nationalist Joseba Elosegi set himself alight in act of protest and throw himself on Franco in 1970; it famously received the historic Basque nationalist leader Telesforo Monzón and many others on his return from exile in 1977; it hosted several funerals held by the left-wing nationalists, *abertzales*, as well as demonstrations both in favor of and against the armed organization ETA. All these images remain recorded in the memories of those who experienced these events in situ, and those who remember them through the medium of the space. The fronton, like Proust's Madeleine, contains within it the collective memory of Basques, a memory that, like any other, is constructed on the bases of present events. This is why the fronton has a central role in the 2003 documentary *La pelota vasca: la piel contra la piedra* ("The Basque Ball: Skin against Stone") by Julio Medem; a documentary that features the conflicting voices of Basque society set against the sights and sounds of pelota, perfectly understanding the symbolism of the fronton.

The fronton is a space in which differences are suspended, the place in which communal unity is proclaimed superior to them. This is why there is such a strong feeling of opposition to anything that would "stain" the fronton, an opposition that emanates from a strong awareness of what the space signifies; any appropriation of the space either goes beyond or exploits community consciousness. Any attempt to monopolize the communal space through partisan messages that may alienate certain sectors provokes the public's rejection, especially that of the more traditional spectators, whether or not they agree with what the messages proclaim. They are interfering with harmony and, no matter how illusory that harmony may be, they go against the primordial narrative of the place: *Huna zer emaiten ahal duen herrian batasunak* (this is what gives unity to a people).

Agon: The Foundation of Culture

> Reconciliation is there, even in the midst of strife, and all things that are parted find one another again.
>
> — Friedrich Hölderlin (*Hyperion*)

Conflict is a latent danger in every society, even if sometimes it is considered as a civilizing impulse. Conflicts are present in foundational myths and rites in vastly distant cultures both in time and space. Beyond poetic fiction and folkloric expressions, these manifestations of community stage a problem of civilization, a problem that almost always seems to be linked to the control of intra-social, domestic violence.

Many cultures have a mythical or ritual narrative that features internal conflict followed by a period of reconciliation and abundance termed a Golden Age, and which is supposedly restored by periodically performed mythical recitation or ritual practices. Most foundational myths and rites revolve around primogenial, cosmogonic struggle through which a period of order is established, recognized as a state of civilization on which culture is based.

The Mayas considered the movement of the ball, *ollin*, as a primordial driving force of life, which unified conflicting forces and represented the synthesis of contraries. There are many relief carvings that symbolize balls in movement: they are composed of the entwined tongues and bodies of fighting serpents, serpents that are depicted as if they were blood springing from the decapitated head of the player sacrificed at play, in which case it constitutes an effective fertility symbol.[9] A similar theme is present in Greek mythology, as Verjat claims: "In the primogenial chaos where serpents fight, the rod of Hermes imposes an order by equilibrating contrary tendencies between reason and irrationality, truth and lie, health and illness, life and death."[10]

In part 2, pelota is found to be a foundational ritual of modern Basque culture; it had its first milestone in the sixteenth century, at the beginning of the modern era, at the beginning of political as well as socioeconomic changes in the Basque Country. From the sixteenth century on the Basque Country underwent fundamental urban development, and witnessed the decline of the hegemony of clans that created constant conflict in the rural areas. A desire for security, partly generated by the economic interests of small towns, lead to the establishment of a juridical police institution: the *hermandad*, or "fraternity." The fraternities were fighting against the powers of feudal lords, many times destroying their towered fortresses, these authentic symbols of political organization in the Late Middle Ages. It is from this transformation that general assemblies and provincial councils emerged. The peasantry seized ownership of land and the rights and privileges of nobility, which Caro Baroja calls the "birth of the concept of the 'original Basque democracy.'"[11] This is

---

9. Taladoire, "El juego de pelota mesoamericana," 27; Ladrón de Guevara, "El juego de pelota en El Tajín," 40.

10. Verjat, *Diccionario de hermenéutica*, 294.

11. Caro Baroja, *The Basques*, 366.

this context in which pelota started to become more important for the community.

At the beginning of part 2, I discussed the coincidence between the colors by which the factions used to differentiate themselves—blue and red in Hegoalde, red and white in Iparralde—and which the players still use today. Once again, it is not my intention to assert here the historic genesis of pelota as a redressive action of late medieval crisis, as symbolic, cathartic representation of the conflict outlined above. Nevertheless, we should not forget that the game was a constant point of reference for several nineteenth-century writers. Comparing the impersonal, fraction-free struggle of the bullfight with pelota, as previously noted, Unamuno says of the latter that it gathers "people of the wars of factions."[12] And, as similarly noted above, in the words of Arriaga, "Ah, if only today's pelotarismo elevated to the *cátedra* had known that permanent faction!"[13]

Seemingly, as chapter 3 argues, until the process of industrialization between the mid-nineteenth and the early twentieth century, rivalries were based on the birthplace of the pelotari, which Juan de Irigoyen terms "localist patriotism."[14] A determining factor in their dissolution seems to have been the emergence of betting, which transformed from binary to multiple oppositions through the establishment of the *momio*. Be that as it may, pelota seems to have maintained a degree of conflict by representation, grouping the male population under emblems that were no longer aligned along warlike patterns, but rather sporting allegiances. This allowed rivalries to conspire in a separate realm at the margins of the political system.

Girard argues that tragic dialogue is a substitution of the sword with the word.[15] The Greeks found in tragedy a consistent symbolic medium of their political conceptions. Above all else, the Greek tragedy consisted of a public confrontation between two figures that briefly exchanged words. It is the *stykomythia*, the "exchange of insults and accusations that corresponds to the exchange of blows between warriors locked in single combat"[16] that constituted *agon*, translated into struggle or competition.

---

12. Unamuno, "Un partido de pelota," 303.
13. Arriaga, *La pastelería y otras narraciones bilbaínas*, 222.
14. Irigoyen, "En los juegos de pelota," 8, 10.
15. Girard, *Violence and the Sacred*, 47.
16. Ibid., 160.

In equal conditions, two persons were facing each other in front of an audience that constituted itself through representing the great authority of their democratic system.

While in time the tragedy would come to occupy its own stage—the theater—at first this representation took place in the *agora*, the nerve center of the city and a place that hosted meetings of assemblies of notables. The *agora* was the physical concretion of the *polis*, of this community that was no longer characterized by kinship relations but by political arrangements. *Agon* was the staging of divergence, which found its conclusion in the *agora*.

Nietzsche argues that the stichomythia, the dialoge in which "two main actors face each other, endowed with the same rights," causing "a rivalry expressed through words and arguments" to emerge,[17] marks the initial decline of tragedy and, as a consequence, the political aspirations of Eurypides in the bourgeois middle class, which from now on took and held the floor. Aeschylus, for example, recreated the old myths in order "to lay the foundations of the new lay, democratic conception of the city."[18]

As I said before, the origins of pelota are profoundly urban, although it was also practiced on the porches of churches located centrally in certain valleys, the ancient form of spatial organization. This agonic fiesta did though require the development of villas (chartered towns or boroughs) to thrive. The game was closely associated with these towns as another representation of *agon*; as a ritual that stages and transcends the latent conflicts and dangers that are inherent to any society, and which becomes the greatest fear of urban configuration: the split, the wound. But just as the tragedy moved as civil powers diversified from the *agora*, the nucleus of the *polis* to occupy its own space, the theater, so pelota moved into its own, autonomous space at the end of the eighteenth century, when the fronton was established.

Pelota was born in the medieval equivalent of the Greek *agora*: the atrium or portico of church buildings that, according to Robert Fossier, were places of communal celebrations, reunions, and decision making.[19] This space was called, and is still called in some villages like Lizartza, the

---

17. Nietzsche, *El nacimiento de la tragedia*, 238.
18. Miralles, *Esquilo*, 15.
19. See Fossier, *The Axe and the Oath*, 141.

zimitorio because it was a place of burial. The Santiago Church of Bilbao was a famous example, from where pelota moved to the *Calle de la Pelota*, "Street of Pelota." The town council met on the tombs of ancestors (who were not necessarily blood relatives) to make its political decisions. In the same place they played a game of pelota, which was nothing but the division of a unity that the plaza itself symbolized. Between the two parties a dialogue was established. In Greece, by way of words; in the Basque Country, by way of balls, which were as different as the persons who played with them. The instrument changed, yet the objective was the same: *sizing up the other*, knowing the other, and knowing oneself.

Like the Greek *agora*, the plaza stages agonic struggles, great confrontations, while it keeps them under the control of representation. It remediates them through representation. The plaza promulgates the unity of the community over tragic polarity. It assumes conflict, accepts it with impartiality and imposes on it its particular sovereignty: authority.

> Stadium games devise and illustrate a rivalry that is limited, regulated, and specialized. Stripped of any personal feeling of hate or rancor, this new kind of emulation inaugurates a school of loyalty and generosity. At the same time, it spreads the custom of and respect for refereeing. Its civilizing role has often been stressed. In fact, "national" games are present in nearly all the great civilizations. The Aztec games of pelota comprise ritualistic festivals in which the ruler and his court participate. In ancient China, archery contests tested the nobles not so much through the results but through their correctly shooting an arrow or consoling an unlucky adversary. In medieval Christendom, tournaments fulfilled the same function. The goal was not victory at any price, but prowess exhibited under conditions of equality, against a competitor whom one esteems and assists when in need, and using only legitimate means agreed to in advance at a fixed place and time.[20]

The civilizing role Caillois attributes to formal games is also emphasized by Huizinga: "the two ever-recurrent forms in which civilization grows in and as play are the sacred performance and the festal contest."[21] In the end, all play is representation and it is in representation where human beings are constructed. They step out of themselves by creating a separate realm in which they interpret and (re)construct their own self.

---

20. Caillois, *Man, Play, and Games*, 108–9.
21. Huizinga, *Homo Ludens*, 48.

This is the symbolic universe, the culture, the realm in which, as Cassirer remarks, human beings acquire their "specific difference," and where "we can understand the new way open to man: the way to civilization."[22]

Philosophy recovers the theme of conflict to explain the origins of civilization: "The interplay of opposites in multiple domains of life and thought is rediscovered by modern critics of identitarian logic."[23] A dialectic conflict that Hobbes had anticipated by citing two subjects who, by desiring to achieve the same goals, become enemies; Hegel would apply this dialectic as the category of the genealogic principle of modern consciousness and the state: "The thread of gold that passes through this trance, epistemological and historical and the same time, constitutive of an era of modern consciousness and of the state, is culture, cultural formation, as historic reality of reason and as dialectics of the civilizing progress."[24] The Hegelian dialectic of the duel establishes for Subirats an "intrinsic relationship between historical violence of domination, individual consciousness, and the general progress of culture."[25]

All that for the Western imaginary constitutes human beings, consciousness, and culture is first and foremost located in this conflictive polarization: "The man has now become one of us, knowing good and evil" (Genesis 3:22). Conflict becomes permanently present: "The sad truth is that man's real life consists of a complex of inexorable opposites—day and night, birth and death, happiness and misery, good and evil. We are not even sure that one will prevail against the other, that good will overcome evil, or joy defeat pain. Life is a battleground."[26] Existence appears as perpetual struggle between the forces of diverse orders; it is precisely in their confrontation that they appear not only *realized* but also conjugated. The Greeks called that confrontation *agony*, a term derived from *agon*, which means gymnastic contest, competition as well as anguish. It is the latter designation that prevails in current language.

The qualitative leap that penetrates culture leads humans from a state of nature, from flowing immediacy with their environment, to a

---

22. Cassirer, *An Essay on Man*, 26.
23. Arnason, *Agon, Logos, Polis*, 8.
24. Subirats, *El alma y la muerte*, 346.
25. Ibid., 352.
26. Jung, *Man and His Symbols*, 75.

state of self-awareness, of nakedness. Humans were banished from Eden for discovering their inevitable reality, their precarious condition; death. This is when agony, struggle enters life and death, a duel in which both appear united and in which the very own destiny of humans is fulfilled—a destiny that only the communal bond the *agora* represents is able to relieve. This is why Subirats says that "dialectics masks the break of the subject split precisely under the unbearable grandiloquence of the Hegelian 'us,'"[27] whose physical image is, in our case, nothing but the plaza. For this author, this process from *I* to *us* "is inadmissible from the point of view of our historical experience of a split and antagonistic society."[28] Nevertheless, it is precisely this obviousness, as Turner would argue, that motivates symbolic representation, the ideal constitution of the community through redressive action, through ritual.[29]

Let us recall the shamanistic cure that Lévi-Strauss discusses in "The Effectiveness of Symbols." The process is the following: offering the sick person an experience, in this case a mythical narration where she accommodates evil, sublimates it, and heals. The illness is perceived as a fractioning, a breaking up, as secession from a totality that the person constitutes.[30] This is why Pierre Clastres affirms that "the form of illness is almost always the same: it consists of the provisional anticipation of that which death affects in a definitive manner: the separation between the body and the soul. . . . To cure the illness, to restore good health is to reconstruct the body-soul unity of the person."[31] Something analogous happens to the community that needs to maintain cohesion, the ideal of itself, despite the separate and finite essence of the members who compose it. This aligns with what Durkheim considers to be the major function of the positive cult: "There can be no society which does not feel the need of upholding and reaffirming at regular intervals the collective sentiments and the collective ideas which make its unity and its personality."[32]

---

27. Subirats, *El alma y la muerte*, 362.

28. Ibid., 361.

29. Turner, *The Forest of Symbols*.

30. Lévi-Strauss, "The Effectiveness of Symbols," chapter 10 in *Structural Anthropology*, vol. 1, 186–204.

31. Clastres, *Investigaciones en antropología política*, 78.

32. Durkheim, *The Elementary Forms of the Religious Life*, 475.

The reconstruction of unity is only possible within the realm of representation. This is the only sphere capable of assembling into a whole subjects that share neither genealogy nor a historical era. The idea of community among subjects that either do not know each other or have not experienced the same conditions of existence is possible due to a cycle of meaning that is produced through representation. This is what Nietzsche called the eternal return: "Everything goeth, everything returneth; eternally rolleth the wheels of existence. Everything dieth, everything blossometh forth again; eternally runneth on the year of existence."[33]

The ideal of the community is based, then, on the interpretive character of everything that takes place in which, according to Manuel Barrios, it is possible to recommence any moment by "cutting the thread of mere lineal succession and the continuation of the preceding, to open oneself to new events."[34] This is exactly what emerges in representation: Maffesoli's eternal instants, which he finds predominant in the character of postmodern societies.[35]

Life in its everyday reality does not normally offer pure outcomes and straightforward resolutions, so human beings seek these in narration, in myth, literature, art, cinema, and ritual. This is why Gadamer argues that

> it is always the case that mutually exclusive expectations are aroused, not all of which can be fulfilled. The undecidedness of the future permits such a superfluity of expectations that reality necessarily lags behind them. Now if, in a particular case, a context of meaning closes and completes itself in reality, such that no lines of meaning scatter in the void, then this reality is itself like a drama.[36]

Ritual, as well as play, is a constant alternation between tension and conclusion. The outcome as the last conclusion exists in fact, it must exist for representation, for the closure of meaning to be possible. But what is relevant is not the outcome in and of itself but the process, this unlimited opening where any path is possible, where everything is open gesture, without conclusion. This tension binds those who are present, it produces the paternal suffering of unity, the magic transformation,

---

33. Nietzsche, *Thus Spoke Zarathustra*, 246.
34. Barrios, *Narrar el abismo*, 197.
35. Mafessoli, *El instante eterno*.
36. Gadamer, *Truth and Method*, 112.

source of renovation, and communal catharsis. At the same time, the outcome is fundamental for memory, for the reconstruction and maintenance of the totality beyond the sphere in which emotions are produced. The outcome is necessary because the process gains meaning by its conclusion. Within the symbolic universe that constitutes humanity, it is not the cause that explains the effect, but the effect that constructs the cause. While emotions are produced in tension, it is the outcome that enables memory and the reconstruction of the succession of time.

The clean slate, a fresh start, only happens in representation, because the only absolute end that awaits human beings in their individuality is death. This is why death (and suffering, its delegate in life) has been considered a fundamental driving force of the consciousness of culture: it constitutes the basic medium of representation through which humans are constituted, something that paradigmatically happens in positive cults.

María Zambrano argues that "the practical meaning of sacrifice was surely a giving place for a kind of 'vital space' for man."[37] Recreating death, real or fictitious, human beings carve a hollow in which they recommence, reinterpret the self. This is why Delgado, following Lévi-Strauss, argued that sacrifice is the creation of a "hollow trap where the cunning of humans causes the gods to fall so that they fill it with their gifts."[38] Delgado builds on this idea: to him, what happens is "generating a hollow space, a marked hole, which implies for the person who occupies it a physical or moral destruction of the self, of one's own body or at least identity."[39] Emptying is the step that precedes filling and starting over: "a little *tabula rasa* of the consciousness, so as to make room again for the new."[40]

Although succession (like rhythm) is always new, although the liminal phase is pure possibility and the ritual admits, endures, and even promotes transformations, meaning is produced precisely because ritual produces an outcome that allows for the interpretation of the process, and for recommencement. In other words, it achieves eternal actuality. Its route is circular. In ritual, as in play, beginning and end coincide:

---

37. Zambrano, *El hombre y lo divino*, 39.
38. Delgado, *El animal público*, 101.
39. Ibid.
40. Nietzsche, *The Genealogy of Morals*, 34.

"with each new game," Caillois says, "even if they have played all their life, the players again face each other from scratch, under the same conditions as the very beginning."[41] This is why it is able to subtract subjects from their everyday reality and integrate them in a "temporary sphere of activity with a disposition all of its own."[42] Hence Gadamer's argument, "all playing is being played." In ritual as in play the subject enters a sphere that Turner calls "cunicular," and which may be compared to being in a tunnel.[43] Outside of the transformations of everyday life, the subject is involved in a task that makes him or her lose their head:[44] "the individual is actuated," Maffesoli argues, "they no longer own themselves, but shine in a greater conjunction."[45]

Pelota and the fronton are precisely an activity and a space upon which this activity is built, this tunnel in which the subject subtracts him or herself from the everyday. The unity of the community is thus reestablished. The very structure of the game, the symmetric split of unity where the two antagonistic parts *size up*, where they discover each other until one overcomes the other, constitutes a key argument for the agonic fiesta. What the agonic fiesta does is basically create a hollow in the game, as well as in its outcome.

When one of the parties *is hunting* for the other during the game, he is discovering the opponent's "hollows" *(huts)*. When one of the players continuously discovers the hollows of the fronton, hollows where he hits the ball, or pressures the other into committing an error *(huts)*, the game is broken *(hautsi)*. One of the parties is definitely hunted down by the other, smashed *(hautsi)*, reduced to ashes *(hauts)*. Zulaika associates the void, *huts*, with ash, *hauts*, and affirms that "emptying, eliminating, reducing to nothing, to zero, turning someone into ashes are formally equivalent and provide the basic performative scheme of the ritual process."[46]

The permanent search for hollows that a pelota game implies, and which affects the reduction of the opponent into ashes, is framed by a scheme that we called sacrificial. One part "gives death" to the other

---

41. Caillois, *Los juegos y los hombres*, 7.
42. Huizinga, *Homo Ludens*, 8.
43. Turner, *Dramas, Fields and Metaphors*, 232.
44. Huizinga, *Homo Ludens*, 13.
45. Maffesoli, *El instante eterno*, 82.
46. Zulaika, *Tratado estético-ritual vasco*, 80.

(wins), devours (embraces) him, reconstructs unity, and exhibits it with closed fists—a symbol of victory and of permanence, of salvation.

This agonic experience of struggle and encounter is staged at the fronton, in the Basque *agora*. Taking shape physically as a great hollow in the nucleus of villages and towns, the fronton is home to the community's ludic, festive, and ritual performances as well as economic (market) and political (rallies) activities. An icon of collectivity, the fronton is a void where the subject is dissolved, where the community is recreated.

Oteiza, who devoted a large part of his long life (1909–2003) to capturing the essence of the void, discovered in the fronton the communal equivalent of his holes in the sand that, as a child on the beaches of Orio, Gipuzkoa, isolated him from the world. In his constant tasks of aesthetic inoccupation, what the Basque sculptor, poet, and thinker achieved was to create an active void of spiritual protection, rather than hollowing. From the point of view of an art conceived not as "artistic perfectioning but [as] significant, symbolic and transcendental projection for life,"[47] Oteiza finds in the megalithic chamber tomb, the cromlech, the conclusion of the artistic process, in which the sculptor "opens a space for his imperiled heart, makes a hole in the sky, and his small head encounters God."[48]

---

47. Oteiza, *Quousque Tandem . . . !*, 118
48. Oteiza, *Oteiza's Selected Writings*, 329.

Before this discovery, Oteiza had concluded his artistic investigations of searching for a spiritual and energetic void, of an internal spatial silence, with his *Metaphysical Boxes*, sculptures constructed by simple thriedrons in which another of the most original Basque constructions are revealed: the fronton. Oteiza himself acknowledged that for his work titled *Homage to Velázquez*, he related the *Las Lanzas* ("The Surrender of Breda") with the *Las Meninas* ("The Maids of Honor"), which configured for him the Basque fronton;[49] a metaphysical insulator, a parking of an educated sensibility.[50]

Oteiza's experimental proposition, now concluded, coincided with the spiritual proposition of the prehistoric sculptor:

> The stones were not placed from reality, but against it, from a metaphysical consciousness defined in space. Previously, in the figurative, the magical hunter from the Paleolithic period controls the image of the animal (the bison history) in his cave paintings from inside his material refuge. Now in the abstract, in this Neolithic cromlech, the artist invents the habitation for his metaphysical root in the precise, external space of reality. Unamuno would call it his intra statue—his soul cupboard—his intra history. Man has stepped outside of himself, outside of time. An aesthetic solution—religious reason—for his supreme existential anguish.[51]

---

49. Pelay Orozco, *Oteiza*, 367.
50. Oteiza, *Quousque Tandem . . . !*, illustration 59.
51. Oteiza, *Oteiza's Selected Writings*, 327.

Joca gaiten onheski, plaça juye bethi, holada ohorezki.
Play fairly, the plaza always judges honorably.

Part 3
Aldude

An Aesthetic:
Play Honestly, the Plaza Is Always Judge

> A tablet of the good hangs over every people.
> — Nietzsche (*Thus Spoke Zarathustra*)

The fact that most cultures have used balls as instruments of play is not to say that they have had the same cultural implications everywhere. We may argue that the physical form of the ball recalls an association with circularity, with movement, with the heavenly bodies, with life. Nevertheless, we cannot conclude from this what these realities really mean for a given culture. Only by observing how this symbol relates to others, and by determining the attitudes toward this specific symbol as well as its importance within the cultural totality, may we conclude how it is conceptualized by a given culture. Merely saying that pelota symbolizes life, that stone stands for permanence, and white for purity does not contribute to the understanding of their meaning for a specific culture, even if they are shared by hundreds of them. In order to understand the particular meanings of culture, we need to identify connections, affects, discordances, and boundaries among its original symbols.

Therefore, the fact that the symbol is not arbitrary, that it has a *certain* connection with what it signifies is not to say that it is universal, nor that we could understand it or observe it. Discussing the arbitrariness of signs, Ferdinand de Saussure affirms that

> the word symbol is sometimes used to designate the linguistic sign, or more exactly that part of the linguistic sign which we are calling the signal. This use of the word symbol is awkward, for reasons connected with our first principle. For it is characteristic of symbols that they are never entirely arbitrary. They are not empty configurations. They show at least a vestige of natural connection between the signal and its signification.

For instance, our symbol of justice, the scales, could hardly be replaced by a chariot."[1]

This is why I would, like Turner[2] agree with Jung that the symbol is the best expression possible of a relatively unknown fact but which claims to be existent.

The fact that the symbol is not arbitrary is no license to merely infer its implications for a specific culture. That the crown symbolically refers to power, that the grabbing function of the hand is an image of possession, of empowerment, is not to say that power is understood in the same way by the Javanese as by the English, as Geertz also argues;[3] nor does it have the same social implications. Therefore, despite the fact that the symbol possesses certain qualities that are intrinsic to that which it represents, it is necessary to contextualize it in order to understand it; ritual is an exceptional realm for the interpretation of symbols, as it is in ritual action that a cathartic effect is paradigmatically produced, an effect that results from the exchange of qualities between the ideological and sensory poles of signification. By way of the same, "norms and values become saturated with emotion, while the gross and basic emotions become ennobled through contact with social values."[4]

---

1. Saussure, *F. de Saussure*, 69.
2. Turner, *The Forest of Symbols*.
3. Geertz, *Local Knowledge*.
4. Turner, *The Forest of Symbols*, 30.

7

Esku:
The Hand as Depository of the Person

> Language is the receptacle of the experience of a people, and the sediment of its thought; the collective spirit of the people have left its marks in the deep creases of its metaphors (that is, the immense majority of its words), like the processes of fauna does in geological fields.
>
> — Unamuno

Anthropological studies have discovered that many human groups use terms that signify or are synonymous with "human" when they refer to themselves, as opposed to those that they use to call their neighbors, normally associated with barbarism and animality:[1] "Every culture," Clastres argues, "performs a division of humanity within itself, which is affirmed as representation of the human par excellence, and the others, who only minimally partake of humanity."[2] As Caro Baroja argues, "in seeing themselves as outstanding, the Basques are essentially the same as the rest of the inhabitants of the world."[3]

In the *Diccionario etimólogico del idioma bascongado* (Etymological Dictionary of the Basque Language), published by Pedro Novia de Salcedo in 1887, there are 131 entries with the root *esku-*, a term that in itself simply means hand or, in another sense, command, authority, power. *Eskudun* literally means "the person who has power:" the competent, skillful person; *eskupe*, or "under the hand" refers to subordination, dependence, and

---

1. See Bartra, *El salvaje en el espejo*; Bestard, *Bárbaros, paganos, salvajes y primitivos*; Redfield, *The Primitive World and Its Transformations*.

2. Clastres, *Investigaciones en antropología política*, 59.

3. Caro Baroja, *The Basques*, 359.

eskuera or "realm of the hand" to jurisdiction. The association between hand and power is clear, and it also becomes patent in some verbs like *eskuratu* (seize), *eskuetsi* (authorize), or *eskua kendu*, literally "remove the hand," translated as "usurp power."

The hand is power and at the same time it is ownership. One need only recall Diogenes and his barrel (or large clay pot),[4] a property that humanized him, and which secured him freedom; he was no slave. He who is "of the hand," *eskukoa*, can either be free ("nire *eskukoa naiz*": "of *my* hand I am"), or a subject ("zure *eskukoa naiz*": "of *your* hand I am"), depending on the possessive pronoun used. An *eskualde*, "boundary," "county," is that which is "by or at the side of the hand"; if *alde* is a spatial notion, *aldi* is temporal, and *eskualdi,* "the turn of the hand," is a play, a cast, and also a handful, all the hand can contain in one grab. For "handful" there is also the term *eskumen*, which is associated with potentiality—a faculty that the hand possesses. This faculty turns into a "right," *eskubidea*, literally "route of the hand," a route of encounter with the other, with everything in general; *eskuarki* is an adverbial phrase that refers to something common, general (probably, generally, commonly).

The hand therefore appears as the norm, the rule,[5] the mold by which humanity is measured; within the context that the Basque language offers us, it is not so far-fetched to argue that *eskualdun* or *euskaldun* (meaning "Basque" or, literally, "one who possesses Basque") is he who "has hand,"[6] or, put another way, he who has the possibility to participate (*esku hartu*, literally "to take hand") or intervene (*esku sartu*, literally "to tackle, to meddle") in public institutions.

In this line of thinking, Eskuara or Euskara (both terms for the Basque language) refers to the way the hand speaks, the way a human being communicates due to the association between hand and humanity, as opposed to *erdalduna* (meaning a non–Basque speaker), one who does not complete humanity, he who remains half (*erdi*) and expresses himself

---

4. Serres, *Atlas*, 49–50. Captured by pirates and sold into slavery, Diogenes the Cynic (412–323 BCE) was a controversial philosopher who flaunted the convetions of his age by, among other things, sleeping in a large clay pot belonging to the temple of Cybele in Athens.

5. Some authors suggest that *escuadra* or "squad" (*esku* + *adrea*) may derive precisely from this, from the rule of the hand. See Novia de Salcedo, *Diccionario etimológico del idioma bascongado*, 567.

6. Iharse de Bidassoet argues that the term *euskaldun* means "hand favorable to those who have it." See the journal *Laurak Bat* 114 (1886), in a translation of Edouard Baudrimont's book, *Historie de des Basques ou Escualdunais primitifs*.

with *erdera* (not Basque), in an incomplete, inconclusive, rudimentary way of speaking. Therefore, the term *euskaldun* (Basque-speaker) goes beyond the definition of "he who speaks Euskara." Both terms are prompted by the human faculty concentrated in the hand, and in which Basques have fixed a symbolic boundary between those who are competent (*eskudunak*) or have rights (*eskubideak*) to participate (*esku hartu*) in matters of the community, and those who do not.

The hand is a yardstick that measures humanity; it is associated with a conception of ownership as emphasized by Michel Serres, and it grants the power of being free (*eskukoa*), the owner of oneself. The *eskualdun* is he who can intervene (*esku sartu*) in situations that have to do with his *eskualde* (region, district). "A tongue without hands! How dare you speak?" as *The Poem of My Cid* reads[7] to discredit the commentary of an incompetent person, of someone who is not *eskuduna*. The hand represents humanity, and it is probable that among the Basques, the hand has been incorporated in the vocabulary to self-designate precisely for this reason.

Frontoiko Ezkertiak (The Left-Handed of the Fronton)

I have argued that the image of woman as a protagonist in the central spaces of Basque culture—those of *bertsolaritza*, of politics, of the plaza, of pelota—is not part of the Basque cultural imaginary. A small minority of women have, however, conquered the public space in the cases of *bertsolaritza* and politics—unlike in pelota, the prototypical activity of the Basques.

Several anecdotes recount stories of women beating men in the plaza throughout the history of pelota. Even Beloki, one of the best pelotaris of the 1990s and early 2000s and who became hand pelota champion at the early age of nineteen, was beaten by Maite Ruiz at the age of thirteen. Years later she became the number one player in *paleta goma* ("paleta rubber") in the trinquet, outside of professional competition. Female superiority at preadolescent age is not surprising, and can be seen in many schools and pelota clubs. As the players get older, mixed games become wildly popular because of their exotic nature. In 1885 the

---

7. Such and Hodgkinson, trans., *The Poem of My Cid*, cantar 3, tirada 143, line 3328 (p. 237). The original line is, "¡Lengua sin manos! ¿cuemo osas fablar?" Quoted in Unamuno, *En torno al casticismo*, 69.

journal *Laurak Bat* quoted news from the daily *La voz de Guipuzcoa* that in the plaza of Lazkao (Gipuzkoa), a twenty-two-year old woman challenged a young man, "of great physique." The bet disputed was an ounce of gold, although her father, "sure of her skill and dexterity," wanted to bet a cow in her favor.[8]

The sisters of the legendary Perkain and his contemporary Azantza were also famous pelotaris. One version of the Perkain myth, rendered by Pierre-Barthélemy Gheusi into an opera that premiered in Paris in the 1930s,[9] featured his sister as the executer of the first "modern" pelotari's most renowned feat. As previously noted, Perkain was exiled in the Baztan Valley in Navarre after the initial triumph of the French Revolution because of his opposition to the new regime. However, one day he learned about an important challenge on the French side and decided to play it. In the middle of the game a guard tried to arrest him; Perkain shot a ball that killed the guard, allowing the pelotari to escape. One version of the legend claims that the lethal shot came in fact from his sister's glove, because she was also present at the game.

One of the qualities they attribute to female players is skill. The female features most associated with this skill are trickiness, dexterity, and astuteness. The supposed absence of the archetypical power of the pelotari, of force, implies the development of a power that may overcome it: astuteness. Clearly, this feature has a symbolic resonance with prototypically female qualities that, while not staged by women, are present in the plaza through the "fox" of the fronton: the left-handed player.

The left-handed player is a serious threat for his opponents, mainly because of his disconcerting playing style. Although the hand modality of pelota requires ambidextrousness, a left-handed player is quickly recognized on the court. It is not only his left-handed shots that reveal him; he employs the art of trickery in its most refined expression. Using the left wall as an ally, the left-handed player hides the ball like no one else. An expert in "breaking waists" or forcing his opponent into quick movements of the torso, he is a virtuoso of the labyrinth, disorienting in it the ingenious right-hand players, who are not necessarily more astute for being right-handed. Arretxe I believed he could beat the left-handed Unanue with shots to the sides in the 1999 four-and-a-half mark

---

8. Laurak Bat, Year VII, no.137.

9. *Perkain*, a lyrical drama in three acts, with music by Jean Poueight (1931).

championship, with a game in the air so unbecoming of a "lion," of long, classic play. But a lion must beat the fox with his great weapon, with strength, and not with the weapons of the fox. Unanue won 22–12.

Robert Hertz associates woman with the left-handed by establishing a relationship between the sides of the body and the sexes: men with the right side and women with the left side. After all, he observes in his book *Death and the Right Hand* (1909), God took a rib from Adam's left side to create Eve.[10] Hertz stresses the tendency to institutionalize the development of the right hand, and to condemn the incompetence of the left.

With the incorporation of the left wall at the fronton, the use of the left hand has completely disappeared from the remonte and jai alai modalities. Even left-handed players hold the *xistera* or basket in their right hand, a common practice since the beginning of the century. In the pala modality there was also a period when the game was restricted to use of the right hand. The left hand of the left-handed Begoñés VI (Ignacio Guisasola) was tied behind his back so that he would not grab the pala in his left hand. At present, ambidextrousness is highly valued, as it has always been in the hand modality.

In his study of the nature of Basque style, Oteiza considered that both hands were important and valuable, as each had a definite role:

> Always it is the same game of a man who carries the rule in his left hand, but it's with the other, the free hand, that he dominates, pronounces and plays. . . . It is the spiritual relationship between something closed and sacred (the cromlech) (the left hand) for his confidence and his free response (the right hand) (life) in Nature.
>
> It's like the court in our game of *jai alai*, with its left wall. . . . His aesthetic and sacred logic ended up on the left, his heart, to the right.[11]

Alfred T. Bryant observed the tendency to separate the functions of the hands among the Zulu, who in their stick fighting game hold a stick in the left hand to protect themselves from the strikes of their adversaries, while they deal with the strikes they receive with their right hand.[12] In the spear-throwing game of the Maori of New Zealand, a dance of presumed military origins, the spear is thrown with the right

---

10. Hertz, *Death and the Right Hand*, 103.
11. Oteiza, *Oteiza's Selected Writings*, 361.
12. Blanchard and Cheska, *The Anthropology of Sport*, 190.

hand and received with the left.[13] The shield in the left hand protects the heart from the throw by holding it on the right. On this account, Roland Auguet notes the dread of left-handed gladiators in the Roman amphitheater.[14]

Hertz calls the separation of functions between both hands "organic asymmetry," a notion that resonates with the incompatibility of contraries in the world of religion: "The whole universe is divided into two contrasted spheres: things, beings and powers attract or repel each other, implicate or exclude each other according to whether they gravitate towards one or the other of the two poles."[15] And that furthermore, "It is a vital necessity that neither of the two hands should know what the other doeth."[16]

Hertz himself claims that in cults the right hand is responsible for offerings and blessings,[17] while confrontation with or distancing from demonic forces is done with the left hand; he does not however recognize their incompatibility, the specialization of functions for a pure corporeal technique. Hertz emphasizes the division between both hands, and the fear of contamination that may result from their mixing, of one hand adopting functions that are not its own. Hertz's conclusions lead to the negative cult, the taboo, as do those of Caillois: "Hertz, who set up this dichotomy, made a profound study of it, in terms of right and left. We can see it applied to the last detail in ritual, in the practice of divination, in customs, and in beliefs. . . . The right hand is for the scepter, for authority, for being sworn, and for good faith. The left is for fraud and treachery."[18] Whether we emphasize incompatibility or complementarity, the fact remains that the body becomes an effective metaphor for the transmission of certain social categories, something that is concentrated even in language: "the different way in which the collective consciousness envisages and values the right and the left appears clearly in language."[19] Indeed, and I quote at length, for Callois:

---

13. Ibid., 180.
14. Auguet, *Cruelty and Civilization*, 172.
15. Hertz, *Death and the Right Hand*, 96
16. Ibid., 98.
17. Something that the Bible also determines. See Genesis, 48: 13.
18. Caillois, *Man and the Sacred*, 43.
19. Hertz, *Death and the Right Hand*, 99.

Language itself manifests this opposition. In the Indo-European family, a special root expresses the concept of *right* in various languages. The *left* side, on the contrary, is designated by multiform and ambiguous terms, by devious expressions in which metaphor and antiphrasis play a large part.

The word *droite* is also the word *adroite*, that which leads the *right* arm to its goal. Thus, attesting not only the adroitness, but the *good right arm* of the warrior, his *uprightness*, it is sign that the Gods protect him. . . . In Greek, the word left, which means to commit an error, a mistake, or even a sin, originally meant "to miss target." We now understand the different meanings of the word "right," designated manual dexterity, the rightness of an argument, a legal norm, rectitude of character, purity of intentions, the basic goodness of an act—in a word, everything that, physically or metaphysically, directs the *right* power to its goal. Conversely, *gaucherie* is a sign of evil intent and an augury of failure. It is at once maladroiteness, at once cause and effect of every tortuous, crooked or oblique power, of every false calculation or maneuver. It is everything uncertain and cause of suspicion and fear, all that is imperfect exposes and involves a tendency towards wrong-doing. Right and adroit manifest purity and divine favor, left and maladroit exemplify defilement and sin.[20]

Euskara also bears this logic that Caillois emphasizes: that of using "devious expressions in which metaphor and antiphrasis play a large part" in order to denominate the left. In the term *ezkerra* (left) there is the negation *ez* (no) with "ker," which in and of itself does not mean anything, but when combined with the verb *joan* (go) to form *ker-ker joan* means "go in the straight line," in other words "directly." Therefore, *ezkerra* could refer to "that which does not go straight," the sinuosity that Caillois refers to, the labyrinth that the *ezkertia* ("left-handed," or more colloquially "southpaw" or "lefty") constitutes to hunt for the other and overcome it.

Eskuma (right) is the hand par excellence, that which through the name itself expresses the very fact of being a hand (*esku*). The left hand does not follow the path of rectitude and seeks to negotiate boundaries and circumstances in order to achieve its own objectives, something that is not necessarily negative. In Spanish, *tener mano izquierda* ("to have left hand") means to know how to deal with something. It is good to know how to negotiate obstacles that the right hand encounters in its way. The

---

20. Caillois, *Man and the Sacred*, 44–45.

hand that executes, blesses, and takes the oath, the social hand, needs the left hand to keep away curses and to defend it in order to be able to act.

To be a good pelota player, especially in the hand modality, it is necessary to know and use the power of both hands. As early as 1884 Enrique Irabien y Larrañaga commented on the tendency to undervalue use of the left hand in the game of pelota: "maybe for human health, development, and perfection, it would be better if it disappeared."[21] Contrary to general expectations, the incorporation of the left wall in the hand modality enormously enhanced the use of the left hand. In an open plaza, without side walls and with only the frontis, the player almost always positions himself to the right, even if the ball goes to his left. The left hand barely scores and is fully defensive. Nevertheless, with the left wall the use of the left hand becomes indispensable; ambidextrousness, or "having two hands" becomes the sine qua non condition to be a good pelota player.

If the pelotari fails to use one of his hands, he is said to be "one-handed." This is an obvious weakness. Without either hand, left or right alike, he is not a complete player. The weakness in one hand leaves the player at the mercy of his rival, who will hunt him down, overcome him precisely at the side where the player is lacking, through this obvious hollow. This is why Oteiza also concludes that "our left hand is the absolute guarantee for freedom."[22]

Far from condemning the inutility of one side, the technique of pelota values the dexterity of both hands; something that, as the concerns of Irabien show, could explain the placement of the wall at the left side of the fronton. Pelota encourages the development of both hands even if, through the perception of left-handedness at the fronton, it shows a tendency to differentiate and hierarchize between them, a tendency that language itself also authorizes. Besides, there emerges a certain symbolic link between the sides of the body and gender based on the two forms of proto-agonic power: the strength, associated with masculinity and the right hand; and cunning, linked to femininity and the left hand.[23]

---

21. Irabien y Larrañaga, "Los partidos de pelota," 248.

22. Oteiza, *Quousque Tandem . . . !*, 141.

23. While it may seem evident, I wish to clarify that not all left-handed players are astute and their right-handed counterparts strong; rather, there is a symbolic association between the cunning of the left hand and the noble strength of the right. To consider a recent example, Olaizola II is a great fox, and he is right handed.

Between these prototypes, the archetypical, ideal pelotari has always been the "lion": he who relies on noble, direct strength to hunt down the other.

Eskuzabaletik Ukabilera: From the Palm to the Fist

Sizing up and the hunt for the other are processes of incorporating the other: first of discovering him, then of overcoming and beating him. The very disposition of the hand during the ritual process shows the intention of seizure, which for the pelotari means victory. The open hand that the player shows when he greets the crowd before the beginning of a game, this hand that disguises nothing and with which the player hits the ball, turns into a fist once he wins the game. In the process of sizing up, when a player struggles to find a hollow in his rival's game and manages to score against him, he normally closes his fists. "Now it's mine," he says to himself in order to motivate himself.

More traditional crowds do not look upon these gestures during the game favorably. Only once he has triumphed, once he has devoured his rival, and once he has overpowered him may he close his hands raising his fist toward the terraces. A fist as a sign of victory before the end of the game is considered a bad gesture by a part of the traditional public, which feels something that Elias Canetti describes as "the hand which never lets go has become the very emblem of power."[24]

The hand that grabs, catches, clearly establishes a relationship between power and ownership. Joseba Zulaika establishes this association by discussing the Basque concept of closure, *ertsi*: "the grabbing functions of the hand are defined as functions of *ertsi*, of closure."[25] In pelota, power through closure, through seizure, through *ertsi*, is absolutely censored as a means, while it becomes the ultimate end, as we saw in part 2.

In the ritualized context of a pelota game the player must demonstrate his power through honest, clean play, and never through *ertsi*, which in another sense means "grab with the hand" or "adhere." As noted, this illegal appropriation of the ball is called *atxiki*, which is the action of adhering, of sticking, and which is termed "retention" in pelota.

---

24. Canetti, *Crowds and Power*, 204.
25. Zulaika, *Tratado estético-ritual vasco*, 30.

The action of closing (*ertsi*) the hand to grab (*ertsi*) the ball, to *seize* the mediating element of the game is "dirty play" and is considered a fault. One needs to "nail down" the hit but never grab the ball. The contact between the hand and the ball must be clean; in other words, there may be no retention of the ball in the hand.

The prohibited *atxiki* shot is harder to identify than one would think. It facilitates control over the ball and disguises the lack of power, strength, and splendor of the hit. Despite the fact that it is normally caught by the referee (who penalizes it) or by the public (who shows its disapproval through various signs of protest), the *atxiki* is executed in all types of hits, whether they are final shots or a simple series of hits. It is especially used in defensive play and hooks where the ball passes over the head of the player. Contrary to what one may think, it is variously executed without distinction by backcourt as well as frontcourt players, although it is normally the latter who are more suspect, given that the shot enables play without great physical resources.

The *atxiki* neutralizes indarra. It makes it possible to control the ball without excessive strength, and foments spectacular play in the *cuadros alegres*, the "happy squares" of the fronton (the frontcourt squares) because it gives the ball direction and velocity. It is a great advantage for "foxes." Nevertheless, one may hit an *atxiki* from the back of the court as well, by slipping the ball on the wrist and the palm in the common but unpopular *caceo*.[26]

Despite its almost permanent presence and the fact that it did not used to be a penalized practice in the game, the *atxiki* is now considered by most an illicit and tremendously hurtful maneuver for the game. It is an obvious disadvantage for those players who opt for a scrupulous, traditional way of playing, as it infringes upon a fundamental precept: the equality of opportuniy. Many of the greatest pelotaris complained about the *atxiki* in the 1970s, a period when this hit was excessively tolerated.

The style of some of the players whose repertoire included the *atxiki* used to delight the crowd. The "happy squares" ignited sparks and the spectacle turned the *atxiki*, retention, into a lesser evil. The players of great power realized that pelotaris who normally would not score two points against them were now beating them, despite "leaving their hands in the game" or playing so hard that their hands suffered. They called

---

26. Translator's note: From *cazo* (ladle), which is how the hand is used.

on the federation to make the companies clarify who played with *atxiki* and who did not, resolving the matter in the following way: *player A* (hand-"atxiki") and *player B* (hand) against *player C* (hand) and *player D* (hand-"atxiki"). This proposal was heavily criticized and the federation ignored the petition. Nevertheless, the clean versus dirty debate continued between players and spectators alike and, despite the companies' reticence, in the late 1980s it was concluded that the *atxiki* constituted a degeneration of the hand modality. It was thus prohibited on courts, just as it had always been in the plazas.

Miguel Pelay Orozco records an anecdote by Luis Ecenarro. The story happened at the *konsejupe* of Elgoibar. A doubles game with an important bet at stake was organized. One of the players, a well-known industrialist in the area, returned a ball with a *slight delay* that flew furiously from the ceiling.[27] The large amount of money riding on the game prevented the public from taking a stand on this, although debate did rage over the issue. The nervous industrialist asked the opinion of the crowd, but all in vain until people noticed that Albixuri, a peasant "famous for his scrupulous nature and philosophic, rural maxims," was also present at the game. The industrialist asked him: "*Zen izan dok?*" (Tell me, then, what was it?) And the peasant, says Pelay Orozco, unable to escape the verdict, responded quietly: "*Txingarra izan balitz, lenago botako zenuan*" (If it was live coal, you would have dropped it sooner).[28]

Grabbing the ball (*ertsi*), the power that closure implies, the feeling of ownership and empowerment, and the effortless direction of the ball where one wants it is a safe, simple, and easy way of hitting. It may result in spectacular play that is impossible to achieve by playing clean, but it is a foul sanctioned each time it is recognized. This is why jai alai, a modality that retains the ball in the tool for a few seconds, was heavily criticized when it first emerged.

One of the rules of the *punta-volea* modality played with the *xistera*, a predecessor of jai alai, is that the ball should not stop in its movement. The moment the ball touches the frame of the tool, it must be lifted up: when the ball stops, or "dies," the game stops. A modality like this, in which the ball died during play and in which the *atxiki* became its most

---

27. The typical *atxiki* is executed when the ball flies over the head of the player. It is impossible to hit it back well so it reaches the frontis, and this is why it is grabbed. It is a clear fault.

28. Pelay Orozco, *Pelota, pelotari y frontón*, 33.

recognizable feature, did not appear very credible. Therefore, when jai alai became popular in frontons in the Americas (especially in Argentina and Uruguay), the game of *punta-volea* against wall that was played in Iparralde came to be called *Joko-garbi* (clean play), to make a clear distinction between the two.

Not that the game that evolved from *punta-volea* would lack the *atxiki*. All the games in Iparralde maintain a discreet affair with retention. After all, the movement of the *xistera* in rebote and *joko-garbi* is called *atxikitxikia* (small retention), as opposed to the *atxikihaundia* (grand retention) of the jai alai basket. The extent of detention nevertheless implies a qualitative difference that is rooted in the ease with which one can control, receive, and strike the ball. There is more time at the body's disposal to return the ball, allowing as many as two steps between the reception and the launching of the ball. Retention enables more forceful hits, and faster and better positioned balls.

With its features of regular, measured movements of the body and the head-spinning speed of the ball, jai alai struck a chord with the tastes of the era and was, for decades, a most profitable spectacle for Basque companies in the Basque diaspora communities. Indeed, in the United States it was termed "the fastest game in the world."[29]

Spectators in the Basque Country, however, were less enthusiastic about jai alai, despite the fact that it came to offer a typical and remunerative career option for many young men in eastern Bizkaia. There is still a certain degree of suspicion about it among fans of the other modalities. They often refer to it as the most accessible of the modalities, the easiest for pelotaris of little talent: "His father made him try all the modalities, but he wasn't even worth it as a *puntista* (jai alai player)." Such disparaging comments show what is considered most deplorable in the game of pelota: laziness and apathy.

In pelota, effort is everything. The Basque language even links it to the idea of work, calling the worker *nekazaria*: "he who tires, who exercises, and produces fatigue."[30] Suffering is considered the ideal itinerary to an honest and noble character whereas jai alai, which allowed many young players to earn prodigious sums of money without great effort, was not considered all that meritorious.

---

29. Jai alai was advertised in the US with this slogan. So much so that a documentary made by Charles Allen in 1984 was titled: "Jai-alai: The Fastest Game in the World."

30. Salaverría, *La gran enciclopedia vasca*, 120.

Maybe this mistrust for jai alai and what it implies—the execution of the *atxiki* in a tool, the paradigm of winning without effort, and embezzlement—contributed to the great obsession with *postures* that exist in the world of this modality. A pelotari who has little capacity to suffer seeks to make the game easier for himself; to this end he would play in postures that are considered "dirty" or "ugly." The purification of style, of the disposition of the body as it receives the ball, thus compensated for the long, extended strikes of jai alai. A jai alai player told me with certain embarrassment that, when he was a child, his father woke him up early on weekends to go and train at the fronton. There, in the middle of the village, in front of everyone, the first half an hour of training was dedicated to doing postures with the basket, without the ball. Measuring steps and positioning the body. Seeking beauty, style.

"Style itself, inasmuch as it is a characterization of a personal way of expressing beauty, is beyond the common people in the areas of painting, literature, music, etc. Nevertheless, they know what is thanks to bullfighting."[31] Tierno Galván is absolutely correct in his assessment, which can be applied equally to pelota. In almost all of the passionate conversations on the game I had with fans, independent of the modality, they ended up acting out with gestures the hits that most captivated them. And these postures were often linked to particular players. With time, I recognized that when an interlocutor jumped up to simulate hits, the memory of its beauty seized him and he needed to externalize emotion by acting it out with his body. At this point, changing the course of conversation was impossible. The only way to continue was if I ended up performing some posture at the request of my interlocutor, who avidly corrected the disposition of my body, my own style.

Pelota's style shows above all in the shot. The way of running the court, of moving around lightly is something much appreciated, but what defines style is the way the player hits the ball, the shape the body takes before the shot. To ensure, as Retegi II did of Barriola, that "the encounter with the ball is an impressive one,"[32] the whole body must act in unison with time toward the ball, with courage, moving toward it, taking all the span of the arm and keeping the trunk straight and solid, while the open hand hits the ball at the approximate height of the body, no matter

---

31. Tierno Galván, *Desde el espectáculo a la trivialización*, 68.
32. Statement to the press.

what span the arm has with respect to it. After all, the larger the *arch* of possible shots,[33] the greater capacity the player has to do damage. If this is allied with a good wrist that directs the ball well and lends it velocity in the moment of the hit, the player will be practically infallible.

Beyond the efficiency of the shot, which no doubt has something to do with its beauty, style defines the disposition of the body with relation to the ball. The clean, tough encounter with the ball is ideal. "One must hit the ball even if it hurts," as suffering is playing clean. An aesthetic I will further discuss in the next chapter.

While playing, therefore, the player must hit the ball and may not grab it. Although it was picked by the player who was favored by chance or by the one who has won the previous set, the mediating element must remain autonomous while it is in motion. The pelotari, who has demonstrated that he is competent (*eskudun*), has raised his hand to the public, and has offered it to his rival, may not grab the ball while it is in play. He may not grab or control it illegally and prejudice the other.

If the ball is hit in a clean way, they say that a noble fight has developed between the pelotaris. Nobleness, as I will show, is the superlative quality used to refer to the three principal elements of the game: pelotari, pelota, and fronton. It is a quality that, while it could define concrete examples, emerges in the contact between them. It is contact that reveals the value of a hit.

---

33. By *arch* I mean the lateral movement of the arm, from the body up to the head.

8

The Ball: Culture Objectified

The ball assumes its role in a game by means of a long process. The first step is its fabrication: a nucleus of rubber wrapped around with wool and thread, on which a leather coat is sewn. Once it is ready, its nature must be discovered and it must be broken in for the game. If the *pelotero* (ball maker) finds it suitable, he sends it along with the other chosen balls to the company, which charges its "material selector" with the task of carrying out his own process of selection. The select balls are displayed in public at the same fronton where the game will be played in a few days. If the game is on Sunday, it is the preceding Thursday; if the game is on Saturday, it is on Wednesday that the players are publicly convened so that they each pick two of the ten selected balls. They put the four balls into a wooden, sealed box, which they trust to the custody of a federation delegate or "keeper of the balls" until the game starts. Once the players have run onto the court and have warmed up, he brings the box onto the court and opens it before everybody's eyes.

The players take *their* balls and try them out for a few minutes, until the referee calls them to put them into a basket, where they will be kept under his custody during the whole game. A coin is flipped to decide the lucky player who may choose the ball with which he wants to execute the privilege that chance granted him: the serve. He bounces it and throws it against the frontis; before serving, he hands it over to his opponent so that he may touch it, try it, and in the end *recognize* it. When the player who returns the serve is ready, he hands the ball over to the one who serves. The server, after bouncing it a few times, walks over to the side line, bounces the ball by the serve line, and hits it against the frontis. From this point on and until one of the players scores twenty-two, the player who wins a point gets to choose any of the four balls in the basket, hands it over to his opponent and, when he gets it back, serves with it. Once the game is over, the balls become an object of desire for the public, with people wanting to take them home with the signatures of players on the leather coat. The ball will always fully evoke the event: the players who participated, their actual physical shape, the fronton in which the game was played, the *pelotero* who made it, and so on.

During the event, the ball is the ultimate indicator of the game: it determines if a shot is good or a fault, if the score goes to one way or the other; the player who gets to serve; if the odds ratio is closing or widening. It mediates between the players, defines their position in the court, drives the actions of the referee, and determines and generates levels of crowd passion. The ball is the baton of the game. Depending of its position, the tools remain expectant or in full action. Every movement at the fronton is determined by the route of the ball. The ball "bows down . . . ordering place and player as in figured dance."[1]

Culture versus Identity

> The conclusion of the cromlech, its role in our tradition, is what Unamuno attempted to find, and which he himself had forgotten: it is by forging the individual soul, producing individual souls that the Basque collective soul is created.
>
> — Jorge Oteiza

One of the most determining characteristics of the game considered by all as *Basque* is precisely the consistency and firmness of the balls. The firmness of the ball has been considered fundamental when it comes to defining the Basque game. There are many games played at frontons that have not been considered Basque pelota precisely because their balls have not come to the expectations of solidity and weight. This solidity is symbolically associated with the leather that covers the ball: leather ball, firm ball, Basque ball. This identification has been primordial during the history of the game; even today, it greatly differentiates one modality from the other. Nevertheless, the leather itself does not forge the character of the pelota. It may differentiate it from *other* games like tennis, but it does not facilitate the understanding either of its practical or symbolic complexity.

---

1. Rilke in De Man, *Allegories of Reading*, 44.

Analyzing the ball in terms of its differences from the balls of other sports or games, we may infer that the Basque ball is different, and it suggests an identification with values like force, suffering, and perseverance. The symbol made icon offers a compact, monolithic image when, in reality and interpreted more profoundly, it is capable of showing us all the explicative powers it has: its proceedings, suitability, versatility, teachings, meanings, and even contradictions.

The pelota is covered with leather, but what makes it solid is not the leather; the *goxua*[2] ball is also made of leather. What gives it consistency is the proportion between its materials (rubber, wool, and leather), and above all its plastic interior, the *potro*. Therefore, what seems revealing from the perspective of understanding the Basque game is that the pelota acquires meaning from its inside, not outside.

We cannot infer the distinctiveness of a pelota by comparing it to the balls of other games; we can, however, compare it to other pelotas and see how it differs from them. Its sound, its relationship with the pelotari, and its character lends meaning to each ball of the Basque game. Beyond these, of course, the pelotas do share features that differentiate them as a group from the balls of other games.

The ball is not defined by its firmness; all professional balls are firm. The ball is defined by its diameter, its bounce—medium bounce, lively, or dead—and, more than anything, its sound and the way it thrusts into the hand of the player; the way it hurts. Emphasizing the hardness of the ball against those of other sports implies defining it against the outside, locating identity in the center of the definition. This way, however, the scope of meaning that this element really concentrates is lost, along with a clear example of what culture really is: not a homogenous whole but rather an open possibility of encounter with the world, of experience.

All the balls used in the Basque game are made of the same material and measure and weigh roughly the same. They differ qualitatively, however, the moment that they are made for use by different subjects, by individuals who want to subtract different powers from them, and who want to communicate with the other, to discover him (*hunt him down*). Players who want to present themselves in their own particular way.

The player does with the ball what each person does with culture: people adjust it to their own singularity, exploit it in their authentic way,

---

2. Literally "sweet." They are softer, and are used by children when they learn the game and by amateur adults.

and make themselves into persons through this acquisition. Culture is identified with the world of Schutzian life where "reality is constituted through the *meaning of our experiences* and not through the structure of objects."[3] Culture is that *through which* we constitute ourselves as subjects; and while culture channels toward a characteristic way of doing, thinking, and acting, it does not determine those activities. Culture is a road that precedes us, yes, but we need to travel through it. To be sure, a road is just a traveled being.

The Ecstatic Personality of the Pelotari

The ball needs the player to develop its own essence as a ball. Anyone may recognize a ball even if it is not used. It is normal for pelotas of important contests to be displayed along with *txapelas* and trophies in the showcases of museums and private collections. Nevertheless, the real personality of the ball is not its roundness, nor its composition, nor its firmness; it is the movement that it acquires in its encounter with the hand or the tool of the player at the fronton. The ball's character, its very nature, reveals itself only when it bounces, when it is hit; later, it is capable of containing and transmitting in its physicality the memory of that movement. That someone should grab it with his hands and strike it against the stone wall of a fronton—this is what lends the ball its real nature.

The pelotari depends on the ball in the same way. The grace that players are assumed to possess manifests itself through the way the ball enters the pelotari's hand. His manner of confronting the ball defines the player's style: he is honest if he does not try to appropriate it, if the ball does not stick to his hand (if he does not grab it), and if the hit is clean. He *has power* if he manages to hit the ball with compulsion, if he controls it with force; he *enjoys his game* if the ball leaves his hand with ease, if he connects with it well, if he hits it long comfortably. He *approaches the ball well* if he correctly calculates the distance he needs before he reaches the ball.

The player plays with the ball, he uses it as the only way to express his attributes, he shows his qualities through the ball. The player executes through the medium of the ball, just as the brain executes through the medium of the hand. The ball is the extension of the pelotari: it fulfills the idea of the player beyond his physical body.

---

3. Lamo de Espinosa, *La sociología del conocimiento y de la ciencia*, 403. Emphasis added.

This acquires significance if we consider that each ball is unique. In case of most sports, the ball is standardized and uniform; yet in Basque pelota each ball is a unique, a distinctive creation. The player seeks for each game a ball that best fits his powers and specific strategies. The balls are handmade, one by one, from beginning to end, without any production-line manufacturing. Each ball is different from the rest, which is why they have a process of selecting the balls: First the ball maker himself, who sends what he considers most suitable for the game to the company. Then the selectors, who choose them depending on the fronton and the players who are going to play the game, always with the interests of the company in mind. And finally the players, who are aware of their own resources as well as those of their rivals and the fronton where the game will be played.

Often when a pelotari is losing a game and then recovers it through a change of serve, it is said that he has encountered the ball. "Encountering" or "finding" the ball is playing with the one that best accommodates your own game and least your rival's. Encountering the right ball is very important, as an anecdote of Jesús Abrego, the magician of the remonte modality illustrates. During a game played in 1942 at the Recoletos fronton in Madrid with Mina I (Martin Olloquiegui) against a trio formed by Azpiroz I (Dionisio Azpiroz), Salsamendi III (Jose María Salsamendi), and Iturain (Juan Iturain), he sent the ball into the buffer (the upper part of the frontis), and it got stuck. He then started to lose to such a degree that he decided to shoot the ball they were playing with toward the same place and another one got stuck; finally, he hit it and managed to get it to rebound off the wall. Once he recovered *his* ball, he won the game with considerable advantage.

It is often the case that once the player has encountered a ball that he likes but which has lost its "ideal state," he tries to remake it or asks a ball maker to remake it. As it is the proportion between the nucleus and the wrapping that gives the ball its quality—and it is precisely this latter feature that wears away and loses consistency—the ball maker readjusts the wool and sews the leather together again. This practice was common even after the game became formalized, because the player was allowed to bring his own balls to a game as long as they matched the required format and were approved by the referee.

The extreme variability of the material becomes a great source of creativity and conflict, inasmuch as the balls may decide a game supposedly played between equals; it may also equalize a game played between rivals of different levels. They are common sources of dispute; so much so that there have been cases in which the balls had to be dismantled and observed to see what they were made of, and to make sure it conformed to the stipulations of the contest. Now, however, the companies determine the type of the balls offered to the players to choose from. The ball therefore becomes for them a fundamental weapon of control. Well selected, unequal players may play against one another; it may enhance the game of the company's favorites, break the meteoric ascension of a player, and thus sooth his constant desire for a pay raise.

Beyond the possible manipulation that it allows, the diversity of the balls constitutes one of the most definite and significant features of the sport. It not only extends to the ritual process and its capacity to congregate, but also acquires a value in the formation of the pelotari's personality.

The pelotari is not searching for a fixed object to accommodate his behavior to it; rather, he adjusts the ball—a ball that, like him, is unique—to his own personality. The ball is a clear reflection of the potential of the player who has picked it. It is ecstatic "I" of the player, his personality beyond himself; this is why much of the player's training and formation as a pelotari is devoted to figuring out what type of ball enhances, and what type debilitates, his powers.

The Dialectics of Experience

> The dialectic of experience has its proper fulfillment not in definitive knowledge but in the openness to experience that is made possible by experience itself.
>
> — Hans Georg Gadamer

Hegel defines self-consciousness, the awareness of oneself as "reflection, the return from *otherness*."[4] It is something like an *alter*ed consciousness passing through the sieve of the other. Recall the child walking toward the fronton, with his ball in his pocket, a ball that he hits against the frontis and learns to control while he is growing up. Such play with the ball falls within the category of *jolas*: noncompetitive play whose pleasure lies in repetition. Any ball will do for this kind of play.

---

4. Hegel, *Phenomenology of Spirit*, 313.

It is when the child confronts other players that he starts finding himself as a pelotari. First he incorporates the other's game as his by copying it; then he seeks to differentiate himself from it, thus creating his own personality as player. He simultaneously discovers the balls most suitable for the maximum enhancement of his personality. The child, now a pelotari, plays in the sphere of *joko*: he has developed his own self through the encounter with the other, another who has separated from him. It is in the engagement between the two where the player encounters his own qualities that manifest themselves in the ball he chooses. Until the incorporation of an opponent, the pelotari does not know if his ball is the most fitting one for the game. Unless there is another present at the game, there is neither pelotari nor ball, evidently.[5]

The player forms his personality as a pelotari through engagement with other pelotaris, an engagement that requires the recognition of the self and the other. His personality is constituted on a borderline that he marks out against other personalities; it is a borderline that, in a situation of initial equality and common objective implied by the game, is only delineable by negating the other, by controlling him. It is the disjunction of "you or me" that sustains the dialectic process in which the player is formed. Facing this disjunction, the player seeks to perfect one of the two proto-agonic powers that I have already discussed, and which Hobbes recognized as suitable for overcoming the other: "there exists no other alternative to safeguard oneself that should be as reasonable as *being ahead*, that is, overcoming each person by means of strength or astuteness until there is no other power sufficiently great to be threatening."[6]

---

5. By talking about the presence of the other in the game I do not simply mean physical presence. The child may play against another and remain in the sphere of *jolas*, and may play alone under the *joko* scheme. *Joko*, as opposed to *jolas*, implies a distinct other, who appears to be integrated in the game even if he is not physically present. In a game played alone with one's own ball, which is considered ideal for the development of the pelotari's qualities, the other is implicit. The ball is the ecstatic "I," outside of the self, when the other is incorporated as other, not before. Pelotari identity is constructed through confrontation, while later it materializes in the ball, and the player may confront himself in the culmination of the solitary play described in chapter 5 that serves to develop his skills and purge his defects.

Through confrontation, he measures his possibilities and understands his own attributes, and this is put to test even in the absence of another player. The ball is now not just any ball but the one that the player considers most fitting for the development of his game, a game that implies the other even if he is not physically there.

6. Hobbes, quoted in Subirats, *El alma y la muerte*, 373.

These powers, which allow the player to get ahead of the other while at the same time developing his own character as pelotari, materialize in the ball, in this object that serves as mediation, as encounter with the other. The ball includes in its composition its own layout, its own presentation; *sizing up*, the incorporation of the other therefore precedes the game itself.

At the selection of material at the four-and-a-half mark finals of 2002, Barriola already knew that it would be very difficult to break Olaizola II. He did not find the ideal balls for the development of his game in the basket, and he expressed his disappointment to the media: "I haven't found what I wanted," "they are balls that are now worn out and by the middle of the game at this fronton they will be even more worn out." When it comes to choosing ball, the fronton becomes an important factor. The Labrit in Iruñea-Pamplona, the fronton that Barriola was talking about, is a rough court that *eats* the ball, that wears it out. Barriola needed a lively ball that would allow him to develop a powerful fast game that wouldn't let the opponent catch his breath, that would not let him think. This was especially important, given that his opponent was Olaizola II, the fox among the foxes who likes heavy balls of medium bounce that allow him to move around and manage the ball with purpose—ultimately "driving the opponent crazy" and "making him lose his footing." Each player, great pelotaris as they are, knows which ball represents him, which ball is suitable for the neutralization of the other; thus it is not necessary for the other to be present when they test the ball. They try the ball out alone in the frontis and they know immediately if it is adequate for the maximum exploitation of their qualities, for overcoming their opponent. Therefore, a power pelotari, with strength, a lion, will look for a ball that makes it difficult for his opponent to reach it, while a fox will choose balls that allow him to move around his rival. In that 2002 final, Barriola complained that he could not find a sufficiently lively ball to fight against Olaizola II. "With these balls, backcourt players like me might as well stay at home," he said, clearly referring to the fact that the balls favored play on the front squares.

The two proto-*agonic* powers of the fight prefer different balls, just as the qualities they use to beat their rivals also differ. Lions usually lean toward balls "with *potro*" or balls that bounce off the frontis forcefully so that the frontcourt player cannot intercept them. Their favorite balls hurt the hand so much and are so little manageable that only strong players can handle them. Foxes on their part prefer balls that *jump* on the frontis, which do not evade them and bounce to the backcourt,[7] and that allow them to execute any intrigue that comes to their mind. The fox wants to *take the ball*, and he does not want it to warm up; if it loses its shine and becomes bouncy, it will allow the other to reach it more easily. The lion tries to prevent the fox from thinking, and the fox tries to prevent the lion from comfortably reaching the ball, thus neutralizing his strength. That said, beyond such generalizations, a lion like Barriola with his exceptional movement is very different from another lion like Beloki, who had the best arms in the league but who moved around less easily on the sides. The former would choose lively balls that trample on the opponent, while the latter would choose ones that fly low and barely rise at all. Similarly, a fox like Titín III, who is famous for his finish-offs and playing in the air, has nothing in common with another fox like Retegi II, who used to control the bounce perfectly. These are important considerations, besides the variable of where one plays, and against whom.

While every pelotari has an idea of the type of ball that most suits him, sometimes they make a mistake and choose better balls for their opponents than they themselves could have chosen. Quite often the chosen ball turns out to be a better weapon for the opponent than for the selector. Many players reach final scores (twenty-two) with the opponent's ball, which suggests that fathoming the ball becomes a principal challenge for the pelotari, and a great mystery for the game. The ball is the result of the construction of the pelotari through the experience of others; this construction is never finalized as the possibility of a new encounter, of a new arrangement of the self against the interpellation of the other, remains open.

The process of understanding the ball and, by extension, understanding oneself as a pelotari never ends. It never ends, it never turns into an absolute control of the object, whether the ball or the opponent. Understanding must be adjusted in each present. They say that a good pelotari knows how to pick the ball conveniently. They also say that an exceptional player knows how to overcome an adverse ball. Retegi II was an expert in playing the rival's ball more than his opponent did, as

---

7. Translator's note: the original Spanish *quitar* "remove, take away." In pelota terms this means not allowing the frontcourt player to enter the game through high and backward balls. The frontcourt player therefore wants balls that do not allow the backcourt player to marginalize or neutralize him in such a manner.

he was able to accommodate to new circumstances and reinterpret them during the course of the game.

The pelotari must be capable of emptying and opening himself to the encounter. He is a liminal being, always susceptible to transformation, to *alte*rnatives, inasmuch as he intensively inhabits this "living through," outside of himself, which for Turner is experience.[8] Retegi II affirmed: "Now that I have retired I realize that pelota is like life. Outside of the court everything happens slowly. Inside, in the tenth of a second."[9]

Like all games, pelota is a privileged realm in which we discover a dialectic process that is experience, and that constitutes life for human beings. But it is mostly in the ball, the mediating element that lends the game its name, where we find one of the most revealing symbols of what culture is: the possibility of encounter and opening up to the other and, simultaneously, an access to oneself, to a consciousness that is always oriented to being *alte*red.

The Aesthetic Ethic

> We are confronted with a series of "affective participations" made of emotions, of sentiments, of anger and joy that we share with those of his tribe within the frame of a generalized aesthetics. In the best of circumstances and in the worst, we "vibrate" together, and enter in a symphony (A. Schutz) with the other.
>
> — Michel Maffesoli

The pelotaris *size each other up*, meet and recognize each other through the ball, an instrument that is a projection of the person who has chosen it. The ball is the ecstatic "I" of the player, his personality outside of himself; it is at the same time the beginning of the encounter between two players. It reveals the self and establishes communication between both persons. Fundamental intermediary of the game, the ball is link, encounter, and relation.

Gadamer interprets play as a dialectic practice that always follows an unusual path; he also stresses that it is independent of those who play. Play imposes tasks on the players that have nothing to do with the very

---

8. Turner, *From Ritual to Theatre*, 18.

9. Julián Retegi II (hand pelota champion), interview by author, Bilbao (Bizkaia), October 16, 2002.

being of the player, but rather with play itself. This is precisely what absorbs the player and thus completes play itself: "Play is structure; this means that despite its dependence on being played it is a meaningful whole which can be repeatedly represented as such and the significance of which can be understood. But structure is also play, because—despite this theoretical unity—it achieves its full being only each time it is played."[10]

Caillois also subscribes to the idea of play as a closed, autonomous, and self-sufficient totality based on one of its secondary meanings: the totality of figures, symbols, and instruments that are necessary for the functioning of the conjunction or the set (for example, card games). The game itself responds to "an idea of totality, complete and immutable, conceived in a way that it functions without any intervention other than the energy that moves it."[11]

Nevertheless, both authors admit that the player is part of a whole that play needs to gain meaning to complete itself. Without the player there is no play. From this necessary originality emerges another meaning, one that Callois takes from the French *jeu*, style, a way a musician or actor interprets a piece; a meaning that the Basque *jo* also shares.

Jo shares many of the meanings that Huizinga relates to play through his overview of terms and their range of meaning in various languages.[12] Probably a descendent of the Latin *iocus, iocari*, whose specific meaning is joke or prank, the Basque *jo*, while it maintains this *jocose* meaning, also refers to struggle, to music, and to sex. Beyond the polysemy of the term *jo*, which could be further elaborated, what is interesting here is that *jo* constitutes the root of words that generally refer to the moral and ethical realm. Therefore, *jokaera*, literally "manner of playing," means conduct; *jokabide*, "process of play," behavior; and *joera*, "manner of hitting," means tendency or inclination. Behavior becomes directly related with ways of play, which may be the reason why the verb *joan* or "go," also shares the root *jo*, a verb whose first meaning is "to hit."

The pelotari's style is revealed by how he connects with the ball, how he confronts it, and how he strikes it. The overall disposition of his body at the encounter with the ball, the posture he adopts, and the

---

10. Gadamer, *Truth and Method*, 116.

11. Caillois, *Los juegos y los hombres*, 9. Translated from the introduction in the Spanish edition, which does not appear in the English edition *Man, Play, and Games*.

12. Huizinga, *Homo Ludens*, 28–46.

vigor of his volleys reveal the pelotari's technique as well as his *jokaera*, his conduct. Various attributes converge in his "manner of play": his dexterity, his art as much as his ethic, and the way he carries himself are all paradigmatically revealed through the encounter with the ball.

Marcel Mauss first reflected on how society marks the individual in his use of the body. He points out out that corporal techniques are a way by which culture imprints itself on the body, by which idiosyncratic modes of conduct are transmitted, which is related to a concept of the world that sustains culture.[13] Some authors refer to this disposition as "memory habit," a memory that allows tradition to be deposited in our body, the same way as style and gestures are not rationalized but are learned and reproduced without thinking about them.[14] The absence of rationalization, however, does not imply automatic incorporation. Each culture has an archetypical way of using the body, a body whose constitution responds to a model as a depository of a characteristic ethos. Within it, there exist prototypes that correspond to classifications of group, gender, class, and so forth, granting each subject a singular way of expression, countenance.

Turner also affirms that the cultural depository of illiterate societies is transmitted orally or by the reiterated observation of standard behavioral patterns. At the same time, he does not pretend to deny each subject's originality in the appropriation of this provision of meanings. Rather, he intends to prove the efficiency of certain mechanisms in their transmission. Technique, as Mauss argues, is one of these mechanisms; it also provides a guide for ethical judgment.[15] Gadamer also ascribes to this conjunction between technique and morality, arguing that both consist of knowing how "to apply what has been learned in a general way to the concrete situation."[16]

It is exactly in the technique, in the ball-pelotari encounter, that the pelotari's own style as well as the real essence of the game is paradigmatically discovered. The spectator experiences the beauty of the game in the *well* executed strike in which the player's energies are all transmitted into the ball. It is certainly a specific contact, a specific style of hitting

---

13. Mauss, *Sociology and Psychology*, 97–105.
14. See Connerton, *How Societies Remember*.
15. Mauss, *Sociology and Psychology*, 97–105.
16. Gadamer, *Truth and Method*, 314.

the ball, which fits the fan's idea of a good strike, even if each hit is unique in its own way. Not all strikes meet this ideal, evidently, but they are easy to identify. They are discovered in the emotions they provoke, because they electrify the spectator, who flings his torso in the air, rests on his chest, and emits a laugh, a yell, or offers applause. They are moves that create moments of communion, moments of *jolas*, in which the crowd undergoes a certain catharsis that makes it sound in unison, something like a collective sigh. Maffesoli refers to these moments of emotiveness as eternal moments, highlighting their effectiveness in case of images. Although individual, the image, he observes, "participates in a common, archetypical treasure that works in favor of the dimension of the communion."[17]

Training the gaze to suffer (and sympathize with) the pelotari's strikes in the spectator's body is extended into the iconography of the phenomenon. Statues, paintings, and photos capture these moments in a primordial way. For Barrios, "taking place is filled with meaning," in which one enters the absolute and "tears the lineal continuity of homogenous time."[18] While these images represent specific players with a personal style and characteristic posture, most of them express an ideal way of contact with the ball, a solid and clean style in which the body manages the ball openly, expansively, and honestly; the leg opposite to the striking arm creates unswerving support and keeps the torso firm and upright, while the extended arm runs the parabola elected for the encounter with the ball. This is the exemplary ball that *hurts*, that *punishes* in the Basque game, something that perhaps explains the sparing repercussion, no matter how hard institutions try, of contests with pelotaris from other games such as Valencian or Irish ball games.

For hundreds of years, Basques and Valencians have occasionally challenged each other to games. In recent years, the Basque Federation has initiated encounters with Irish pelota.[19] Nevertheless, such encounters usually meet with only modest success. In case of the Valencian ball game, the contests are currently modified by adopting the Basque hand modality *a blé*, against wall, but reducing both the length of the court

---

17. Maffesoli, *El instante eterno*, 70.

18. Barrios, *Narrar el abismo*, 98, 101.

19. There are references to late nineteenth-century contests *a blé* in New York against American players from established clubs. They probably played handball, Fives, or likely a game descended from it.

as well as the weight of the ball. Despite the adjustments, however, for the most part the game becomes impracticable. Either the Basque dominates the Valencian through his series of hits, or the Valencian obliges the Basque to rebound, something he is incapable of doing. There is no encounter between equals because they do not play the same game, because their techniques are irremediably different.

The Basque crowd feels that the Valencian's way of hitting the ball is dirty or, what amounts to the same thing, ugly. The spectators are indignant when the player throws himself on the ball and plays it of *botivolea*,[20] with fainthearted arms. Even the serve seems illicit. If the Basque scores as a result of a robust strike, it looks logical; if the Valencian executes a forceful cut that "dries," or dies in the court and does not bounce, it looks unfair. The Basque spectator does not understand the Valencian's game, it does not carry him away, he is not taken by the fronton. A mixed contest of this type may at the very most satisfy the patriotic tastes of the crowd, but it will barely provide them an aesthetic experience. As Maffesoli argues, "aesthetics is a way of feeling in common. It is also a means of recognizing ourselves;"[21] the Basque spectator does not recognize himself in the game of the Valencian player, while he might be able to enjoy it in its own context.

It is when the ideal becomes real that the spectator gets carried away by play. He discovers in the pelotari a hit, a strike, that makes him think that "it is," in the words of Gadamer, "the truth of our own world—the religious and moral world in which we live—that is presented before us and in which we recognize ourselves."[22] The spectator feels this way only when he sees styles that, despite being unique, resemble how he understands the game of pelota. His ideal becomes reality in play, hierophany that corroborates the reality of this ideal, the validity and permanence of his convictions. This belief turned certainty is, moreover, shared by the rest of the crowd that, like him, gets exalted by contemplating the beauty of the encounter between player and ball.

A holistic recognition is thus produced, a kind of mystic participation in which everything becomes one: the spectator, the rest of the spectators who, like him, experience the ideal in a hit that is part of the whole, just

---

20. Translator's note: *botivolea* refers to a hit at the height of the chest once the ball has bounced. It is a controversial hit inasmuch as it is associated with the *atxiki*.

21. Maffesoli, *The Time of the Tribes*, 77.

22. Gadamer, *Truth and Method*, 124.

as the player who strikes, as well the ball, the fronton, and the rest of the game's components. Everything enters into a communion, becomes united in a totality that remains one in each of its elements, beyond the moment and space in which it is produced.

The total contexture through a shared feeling is what Maffesoli calls "the ethic of aesthetics," an aggregating force, a *glutinum mundi*, which varies through time and culture.[23] Nietzsche refers to it as a "table of values," and exemplifies it with four cultural styles: Greek, Persian, Jewish, and German. Of the Greek case Zarathustra says: "'Always shalt thou be the foremost and prominent above others: no one shall thy jealous soul love, except a friend'—that made the soul of a Greek thrill: thereby went he his way to greatness."[24]

If we recognize pelota as one of the rituals in which Basque aesthetic ethics is expressed, we must mention nobleness as the value that all the elements of the whole share. It is an agglutinating value par excellence, whose preeminent meaning is just that: the fact of agglutinating in itself. In the Basque game, the adjective noble is used to qualify persons, frontons and balls.

According to Victor Turner, the holy and sacred objects of different societies function as mnemonic exercises in order to remember cosmologies, values, and cultural axioms. They serve to affect the transmission of profound knowledge from one generation to the other.[25] Cassirer also sets forth the necessity to transubstantiate certain pure significations into beings or things so that consciousness may register them. The meaning of the adjective *noble* is embodied, is understood precisely when it qualifies a fronton or a ball as such.

There are many types of balls: sprouting, lively, moderate bounce, dead, dancing, delicate, middling fine, or reinvigorated. All of them, however, are expected to have a requirement in common: that they are noble. This is why the pelotari *tames* them. A noble ball does not have strange ways; it bounces directly and follows the player's directions. A noble ball "allows playing." It must submit itself to the mandates of the player, move when it is ordered to, and depart as intended by the player's strike. Its ultimate mission is to make the encounter possible, to facilitate

---

23. Maffesoli, *El instante eterno*, 34.
24. Nietzsche, *The Gay Science*, 55.
25. Turner, *Dramas, Fields and Metaphors*, 239.

it. The ball thus demonstrates its nobleness and becomes an exemplary model.

The ball is an element that represents and links all that composes the ritual in a most effective manner. As a fundamental mediator, the ball guides the narrative plot; not only the narrative of what precedes the game, as I argued before, but also that of the game itself. In the game, the point on the scoreboard depends on it, on where it is, and where it bounces. It is through the medium of the ball that the pelotaris reveal themselves. The player suffers the strength or the astuteness of his rival not directly but through the ball; through the ball's direction, velocity, and effect. The ball also incorporates in its constitution the characteristics of the player who chose it. The ball regulates contact between the player and the referee, which engages or silences the crowd. As the spine of the game, it connects the court brain with terrace nerve endings. Striking the iron sheet destroys the hopes of many bettors; through its defiant route on the fronton, the ball provokes uncontrollable emotions or absolute boredom. The ball is also the element that exemplifies, through its direct bounce, how the player should conduct himself. The ball must be noble: it must depart as desired by the pelotari. It may not have strange ways; it must facilitate an honest, open encounter. The player must behave the same way.

This stock of meanings and significations endows the ball with great importance: it endows it with the capacity to become the element that lends the ritual its name. The ball is the element that summarizes the game: its era, the fronton, the physical condition of the player who chose the ball and also his rival's, the person who fabricated it, the particular interests of the company who entrusted him with the job, and many other things that may be deduced from its meticulous analysis.

Retegi II, fourteen-time hand pelota champion, keeps the balls with which he played these finals. When he takes one of these balls in his hands, the ball is not merely an object with which he played the final of this or that year; the ball *is* the final of that year. He sees in it his physical condition during that moment, the attributes of his rival, the fronton, and the era in which the game was played. A review of the balls may demonstrate the changes the game has generally undergone, as well as the particular evolution of the champion. It would be hard to find a more significant concretion of such moments.

9

The Plaza: The Embodiment of Society

> Urban structure is nothing but a topologic projection of styles of liberties into urban space and time.
> — Abraham A. Moles

The pelotaris meet and recognize each other through the ball. It is in the alternative interchange of the ball where the player's personality is constructed—a personality that emerges in the type of ball he prefers. Despite this unshakeable and definite link between ball and player, it is not the ball that represents the pelotari; rather, it is the hand, that open hand that greets the public before the beginning of the game, and which concentrates his entire being as a pelotari. On the webpage of the hand modality players' union Eskutik ("from the hand"), the photos of the players appear together with images of their hands. It is the hand that shakes that of the rival, that swears honesty in the game and, most importantly, it is the hand that hits the ball.

The pelotari's hand perpetuates contact with the ball. His hand is living memory of the continuous blows to which it is submitted. Sports medicine specialist Ander Letamendia asserts that "the simple inspection of a hand is enough to determine if a person has played the hand modality for an extended period of time or not. There is a host of typical deformations that the dominant hand or, if he is ambidextrous, both hands of the player show. The most frequent bone-related deformation is a deviation of the third phalanx bone of the little finger toward the center of the hand."[1] This deformation constitutes one of the most marked features

---

1. Letamendia, *El pelotari y sus manos*, 138.

of pelotari identity[2] and, as such, it is a source of pride for he who possesses it. It is thus not surprising that the fingers should be displayed with the aim of legitimizing a particular opinion. This crooked little finger is an accrediting record of the experiences of its owner, revealing in and of itself an *expert* and therefore authorized opinion.

The hand represents the pelotari. But it is only through contact with the ball that his personality, his style, is revealed. Because of its crucial importance in the process of player formation, the ball itself has been associated with the pelota's culture. An essential mediator of the game, the ball is revered as the principal symbol of the event.

Hand and ball, subject and culture, action and symbol—a third element is missing to complete the basic agreement between the game of pelota, life worlds (Alfred Schutz), and cognitive development (Jean Piaget).[3] Fronton, society, and rule, respectively, constitute the totality, the conjunction, and the articulation of boundaries and their resulting possibilities. It is on their bases that subjects *are*.

I have already discussed the meanings of *jeu*, which Caillois borrows from everyday language to understand play: "in general, these distinct meanings imply ideas of totality, of rule and liberty."[4] The idea of play that establishes and thickens a mutual dependence between law and liberty led Huizinga to postulate that "civilization arises and unfolds in and as play," and that "authentic, pure play is one of the main bases of civilization."[5]

The *joko* play is a paradigmatic example of the imposition of boundaries, because in *joko* a group of individuals submit themselves to fully accepted, shared rules: "all players and spectators must subordinate themselves to rules."[6] The intersubjective acceptance of boundaries is the beginning of any group formation, of any community. As Bernardo Estornés Lasa says, "boundary supports rights and the normative,"[7] something that Lévi-Strauss also claims by considering the rule as a

---

2. The protection that hand pelota players use nowadays prevents this malformation. Even so, most frontcourt players still suffer from the problem.

3. See Schutz, *The Problem of Social Reality*; and Piaget, *The Origins of Intelligence in Children*.

4. Caillois, *Los juegos y los hombres*, 14.

5. Huizinga, *Homo Ludens*, foreword, 5.

6. Duncan, *Symbols in Society*, 328.

7. Quoted in Oteiza, *Quousque Tandem . . . !*, 38.

constitutive phenomenon of society, as a primary manifestation of order.[8]

Norms are most clearly demonstrated at the fronton by the *eskas*, or fault lines. These are the exterior contours of the court, and they establish the limits of where the ball may bounce, the lines themselves being excluded from play.

In games of *blé*, against a wall, the boundaries are fixed. The distance between them depends on the modality, but it is agreed upon it before the game starts, and is not modified during the game. In the long modality games, however, there are some *eskas* or lines that change position depending on how the game develops, and which divide the court in one way or another. Without going into the process of their arrangement, which I have described in chapter 1, these lines have been traditionally called *chazas*; a term that refers to the place where the ball is stopped before it crosses the line at the very back of the court,[9] as well as to the mark that indicates the place in which the ball stops.

The *chaza* commonly exists in most pelota games, and the term has been interpreted in various ways.[10] Without going into these in detail, the *chaza* determines the possibilities of each player to win the point. In the modality of *rebote*, because the fields of serving team and the returning team are unequal, there is the opportunity of changing the field. It is the occasion for the serving team to win the more advantageous field, the area of the return. The line thus assumes a fundamental significance: that of chance.

The rules of a game are a set of possibilities that the game admits, that which may or may not be done within the context of the game. They are the regulation.

There have always been regulations in pelota. Some rules regulate court itself, stipulating the measurements of the fronton, the weight of the balls, and the basic rules of execution, with reference to the pelotaris' instruments. Other more general rules include those on bets and the

---

8. As Eliseo Verón indicated in the "Prólogo a la edición española" of Lévi-Strauss, *Antropología estructural*

9. If it was not stopped, the move would turn into a point, namely, "fifteen." That is why there is a Castilian saying no longer in use to express the fact that one person excels another in a given skill or merit: "*Dar quince a fulano y raya a mengano*" (to give fifteen to so-and-so and to give a line to (keep at bay) so-and-so).

10. See, among others, Arramendy, *Le Jeu, La Balle et Nous*, 86–94; and Taketani, *Investigación sintética sobre la cultura deportiva en el País Vasco*, 129.

responsibilities of referees, bookmakers, *botilleros*, and other actors, even including spectator behavior. Some rules are limited to specific frontons, others to specific modalities, and a few to pelota in general.

Nevertheless, the written rules of the game are little consulted. While they have existed for centuries, the game has not needed them for legitimizing itself. A general consensus about the rules of the game, some rules transmitted from fathers to sons and learned at the fronton, have been until recently sufficient for posters to announce great contests in the following way: "Customary rules will govern": rules that are adjusted to the fronton where the game was to take place.

While pelota has always possessed nomothetical regulation, each space or fronton tailors it to its own configuration. *Locus, regit, actum.* The specific place makes the rules unique, which is logical considering that the properties of the game depend on the very characteristics of the plaza, which may differ significantly from one to the other. Many games rule that it is a point if the ball bounces off the *xare* or roof net without previously bouncing in the court, while in other places a bounce in the court is necessary. There are also frontons like the *konsejupe* of San Nicolás in Algorta, where the lines count, and others where certain strikes are forbidden. The configuration of the plaza thus conditions the rules of the game, the possible conditions that the game offers the players.

This peculiarity was lost with the industrialization of the game, whose perhaps most conspicuous feature is the standardization of frontons. A type of court is established for each modality, and measures and materials regulated. Standardization, however, does not eliminate the exclusive uniqueness of each fronton. Some frontons are faster than others, frontis differ according to their robustness; there are an infinity of variables that render a fronton original. Therefore, although the industrial fronton does not adapt the rules to its structure, the game's possible conditions depend on its idiosyncrasies. The players thus devise and adjust their strategies depending on the fronton in which they have to play. If they play at a rough fronton like that of Labrit in Iruñea-Pamplona, they choose a ball somewhat faster than the one they would choose if they played in Ogueta in Vitoria-Gasteiz. Just as each player has preferences for a specific type of ball, so he will also prefer one fronton over another, depending on his game.

Nevertheless, beyond personal preferences, some frontons are more appreciated than others. They are the rough, hard frontons like the Astelena of Eibar or the Beotibar of Tolosa, frontons where "the ball becomes more ball. "One might say of them that they "invite one to play," that they are *noble* because they facilitate the game: they do not cheat, and they get the best out of the player and the ball.

Again the symbol maintains a tension between its own uniqueness and the very ideal that it supports, and which in certain specific cases appears condensed. Even so, whether in its specific or archetypical aspect, the fronton abides by the rule as a precept of play. Its concrete spatial configuration as well as the generic idea that it expresses the point at the very boundaries within which the game *takes place*. This is why the plaza is a representative image as well as an effective manifestation of the set of rules of pelota.

Postures at the Fronton

> Even if a gentleman should lose his whole substance, he must never give way to annoyance. Money must be so subservient to gentility as never to be worth a thought.
>
> — Fyodor Dostoyevsky, *The Gambler*

In principle, the bodies of the spectators constitute the boundaries of the play sphere, a space that because of its popularity became the public space par excellence, the plaza. The public as a group of spectators is so inherent to the fronton that players often refer to the crowd when they are asked which fronton they prefer. The public of the Astelena in Eibar is famous for its severity; that of the Adarraga in Logroño for its fervor; and that of the Labrit in Iruñea-Pamplona for its cordiality.

Just as the fronton may be considered independent of its crowd, so the latter maintains its particular idiosyncrasy beyond the fronton that it considers its own. Each spectator is a reserve of the exclusive ethos of his province: "I would say that [spectators] from La Rioja are very passionate; Gipuzkoans are more serious and demanding; the Navarrese assimilate well, they are happy and not aggressive; the Bizkaians are very Bizkaian, they love everything; those from Araba I can't comment as the game has lost much of its fan base there."[11]

Just as the uniqueness of each fronton does not contradict the archetypical ideal of the same, so there exists a type of crowd that considers itself the game's very own. This is the crowd that I have labeled

---

11. Retegi II in his comments to Mendigorria, "Julian Retegi."

"traditional"; it is the spectator that is most likely to demonstrate his erudition, respect, and admiration for the game, instead of some unconditional allegiance to a particular player. The traditional spectator is the pride of every *pelotazale*: "There is no public like that of pelota." Serious and respectful of the game as well as the decisions of the referees, the traditional pelota crowd stands out for its impartiality.

Vincente de Monzón praises the composure and moderation of the spectators at a rebote game in Donibane Lohizune (Lapurdi): "the numerous public is waiting impatiently, but without showing it, the referee's decision."[12] He depicts how, despite the great sums of money at stake, the tension created by the bet remains hidden; the fronton teaches self-composure.

Within this general self-composure, however, there are different types of bettors according to the way they wager on the game. The *posture* the bettor adopts, the stand he takes, determines the level of respectability he gains. It becomes a posture in a general sense, which is expanded into two interconnected meanings: one has something to do with the bettor's "knowing how to behave himself," his poise, and his composure; the other with the amount of the bet wagered.

The strong gambler, the *punto* (odds-giver), barely shows his emotions, his inquietudes, his happiness or unease: "no one knows who is suffering. Defeat and victory are assumed with tranquility."[13] Outside, he appears impassive even if a torrent of unease is shaking him within. At most, one perceives his eyes to fall somewhat and he snorts; he might even gently swing his body following the ball, telepathically pushing it toward the frontis during a crucial game.

The *momista* (odds-taker) is a whole different affair altogether; he risks little with the hope of making it big. Many of these kinds of bettors are easily recognizable for their furious gesticulation, their shouting at the players, and challenging the referees' decisions. The television cameras seek out this kind of spectator, the one who jumps up from his seat at the slightest stimulus. However, the really tense bettor is next to him, the one who doesn't move but sits still because he is playing big, maybe bigger than he handle. He is not heard talking about what he has lost, nor does he brag about what he wins. After the game, if asked, he would

---

12. Monzón, "Zazpiak bat."

13. Interview with pelota bettor (names of bettors in the text are withheld by mutual agreement), Bilbao (Bizkaia), February 22, 2002.

answer *parra* ("grapevine"), which means he has neither won nor lost, or *casa* ("house"), which means he has hit the percentage, which may amount to a great sum of money. Either way, he will answer with the most neutral of his entire registry of gestures.

Let's see now the crowd, which I previously divided into two groups. The first type is the person who bets through the bookmakers and principally goes to the game to see if he can cash in some money. The second type goes to the fronton because he is attracted by the novelty and the interest that pelota games offer. Within the first group a fantastic group stands out: the *cátedra*. It is a person that, with a judgment prompted by the contest to take place, comes to fish for the gullible, previously offering smaller or greater odds for this or that faction, depending on his confidence in the skill of the players.

It is a mathematical calculation that cannot fail: *A*, as frontcourt player, will do this and that and will be all over the place; *B* will not be able to counteract his pressure; *C* will defend himself splendidly, and *D* will go crazy and it will be impossible for him to play his game.

Then comes the odds-calling followed by loud cries, and the *wise* ones quickly realize that everything happens the opposite way they anticipated, which results in a tough situation for them. They have to turn their coats, intend to cover their bet with another one in great haste—manipulations whose secrets only those who are extremely knowledgeable about the *art* of betting possess. This is the *cátedra*, perhaps named so as an antiphrasis, given the losses it suffers, and which it will be always ready to suffer. Generally the *cátedra* is composed of serious people who do not scream, intelligent spectators who go to the fronton with the same or only a bit less formality as though they were going to mass. They are people who do not give in to emotions; when they lose they endure the hit, when they win they cash in their price without a word.

The restless public, the real usurers, are those that take the odds and, delighted with the perspective of winning double or more the amount of money they risked, become indignant. They then shout and insult the players because they did not make them win. The suspicion of *tongo*, or the game having been fixed, as a consolation for defeat is common to wise and ignorant bettors alike, but it becomes most odious in that segment of the public that I have called *usurer*.

They are those who, when they win by chance *twenty* five-peseta coins by risking *one*, are dead silent; but they scream blue murder and they call just about everybody a cheat if luck abandons them.[14]

---

14. Peña y Goñi, "El pelotarismo moderno."

These two postures that Peña y Goñi portrays, and to which any *pelotazale* would subscribe, have no doubt influenced the two-sided and contradictory evaluation of the bet; at times it is considered an antisocial element, other times a phenomenon representing one's moral compass. It is either seen as vice, a symptom of egoism and avarice, or as virtue that expresses detachment and a surrender to the event. In fact, until a little while ago it was the *puntos*, the strong bettors, who maintained pelota; even today they are one of the game's major income sources.

There is a difference of status on the terraces as evinced in the postures of the bettors, this time in an economic sense. In other words, the amount of the bet determines the character of the bettor, from the casual to the real *gambler*, by way of those who like a moderate wager. A regular gambler put it to me in the following way: "There are those who come to spend the afternoon, play a few cents low bound, and they leave. They are a delicacy for the bookmaker. They help him cover the *punto*.... Another type is the moderate bettor, the one who enjoys it but can't bet much and he puts limits on himself. And finally, there is the gambler, the one who always plays beyond his means. A unique class. He is born a gambler, he makes and perfects himself."[15]

There is a certain fascination with the *punto*, despite the fact that his addiction to the game is often the subject of gossip, criticism, and jokes—an addiction that the gamblers themselves recognize. Even if he has lost inestimable amounts of money ("it would be nice to make money by doing things you like"), the gambler does not abandon the game because it is for him "vital." Sometimes the bookmaker "does not give you more than what he thinks you can lose," acting absent-mindedly: "he is like your guardian angel." For this type of bettor, going to the fronton "is like going to mass; it is inevitable."[16]

> In a paradoxical way, some people attribute a value of moral formation to the profound anxiety which they deliberately accept. Experimenting pleasure and panic; exposing oneself at one's own will in order not to succumb to anxiety; having the image of losing in front of one's eyes; knowing the inevitable and yet not looking for an exit other than the possibility to mime indifference is, as Plato says of another bet, a beautiful risk that is worth running.

---

15. Interview with pelota bettor (names of bettors in the text are withheld by mutual agreement), Bilbao (Bizkaia), February 22, 2002.

16. Ibid.

Ignatius of Loyola professed that it was necessary to act in a way that one only with oneself, as though God did not exist, while always bearing in mind that everything depends on His will. Play is no less rigorous a school. It orders the player not to neglect anything for triumph, and at the same time to keep a distance from it. What has been won may be lost again; it may even be destined to be lost. The manner of winning is more important than victory itself and, in any case, it is more important than that which is at stake. Accepting defeat as mere mishap, accepting victory without intoxication or vanity, with indifference, with this last reserve with respect to the act, is the law of the game. Considering reality as play, gaining more ground with this fine education that makes miserliness, greed and hatred retreat, is carrying out an act of civilization.[17]

The game "teaches you to pay what you owe, to become responsible for your actions, it makes you appreciate the real value of money, and it teaches you to quit once you reach the limit."[18] This is why one of my informers argued that the best thing that had happened to him was "becoming a gambler," because this is what has brought him the most authentic experiences, the greatest satisfaction—besides suffering and anxiety.[19]

Life is considered analogous to wagering to such an extent that the latter has become somewhat like a school. Besides his notable interest in knowing every factor of the game, the bettor is reckoned to possess extremely instructive experiences. After all, a profound but according to him almost always fruitless analysis precedes each bet in consideration. Perhaps this is why, despite being absorbed and possessed by something that in principle appears to be nonproductive, the *puntos* enjoy a prestige and credibility that is difficult to assume without active participation in the bet. The bet is not considered a cause of one's delegitimization and loss of authority, quite the contrary. The bettors are and have always been an integral and enormously relevant part of pelota.

> The heads of the spectators move simultaneously and rhythmically, following the flight of the ball; robust voices are heard offering bets with energetic intonation that, at the end of the fifteens, ring out clearly and expressively,

---

17. Caillois, *Los juegos y los hombres*, 20. Translated from the introduction in the Spanish edition, which does not appear in the English edition *Man, Play, and Games*.

18. Interview with pelota bettor (names of bettors in the text are withheld by mutual agreement), Bilbao (Bizkaia), February 22, 2002.

19. Informal conversation with an informer, Eibar (Gipuzkoa), February 13, 2000.

dragging the syllables, the intoxication of the scoreboard: *Fifteen* love; forty thirty and *raya*; *ona arrayá jaunak!* (Here's the *raya*, gentlemen).

The priest was there, among the masses, rubbing shoulders with the people of the court, fully immersed in the contest, whose smallest incidents he followed with growing interest and commented seriously, peaceably, without fury or passion.

He brought there ounces and napoleons [currency at that time], he betted them, calculating the dexterity of the pelota players; and his skill in betting was so great, he had tried it in so many games, that he rarely lost; resigned, at the same time, when fortune turned his back on his favorites and the accounts turned out to be the opposite.

The players loved and respected him, and enthusiastically defended his money; in the lively polemics about the main incidents of the game, the priest's voice was heard with religious respect and was approved with fervor, as though he was addressing his parishioners from the sacred *cátedra*.[20]

Discussing the figure of the referee in previous chapters I argued for the mutual dependency of his two attributes: impartiality and authority. Note that the priest cited above had explicit interest in the game and had positioned himself financially in favor of a player; and yet he maintained sufficient authority to resolve a case if needed.

Nowadays bettors maintain a certain distance from the pelotaris in order not to have the cleanness of the bet called into question. In no way do they influence the decisions of the referee. Nevertheless, the authority of strong bettors, as I argued before, is indisputable. It is not without reason that they are called the *cátedra* of the fronton.

In a similar way to the pelotari when it comes to a victory, it is not the fact of betting that grants respectability or generates mistrust at the fronton; rather, it is the manner of betting, the style of the bettor.

In the game, the player is inserted in a sphere where, as Caillois says, "nothing that takes place outside this ideal frontier is relevant."[21] He is absorbed by a self-maintained system, and which presents him with conflicts that he has to resolve immediately. If it is before decision-making that the subject feels most naked, that desires and motivations emerge most notoriously, there is no point denying that they are produced in situations of great physical and psychological tension. This is why Fran-

---

20. Peña y Goñi, *La pelota y los pelotaris*, 63–64.
21. Caillois, *Man and the Sacred*, 6.

cisco Amorós says that it is at play "where the vices of the heart are best revealed."[22]

Pelota is one of the privileged realms in which the essence of a person may be discovered: "What one shows at court has a lot to do with what he is outside of it."[23] The game becomes a fundamental weapon of understanding the other, of encounter, of recognition.

A pelotari is expected to do his best in order to win, to suffer, and to work for the points. The law of minimal effort is least recommended and most criticized at the court. Equally, when a player fails on purpose, thereby giving the point to his rival and in order to counteract an erroneous call by the referee, this is valued enormously. This barely happens nowadays; when it does, however, a profound feeling of moral greatness overtakes the fronton. Indeed, any player who plays dumb in such a situation is severely reprimanded, and the crowd frequently whistles as he prepares to execute the next serve; it is a serve that under ideal conditions is not his right, and which the public thinks he has usurped from his opponent.

Something analogous happens on the terraces as well. The attempt to strike it rich and lose composure at the fronton, or counting your chickens before they are hatched is not ideal for the bettor. He is expected keep his cool so that the direction of his bet does not make him lose sight of the game. The *momistas* are in this sense the inevitable opposite of the typical bettor, of he who *bets strong* and *plays hard* for the pelota game. They want to hit the jackpot by risking little, and when this does not happen it is difficult for them to accept. Ambition blinds their vision and they show their distrust in pelotaris and referees alike at the slightest setback.

Just as there are ideal pelotaris and bettors, so as noted is there an ideal public as well. It is a passionate public, but one capable of discerning the game no matter who is playing. The postures at the fronton turn into clear, moralizing examples; they partly reveal what the ideal *pelotazale* is like, no matter what role he has at the fronton.

Participating in the Plaza

Gadamer emphasizes the communion that underlies the term *theoria*, which is understood as real participation in what really is, noticing that

---

22. Amorós, "El último tanto," 51.

23. Errandonea's statements to Jon San Sebastián in *Mutxo* 28 (December 28, 2000): 15.

theoros is someone who participates in a festival: theoria, then, is "not something active but something passive (pathos), namely being totally involved in and carried away by what one sees."[24]

Participating in pelota is not merely about hitting balls. It is about understanding the game and understanding oneself within it. This suggests a profound internalization of the very possibilities of the game, of its rules, which implies that anyone may become its judge, anyone may freely comment on the validity of its outcome.

The widely shared passion that Basques feel for pelota has, contrary to what one might think, contributed to its impartiality; an extended impartiality that grants anyone sufficient authority to judge the game. In fact, at the informal plaza games, it is normal to ask the people gathered there in case of a doubtful hit, whether or not it was procured by one of the players. Even in the absence of a public the contenders resolve the game with little room for dispute.

The profound knowledge of both the rules and the conditions in which they are verified understands the margins of possibilities the game affords. This is why, despite not having seen the hit directly, the player normally knows if it was possible or not, if it was a score or not. This capacity is carried to the extreme in a game that some informants claim to have played as children, a game without any ball and without a fronton, one that only relies on the corporal movements of the participants, and which does not create greater discrepancies than the real court game.

This game of *as if* is played like any normal game. One serves, the other returns, and the alternative hitting of an imaginary ball continues until one of the players scores, commits an error, or detects an impossible hit, which is immediately recognized by all. "You didn't return that *sotamano*, not even as a joke;" "where did you get this posture from?" "this one went below the iron sheet;" "two bounces," "from there below you didn't catch that ball, it went like a bullet." The action happens simultaneously in the minds of the players, which is possible because they all share a *common sense* for the game, an embodied understanding that enables them to judge any of the strikes that belongs within the conjunction that the game constitutes.

We may consider the *sensus communis* in an analogous sense; Gadamer refers to it not only as a human capacity but also as a meaning

---

24. Gadamer, *Truth and Method*, 122.

that underpins the community.[25] Common feeling creates an original sense of participation, which facilitates the understanding of everything that happens within the totality of which we partake. Bourdieu calls it "habitus," and refers to the totality as "field"; he argues for an ontological complicity between them,[26] something similar to what Geertz establishes between ethos and cosmo-vision.

The referee is charged with observing the rules in pelota; he is a person whose impartiality and understanding of the game is recognized. This, which is often cited as the honesty of the referee, is just the extraordinary accommodation of his judgments to common sense. It is a common understanding shared by all those who participate in pelota, but which only the referee may dignify through each one of his decisions.

The common sense that the referee proudly embraces allows him to govern the rules, rules that result from practice, from custom. A radical confluence is thus produced between the normative and the traditional, a confluence that becomes effective in the common sense of each person, and which becomes a basic support of authority: "That which has been sanctioned by tradition and custom has an authority that is nameless, and our finite historical being is marked by the fact that always the authority of what has been transmitted—and not only what is clearly grounded—has power over our attitudes and behavior."[27]

It is precisely this confluence that culminates in the very image of the fronton, of the plaza, which becomes an icon of the permanent order that the subject recognizes as superior (authority), but which at the same time belongs to him, because it is part of him (common sense).

Plaza-Gizon

> To live as one likes is plebeian: the noble man aspires to order and law.
> — Goethe

The fronton as element of social cohesion and pelota as reinforcement of the physical and moral countenance of those who practice it have been one of the most reiterated convictions about the game over the centuries.

---

25. Gadamer, *Truth and Method*, 20.
26. Bourdieu, *Practical Reason*, 85.
27. Gadamer, *Truth and Method*, 281.

As early as 1599, the preface to the regulations of the *juego de palma*, or palm game, reads as the following:

> The noble game of the fronton, noble among all games
> Trains man's body, as well as his spirit and eyes;
> Playing skillfully, the body moves into action
> And the mind yields to a new affection.
> We are thus seeking pleasures, as opposed to boredom
> To be at work more gallant.[28]

In the late century Jovellanos also praised pelota for being honest: "it offers honest recreation for those who play it and those who watch; it makes its practitioners agile and robust, and it improves the physical education of the youth."[29] A century later, the London newspaper *The St. James Gazette* published an article titled "The Game of Pelota," which ends with the following: "The game of pelota is hygienic and demonstrative of the strength of man; it enhances skills of art and agility; its introduction in England is well desired."[30]

The "noble and hygienic game of pelota"[31] was considered the ideal recreation for the constitution of the strong, tenacious, and honest man. So much so, that it provoked the admiration and affect of its congeners: it came to embody the most exalted communitarian values, and it turned into a living icon as a legitimate representative of the people and the village. This prototype, which is not only related to the pelotari, acquires in Euskara an expressive epithet: *plaza-gizon* or "plaza-man," a qualifier also used to express the fact that a young person is now educated and trained—that he has become a worthy man.

While the phrase is revealing in itself, it is important to sketch here two of the primordial meanings that the term acquires, and which make perfect sense in the context of pelota. The first of them has to do with what I have already discussed and what is eloquently portrayed by a monument in the plaza of Sara, Lapurdi. It exemplarily synthesizes the idealized virtues attributed to the pelotari.

The monument in question is a commemorative monolith of a hero of the French armed forces, who died in battle in World War II. The

---

28. Gillet, *Historia del deporte*, 48.
29. González Alcantud, *Tractatus ludorum*, 164.
30. *Euskal-Erria* 25 (1891), 54.
31. Paxaka, "Miscelánea."

young Basque man was called Victor Ithurria (1914–1944), and he was a well-known pelotari of the area. The monolith is a double relief: on top is the soldier Victor Ithurria, ("hero of the Free French Forces"); behind him is the pelotari Victor Ithurria, the *pilotari zintzoa* (noble pelotari). Both figures are in the same posture, with the robust torso turned toward the viewer, looking ahead (displaying his profile), his right arm raised in a throwing position. The soldier with the hand closed, grabbing a grenade; the pelotari with the hand open, hitting a pelota. In the background a curved frontis; in the foreground the rays of the imperial sun.

In an article titled "Los nidos de los pelotaris" (The nests of the pelotaris), José María Salaverría writes: "Between the mountains and the sea, over the hills, a feature of the Basque temperament comes into the foreground: agility. A complicated agility with great strength. An admirable complication that yields the terrible type of the factious guerilla, as well as the beautiful example of the pelotari."[32] The prototype of the soldier and the pelotari shares the attributes—agility and strength—of lions and foxes, but also the fertile fundamentals of nobleness: the capacity to endure suffering and the respect for authority.

This epic scope of nobleness includes its perhaps major significance, a meaning that José Ortega y Gasset determined by saying that "the excellent man . . . is the one who makes great demands on himself,"[33] and who "is impelled by his very nature to seek a norm higher and

---

32. Salaverría, *La gran enciclopedia vasca*, 645.
33. Ortega y Gasset, *The Revolt of the Masses*: 44–45.

superior to himself, a norm whose authority he freely accepts."[34] It is the tenacious person who does not shy away from adversity; who can endure suffering to achieve his goals; who does not lose hope of victory; and who always acts according to a law he recognizes superior, and which his own personality exalts.

The *plaza-gizon* balances his glory with the glory of a reality that transcends him. He conjugates the full development of his potential with the exaltation of that to which he belongs.

> *Zilar finaren pare da Pilotaria*
> *gorpitza sano eta zohardi begia*
> *xerkatzen du leialki plazan jokatzia*
> *bere Eskual Herria gora laidatzia.*
>
> *Zelüko Jenko Jauna*
> *gütaz orit zite;*
> *Pilotarien Biltzarraren*
> *zü jar zite jabe.*
> *Gazte hoiek ondotik*
> *har dezaien parte.*
> *Zer litzateke Eskual Herria*
> *Pilotarik gabe.*
> *Eijer pilotaria agertzen delarik*
> *aingüru baten gisa xuriz beztitürik*
> *gogua arin eta kuraiez beterik*
> *harek ez dü ordian nihuren beldürrik.*
>
> *Perkainen denboratik, bai eta orai da,*
> *plazetan zunbat ürrats eginik izan da;*
> *zunbat xapeldun jelki, heben anitx bada.*
> *Nihuntik ez leiteke Pilota galtzera.*
>
> The pelotari is like fine silverware
> Of healthy body and vigilant eyes
> Who seeks to play faithfully in the plaza
> In praise of Euskal Herria

---

34. Ibid., 52.

> Lord God of the heavens
> Remember us;
> Be president
> Of the assembly of pelotaris,
> By the side of the youth
> Who participates
> What would become of Euskal Herria
> Without pelotaris.
>
> When the fine pelotari appears
> Dressed in white like an angel
> With light spirit and full of courage
> He then fears no one.
>
> Since the times of Perkain until now,
> They have made great progress in the plaza;
> With so many champions *jelki*, that have been here
> It is impossible to lose pelota.

This song, "Laida Pilotaria," expresses the position the *plaza-gizon* occupies in the *pelotazale* imaginary: they are loyal players who get involved, who take part in the exaltation of their nation, and who fear nothing in the court. It is the adjective *jelki* that best expresses this primary signification. "Jel" refers to the initials of the slogan *Jaungoikoa eta lege zaharrak* ("God and the old laws," with reference to the *fueros*, or customary laws). While this acronym was invented by Sabino Arana, and was monopolized by the Basque Nationalist Party that Arana founded and which called its members *jelkides*, here the poet refers to the noble pelotari, to he who observes and exalts the laws of his forefathers, laws that ideally constitute the foundations of his nation. The adjective *jelki* refers to the person who is able to put a higher purpose first, whether God or tradition. He does so through the observance of the law, of shared norms: "pelotari, pelotari image of a vigorous race, consecrate your game to God and to your homeland, offer up your triumph with glory in the heavens and human peace on the earth, our racial virtues are imprinted in your game."[35]

---

35. Last verse of the "Himno al pelotari" (Hymn to the Pelota Player), quoted in Cercadillo, *Manual completo de la pelota vasca*, 13.

The word *plaza-gizon* expresses a conjunction between particular and collective interests. It refers to a man who excels in endeavors that are a source of pride for the community, and who represents fundamental pillars of their cultural bonds.

The plaza stages all the manifestations that celebrate community *being*. Those who know how to exalt them through their own beautiful style will be recognized and acclaimed by the rest, as long as their contribution accords with the idea that the manifestation itself transmits. They thus become worthy representatives of the village, which celebrates in itself the collectivity—a collectivity whose sediment is the plaza. Hence the word *plaza-gizon*.

The range of meanings of *plaza-gizon* is not exhausted in this glorified interpretation. A popular meaning discussed by Zulaika envelopes the person who grows up in the plaza,[36] in the public space par excellence. Even if displaced from the iconography of the pelotari, this common feeling resonates with the competitive naturalness of the *plaza-gizon*, thus extending the meaning of the plaza. This meaning, in turn, maintains an essential tension between the quietude that the container expresses, and the dynamism it contains.

In the introduction to this chapter I discussed the boundaries, the sphere of play, of the court; fixed, unmovable boundaries that nevertheless constitute infinite possibilities of action. The *plaza-gizon* in this sense is the person who exploits the possibilities the plaza offers, as well as his own potentialities, to the maximum. For him, and those who are like him, the limits are challenges, and the will to win he possesses leads him to negotiate boundaries. As Retegi II, a born winner, said: "the essence of pelota lies in people whose faculties fail them, but who have a craftiness that they also inculcated in me."[37]

For this type of pelotari, *plaza-gizon* in the second meaning of the word, the game does not end with the *eskas*, lines, of the plaza, since it is with them that they construct their game. They play with the limits and trap their rivals in them. It is basically these types of players who we have called foxes, and whom are popularly termed "artists," because they are capable of devising unpredictable, magic, plays that confuse their rival's minds. They are said to make the game grow, to keep the plaza alive.

---

36. Zulaika, *Basque Violence*.
37. Interview with Julián Retegi II, Atxondo (Bizkaia), November 20, 2000.

Sometimes they are accused of playing dirty, of demonstrating excessive competitiveness; as a result, some fans deny these players the qualifier *plaza-gizon*, reserving it for those who demonstrate the ideal behavior expected of the pelotari yet that is nevertheless endorsed by many foxes. But, beyond the power that the pelotari uses to overcome the other, the *plaza-gizon* in this second sense of the word is he who knows how to make the most of the plaza, something that is directly related to triumph. Once again, the desire to win becomes essential in the recognition of the pelotari.

The *plaza-gizon* is definitely he who carries within him the spirit of the plaza, whether a community ideal, the permanence of certain idiosyncratic ways of being, or the capacity of action, of cultural dynamism. The point is to celebrate the plaza, this epitome of tradition and the possibility of action.

Play Honestly, the Plaza Is Always Judge

> There is an intrahistoric, unwritten social contract that is the effective internal constitution of each people.
>
> — Miguel Unamuno

Mary Douglas argues that, if a group of subjects can consider themselves a society, "it is because of the legal theory that endows it with fictive personality. Yet, legal existence is not enough."[38] Part 3 of this book intended to decipher the nature of the fundamental connection, the bond, that pelota implies. It set out to understand what values and ideals are hidden behind specific symbols, and how they come into harmony until they produce the cultural message that the ritual transmits. Understanding this resort to values is what Nietzsche referred to, to this intrahistoric social contract that Unamuno proposed, and which takes form in a specific way of conceiving the world and being in it, in aesthetics.

Each of the three chapters that make up part 3 concentrates on one of the necessary elements the game requires to take place: the hand (the concretion of the pelotari himself), the ball, and the plaza or fronton. Each chapter discusses the significance of these elements as well as their role in the ritual process.

---

38. Douglas, *How Institutions Think*, 9.

In examining the importance of the hand (*eskua*), I reviewed the classic conception of a person—which highlights ownership as a basic principle of definition—to establish a fundamental relation between the hand, and elemental symbolic concretion of seizure, of power, and of humanity. I postulated that the hand is the clearest image of rights (*eskubideak*) and obligations that an individual acquires as member of a collectivity, and which grant him or her condition as a person. The hand symbolizes competence itself, the capacity to participate (*esku hartu*) or intervene (*esku sartu*) in the affairs of the community.

Leaving aside the connotations that this could have in relation with the very etymology of *eskualdun* or *euskaldun*, within the ritual itself, the fact that the player shows his hands to the public before starting the game denotes, beyond other questions like cleanliness and honesty, his own capacity (*eskumen*) to take a leading role in the ritual. Similarly, the referee, the maximum authority, shows his hand to demonstrate his jurisdiction (*eskuera*) over everything that happens at the court. A clear division is thus established among those who are competent (*eskudunak*) to occupy this space and represent the community, and those who are not. Among the latter are, for example, women.

Despite being absolutely excluded from the formalized ritual, women have been protagonists of numerous legends that link them to one of the proto-agonic powers, to astuteness. At the fronton, the left-hand player, the *ezkertia*, also known as "he who does not go straight," paradigmatically represents astuteness. Without going deeply into what I have sufficiently discussed, the bodies thus turn into moralizing tropes. Far from the real practice of the game, where the predilection for one or the other is a mere personal matter, there exists a preference, a cultural preference if you will, for pelotaris of power, of strength. They represent honesty and stand above those who use astuteness as a means to hunt down the other.

This preference, which is clearly detectable in the iconography on pelota (in the paintings, posters, and *bertsos* that show a strong, robust pelotari, definitely a lion) does not at all condition the practice itself, in which astute pelotaris are historically recognized as the greatest players of the game. Atano III and Retegi II are the most important examples of this. When someone says that this or that player is "very pelotari," there is an implicit reference to this astuteness, this absolute domination of the space of the court that the fox executes in an exemplary way; they are called "artists" because of their capacity to constantly appeal to the unforeseeable. Therefore, while there is certain suspicion about the fox's game, and the lion's honest and direct force remains an indisputable moral imperative, *pelotazales* do recognize the real value of the two types of power in the constitution of the pelotari's personality.

The hand is nevertheless the fundamental symbol of the pelotari's competence, it is his tool of action. This is why he shows it to the public and offers it to his rival before starting the contest. In the handshake the pelotaris recognize each other as equally equipped for the game. They recognize each other as competent, *eskudunak*, possessors of the hand.

It is nevertheless through the ball that the players recognize each other as executors, as interpreters of the game through their own style and personality. It is through contact with the ball—the pelota, the instrument of mediation and object that lends the game its name—that the personality of the pelotari is constructed, a personality that is embodied by the type of ball he chooses.

In the Basque game, the ball adapts to the attributes of the player who chose it. It becomes his ecstatic "I," a reflection of his personality beyond his physical body. Individuals who are very experienced in the game are able to sense by the mere analysis of the ball—by bouncing and hitting it—the attributes and strategies of the player who will use it in his game.

This feature—the singularity of the material of exchange, of the encounter—shows the value that the ritual grants the personality of the pelotari, and constitutes a strong stimulus on the process of the construction of his own self as a player. In the process of the game, in sizing up, as well as in the very own progression of the pelotari in his professional career, a dialectic process becomes evident: a process in which the player's experience, his personality as a pelotari, is constructed. In order to recognize the ball that ideally matches his style of play, the player must know his attributes, qualities that he is unaware of until he encounters and confronts others, which he does through the medium of distinct types of balls.

This process is always open to the interpretation of the other, and takes shape in the ball as the player learns about his attributes. It becomes a major metaphor for the socialization process, for the constitution of the personality of the subject, thanks to its active incorporation in the culture. Just as the pelotari adapts the ball to his own attributes, which develop and become conscious through his struggle against others, so the subject adjusts culture, and thus creates his personality. For the construction of the self through the other to be possible, there is a need for a certain convention of meanings. Therefore, despite the fact that culture does not determine the personality of the subject but enables the process of necessary experiences to conform to it, there are supra-individual cultural styles that proceed precisely from this convention of meaning that serves as mediation.

Beyond internal diversity, each culture promotes certain corporal techniques and distinctive styles that it considers harmonious with an idiosyncratic ethos. Basque pelota prefers clean and powerful postures, and honest contact with the ball. The crowd finds in these postures aesthetic emotion and affective participation in the ideal representation of what pelota means.

The ideal that the spectator encounters in the style of the pelotari is almost always accompanied by a virtue that Basques have considered a representative attribute of their own character, and which extends through all the substantial elements of the game: nobleness. Sober elements of a purified simplicity and extreme solidity—both the ball and the fronton are considered noble when they respond to the stimulus, when they avoid *rarities*, when they produce no irregular trajectories with respect to the hit. While their uniqueness is recognized, balls and frontons must facilitate the encounter, incite play, with a calculable and commensurate behavior that abides by the rules.

The personification of the primordial elements of the game facilitates the understanding of meanings that, exclusively applied to persons, could be confusing. The classification of balls and frontons on the basis of their nobleness constitutes a model of moral knowledge for the pelotaris and the public, who recognize a noble person in his transparency and respect for the principles of authority, of common norms; norms, as noted above, that are rooted in a common consciousness. Physically embodied in the *eskas* or fault lines, and administered by the referee, the norm is a conjunction of possibilities for action by the pelotari, unquestionably linked to the public.

The public, as a group of spectators's bodies, was probably the first element to constitute the boundaries of play, and the referee was just its appendage. It is the public as a graphic representation of society from which norms emanate; and it is the plaza, the firm sedimentation of the public and of society, which embodies them spatially. Norms, public, society, and plaza are aspects of the same thing: of the boundaries and as such of the subject's possibilities of action, of the context wherein the subject encounters others and shapes his own personality. Therefore, those whose judgments accommodate these norms in an exemplary manner, norms that emanate from a common consciousness, acquire the necessary authority to resolve questions and become judges, thus embodying government at the plaza.

Although a physical place, the plaza is not only the space of encounter and representation that can be found at the center of Basque towns and villages. The plaza is also part of the conscience of each subject that participates in it. It is nothing but society hypostasized and taken place; it evokes the link that turns a group into a community. Therefore, anyone who expresses in his very being features that the community considers a source of union is called a *plaza-gizon*.

According to Geertz,

> The Balinese, not only in court rituals but generally, cast their most comprehensive ideas of the way things ultimately are, and the way that men should therefore act, into immediately apprehended sensuous symbols—into a lexicon of carvings, flowers, dances, melodies, gestures, chants, ornaments, temples, postures and masks—rather than into a discursively apprehended, ordered set of explicit "beliefs."[39]

Something analogous happens with Basques and pelota. Hand, ball, and plaza; besides being the minimal elements the game requires, they are consecrated as primordial symbols that ritual will use in order to transmit essential meanings about the constitution of the community that holds them together. Their interpretation and interrelations contribute to the revelation of a character that permeates all the elements, allowing us to identify a bond that connects them, and which the conjunction displays.

Immaterial although physical in each one of its parts, this ethereal whole, which is of a symbolic order in an allegorical sense as well as in its meaning as formal suture, is nothing but the ideal of culture, its conception of the world. It assembles distinct components into a coherent whole, giving them a characteristic style that determines its own cognation. This bond has to do above all with the constitutive principles of the group, and is embodied in representation, in the distinctive levels of aesthetic expression that society generates, through which the subject experiments, learns, incorporates, and recreates the culture in which he

---

39. Geertz, *Negara*, 103.

or she participates. As Durkheim observes, "society is not simply constituted by the mass of individuals who compose it, by the land they occupy, by the things they use, by the movements they make, but above all by the idea that it fashions of itself."[40] In fact, it is this ideal that agglutinates and pulls together all the elements of life into a thinkable concept, filtering into them and endowing them with extraordinary quality.

I have argued that pelota represents a central ideal in the Basque imaginary, an ideal that has to do above all with a concept of nobleness. In its most archaic sense, nobleness appears to be related to possession and thus with the hand, with authority, possessing a meaning that Serres would express in reference to Diogenes' barrel, his property that made him free and human.[41] In Euskara this meaning is embodied in the word *eskukoa*, literally "he of the hand," which may mean free man and subject alike, depending on the pronoun that precedes the noun. It is a liberty that, unlike *aske*, free inasmuch as liberated—separate, empty—hides a fundamental reference to rights (*eskubidea*), to the common (*eskuarki*): "liberty is but the conscience of the law as opposed to the submission of imposed rule," Unamuno declared.[42] The noble person is *jelki*, who respects traditional laws; he or she is also *zintzoa*, loyal to oath, to law, and to common norms.

The reconciliation between one's autonomy, one's own style of behavior, and the observance of the common norms appear exemplified by both the fronton and the ball—elements that, despite their originality, must be tailored to measure. They are the ball with a straight bounce, which responds to the pelotari's hit, and the fronton that respects the trajectory and force of the ball. Nobleness has to do with "facilitating the encounter," with "inviting to play." The conjugation of one's own independence and respect for the common norm paradigmatically defines the virtue of nobleness, a virtue that is culturally extolled and that is linked to effort and struggle. Therefore, in order to capture in one sentence the set of values that constitutes the Basque imaginary, let me refer to the legend that honors the plaza-fronton of Aldude in Lower Navarre. It reveals the intrahistoric contract, the cultural message that pelota trans-

---

40. Durkheim, *The Elementary Forms of Religious Life*, 317.

41. In Roman law the slave, as he has no possessions, was a *res mancipi* and therefore was not considered a person. See Mauss, *Manual of Ethnography*, 143.

42. Unamuno, *Estética como ciencia de la expresión y lingüística general*, 24.

mits and that is summarized in this maxim: "Play honestly, the plaza is always judge."

Conclusion

> Conflict identifies the positive moment that is interwoven with its negative character in a unity that is only apparently but not actually breaking up.
> — Georg Simmel

> Really to play, a man must play like a child.
> — Johan Huizinga

Struggle has been one of the most effective images to think communitarian genetics. The conciliation of forces in conflict constitutes one of the dominant arguments of an infinite number of myths and foundational rites. Perhaps this is why F. J. J. Buytendijk observes the possibility that "at their inception, for many cultures ball games served as a medium to represent old myths."[43]

As penal documents and travelers' testimonies demonstrate, pelota enjoyed extensive diffusion within the Basque population as early as the sixteenth century. This coincided, on the eve of the modern era, with the emergence of a Basque imaginary. This imaginary partly emerged from the necessity for structural political changes—which would not come into effect until later centuries—and partly from the influence of essayists of the epoch who theorized it. Some observers (Otazu y Llana) term this imaginary "egalitarianism," others (Caro Baroja) see it as "original Basque democracy." This ideology was mainly based on the concept of universal nobility and in a judicial equality in decision-making. While its historical reality is strongly questioned, it has come constitute one of the most solid bases of the Basque cultural imaginary to this day. Some have even considered it as an original Basque feature that has been present since time immemorial, since prehistory.

The historical genesis of this ideological construct is nevertheless traceable: it is the moment when medieval societies dominated by warring factions or clans began to disintegrate. This does not mean that feudal structures disappeared overnight; according to Otazu y Llana, they were maintained even centuries later. A fundamental milestone was, however, established in the configuration of the Basque imaginary that

---

43. Buytendijk, "El jugar en el hombre," in *Nueva Antropología*, 102.

remains predominant today. In this context, pelota may have constituted an essential ritual in strengthening a community whose relations began to be founded on a new conception of the world: a conception that did not necessarily reflect a social reality, but which practice itself fomented alongside other practices and discourses, thus contributing, in time, to the materialization of this conception.

The sixteenth century was thus an era marked by factious wars: essentially agonic fights between symmetric groupings of analogous structure and equal power. At a representative level, pelota presents an argument that is equivalent to these fights, although this does not mean that they they gave rise to it. In the Basque territories pelota games had been known long before the factional or clan wars. Such games were typical throughout most of Europe in the Middle Ages, and perhaps even before; their rules were similar to those that the first Basque documentation of the game describes, and which still prevail in long modality games, *laxoa* and rebote: a score system of four fifteens and a system of lines (*raya*) that depend on where the ball is driven and where it stops, besides the alternative interchange of a ball with the hand or a handheld instrument.

The growing popularity of the game was due to the development of villas (chartered towns or boroughs), which were largely nourished by marginalized sectors of the rural nobility's lineage system, and by a large number of outsiders.[44] Pelota now constituted not only a form of representation and the overcoming of a patent, historic conflict, but also and fundamentally an effective practice of sociality that planted in the symbolic order the latent conflict in every public structure: the division, the wound.

Tierno Galván establishes the relation between the words *polis* and *poleo*, fighting.[45] This relation recalls theories that trace the origins of *polis* to sacred lynching, to the sacrifice of the tyrant, of the serpent, or of the male goat, *tragos*; sacrifices that could be also represented as a primogenial struggle, as *tragedies* among equals, among brothers.[46] Disjunction and the outbreak of violence in the heart of the community constitute one of the most disconcerting threats for any society. Myths

---

44. See Caro Baroja, *The Basques*, chap. 1.

45. Tierno Galván, *Desde el espectáculo a la trivialización*, 6.

46. Lloyd, *The Agon in Euripides*; Arnason, *Agon, logos y polis*, Miralles, *Esquilo*.

as well as rituals are bridges that aim to save it from such splits, bridges that Simmel or Turner would consider as proof of the split itself. Hence the morphology of ritual, which determines its plot.

The game of pelota is a representation of *agon*, of a competitive fight. Without discussing again the Greek etymology of the word, we sometimes use the word *partido* ("split" in Spanish, "game") and other times *encounter* when we refer to the spatial-temporal embodiment of essentially agonic sports—despite the fact that in pelota the word "encounter" (*encuentro*) is not frequently used. Struggle and reunion, the *agon*, is the context in which forces of conflict meet and get resolved; its physical embodiment is *agora*, or *agon* taking the form of place.

Pelota and fonton, respectively, constitute the ritual and the monumental embodiment of a myth that has not been formulated in terms of communitarian function. Here I mean myth not in a merely explicative sense, but in the practical sense of being a medium of orientation and installation whose function is, according to Manuel García Pelayo, "maintaining and conserving a culture against disintegration and destruction."[47] The game of pelota is narration in the form of action, formalized in expressive acts that recreate the process by which, based on a field of struggle, a supposed original unity is constituted, a unity that only the exchange of the ball can produce.

The term that in Basque is closest to the meaning of *agon* is *joko*. *Joko* is competitive and essentially disjunctive play.[48] It sustains the logic of a *partido*, an event where two players confront each other—individually or in doubles—by starting out from a state of withdrawal that is symbolically embodied in the whiteness of the players' garments. Attire also marks, by means of the distinctive colors of their *gerriko* (sash) and jersey, the split (red or blue) of the totality that involves the *partido*. This distinction coincides with the colors medieval factions used to differentiate themselves, and which they exhibited in the same way that pelotaris do today in their belts. It is on the basis of this distinction that the public takes *posture*, positions itself at the event, a positioning that the development of the game may change.

The public positions itself before the game. The pregame bets among the fans, which almost always take place in a jocose tone, are

---

47. García Pelayo, *Los mitos políticos*, 19.
48. *Joko* also means "conjugation," which is the equivalent of the meaning of *agon*.

essential parts of the game. They facilitate sociability and participation. The public must feel itself implicated; it must take a posture. This is why there exists a tradition of wagering, from the most spontaneous to the most formalized ways of betting at the fronton.

The essential difference between preliminary bets and those made during the game is that the latter allow the gambler to "turn his coat," to change the direction of the bet and rectify his original positioning. The possibility to change the direction of one's bet smoothes fanatic rivalry and works toward creating a public that adjusts its judgment according to the proceedings of the game rather than its initial inclinations. Therefore, once the game has started, the gambler does not bother to have his predictions confirmed by cheering his player or by booing the rival. Rather, he surrenders to the game and judges with impartiality the struggle between the pelotaris. Indeed, ultimately the pelotaris are responsible for resolving the contest and the public feels like a judge rather than part of the conflict. The public will therefore cheer the merits of both players, rather than just its original choice.

Distant from factions, from mere rivalry, the public is no longer in the sphere of *joko*, of struggle, a responsibility that belongs to the pelotaris alone. Rather, the game tends toward the sphere of *jolas*, of dissolution, of magic transformation, which is not always achieved, but which is an essential motive for the crowd to periodically return to the fronton.

The game of pelota in a court stages a communion which is culminated by ritual. The process of *sizing up*, by which the game is resolved, is just the incorporation of the other, mutual recognition between equals; it will eventually turn into a hunt in which one will be hunter and the other hunted down. When one of the players discovers the hollows, the weak spots of the other, he *hunts him down*, he takes possession of him. The incorporation that sizing up supposes is materialized in the hug the players give each other after the game. The winner symbolically devours the loser, and proudly presents his achievement to the public through his closed fist, which is an effective image of power. He fought clean and honest during the game with an open hand, without grabbing the ball, which is the material for mediation, for the *encounter*. Now, once he has hunted down the rival, he embraces him and shows his prey to the public with a closed fist, as though his victim was inside it. The public surrenders through its applause to the winner and consecrates his triumph. That triumph is the unity of those present, which the winner himself—with his fist in the air—symbolizes.

The ritual starts with the *joko* scheme: with split, with disjunction. It is then resolved in the scheme of *jolas*: of communion, of suture, where there is no difference between the parts, where all are one. In Basque the word *jolas* refers to children's games. Some authors have emphasized a kind of return to a state of candor that ritual effervescence implies. For Romano Guardini, for example, the practice of the liturgy is "becoming like children."[49] Periodically performed ritual reproduces the reconstruction of unity, the return to a primogenial totality, to the community. It smoothes the consciousness of *being* split, splintered.

Pelota is a ritual representation of the latent conflict in every human experience, whether individual or collective, social or personal, or historic or mythic. Struggle constitutes in fact one of the most effective images to express the first, foundational act. It also warns about an intrinsic danger: dismemberment as a consequence of its nonresolution. If it is staged in a definite context that conspires to an outcome, struggle reserves its regenerative value because it is a positive expression of life, of movement, of transformation.

Pelota constitutes therefore a positive cult of the first order. It periodically recreates the foundation of the community, a reality completely intangible; ritual, however, makes it effective by granting it spatial-temporal coordinates and by creating bonds of emotion among the participants.

Eugenio Trías emphasizes the coincidence of the root *tem-* in the word "temple" with that of the verb *temnein*, "to cut." According to him, a temple merely a demarcation, a "cut by means of which cleared space is marked out, and which is assigned *sacred* character."[50] From this he infers that the verb "contemplate," *cum-templare*, would refer to producing a cut, a demarcation,[51] in such a way that it delimits and abstracts from the environment that it is concerned with, in order to establish a connection with it, to affect and to be affected by that which is contemplated.

The very act of group contemplation establishes in its own physical configuration a cut. The bodies, orienting their gaze toward the object of contemplation, constitute a primary demarcation. They turn their back on the city and create a center, an interior, in which they are directly

---

49. Quoted in Buytendijk, "El jugar en el hombre" in *Nueva Antropología*, 103.
50. Trías, *La fundación de la ciudad*, 14.
51. Ibid., 16.

implicated. An essential relationship is thus born between the contemplated and the spectators, because their own bodies grant the former its place. If this relation is consolidated and the spectator returns periodically to con-template the con-templated, whom he himself has situated, it is because he finds within it something that touches him, something in which he recognizes himself.

From the perspective of this unshakeable link between the spectator and the contemplated, one understands Gadamer when he says that "in being played the play speaks to the spectator through its representation; and it does so in such a way that, despite the distance between it and himself, the spectator still belongs to play."[52] This original feeling of participation in the event is what I termed *sensus communis*, a common consciousness that founds community. Common consciousness also becomes an essential foundation for the capacity to judge, since it creates the most efficient principle of authority that exists, given that it is born within the conscience of each person who shares it.

Durkheim defended morality as a result of affective participation in a certain idea of the community. Durkheim, as Eduardo P. Archetti remarks, "did not accept that a rational definition of duty, or a utilitarian respect for sanctions, are sufficient as a basis for moral commitment. Morality requires compassion, fervor and a sense of engagement."[53] Those values that the group considers the substance of its constitution are most efficiently incorporated or ratified in moments of effervescence, of full participation, and of common union. It is in this sense that Turner says that "the biological referents are ennobled and the normative referents are charged with emotional significance,"[54] something to which Albert Camus testifies: "All I know most surely about morality and obligations, I owe to football."[55]

Rituals are merely dramatizations, *performances*, experiences that endow with meanings and emotions the very being of the subject and the community. Therefore, the postures that are adopted in them are charged with significance; they become moralizing examples, enlightening metaphors of the way different behaviors are ordered.

---

52. Gadamer, *Truth and Method*, 115
53. Archetti, *The Ethnography of Moralities*, 101.
54. Turner, *Secular Ritual*, 55.
55. Meynaud, *El deporte y la política*, 230.

Pelota is one of the contexts in which an idealized Basque ethos emerges, evoking a credo for many Basques that would otherwise have to be defined in political terms. Lacking any corroborating statistics, I would have to speculate that, on the basis of my fieldwork, the practice of pelota does not subscribe to any of the major factions in the current Basque political arena, which in Hegoalde is profoundly polarized between Basque nationalism and what has recently come to be known as Spanish "constitutionalism."[56] As an icon, however, pelota has formed an essential part of the Basque nationalist imaginary, which has considered it a fundamental pillar of Basque difference. Iñaki Anasagasti, congressman of the Basque Nationalist Party proudly reacted to a comment intended to be degrading by an opposing member of parliament in Madrid, who blurted out loudly: "I don't understand what these four pelotaris want" (referring to Basque representatives in a demeaning way as pelotaris). In an article titled the same, he concluded the following: "If someone wanted to do a synthesis of the basic morals of the Basques, a practical synthesis of their idiosyncrasy, it would not be surprising if the result would be a fronton and a game between pelotaris."[57]

To begin, I would list the essential morals Anasagasti discusses. Among others, they are honesty, diligence, respect for the principles of authority, and loyalty to the given word. All of these find idealized expression in pelota, especially in the formalized acts of the ritual process. A whole narrative is constructed around these morals that exhibits the pillars on which an edifice of meaning rests. It is nevertheless in the open process of the game where the diverse manners of conduct reveal themselves. Therefore, formalized acts, despite having a determining message, serve above all to create a context in which what really matters is enabled, and which constitutes the most effective enhancer of ritual: the game itself. In the game the real character, the original genius of all those who play, emerges.

The style of the pelotari manifests itself in the way he hits the ball—a style that is believed to denote his conduct. In the same way, the manner of wagering reveals the bettor's character, just as the way of appreciating the game reveals the public's character. Language itself reveals this

---

56. The verb "polarize" refers here to concentrating in two opposing poles. There are few options nowadays outside of this dialectic in the political spectrum. Outside of politics, however, there are many.

57. *Deia*, September 12, 1988.

confluence between the manner of playing and morality, and indefectibly links the technique, the "procedures of the game" (*jokabide*) with behavior (*jokabide*); the *jokaera*, or "manner of playing" with conduct; and the *joera*, "manner of hitting, moving around" with tendency or inclination.

The pelotari's manner of playing, his *jokaera*, is revealed in how he moves around in the court, in his encounter with the ball, in his capacity to surprise and to deceive, in his reactions to critical moments, and so on. The way the body of the public moves with the distinctive actions of the pelotari offers an essential key to understanding what the crowd celebrates, and appreciates. Comparing the reflexes of the terraces with the iconography of the phenomenon, it is possible to see agreement and disagreement between that which the fans value and that which has been idealized: between the archetype pelota holds and that which it applauds within, which do not necessarily coincide.

I have already argued that sizing up clearly represents the process of constructing personality. It entails the exploration of possibilities, the search for a position with reference to the other. This is why it is in sizing up, in this permanent rehearsal, that the game is implied; it is here that the pelotari and a large part of the crowd discover what his strengths, skills, and talents are.

Two powers dominate among these attributes: strength and astuteness. They are powers that are allegorically linked to different categories of people—whether they are left- or right-handed, men or women, and so on. These powers are constituted in examples of moral knowledge. Direct, solid, open strength without tricks, and the force of cunning, and of calculus and rapidity (as Unamuno defined it) might be equally valued in the game. They, however, stand in a hierarchical relationship. The power of strength emerges as a paradigm for nobleness; astuteness, on the other hand, always connotes a certain suspicion about moral impurity, sophism, shadiness, of tricks used in order to win, to hunt down the other, to discover him and incorporate him. In the iconography of the pelotari, it is the lion who becomes a model, an example to follow—despite the fact that one is a pelotari to the extent he has developed the art of trapping.

Saying that someone is "very pelotari" means that he has great control of the court, as well as a pure technique of hitting the ball wherever he wants. But above all "very pelotari" means that the player is capable of designing unpredictable, magical play; that he is an "artist." He is, as

Martín Ezkurra said of the young Martínez de Irujo, "imaginative to the point of recklessness."[58]

Following the terminology Zulaika employs with reference to the two types of energy—potential (*ahal*) and actualized (*indar*)—that take place in ritualized behavior,[59] the lion relies mostly on *indarra*, the power of the hit, an energy that *radiates* impetus to the ball, and which *extends* the hit. The fox, in turn, possesses *ahala*, the power of ingenuity as the capacity to find hollows, holes (*huts*), the discontinuity where the ball should be hit. During the television coverage of the game I referred to in chapter 4 between Beloki and Olaizola II, the commentator Eguskitze referred to Olaizola II's vision of game by crying out: "*Hori da, ahala, hori!*" ("that's it, that is power!"), while without a doubt he would call the strength of Beloki's arms *indarra*, never *ahala*.

The mechanical model of the execution of *indarra* is, according to Zulaika, the *jo* (hit).[60] At the fronton, the player must give himself over to the struggle by hitting the ball, a struggle that the public has now renounced. "*Jo pilota!*" they shout to the player so that he gives his game greater strength, so that he deploys the essentially masculine *indarra*.

The iconography of the pelotari almost always shows him in the moment of hitting, the best expression of his power, his *indarra*. It is therefore the lion, the *indartsua*, who constitutes the archetypical image of the pelotari. It is the lion who is charged with the personification of struggle; it is his fist that becomes its icon as it is lifted in the air, a gesture habitually used in the political context. This fist is an energetic symbol of *indarra*, as well as of the effective union of the community.

This cultural archetype of the pelotari, however, shares importance with another prototype that *is* for the public "more pelotari" than the example I just outlined. We see therefore an obvious discrepancy between the ideal type that sustains the image of the pelotari, and the type that comes from the real practice of the game. This supposed contradiction emerges in other elements as well, which reveals a necessary and culturally fertile tension between prototypical ideals and ideal counter-types: "Culture counterposes the 'positive' causality *jo* (to hit) of *indar* against the 'negative' causality of *ahal* situated in the terrain of potentiality and

---

58. Statement to the press after a match, Iruña-Pamplona, date unknown.
59. Zulaika, *Tratado estético-ritual vasco*, 96–104.
60. Ibid., 102.

working by attraction. At the level of signs, a containing object governed by *ahal* is necessary for the hit *jo* to take place. Ritual action causes both forms of causality to interact."[61] In pelota, the potential energy *ahal* appears to be iconically represented by the plaza, because *ahal* is the prototypical power of foxes, of the pelotaris that know how to exploit the potentialities, the possibilities (*ahalbide*) of action that the very limits of the plaza engender.

In chapter 7, I compared the figure of the fox to women. Zulaika also argues that *ahal* energy is essentially female. In this sense, the plaza is conceived of as a field, as a return to origins and as a place of recreation, where bodies dance in disorderly fashion and give themselves over to commensality. Thus, the ideal of the plaza is embodied as a maternal lap that *attracts* the bodies of the community, and which represents the *common consciousness* that assembles them. The open hand, its hollow that hides the ball is also power, faculty (*ahalmena*), and the image of *ahala*. This is why the pelotari shows it to the public before the game starts; he shows that he "has hand," that he is competent (*eskudun*), that he is equipped (*ahaldun*) to play. No doubt, competence depends fundamentally on the hands' capacity to hit the ball, to realize itself in *indarra*, to turn into a fist. The same happens with the plaza and its limits, which are both possibilities of action as well as the physical concretion of the norm.

The moment bodies organize themselves to contemplate struggle, whether the verbal contest of *bertsolaris*, the physical contest of *aizkolaris* or *harrijasotzailes*, or a game of pelota, the plaza is converted into a temple, and all feminine elements disappear. It is the "sons" who concentrate around the fist, this *indarra* that represents them, and of which they form a part. The *communitas* is transformed into a political community, into *potestas*; and the plaza, born from and nourished by this consensus, now exemplifies the principle of authority.

John Berger describes the two aspects of these types of communitarian places:

> It was a mystery why there were always so many people on Alexanderplatz. There was the bus station, but this couldn't explain the crowds at night. Perhaps people went there simply because it was so big. Perhaps the bare, empty place, which was not like that of a park, compelled crowds to gather there, according to some natural law of men and streets

---

61. Zulaika, *Tratado estético-ritual vasco*, 103–104.

and Man. All cities have one such space, where victories are celebrated, where crowds dance at the new year, where political marches begin and end, a space that belongs to the people ... When you cross it it's like crossing a stage. On this stage, in times of summary justice, tyrants and traitors are hanged from lamp posts.[62]

The public center par excellence, the plaza is a place of concurrence that welcomes equally institutionalized as well as institutionalizing events and spontaneous actions. This is why the dual condition of the plaza has been discussed: on the one hand, as a field (an explosion of the communitarian, a return to origins, amusement, and recreation); and on the other as a temple (a receptive void in which periodic acts of the community foundation are formally represented).

The plaza, founded through the union of bodies in space, thus constitutes an image of meaning (*sinnbild*) of the community; a symbol (*sinnbild*) that "not only points to the fact that people belong together, but demonstrates and visibly presents that fact."[63] This converts it, as Mauss would say, into a permanent rite.[64]

In conclusion, the game of pelota diffuses fundamental cultural meaning. It expresses a conception of the world, on whose basis prototypical behaviors are ordered, and embodies this conception in fundamental symbols. Its effectiveness as a communal, agglutinating factor comes, nevertheless, from a state of emotiveness, from this return to candidness, from this acting like children that the game itself creates, and which maintains the power of convocation despite the appropriations, the changes, and the renovations that the narratives concerning the game have to experience.

The "total social phenomena" of game and ritual constitute in fact an integral order, autonomous from other spheres of social life. This defining character implies the abandon of everyday order, just as in a certain way it is, as Gadamer suggests, the abandon of the self to the task and spirit of the game. This is what makes ritual effective, what makes it endure beyond the changes that happen at its core. The kingdom of pure possibility that opens up renders them effective, and ensures their continuity beyond the transformations that the society in which they are embedded undergoes.

---

62. Berger, *Lilac and Flag*, 124–25.
63. Gadamer, *Truth and Method*, 147.
64. Mauss, *Manual of Ethnography*, 184.

From the sixteenth century to this day, Basque society has transformed profoundly—yet what pelota fans feel before a sensational game has hardly changed at all. The formalization of the game has changed, yet its essence has not. New materials have been incorporated, new modalities have appeared, the plazas and frontons have changed, but the game is essentially the same: two teams, in pairs or individually, alternatively exchange a ball within some predetermined boundaries until one of them fails. Recall the rhythm: everything changes so that that nothing changes. What has never changed and never will is precisely its open, pure possibility, this always new contingency out of which, in determined moments, flows eternal actuality, the magic of the event.

In any moment, between pelotari, ball, and fronton magic may emerge, a moment of beauty unbound, of constituting harmony, in which the subject feels they are completely participating in something. It does not always happen; quite the contrary. But when it does, when the crowd is captured, there emerges what they came for: *jolas*, or magic transformation. The enthusiasm for this feeling of total comprehension, in a full sense, is so real and so liberating that one cannot but return to the fronton to experience it time and time again.

The game of pelota is an event whose effectiveness lies in the fact that it is capable of completely absorbing those who gather around it. The agonic setting has turned out to be extremely powerful to achieve that. Without the aesthetic comprehension of struggle, however, emotions would only precariously overtake the terraces.

Meanwhile, aesthetic understanding is a precept to a sensation of participation in something that transcends the contours of the self, but which is difficult to avoid as it radically belongs to the self. It comprises a being felt with others, this *sensus communis* that emanates from the most profound sources of understanding, from meanings. It results from a feeling of inclusion in an order, in a concrete mode of understanding the world and acting in it, of sharing it with others; ritual, on specific occasions, makes it real in the heart of each participant, dissolving them in common palpitation. The game of pelota constitutes an activating nucleus of meaning despite the changes and fissures its core has had to endure.

This work aims to understand the symbolic system that pelota constitutes, the signification that its forms suggest. This is why I have fundamentally referred to discourses and practices in which it is expressed. It is possible to identify a conceptualization of the world within a studied phenomenon; this is, however, not to say that pelota constitutes a harmonic conjuncture. The meanings that are constructed in it differ according to several variables among them the subject's own position in the framework itself. Time and time again, *pelotazales* confirm a sensation of loss and corruption in the game that finds its idealized expression in the past, and which looks into the future with concern. Disagreement and controversies can arise at any moment: balls that are not convincing, accusations of cheating, disappointed crowds, and so on. Nevertheless, sooner or later the game will produce the moment, this "eternal instant" that makes everything come together in a totality that becomes real, a totality made vital in each one of the bodies touched by it. It is a communion that has taken place. The struggle achieves its objective: to resolve itself, to return to the unity from which it departed, and cultural meanings are refounded within the present conjuncture, enabling change within permanence. Pelota thus fulfills its performative essence, and is constituted in an experience that is constitutive of community *being*. It will not lose its efficacy as long as it is played (*jokatu*), and fans continue to be con-jugated[65] by it (*jokatuta*).

---

65. Translator's note: *con-jugado* is a word play on the author's part, *jugar* meaning "play," and *jugado* "played."

Epilogue

By founding the first soccer team of Lekunberri, and by upgrading a meadow into a soccer field in 1940, the village had a modest rival from Iruñea-Pamplona. In it [there was] a player called Urtasun, from the Roncal-Erronkari Valley. This center forward ruined the game for the fans of Lekunberri, who did not stop shouting at him and insulting him.

After getting the fifth goal, the Lekunberri goalkeeper, tired of such humiliation, turned to Urtasun with these words: "Listen! In this you will win because I'm just a beginner; but since you are such a show-off here, I bet you will not have the guts to play hand pelota with me. Five five-peseta coins, if you will."

As the game resumed, neither the Lekunberri goalkeeper nor the Iruñea-Pamplona center forward showed up. Someone remarked that they were at the fronton playing a challenge game. Players and public all ran over there "to witness a contest of a sport *they understood and felt*, and which impassioned them."

Apparently, Urtasun was as dexterous with the pelota as with the soccer ball, and was clearly dominating the goalkeeper. "All the provocative harshness and vulgarity of the soccer field transformed at the fronton into enthusiastic admiration and fraternal *txalos* [applause]. That afternoon, Urtasun was the adored hero after having been a hated footballer. *Lekunberri had found itself again.*"[1]

This anecdote demonstrates a key argument of the book: the affective implication that pelota has for its fans, and the radical experience that it constitutes in the configuration of their *common sense*.

However, the anecdote is used here to exemplify something that has been apparent during my fieldwork: a transformation that has been sweeping pelota in recent years, and which shows a qualitative leap with respect to this common consciousness. This leap is not so much the

---

1. Bombín, *Historia, ciencia y código del juego de pelota*, 278–79. Emphasis added.

consequence of the privatization of organizational structures, something that had already taken place at the end of the nineteenth century or even earlier; rather, it has to do with what Daniel Lizarralde, writing in 1887, had identified in other societies, but which he did not expect to find in his own: "The principle of authority has not experimented yet, nor is it to be expected that it will in the future, such a frequent dislocation, which consists of moving from collectivity to a few persons or only one, who set themselves up as judges of the community making use of its desires and without counterweight of its elements."[2]

This dislocation, which may be easily identified at a political-institutional level in the steps taken at an organizational level in recent years, especially in the displacement of public institutions from decision-making, is evident when one interprets the behavior of agents, starting with the public.

The traditional pelota spectator, who still forms the majority of those who watch the game, is a spectator who enters the fronton alone or with his friends; he has a drink in the bar, greets the people he has not seen for a while or whom he saw the night before; he comments on previous games, on the game he is going to see, on personal questions, political matters, or any other topic; then he sits down. During the game he talks with those around him, applauds the points, comments on failures, and even jokes about the blunders of the pelotaris. He does not reproach the referee for his decisions, nor does he pay more attention to the court than necessary. If he is entangled in a conversation, he readily sacrifices a couple of points for its sake, and then asks the people around him about what happened if he missed something. If he finishes his drink and wants another one, he will wait until the point is over, and then he will go for another one. He might miss out on a few points because he may run into an old friend in the bar, and he returns to his seat once the play is finished. He keeps silent unless the court captures his attention to such an extent that he gets absorbed by it; he would only rise from his seat in celebration of a point if he considers that the player, independent of who he is and if he is against his bet, has executed a shot that merits it.

Today, however, a new kind of spectator is clearly attending games at the fronton. While he is still in the minority, and is only present at championship games or major contests, this type of spectator is usually

---

2. Lizarralde, "El principio de autoridad," 170.

young and comes to the fronton as part of a group. He normally sits in the higher terraces, where seats are cheaper, and he or she does not usually have access to the bookmakers, although at times their tennis balls, with their betting slips, do fly to these heights. These spectators might bring some kind of banner with them, and may wear signs of allegiance to one of the pelotaris, whether T-shirts with his name or a photo, with the name of a home village, or some other type of distinguishing feature that links them. These groups disregard the traditional rhythms of the fronton: they whistle the opposing player when he is about to serve, and applaud and chant the name of their own player when his rival makes a mistake. They pay close attention to everything that takes place on the court, as though following all the movements of their idol might strengthen him, and as if the launching of telepathic curses might weaken the opponent. They cheer their own score even if it results from a mistake by the opponent, and whistle opposition scores. They incorporate chants that they sing together, and inundate the fronton regardless of the result being favorable or not, since they must support their pelotari.

This type of spectator started going to the fronton in the late 1990s, and differs enormously from what I describe as the traditional spectator. The uniformity of clothes, the flags, banners, the chants sung together, the measured applause, and the fanaticism has little to do with the rowdy, chaotic public that does not act in unison unless it thinks the score deserves it, that applauds when it thinks the game merits it, and that tries not to manifest its unconditional allegiance to any of the pelotaris.

When a spectator applauds a mistake, he is applying behavioral schemes that have nothing to do with those of traditional spectators. In the past, if someone applauded a clear failure, he was looked upon as someone who did not understand the game, or as a disrespectful person. Today, however, it is a standard practice at important games, at least at hand pelota games. If one's player scores, he is applauded; if the opponent does, he is not. It is even possible to boo the good play of the rival or whistle him when he prepares to serve. This goes against the traditional logic of the applause, which responds to the good execution of a play or shot.

This transformation in the behavior of the crowd cannot be understood without contextualizing it. The general view is that the emerging fanaticism is due to importing behavioral patterns from other games, something that is without a doubt influential. Nevertheless, it may also be down to the very workings of internal structures, and to the agents of pelota themselves, pointing at the transformations in the referee's powers of competency, as well as those aspects that Lizarralde outlined and which the referee embodies: the principle of authority.

As I have argued in chapters 3 and 9, not too long ago the advertising posters of the games would read: "the customary norms will govern," norms that emanated from cultural heritage, from a common sense of being felt with others, from a con*sense*. Before making a consequential decision, however, the referee would turn toward the crowd with a respect that today has totally disappeared, and which is reduced to the greeting the referee performs together with the pelotaris before the game. The clothing of the referee himself, as well as his gesticulation, would show this deference toward the public.

> With what restraint they carried themselves, moving their left shoulder to raise the cloak [a typical garment worn on holidays in late nineteenth-century Buenos Aires and Montevideo], when there was a doubtful score and the players asked for judgment! All gathered in the middle of the plaza, put their heads together so that they did not have to raise their voice and nobody would hear their particular opinion, and the responsible person announced the resolution to the public, a resolution that was accepted and respected by all. The judges then sat down and the game continued.[3]

The solemnity of their act, the ceremony that sustained their authority, the testimony of respect surrounding their ministry, met with a similar response on part of the public: the crowd felt respected and its interests protected by this notoriously impartial figure, in whom they delegated their powers. The acknowledgement of the deliberations of the referee by the crowd constitutes a clear example of this:

> Such was the respect that this Judge and his resolutions had, that the greatest silence was maintained while he was at deliberation; and such was the submission to his judgments that, in the mist of so much interest at play, no voice ever rose against him, which made one of our well-known political figures acclaim at a game in Hernani: "*The Supreme Council of Castile* [in other words, the Spanish government] *enjoys no greater respect in its decisions.*"[4]

---

3. *Laurak Bat.* Year IV, no. 81.

4. Santiago Domingo, "Apuntes sobre el juego de pelota," 176.

The transformation of fan behavior took place as organizing companies started to freely establish regulations and substitute the collective feelings of the public as the principal source of authority for appointed officials. Today the referee is largely unknown to most spectators. He will have obtained the title of referee from the federation, and is contracted by the company that organizes the game; the same company also has pelotaris and bookmakers on its payroll, and collects an entrance fee from the public who wants to see the game. Today, the referee belongs to the company. It is the company that pays his salary and supplies his clothing, which also implies that his authority no longer comes from his exceptional adjustment to the collective desires of the public, but from regulation; a regulation that the company is free to establish.

Traditionally, the referee dressed in a similar way to most of the crowd, wearing the typical attire of the Basque adult male: flannel pants and marine blue jersey with white shirt and a beret, a beret that he took off each time he turned to the public or entered the court for deliberation. With the exception of the beret, this attire is maintained in the majority of the professional modalities, just as in amateur categories. It is not the case in the professional hand modality: since 2003, the referee has worn a brown tracksuit, a short-sleeved shirt, sweatpants, and sneakers.[5] This sports attire clearly points at the definite segregation of the referee from the public; the norms he represents do not emanate from a common consciousness, from *consensus omnium*, but from the very regulations established by the company, by which he is principally owned.

Today, this segregation produces incomprehensible decisions for the public. This is how, for example, at the finals of the four-and-a-half modality in 2002, the line judge who was supervising the line that defined the category slightly raised his hand before the ball hit by Olaizola II bounced. The head referee indicated a fault immediately. The assistant referee ran over to the head referee and told him he had been mistaken. It did not matter. According to the rules, once the head referee signals the point for the scoreboard, it is fixed. The crowd was outraged. The protests continued through various plays and were manifested through whistling the opponent Barriola for not taking a stand, and the referees, who maintained an absolutely indifferent attitude against the reprobation of the public.

---

5. As I write these lines (2012), the referee has returned to wearing traditional clothing in marine blue and black tones.

With the loss of any connection to the public and his subordination to the regulations and to the company that freely controls him, the referee feels unable to resolve questions that traditionally were his competence. This is why, for example, while the referee does have the necessary authority to remove a ball he considers unsuitable for the game from the basket, he never exercises this competence now. Despite the fact that sometimes bad play is attributed to the ball, it is unusual, if not impossible, for a referee to remove a ball from the basket. Because he lacks the support of his own charisma and the sympathy of the crowd, by removing a ball he would seriously damage the only pillar of his authority: impartiality. The ball is connatural with the player to such an extent that removing one of the balls could appear as a serious infringement on the player's freedom of choice. Equal opportunity would also be at least apparently jeopardized. The referee thus prefers not to exercise this competence that otherwise moves a whole protocol and numerous agents: the ball maker, the selector of the balls, the pelotaris themselves and their *botilleros*, and, finally, the keeper of the balls. By exercising that competence the referee could be accused of partiality and as such, could be disqualified.

The increasing number of agents at the fronton and the diversification of their functions have notably reduced the competences of the referee, something which might appear to be a logical consequence of the modernization of the game. What becomes most patent, however, is the fact that the public has been completely removed from the decision-making process, a capacity that now entirely belongs to the company. The company buys the balls, chooses them, contracts the referees, pelotaris, and bookmakers, and nothing stands in its way when it comes to changing the regulations.

The declining authority of the referee, whose sole responsibility today is watching if the ball bounces between the fault lines, within the court, also denotes a certain laxity with respect to the precepts of the game. The loss of the referee's capacities results in the almost total lack of penalization of the pelotari's play, and in the total absence of control over the companies' excesses. Dirty play thus flourishes; even the illegal *atxiki*, retaining the ball in one's hand, has become common again, and insistent rumors of cheating persist.

In this context it is not difficult to understand the spectators' change of behavior. They no longer find their own representation in the figure of the referee—they only find it in the figure of the player. The player is the only agent who represents the crowd at the fronton, principally because fans share a local geographical identity with him. This is why the spectator has succumbed to the satisfaction of his agonic instincts, returned to the logic of factions, and lost his capacity of criticism as spectator.

The New Game Regulations of Iruñea-Pamplona (1847) makes it clear, as I partly outlined in chapter 3, that partiality implies exclusion from the decision-making process. The privatization of and monopoly over all the elements that make up the pelota industry—balls, players, bookmakers, referees, and frontons—necessitates a partial and essentially agonic public to perpetuate itself, something that may end up seriously damaging the system of betting.

The bet is maintained above all by the *puntos*, or strong bettors. They are not accustomed to betting from the heart; at the very least they intend to rationalize their posture. They need to have confidence in the honesty of the players and the authority of the referee, as well as in the seriousness of the company when it comes to organizing games. This seriousness has not yet been called into question, despite the fact that the arrangements for the last hand pelota championships received a lot of criticism by the *pelotazales*.

The 2003 hand pelota championship left a bad taste in the public's mouth. Its regulations were established for the occasion and, according to the president of the LEPM, were "unalterable." These regulations maintained the immobility of the dates: the postponement of games was not possible, something that has been customary in pelota. It also convoked a brutal eliminatory semifinal in which the sudden-death system and in fact the only game was substituted by a mini-league among the semifinalists. Each player had to play three games to qualify for the finals. The company thus ensured six games, with all that it implied in terms of entrance tickets, bets, broadcasting rights, and advertising at the fronton. The new regulation depreciated the presence of the best players in the finals, a desire in keeping with the *pelotazale* tradition; a tradition that maintains that a solid champion should participate in great hand pelota contests throughout the year.

In 2003, Olaizola II, the player who had defeated three champions by large margins—among them the champion of the previous year, Barriola—had injured his triceps at the game against Beloki described in chapter 4. Faced with the horror of going against the traditional wish that the best should play the final, which was felt to be an integral feature of pelota, the championship organizers decided to break the rules: Olaizola II was allowed to postpone the game.

Nevertheless, the LEPM itself, because it is comprised of two companies with particular interests, of which only one controlled the pelotari in question, did not agree on the matter; and eventually, the conflict was only overcome by the establishment of a date too tight to enable the full recuperation of the player. In short, he had to play within three weeks at the latest. It was the last game of the semifinals against Patxi Ruiz, which Olaizola II did not need to win given that victory in the previous games had already qualified him. There were doubts about the organization of the game that, by not being played, would have led to qualification for Ruiz and passage to the finals against Beloki. Not playing the game would have also implied a substantial loss of money for the Asegarce company, to whom both players belonged.

Olaizola II decided to play. At 14–8 in his favor, however, he had to retire with his arm completely "dropped"[6] which resulted in the suspension of the game. The bets were resolved by apportionment, and the company appropriated the entrance tickets, the broadcasting rights, and advertisement fees, keeping these two players in the finals: Olaizola II and Patxi Ruiz. The next question was when to play the finals, which again ignited controversy. The issue was whether to wait until Olaizola II had completely recovered (something absolutely contrary to the rules, to which Patxi Ruiz was holding on to in order not to postpone the game); or setting a specific date and, if Olaizola II was still injured then, substituting him with another pelotari, in this case Barriola.

The *pelotazales* were disconcerted.[7] Every option went contrary to the rules. If they waited, which had been the most typical solution in the past, they would be going against the regulations that, although now disregarded, all players, not without protest, had accepted at the beginning of the championship, and behind which Ruiz had every right to hide. If they established a date within a period of three weeks, either someone other than the one qualified pelotari would have played the final (something unheard of), or the game would be suspended and Ruiz crowned; or they assumed the risk that Olaizola II would play injured because his doctor, employed by the company, had doubts about his full recovery, especially after the second injury.

---

6. This type of tricep injury, one of the most serious injuries a pelotari can suffer, is traditionally called "*brazo caído*" (dropped arm).

7. They continued disconcerted in 2011, when the companies decided to substitute the singles finalist Xala with Bengoetxea III. This decision became an issue in the Basque press for days and at the end social pressure forced the companies to withdraw.

The second option, lying between fixing a specific date and directly crowning Ruiz, would have been more in tune with tradition, but not with the current regulations that leaned more toward substitution. However, the company, following its own entrepreneurial logic, did not even consider it. Either Olaizola II would play, or his place would be taken by Barriola, who had also made it clear that since he had not qualified for the finals, he was not going to play.

Olaizola II, who had already played half a game injured against Beloki and had won, wanted to take his chance. If he recovered sufficiently, he could maybe endure it, thus closing an extraordinary year in which he was indisputably the best pelotari. Besides, the injury could ease in the intervening three weeks, but even so, in no case could he really have contemplated playing a final, as those who already had a similar injury anticipated.[8]

The game day arrived and the coin turned out favorably for Olaizola II, who had declared that he was fine, although he reached the finals without practically touching a ball. A few scores into the game, people were watching him with concern. Some had noted it right from the beginning: "he is protecting his right. He carries it instead of hitting it." Patxi Ruiz, on his part, took his game seriously. He played with fury because he was tired of people questioning his merits in getting to the finals. He deployed all he had, all a lion has, neutralized the cunning game of the fox and, granting that the other was injured, he won the game. Although the game was played to the end and Ruiz did everything fine, it was not a contest between equals, and the *txapela* fell under suspicion: "Now they have a champion, let's see how they defend him during the year," a hand pelota champion commented to me as he departed from the game.

Ruiz did not have a brilliant year in the red jersey of the champion. Nor did Barriola for that matter, after deservingly becoming champion in 2002. And probably neither did many others before. The aims behind certain decisions are not always realized. Nor are expectations. Deserving *txapelas* have yielded flat champions. Solid champions have closed

---

8. Retegi II wrote an op-ed article in the *El Correo* newspaper saying that he had played several finals injured, declarations that, according to some of the public, were the result of his new position as technical director of the LEPM and creator of the championship more than as a consequence of his championship record. In ten out of fourteen hand pelota finals that he played he entered directly in the final as defender of the *txapela*, as reigning champion. This was the traditional system and it is still practiced in instrument modalities today.

years of authentic drought. And disastrous championships have offered the public fantastic encounters.

Reality does not respond to a priori planning. It may coincide with them, but plans don't guarantee any outcome. As Jesús García Ariño said to Fortún Garcés: "The game carries with it all the tricks that players want to put in practice,"[9] wherein rests its enchantment. Because it is like life, only captured. The game, as opposed to life, can always start again.

During my fieldwork, I have been able to confirm a radical change in pelota since 1998. Today, the motivations that used to drive what have been termed here the traditional public have nothing to do with the motivations of companies that regulate the game, which are driven by pure financial interests. Today, authority is maintained by criteria that, while they may be generalized, do not respond to traditional sensibilities; something that I suspect was not all that unusual before but indeed another easily verifiable historical fact.

I do not think, however, that all this can make a dent on passions for the game. As long as pelota keeps filling people with enthusiasm, it matters little what the companies do to it. The reporter Juan Irigoyen expressed it in the following way in 1944: "The game of pelota, if it wants to stay alive, has to be forcefully aided by the popular spirit that has nourished it outside of industrial courts, even if they will harvest the benefits of the advantages of this popular assistance, which will supply the continuity and renovation of players."[10]

There may be a time when the *pelotazale* tradition will count for more than renovating aspirations when it comes to deciding about regulating the game. Perhaps there will be a feeling that, by endorsing again the traditional elements of the game, there will be greater financial benefit. Or just the opposite, and pelota will continue to resemble the organizational pattern of other professional sports. What appears certain is that pelota, so long as it offers magical moments and carries the public at the frontons away, will continue, whatever the current circumstances are, and will constitute an ideal context for interpreting the worldview of those who practice and celebrate it.

---

9. Garcés, *Campeones manomanistas, 1940–1990*, 144.

10. Irigoyen, "La pelota, como deporte y espectáculo," 9.

Glossary

ancho. "Width," the front right side of the court. It is one of the "hollows" of the fronton, where players hit the ball in order to score or to move the opponent off court.

a *punto*. A ball game, generally played informally by youth, where the best player wins by the gradual elimination of the rest from the game.

arkupe. In Basque it literally means "under the arches." They are frontons situated in the atriums of church buildings.

artekaria. In Basque, literally "intermediary," with reference to bookmakers.

at par. A phrase that refers to the bet when it is even, that is, when it costs the same to bet on both players.

atxiki. In Basque, literally "to hold." In the hand ball modality, it refers to the fault the player commits when he grabs the ball instead of hitting it. In modalities with instrument, *atxiki* refers to the time of contact between the instrument and the ball. We distinguish between two types: the *atxikihaundia* ("great *atxiki*") of the jai alai, which retains the ball for a few seconds with each hit; and the *atxikitxikia* ("small *atxiki*") of the games in Iparralde—the joko-garbi, rebote, and xare modalities.

besagain. In Basque, literally "arm in the air." It refers to the volley the player executes with arms extended to the side.

blé. Refers to indirect games against a wall. All the professional modalities of Basque pelota (hand, pala, remonte and jai alai) are played *a blé*.

botepronto. Hitting the ball as soon as it bounces in the court.

botillero. Literally "bottle keeper." Assistant of the *pelotari* who provides counsel during individual games.

botivolea. Hitting the ball as though it was a volley, that is, above the head once it has bounced in the court.

buruz-gain. In Basque, literally "above the head." It refers to the shot that flies over the head of the opponent, making it impossible for him to return it.

cancha. "Court," space of the fronton where the pelotari's game takes place. It is marked by the *eskas* or fault lines.

cátedra. "Cathedra." Part of the pelota public that is composed of the *puntos*, or strong bettors, who deteremine the *momio* or odds ratio.

cesta-punta. Professional modality known as Jai-alai (in Basque, literally "happy fiesta"), which is played with a wicker basket with a big belly, attached to the right hand. The ball enters and leaves by the tip of the instrument after it remains for a few seconds in the belly. This action is called *punta-volea* or "tip volley." Exclusively masculine.

cestaño. It is composed of the four or six select balls that the players may use during a game. It also refers to the basket where the balls are kept, and which is guarded by the head referee during the game.

colored. A term that means red in the pelota game and, as an extension, it refers to the player who plays in this color, identified as the color of the champion.

counter-court. The area of the fronton between the court and the terraces. The referees and the bookmakers are situated there.

cuadrilla. A goup of friends of the same age, to which one belongs all his or her life and which gains its cohesive and referential strength principally during youth. It is a typical form of solidarity in the rural Basque Country.

cuadro. "Square" of the court. Each of the areas that longitudinally divide the court. They measure about 3.5 meters, and are marked with a white line and a number on the left wall.

cuadro. "Squad," "team" of pelotaris. A group of professional pelotaris that play for the same company or at the same fronton.

cuadros alegres. "Happy squares." The front squares of the court situated closer to the frontis (front wall), where the front court players develop their game with varied and rapid strikes.

chapa (coin). A coin that the head referee flips into the air at the beginning of the game in order to decide which player will execute the first serve. It is normally a coin whose two faces are red and blue. It is also called "lion castle" as they would use this typical Castilian coin.

chapa (of the fronton). A 10 cm (3.9 in) wide iron sheet that stretches horizontally at the frontis at the height of 1 m (3.28 ft). If the ball touches it or hits the wall below it, it is considered a fault. When a ball hits it, the *chapa* gives off a sound, for which it is also called "*la chismosa*" or "the gossipy," for it tells the players the point is lost.

chaza. Point where the ball is driven back, or where it stops. Proper and central to long modality games, in which an imaginary line serves to temporarily divide the game area in order to contend a fifteen. For a description of the rules of long modality games, see the part titled "The Establishment of Pelota" in chapter 2 "The Pelota of the Basques."

direct game. A term that refers to modalities where the pelotaris are positioned facing each other, without sharing the same play area. Direct games are the long modalities—laxoa and rebote—and the paxaka.

eskas. In Basque, literally "insufficient, faulty." Lines that mark the court area. The Basque games differ from other pelota games inasmuch as it is considered a fault if the the ball bounces on the *eskas*.

four-and-a-half. A hand modality where the ball, once the serve is executed, may not bounce in the court beyond the four-and-a-half square. It is also called *jaula*, "cage."

frontenis. A nonprofessional modality played with a racquet, a solid rubber ball at a 30 meter (98.4 ft) fronton. There exist a female modality.

frontis. The front wall of the fronton for games against wall, or games *a blé*. The ball must rebound on the wall with each strike.

fronton. Generically it is the space for the Basque pelota game. There are many types of fronton, while the one that this designation most readily evokes is the fronton with a left side wall, let it be 30 m (98.4 ft), 36m (118.1 ft) or 54 m (177.1 ft), depending on the modalities it homes.

fronton, industrial. See "industrial fronton."

game, direct. See "direct game."

game, indirect. See "indirect game."

gerriko. In Basque literally "of the waist." A sash the pelotaris wear, and which marks the disjunction between them: either blue or colored (red).

gozar. "To get it right" when hitting the ball. They say the pelotari "gets it right" when he hits the ball energetically and efficiently.

grand xistera. A term that designates the instrument of the jai alai in Iparralde. It is also the name of the typical modality that is played here with this instrument, in an open plaza, three against three.

guante. "Glove." A leather instrument that is attached to the hand, and where the ball enters at the hight of the wrist, and exits at the tip of the glove in an action that is called *remontar* or "soaring." There are two types of gloves: the long glove, which only the back court players of the laxoa game use; and the short glove, which the front court players use in both the laxoa and the rebote games, and it is an instrument used in the paxaka game.

hand ball. A professional and amateur modality where the ball is hit directly with the hand, which is recently protected by "tacos," pads of one square centimeter, attached with band aid. The ball used in this modality is solid and weighs about 105 grams if it is played on a fronton with a left wall, and some 90 grams if played on trinquet. Exclusively masculine.

Hegoalde. In Basque literally "the south side." It refers to the southern part of the Basque country, and belongs to Spain. It is composed of the provinces of Araba, Bizkaia, Gipuzkoa, and Navarre.

Hermandad. Literally "brotherhood." A Medieval judicial-police institution that are constituted in the Basque Country at the end of the fifteenth century in order to pacify the rural areas that were characterized by factious conflicts.

hordago. In Basque, literally "there it is." A phrase used in the card game called *mus* to express that the player wants to bet everything on the next play. To "throw an ordago" (*lanzar un órdago*) is an expression that means risking a lot or betting everything, depending on the context.

instrument. Any instrument that is used for the pelota game, and which differentiates between the modalities. There are many types of instruments, among them are: *cesta, remonte, xare, guante, xistera, raquet, paltea, short pala, long pala.*

indarra. "Force" in Basque. This monograph uses the concept as described by Sandra Ott, which relates the term with the notion of sacred power. In anthropology, it is also known as mana, wakan, etc.

indirect game. A term that refers to modalities where the players are positioned facing the frontis, the front wall, sharing the same play area.

They are also called games against wall, or *a blé*; the majority of Basque pelota games are indirect games.

industrial fronton. Closed fronton where the professional modalities of hand pelota, pala, jai alai, and remonte are played.

Iparralde. In Basque, literally "north side." It refers to the northern part of the Basque Country, which belongs to France. It is composed of the provinces of Lapurdi, Lower Navarre, and Zuberoa.

jai alai. In Basque, literally "happy fiesta." A term coined by Serafín Baroja in order to name the fronton of Donosti-San Sebastián, built in 1887 on the promenade of Astigarraga. Today it principally refers to the game of the *cesta-punta* or jai alai, and the frontons that home this modality.

joko-garbi. In Basque, literally "clean game." A typical modality of Iparralde played with a a xistera that is shorter and has smaller belly than the cesta. It is played in an open plaza, three against three players. The term joko-garbi was first used to differentiate the traditional xistera game from that which arrived from Argentina at the end of the nineteenth century, and which is the actual jai alai. It was considered in its moment a dirty game for its excessive retention of the ball in the cesta.

joko. One of the senses of "play" in Basque. It refers to competitive, principally disjunctive play: win or lose. It is submitted to rules and related to play and game among adults. See *jolas*.

jolas. One of the senses of "play" in Basque. It refers to noncompetitive, illusory, unregulated play characteristic of childhood. See *joko*.

kaiola. In Basque it means "cage." It is a small fronton closed by the four sides, where the ball may bounce on every wall.

kiski. See "potro," "colt."

konsejupe. In Basque, literally "under the town council." They are frontons situated in the atriums of town councils.

kontatzaile. In Basque, literally "he who counts." During the pelota game, he keeps the score and announces the point at a normally singing, loud voice. This figure has disappeared from the majority of the modalities, especially from those that are played on industrial frontons. They are still present, however, in long modality games and modalities typically played in open plazas in Iparralde.

laxoa. Traditional long modality game that is played in the Navarrese valleys of Baztan and Malerreka. It is played in an open plaza that is between 80 and 100 meters long (87.7 yd—109 yd), and 15 m wide (16.4 yd), with glove (short for the front court players, long for the back court players), and in teams of four pelotaris. For a description of *laxoa*, see the part titled "The Establishment of Pelota" in chapter 2 "The Pelota of the Basques."

long games. Long games are direct modality games played in plazas that measure between 80 and 100 meters (87.7 yd—109 yd), like the laxoa and the rebote. For a description of long modality games, see the part titled "The Establishment of Pelota" in chapter 2 "The Pelota of the Basques."

manomanista (hand ball championship). Singles hand modality championship in fronton with a left wall, organized once a year in spring. It is the major championship of the modality, as it yields the champion.

momio. Odds ratio. Initial deliberation of the bet, calculated in proportion to what the cátedra considers are the possibilities of victory for both pelotaris or couples. For a description of wagering in pelota game, see the part titled "The Wager with Bookmakers: Turning the Coat" of chapter 3 "The Control of *Indarra*."

momista. A term that comes from *momio*, "odds ratio." A bettor who usually plays downbound, in favor of the player who at the beginning has less chance to win. That is to say, the momista bets for the cheaper player who, if he wins in the end, will make the momista win more money by risking less. For a description of the various types of bettors see the part titled "The Wager with Bookmakers: Turning the Coat" of chapter 3 "The Control of *Indarra*," and the part titled "Postures at the Fronton" of chapter 9 "The Plaza: The Embodiment of Society."

nerve, *nervio*. The vitality of a strike. They say the player "has nerve" when he is able to to strike the ball with strength, force.

open plaza. A type of fronton typical in Iparralde; it only has one wall, the frontis or front wall.

pala. Solid wood instrument of an oblong shape, with which the player strikes the ball in the modality called the same. The pala modality is professional and is played on a fronton with a left wall. Exclusively male game.

paleta. A flat instrument made of wood, with a similar shape as that of the typical pala of paddle of the game in Argentina.

pelota goma. "Rubber paleta." An amateur modality played with a small, shovel-shaped instrument and with a solid rubber ball on trinquet as well as on frontons with a left wall. There are female modalities.

paleta cuero. "Leather paleta." Amateur modality that is played with a small, shovel-shaped instrument and a solid leather ball on trinquet as well as on frontons with a left wall. Exclusively male modality.

par, at. See "at par."

paxaka. A traditional modality of direct game played with a short glove and a large leather ball of great dimensions. The most characteristic feature of this modality is that a net divides the play area, where two trios confront each other.

pelotari. In Basque, literally "he who practices pelota." Pelota player.

pelotazale. In Basque, literally "fan of pelota."

pelotero. The person who prepares the balls for the pelota game.

pido. "Request." A petition by a pelotari that demands the recognition of a fault by during the game.

plaza. Central place in the public space. In the Basque Country, it is a term that is also used to refer to the place where pelota is played, the fronton.

plaza-gizon. In Basque, literally "plaza man." It is a polysemic term, with a clear connotation of a public man. See the part "plaza man" in chapter 9 "The Plaza: The Embodiment of Society."

plaza, open. See "open plaza."

poder. "Power." "Having power" means hitting the ball strongly and dominating the game.

potro (also kiski). The nucleus of the pelota formed by a small miter ball wrapped in rubber. The greater or smaller quantity of the rubber will determine the type of the ball, its personality. In order to understand the importance of the diversity of balls, see the part titled "The Box of Weapons" of chapter 3 "The Control of Indarra."

primis (play primis). A game played in groups typically in childhood. All those who want to play are in the court; the ball must be returned by the player who is closest to it as it bounces, or the one who is considered to be in the most optimal position to return it. The game develops through the elimination of those who fail to return the ball, or those who do not hit it even if they are closest to it. When only two players remain at play, they hit the ball alternatively as it is done in serious play. The person who wins gains a primi or point, which will save them from elimination the next time they make a mistake.

punta-volea. "Tip volley." A movement typical of the xistera and jai alai modalities, as in them the ball enters and exits the instrument at its tip, thus executing an *atxiki* or retention. It differs from the *remontar*, the "soaring" of the guante and remonte modalities.

punto. Central bettor in the pelota game. He is part of the cátedra. It is a bettor who plays upbounds, betting on the favorite. For a description of the types of bettors, see the part titled "The Wager with Bookmakers: Turning the Coat" of chapter 3 "The Control of *Indarra*," and the part "Postures at the Fronton" in chapter 9 "The Plaza: The Embodiment of Society."

punto (play punto). See "Primis".

quinze. The worth of a score in long modalities, which compose games. A game includes 4 "fifteens:" 15, 30, 40, and game.

raquetista. "Racquetist." Women who played professional pelota since the 1910s until the 1980s. They played racquet with a leather ball in industrial frontones all over the world.

raya. "Stripe, line." A central feature in long modality games, in which an imaginary stripe or line temporarily divides the game area in order to play a fifteen. They also call "raya," "line" the artefact they use to mark this imaginary line, which is located at the side of the game area. For a description of the regulations of long modality games, see the part titled "The Establishment of Pelota" in chapter 2 "The Pelota of the Basques."

rebote. "Rebound." A traditional long modality game that is principally played in Iparralde and the locations of Villabona (Gipuzkoa) and Zubieta (Navarra). It is played in an open plaza that is is 100 m long and 15 m wide, in teams of five pelotaris, two front court players with short gloves, and three back court players with xistera. For a description of the rebote, see the part titled "The Establishment of Pelota" in chapter 2 "The Pelota of the Basques.

rebote. Main rebound wall of the plaza where the serve is directed. In frontons with a left wall, the back wall of the fronton is called rebote or rebound wall.

rebotear. "To rebound." The action of returning the ball once it hit the back wall or rebote of the fronton.

remontar. A movement typical of the guante and remonte modalities; the ball enters the instrument by the wrist and exits at its tip, without any retention. It differs from the movement called *punta-volea*, or "tip-volley" characteristic of the xistera and the jai alai.

remonte. Professional modality typical of the north of Navarre and Gipuzkoa. It is played with a long wicker basket that has little curvature. The ball enters the instrument by the wrist and exits at its point, without retention.

sotamano. Hitting the ball in the air; as opposed to the volley, it is executed upwards from below.

tacos. Small protective pads.

tanteo. The succession of necessary points in order to win the game. The number of points depends on the modality: 22 in hand ball, 35 in jai alai, 45 in pala etc.

tanto. "Point." Each one of the points of a game. They also call *tanto* the interval of the game from the serve until the resolution of the point.

trinquete. Trinquet. A space closed at four sides, where the ball may bounce on every wall. Besides the right side wall, it has a series of features that differentiate it from the fronton: the *tejadillo*, spectator's gallery that stretches along the whole left side wall; the *fraile*, a bevel in the corner that connects the right side wall and the frontis; and the *xilo*, a hole on the right side of the frontis, about 45 cm above th *chapa*, which renders unpredictable the departure of every ball that hits it. In the trinquet they play hand modality, paleta and xare, modality that is only played at these spaces.

txapela. In Basque it means "beret." This is the maximum trophy a pelotari may aspire for. He is crowned with it when he is proclaimed champion, *Txapelduna*, literally "He who possesses the beret."

Txapeldun. In Basque, literally "he who possesses the *txapela,* the beret;" it means champion. The *Txapeldun*, besides being crowned with the *txapela* of the champion, also has the honor to play colored (red) in every game that he plays during the year until the finals.

txik-txak. Typical move of the jai alai modality. The ball brounces very close to the angle that the floor and the back wall form, it lacks the necessary projection, which renders its return impossible. It's a point. In the *txik-txak*, as opposed to the *txula*, the ball impacts fisrt in the floor and then on the back wall.

txoko. Left front part of the court right by the left side wall. It is one of the "hollows" of the fronton, where the ball is hit in order to make it difficult for the opponent to return it.

txula. Characteristic move of the jai alai modality. The ball bounces very close to the angle formed by the floor and the back wall, does not take the necessary trajectory, which makes it impossible to return. It's a point. In the *txula*, as opposed to the *txik-txaka*, the ball first hits the back wall, and then dies by crashing into the floor.

xare. Instrument of the form of a pala, with a chestnut or hazelnut frame within which there is a loosely knit net. It is also known as "Argentine raquet." They also call *xare* the modality that is played with this instrument, and which is exclusively played in a trinquet.

xistera. Instrument made of wicker; it is somwhat smaller and has a smaller belly than that of the jai alai. It is used to play the rebote and joko-garbi modalities.

Bibliography

Abril, Enrique. *Dos siglos de pelota vasca.* Donostia-San Sebastián: C.A.M, 1971.

Aguirre, Rafael. *Juegos y deportes del País Vasco.* Donostia-San Sebastián: Kriselu, 1989.

Amorós, Francisco. "El último tanto." *Euskal-Erria* 27 (1892): 51.

Anasagasti, Iñaki. "No sé lo que querrán estos cuatro pelotaris." *Deia,* September 12, 1988.

Aralar, José de. *La victoria de Munguía y la reconciliación de oñazinos y ganboinos.* Buenos Aires: Ekin, 1949.

Aranzadi, Juan. *Milenarismo Vasco: Edad de oro, etnia y nativismo.* Madrid: Taurus, 1982.

Archetti, Eduardo P. "The Moralities of Argentinian Football." In *The Ethnography of Moralities,* edited by Signe Howell, 98–123. London: Routledge, 1997.

Armistead, Samuel G., and Joseba Zulaika, eds., *Voicing the Moment: Improvised Oral Poetry and Basque Tradition.* Reno: Center for Basque Studies, 2005.

Árnason, Jóhann Páll, and Peter Murphy, eds. *Agon, logos y polis: The Greek Achievement and Its Aftermath.* Stuttgart: Steiner, 2001.

Arpal, Jesús. *La sociedad tradicional en el País Vasco.* Donostia-San Sebastián: L. Haranburu, 1979.

———. "Solidaridades elementales y organizaciones colectivas en el País Vasco." In *Processus sociaux, idéologies et pratiques culturelles dans la société basque,* edited by Pierre Bidart (dir). Pau: Université de Pau et des Pays de L'Adour, 1985.

Arramendy, Jean. *Le Jeu, La Balle et Nous.* Biarritz: Atlantica, 2000.

Arriaga, Emiliano de. *Lexicón etimológico naturalista y popular del bilbaíno neto*. Bilbao: Ayuntamiento de Bilbao, 2001.

——. *La pastelería y otras narraciones bilbaínas*. Bilbao: El Cofre del Bilbaíno, 1962.

Augé, Marc. "Espacio y Alteridad." *Revista de Occidente* no. 140 (January 1993): 13–34.

——. *Las formas del olvido*. Barcelona: Gedisa, 1998.

——. *Los no-lugares*. Barcelona: Gedisa, 1996.

Auguet, Roland. *Los juegos romanos*. Barcelona: Ayma, 1972.

Aulestia, Gorka. *Improvisational Poetry from the Basque Country*. Reno: University of Nevada Press, 1995.

Azcona, Jesús. *Para comprender la antropología: vol. 2: La cultura*. Estella: Verbo Divino, 1991.

Balandier, Georges. *Political Anthropology*. Translated by A. M. Sheridan Smith. London: Allen-Lane, 1970.

Barandiaran, Miguel. *Obras completas I: Diccionario ilustrado de mitología vasca y algunas de sus fuentes*. Bilbao: Editorial de la Gran Enciclopedia Vasca, 1972.

Baroja, Pio. *Guía del País Vasco Español-Francés*. Madrid: Caro Raggio, 1940.

Barrios, Manuel. *Narrar el abismo: Ensayos sobre Nietzsche, Hölderlin y la disolución del clasicismo*. Valencia: Pre-textos, 2001.

Bartra, Roger. *El salvaje en el espejo*. Barcelona: Destino, 1996.

Basas, Manuel. "La calle de la pelota." *Bilbao*, May 30, 1988.

Bateson, Gregory. *Mind and Nature: A Necessary Unity*. New York: Dutton, 1979.

Bazán, Iñaki. *De Túbal a Aitor: Historia de Vasconia*. Madrid: La esfera de los libros, 2002.

Bell, Catherine. *Ritual: Perspectives and Dimensions*. New York: Oxford University Press, 1997.

——. *Ritual Theory, Ritual Practice*. New York: Oxford University Press, 1992.

Beristain, Jose María. *Azkoitia, cuna de pelotaris: 100 años de pasión por la pelota*. Donostia-San Sebastián: Ayuntamiento de Azkoitia, 2000.

Berger, John. *Lilac and Flag: An Old Wives' Tale of a City*. New York: Vintage Books, 1992.

Bertsolariak. *Pelota, euskal jokoa*. Temas guipuzcoanos 8. Donostia-San Sebastián: Caja de Ahorros Municipal de San Sebastián, 1975.

Bestard, Joan, and Jesús Contreras. *Bárbaros, paganos, salvajes y primitivos: Una introducción a la Antropología*. Barcelona: Barcanova, 1987.

Blanchard, Kendall, and Alyce Taylor Cheska. *The Anthropology of Sport: An Introduction*. South Hadley, MA: Bergin & Garvey, 1985.

Blazy, Edmond. *La Pelote Basque*. Baiona: N.P., 1929.

Bombín, Luís. *Historia, ciencia y código del juego de pelota*. Madrid: Lauro, 1946.

Bombín, Luís, and Rodolfo Bouzas. *El gran libro de la pelota*, 2 vols. Madrid: Caja de ahorros municipal de San Sebastián, 1976.

Bourdieu, Pierre. *Practical Reason: On the Theory of Action*. Cambridge: Polity, 1998.

———. *¿Qué significa hablar? Economía de los intercambios linguísticos*. Madrid: Akal, 1985.

Bruner, Edward M. "Experience and Its Expressions." In *The Anthropology of Experience,* edited by V. Turner and E. M. Bruner. Chicago: University of Illinois Press, 1986.

Bullen, Margaret. *Basque Gender Studies*. Reno: Center for Basque Studies, 2003.

———. "Gender and Identity in the *Alardes* of Two Basque Towns." In *Basque Cultural Studies*, edited by William A. Douglass, Carmelo Urza, Linda White, and Joseba Zulaika, 149–77. Reno: Basque Studies Program [Center for Basque Studies], 1999.

Bullen, Margaret, and José Antonio Egido. *Tristes espectáculos: Las mujeres y los Alardes de Irún y Hondarribia*. Bilbao: UPV/EHU, 2003.

Buytendijk, Frederic Jacobus Johannes. "El jugar en el hombre" In *Nueva Antropología*, edited by Hans-Georg Gadamer and Paul Vogler. Translated by Margarida Costa. Barcelona: Omega, 1976.

Caillois, Roger. *Los juegos y los hombres*. México: FCE, 1994.

———. *Man and the Sacred*. New York: The Free Press, 2001.

———. *Man, Play, and Games*. New York: Free Press of Glencoe, 1961.

Candau, Joël. *Anthropologie de la mémoire*. París: Presses universitaires de France, 1996.

Canetti, Elias. *Crowds and Power*. New York: Farrar Straus Giroux, 1988.

Caro Baroja, Julio. *The Basques*. Reno: Center for Basque Studies, University of Nevada, Reno, 2009.

——. *Introducción a la historia social y económica del pueblo vasco*. Donostia-San Sebastián: Txertoa, 1974.

Cassirer, Ernst. *Antropología filosófica*. México: FCE, 1963.

——. *The Philosophy of Symbolic Forms*. New Haven: Yale University Press, 1953, 1996.

Cátedra, María. "Símbolos." In *Ensayos de antropología cultural*, edited by Joan Prat and Ángel Matínez. Barcelona: Ariel, 1996.

Cecilio, Manu. *Antología fotográfica de la pelota a mano*. Bilbao: El Correo and Sociedad Vascongada de Publicaciones, 2003.

Cercadillo, Manuel. *Manual completo de la pelota vasca: De interés para iniciarse en la pala y raqueta*. Bilbao: Editorial de la Gran Enciclopedia Vasca, 1981.

Cheska, Alice T. *Play as Context*. New York: Leisure Press, 1979.

Clastres, Pierre. *Investigaciones en antropología política*. Translated by Estela Campo. Barcelona: Gedisa, 1981.

Coca, Santiago. *El hombre deportivo*. Madrid: Alianza, 1993.

Connerton, Paul. *How Societies Remember*. Cambridge: Cambridge University Press, 1989.

Coromines, José. *Diccionario crítico etimológico castellano e hispánico*. Madrid: Gredos, 1992.

Csikszentmihalyi, Mihaly. "Some Paradoxes in the Definition of Play." In *Play as Context*, edited by A. T. Cheska. New York: Leisure Press, 1979.

Cushman, Horatio Bardwell. *History of the Choctaw, Chickasaw and Natchez Indians*. Greenville, TX: Headlight Printing House, 1899.

D'Elbée, Christian. "L'epoque de Perkain." *Gure-Herria* (1922): n.p.

——. "Les jeux de pelote basque." *Gure-Herria* (1921): n.p.

Delgado, Manuel. *El animal público*. Barcelona: Anagrama, 1999.

De Luze, Albert. *Le magnifique histoire du jeu de paumme*. París: Bossard, 1933.

De Man, Paul. *Allegories of Reading: Figurative Language in Rousseau, Nietzsche, Rilke and Proust*. Yale: University Press, 1979.

Del Valle, Teresa, dir. "La liminalidad y su aplicación al estudio de la cultura vasca" *Kobie* 2 (1987): 7–12.

———. *Mujer vasca: Imagen y realidad*. Barcelona: Anthropos, 1985.

Diáz Cruz, Rodrigo. *Archipiélago de rituales: Teorías Antropológicas del ritual*. Barcelona: Anthropos, 1998.

Douglas, Mary. *How Institutions Think*. London: Routledge & Kegan Paul, 1987.

Douglass, William. A. *Death in Murelaga*. Seattle: University of Washington Press, 1969.

Duhour, Pierre. "Hazpandar bi pilotari." *Gure-Herria* (1922): n.p.

Dumezil, Georges. *El destino del guerrero: Aspectos míticos de la función guerrera entre los indoeuropeos*. México: S. XXI, 1971.

Duncan, Hugh Dalziel. *Communication and Social Order*. New York: The Bedminster Press, 1962.

———. *Symbols in Society*. New York: Oxford University Press, 1968.

Dunleavy, Aidan O., and Andrew W. Miracle, Jr. "Sport: An Experimental Setting for the Development of a Theory of Ritual." In *Play as Context*, edited by A. T. Cheska. New York: Leisure Press, 1979.

Dunning, Eric. "Preface." *Sport and Leisure in the Civilizing Process: Critique and Counter*-Critique, edited by Eric Dunning and Chris Rojek. Toronto and Buffalo: University of Toronto Press, 1992.

Durkheim, Emile. *The Elementary Forms of the Religious Life*. New York: Free Press, 1965 [1915].

Eagle, Sonia Jacqueline. *Work and Play among the Basques of Southern California*. Ph.D. dissertation, Purdue University, 1979.

Echevarría, Javier. *Sobre el juego*. Barcelona: Destino, 1999.

Edouard Baudrimont's, Alexandre. *Historie de des Basques ou Escualdunais primitifs*. Paris: Chez Benjamin Duprat, 1854.

Eliade, Mircea. *Mito y realidad*. Barcelona: Labor, 1994.

———. *Lo Sagrado y lo Profano*. Madrid: Guadarrama, 1967

Elias, Norbert, and Eric Dunning. *The Quest for Excitement: Sport and Leisure in the Civilising Process*. Oxford: Blackwell, 1986.

Elissalde, Jean, and Louis Dassance. "Erreboteko jokoa." *Gure-Herria* (1921): n.p.

Enríquez, Javier, Concepción Hidalgo, Araceli Lorente, and Adela Matínez. *Ordenanzas municipales de Bilbao (1477–1520)*. Fuentes documentales medievales del País vasco. Donostia-San Sebastián: Eusko Ikaskuntza, 1996.

Esteban, Mari Luz and Mila Amurrio. *Feminist Challenges in the Social Sciences: Gender Studies in the Basque Country*. Reno: Center for Basque Studies, 2010.

Estoquera, José María. "Símbolo." In *Diccionario de hermeneútica*, edited by Andrés Ortiz-Osés and Patxi Lanceros. Bilbao: Deusto, 1997.

Fernández de Larrinoa, Kepa. *Hitzak, denbora eta espazioa*. Donostia-San Sebastián: Elkar, 1991.

Firth, Raymond. *Symbols Public and Private*. New York: Cornell University Press, 1975.

Fossier, Robert. *The Axe and the Oath: Ordinary Life in the Middle Ages*. Translated by Lydia G. Cochrane. Princeton, NJ: Princeton University Press, 2010.

Frazer, James G. *La rama dorada*. La Habana: Instituto Cubano del Libro, 1972.

Gadamer, Hans-Georg. *Truth and method*, second revised edition. London: Continuum, 2004.

Galbete Guerrendiain, Vicente. "Miscelánea de datos para una historia del juego de pelota." *Cuadernos de Etnología y Etnografía de Navarra* 6 (1974): 89–116.

———. "Reglamento del 'juego nuevo' de pelota en Pamplona" *Cuadernos de Etnología y Etnografía de Navarra* 6 (1974): 295–310.

Gallop, Roger. *A Book of the Basques*. Reno: University of Nevada Press, 1970.

Gámez, Javier, David Rosa, Enrique Alcántara, Antonio Martínez, María José Such, Juan Vicente Durá, Jaime Prat, and José Ramiro, "Measurement of Hand Palm Pressures in 'La Pelota Vasca' Game." *The Engineering of Sport* 6 (2006): 17–22.

Garcés, Fortún. *Campeones manomanistas, 1940–1990*. Burlata: N.P., 1991.

Garcia, Manuel, Núria Puig, and Francisco Lagardera, comps. *Sociología del deporte*. Madrid: Alianza, 1998.

García Pelayo, Manuel. *Los mitos políticos*. Madrid: Alianza, 1981.

Garzia Garmendia, Joxerram Jon Sarasua, and Andoni Egaña. *The Art of Bertsolaritza: Improvised Basque Verse Singing*. Donostia-San Sebastián: Bertsozale Elkartea, 2001.

Geertz, Clifford. The Interpretation of Cultures. New York: Basic Books, 1973.

———. *Local Knowledge: Further Essays in Interpretive Anthropology*. New York: Basic Books, 1983.

———. *Negara: The Theatre State in Nineteenth-Century Bali*. Princeton, N.J.: Princeton University Press, 1980.

Gil Calvo, Enrique. *Estado de fiesta*. Madrid: Espasa-Calpe, 1991.

———. *Función de toros*. Madrid: Espasa-Calpe, 1989.

Gillet, Bernard. *Historia del deporte*. Translated by Ma. Dolores Lamarca. Barcelona: Oikos-Tau, 1971.

Girard, René. *Violence and the Sacred*. Translated by Patrick Gregory. London: Continuum, 2005.

González Abrisketa, Olatz. *Bodies Out of Place: Gender, Space and Community in the Basque Sport of Pelota*. Forthcoming.

———. *Frontones de Bizkaia*. Bilbao: Diputación Foral de Bizkaia, 2001.

González Alcantud, José A. *Tractatus ludorum: Una antropológica sobre el juego*. Barcelona: Anthropos, 1993.

Graeber, David. *Toward an Anthropological Theory of Value*. New York: Palgrave, 2001.

Greimas, Algirdas Julien. "Pour une sémiotique topologique." In *Semiotique et Sciences Sociales*, edited by P. Hammad / Sociales, edited by P. Hammad, 129–57. Paris: Le Seuil, 1976.

Guilmette, Ann Marie, and James H. Duthie. "Play: A Multiparadoxical Phenomenon." In *Play as Context*, edited by A. Cheska. New York: Leisure Press, 1979.

Guttmann, Allan. *From Ritual to Record: The Nature of Modern Sports*. New York: Columbia University Press, 1983.

Halbwachs, Maurice. *La mémoire collective*. Paris: Press Universatiries de France, 1968.

Harris, Janet C. "Beyond Huizinga: Relationships between Play and Culture." In *Play as Context,* edited by A. T. Cheska. New York: Leisure Press, 1979.

Heers, Jacques. *"Fêtes, jeux, et joutes dans les sociétés d'occidente à la fin du moyen-âge."* Montreal: Institute d'etudés médiévales, 1982.

Hegel, George Wilhelm Friedrich. *Phenomenology of Spirit.* Delhi: Motilal Banarsidass, 1998.

Hertz, Robert. *Death and the Right Hand.* Translated by Rodney and Claudia Neeham. Glencoe, IL: The Free Press, 1960.

Herzfeld, Michael. *Anthropology.* Oxford: Blackwell, 2001.

Hess, Andreas. "The Social Bonds of Cooking: Gastronomic Societies in the Basque Country." *Cultural Sociology* 1, no. 3 (2007): 383–407.

Huarte, Ángel de. "La pelota en Navarra." *Euskalerriaren alde* 268–269 (1926): 121–28.

Hubert, Henri, and Marcel Mauss. *Magia y sacrificio en la historia de las religiones.* Buenos Aires: Lautaro, 1946.

Huizinga, Johans. *Homo Ludens: A Study of the Play Element in Culture.* New York: Roy Publishers, 1950.

Humboldt, Wilhelm Von. *Los vascos.* Donostia-San Sebastián: Roger, 1998.

Ibáñez, Jesús. *Nuevos avances en la investigación social II.* Barcelona: Proyecto A Ediciones, 1998.

Irabien y Larrañaga, Enrique. "Los partidos de pelota." *Euskal-Erria: Revista Bascongada* 11 (1884): 247–48. Available at http://meta.gipuzkoakultura.net/handle/10690/65458.

Irigoyen, Juan. "En los juegos de pelota" *Avante* 8, May 20, 1944.

——. *El juego de pelota a mano (1900–1925).* Bilbao: Editorial de la Gran Enciclopedia Vasca, 1980.

——. "La pelota, como deporte y espectáculo." *Avante* 1, March 30, 1944.

——. "Sobre el origen vasco del juego de pelota." In *La Gran Enciclopedia Vasca,* volume 2, 671–673. Bilbao: Editorial de la Gran Enciclopedia Vasca, 1967.

Jarvie, Grant, and Joseph Maguire. *Sport and Leisure in Social Thought.* London: Routledge, 1994.

Jeu, Bernard. *Análisis del deporte*. Barcelona: Bellaterra, 1988.

Jovellanos, Gaspar Melchor de. "Memoria sobre la policia de los espectáculos y diversiones públicas y su origen en España." *Euskal-Erria* 15 (1886): 275.

Juaristi, Jon. "Introducción." In Miguel Unamuno, *En torno al casticismo*. Biblioteca Nueva, Madrid: Biblioteca Nueva, 1996.

Jung, Carl Gustav. *Man and His Symbols*. New York: Doubleday, 1964.

Ladrón de Guevara, Sara. "El juego de pelota en El Tajín." *Arqueología Mexicana* 8, no. 44 (July–August 2000): 36–41.

Lamo de Espinosa, Emilio, José María González Garcia, and Cristobal Torres Albero. *La sociología del conocimiento y de la ciencia*. Madrid: Alianza, 1994.

Lanceros, Patxi. "Ethos y libertad." In *Diccionario de hermeneútica*, edited by A. Ortiz-Osés and P. Lanceros. Bilbao: Deusto, 1997.

———. "Religión." In *Diccionario de hermeneútica*, edited by A. Ortiz-Osés and P. Lanceros. Bilbao: Deusto, 1997.

———. "Sentido." In *Diccionario de hermeneútica*, edited by A. Ortiz-Osés and P. Lanceros. Bilbao: Deusto, 1997.

Larramendi, Manuel. *Corografía de Gipuzkoa*. Bilbao: Larrun, 1982.

Lasén Díaz, Amparo. "Ritmos sociales y arritmia de la modernidad." *Política y Sociedad* 25 (1997): 185–203.

Leach, Edmund. *Culture and Communication: The Logic by which Symbols Are Connected*. Cambridge: Cambridge University Press, 1976.

———. "Two Essays Concerning the Symbolic Representation of Time." In *Rethinking Anthropology*, 125–36. London: London School of Economics, 1962.

Lefebvre, Henri. *Rhythmanalysis: Space, Time, and Everyday Life*. Translated by Stuart Elden and Gerald Moore. With an introduction by Stuart Elden. London: Continuum, 2004.

Le Goff, Franck. "Formes et usages d'un jeu: Le palet sur terre en Centre-Bretagne." *Ethnologie francaise* 39, no. 1 (1999): 79–85.

———. *Jeux, identités, pratiques: Le palet sur terre en Basse-Bretagne*. Ph.D. dissertation, Université de Nantes, 1996.

Le Goff, Jacques. *El orden de la memoria*. Barcelona: Paidós, 1991.

Leif, Joseph, and Lucien Brunelle. *La verdadera naturaleza del juego*. Buenos Aires: Kapelusz, 1978.

Letamendia, Ander. *El pelotari y sus manos*. Bilbao: Ikastolen Elkartea, 1995.

Lévi-Strauss, Claude. "Introducción a la obra de Marcel Mauss." In *Sociología y Antropología*, edited by M. Mauss. Madrid: Tecnos, 1971.

———. *The Savage Mind*. Chicago: The University of Chicago Press, 1966.

———. *Structural Anthropology*. 2 volumes. New York: Basic Books, 1963, 1976.

Linazasoro, José Ignacio. *Permanencias y Arquiterctura urbana*. Barcelona: Gustavo Gili, 1978.

Lizarralde, Daniel. "El principio de autoridad." *Laurak Bat* 170, January 1, 1887.

Lloyd, Michael. *The Agon in Euripides*. Oxford: Clarendon Press, 1992.

López Rodríguez, P. *Para una sociología del juego*. Ph.D. dissertation, Universidad Complutense, Madrid. 1988.

Lukes, Steven. "Political Ritual and Social Integration." *Sociology* 9 (1975): 289–308.

Madariaga Orbea, Juan, ed. *Anthology of Apologists and Detractors of the Basque Language*. Translated by Frederick H. Fornoff, María Cristina Saavedra, Amaia Gabantxo, and Cameron J. Watson. Reno: Center for Basque Studies, 2006.

Maffesoli, Michel. *El instante eterno: El retorno de lo trágico en las sociedades posmodernas*. Buenos Aires: Paidós, 2001.

———. *The Time of the Tribes: The Decline of Individualism in Mass Society*. Translated by Don Smith. London: Sage, 1996.

Maisonneuve, Jean. *Ritos religiosos y civiles*. Translated by María Colom de Llopis. Barcelona: Herder, 1991.

Manning, Frank. *The Celebration of Society: Perspectives on Contemporary Cultural Performance*. Ohio: Bowling Green University, 1983.

Markale, Jean. *Druidas*. Madrid: Taurus, 1989.

Martínez Montoya, Josetxu. *La construcción nacional de Euskal Herria: Etnicidad, política y religión*. Donostia-San Sebastián: Ttarttalo, 1999.

———. *Pueblos, ritos, y montañas*. Bilbao: Desclée de Brouwer, 1996.

Mauss, Marcel. *Manual of Ethnography*. Edited and introduced by N. J. Allen. Translated by Dominique Lussier. New York: Durkheim Press, 2007.

———. *Lo sagrado y lo profano*. Translated by Juan Antonio Matesanz. Barcelona: Barral, 1970.

———. *Sociology and Psychology: Essays*. Translated by Ben Brewster. London: Routledge, 1979.

Mayr, Franz. *La mitología Occidental*. Barcelona: Anthropos, 1987.

MacClancy, Jeremy, ed. *Sport, Identity & Ethnicity*. Oxford: Berg, 1996.

Mendigorria. "Julian Retegi." *Mutxo* 1 (September 1998): 12–18.

Mendiola, Ignacio. *Movimientos sociales y trayectos sociológicos: Hacia una teoría práxica y multidimensional de lo social*. Bilbao: UPV, 2000.

Meynaud, Jean. *El deporte y la política*. Barcelona: Hispano europea, 1972.

Middleton, David, and Derek Edwards. *Memoria compartida: La naturaleza social del recuerdo y el olvido*. Barcelona: Paidós, 1992.

Miguel, Amando. *Introducción a la sociología de la vida cotidiana*. Madrid: Edicusa, 1969.

Miralles, Carlos. "Introducción." In Aeschylus, *Esquilo: Tragedias Completas*. Madrid: Planeta, 1993.

Moles, Abraham, and Elisabeth Rohmer. *Psicología del espacio*. Translated by Enrique Grilló Solano and María José Méndez Tihista. Madrid: Ricardo Aguilera, 1972.

Molina, Pedro, and Francisco Checa. *La función simbólica de los ritos*. Almería: Icaria, 1997.

Monzón, Vicente. "Zazpiak bat." *Euskal-Erria* 31 (1894).

Moore, Sally F., and Barbara G. Myerhoff. *Secular Ritual*. Assen/Amsterdam: Van Gorcum, 1977.

Muntión, Carlos. *50 años de pelota en La Rioja*. Logroño, 1993.

Needham, Rodney. *Right and Left: Essays on Dual Symbolic Classification*. Chicago: The University Press of Chicago, 1973.

Nietzsche, Friedrich Wilhelm. *The Birth of Tragedy and Other Writings*. Cambridge: Cambridge University Press, 1999.

———. *The Gay Science (The Joyful Wisdom)*. Translated by Thomas Common, Paul V. Cohn, and Maude D. Petre. New York: Barnes & Noble, 2008.

———. *The Genealogy of Morals*. New York: Dover Publications, 2003.

———. *On the Genealogy of Morality*. Revised student edition. Cambridge: Cambridge University Press, 2007.

———. *Thus Spoke Zarathustra: A Book for Everyone and No One*. New York: Penguin Books, 1961.

Ortega Ruiz, Rosario. *El juego infantil y la construcción social del conocimiento*. Sevilla: Alfar, 1992.

Ortega y Gasset, José. *Meditations on Hunting*. Bozeman, MT: Wilderness Adventures Press, 1995.

———. *The Revolt of the Masses*. Notre Dame, Ind.: University of Notre Dame Press, 1985.

Ortiz-Osés, Andrés. *El matriarcalismo vasco*. Bilbao: Universidad de Deusto, 1988.

———. "Mitología del héroe moderno." Edited by Joseba Zulaika. *Revista Internacional de Estudios Vascos* 40, no. 2 (1995): 381–93.

Otazu y Llana, Alfonso. *El "igualitarismo" vasco: Mito y realidad*. Donostia-San Sebastián: Txertoa, 1986.

Oteiza, Jorge. *Ejercicios espirituales en un túnel*. Donostia-San Sebastián: Hordago, 1984.

———. *Oteiza's Selected Writings*. Edited by Joseba Zulaika. Reno: Center for Basque Studies, University of Nevada, Reno, 2003.

———. *Quousque Tandem . . . !: Ensayo de interpretación estética del alma vasca*. Donostia-San Sebastián: Txertoa, 1975.

———. "Revelación en frontón vasco de nuestra cultura original." Prologue to Miguel Pelay Orozco, *Pelota, pelotari y frontón*, 5–25. Madrid: Ediciones Poniente, 1983.

Ott, Sandra. *The Circle of Mountains: A Basque Shepherding Community*. New York: Oxford University Press, 1981.

Padiglione, Vicenio. "Antropología del deporte y del ocio" In *Ensayos de Antropología socio-cultural*, edited by J. Prat. Barcelona: Ariel, 1996.

Pareto, Vilfredo. *The Mind and Society*. Translated by Arthur Livingstone. New York: Harcourt, Brace, and Co., 1935.

Paxaka. "Miscelánea." *Euskal-Erria* 13 (1885).

Pelay Orozco, Miguel. *Oteiza: La Gran Enciclopedia Vasca*. Bilbao: Editorial de la Gran Enciclopedia Vasca, 1979.

———. *Pelota, pelotari y frontón*. Madrid: Poniente, 1983.

Peña y Goñi, Antonio. "Beti-Jai." *Euskal-Erria* 29 (1893): 81.

———."Los corredores." *El pelotari* 29, year 2 (1894): 227–28.

———. "El pelotarismo moderno." *El pelotari* 11, year 1 (December 1893): 26.

———. *La pelota y los pelotaris*. Madrid: N.P., 1892.

Pérez-Agote, Alfonso. *The Social Roots of Basque Nationalism*. Reno. University of Nevada Press, 2006.

Piaget, Jean. *The Origins of Intelligence in Children*. New York: International Universities Press, 1952.

Pilota Kantuz. Pilotarien batzarra, 1993.

Redfield, Robert. *The Primitive World and Its Transformations*. Ithaca, NY: Cornell University Press, 1953.

Rof Carballo, Juan. "La pelota y el laberinto." In *Entre el silencio y la palabra*. Madrid: Aguilar, 1960.

Rothenbuhler, Eric W. *Ritual Communication: From Everyday Conversation to Mediated Ceremony*. London: Sage, 1998.

Rowe, Sharon. "Modern Sports: Liminal Ritual or Liminoid Leisure." *Journal of Ritual Studies* 12, no. 1 (Summer 1998): 47–60.

Rudie, Ingrid. "Making Persons in a Global Ritual? Embodied Experience and Free-Floating Symbols in Olympic Sport." In *Recasting Ritual*, edited by F. Hughes-Freeland and M. Crain. London: Routledge, 1998.

Rull, Enrique. "Introducción." In Manuel de Unamuno, *En torno al casticismo*. Madrid: Alianza, 2000.

Salaverría, José María. "Los nidos de los pelotaris." In *La gran enciclopedia vasca*. Bilbao: Editorial de la Gran Enciclopedia Vasca, 1966.

———. "El pelotari." In *La gran enciclopedia vasca*. Bilbao: Editorial de la Gran Enciclopedia Vasca, 1974.

Sales, José Luis, and Isidoro Ursua. *Catálogo del archivo diocesano de Pamplona*. Iruñea-Pamplona: Institución Príncipe de Viana, 1988.

Salter, Michael. *Play: Anthropological Perspectives*. New Jersey: Leisure Press, 1979.

San Sebastián, Jon. "Entrevista a fondo: Inaxio Errandonea." *Mutxo* 28 (December 2000): 10–16.

Santo Domingo, Félix. "Apuntes sobre el juego de pelota." *Euskal-Erria* 11 (1884): 168–76.

Satrustegi, José M. *Mitos y Creencias*. Donostia-San Sebastian: Orain, 1995.

Saussure, Ferdinand, and Charles Bally. *Ferdinand De Saussure: Course in General Linguistics*. London: Gerald Duckworth & Co. Ltd., 1983.

Schutz, Alfred. *The Problem of Social Reality*, fourth edition. Edited and introduced by Maurice Natanson. With a preface by H. L. van Breda. The Hague: M. Nijhoff, 1973.

Serres, Michel. *Atlas*. Madrid: Cátedra, 1995.

Simmel, Georg. *Sociología: Studios sobre las formas de socialización*, vols. 1 and 2. Madrid: Revista de Occidente, 1977.

Smith, Philip. "The Elementary Forms of Place and Their Transformations: A Durkheimian Model." *Qualitative Sociology* 22, no. 1 (1999): 13–36.

Soraluce, Inocente. "Sobre la pelota." *Euskal-Erria* 20 (1889): 533–36.

Such, Peter, and John Hodgkinson, trans. *The Poem of My Cid*. Warminster, UK: Aris and Phillips, 1987.

Subirats, Eduard. *El alma y la muerte*. Barcelona: Anthropos, 1983.

Taketani, Kazuyuki. "Sobre laxoa y chaza." In *Investigación sintética sobre la cultura deportiva en el País Vasco*, edited by K. Taketani. Kobe: N.P., 1998.

Taladoire, Eric. "El juego de pelota mesoamericana." *Arqueología Mexicana* 8, no. 44 (July–August 2000): 20–27.

Thalamas Labandibar, Juan. "El origen sacro de las primeras instituciones vascas." *Boletín de la Real Sociedad Vascongada de Amigos del País*. 31, no. 30 and 40 (1975): 305–43.

Tierno Galván, Enrique. *Desde el espectáculo a la trivialización*. Madrid: Tecnos, 1987.

Trías, Eugenio. *Tratado de la Pasión*. Madrid: Taurus, 1984.

———. "Prólogo." In *La fundación de la ciudad: Mitos y ritos en el mundo antiguo*, edited by P. Azara, R. Mar, E. Riu, and E. Subías. Barcelona: UPC, 2000.

Turner, Victor. "Dewey, Dilthey and Drama: An Essay in the Anthropology of Experience." In *The Anthropology of Experience*, edited by Victor Turner and Edward M. Bruner. Chicago: University of Illinois Press, 1986.

———. *Dramas, Fields and Metaphors*. Ithaca: Cornell University Press, 1984.

———. *The Forest of Symbols: Aspects of Ndembu Ritual*. Cornell University Press, 1970.

———. *From Ritual to Theatre: The Human Seriousness of Play*. New York: PAJ, 1982.

———. *On the Edge of the Bush: Anthropology as Experience*. Arizona: University of Arizona Press, 1985.

———. *The Ritual Process: Structure and Anti-Structure*. Chicago: Aldine Pub. Co., 1969.

———. "Variations on a Theme of Liminality." In *Secular Ritual*, edited by Sally F. Moore and Barbara G. Myerhoff. Assen/Amsterdam: Van Gorcum, 1977.

Unamuno, Miguel. *La agonía del cristianismo*. Madrid: Alianza, 1986.

———. *Del sentimiento trágico de la vida en los hombres y en los pueblos*. Madrid: Alianza Editorial, 2001.

———. *En torno al casticismo*. Madrid: Alcalá, 1971.

———."Prólogo" In *Estética como ciencia de la expresión y lingüística general: Teoría e Historia de la estética*, edited by B. Croce and Francisco. Madrid: Beltrán, 1912.

———. "Un partido de pelota." *Euskal-Erria* 20 (1889): 301–11.

Uribarri, Ignacio, and Javier Uribarri. "La fiesta de la pelota vasca." *Fiestas, ritos y espectáculos* (1982): 35–38.

———. *El moderno juego de la pelota vasca*. Colección de Temas Vizcaínos. Bilbao: BBK, 1991.

Urquijo, Julio de. "Cosas de antaño: II." *Revista Internacional de Estudios Vascos* 26 (1923): 339–46.

———. "La pelota y el mus." *Euskalerriaren alde* 7, no. 149 (1917): 113–6.

Van Gennep, Arnold. *The Rites of Passage.* Translated by Monika B. Vizedom and Gabrielle L. Caffe. Introduced by Solon T. Kimball. Chicago: University of Chicago Press, 1960.

Verjat, Alain. "Hermes" In *Diccionario de hermeneútica*, edited by A. Ortiz-Osés and P. Lanceros. Bilbao: Deusto, 1997.

Verón, Eliseo. "Prólogo de la edición española." In *Antropología estructural*, edited by C. Lévi-Strauss. Buenos Aires: EUDEBA, 1968.

Ward, Russell E. "Rituals, First Impressions, and the Opening Day Home Advantage." *Sociology of Sport Journal* 15 (1998): 279–93.

Whannel, Gary. *Fields in Vision: Television Sport and Cultural Transformation.* London: Routledge, 1992.

Wunenburger, Jean-Jacques. "Mythe urbain et violence fondatrice." In *La fundación de la ciudad: Mitos y ritos en el mundo antiguo*, edited by Pedro Azara, Ricardo Mar, Eduard Riu, and Eva Subías, Barcelona: UPC, 2000.

Wyer, Robert, and Thomas K. Srull. *Memory and Cognition in Its Social Context.* New Jersey: LEA, 1989.

Zambrano, María. *El hombre y lo divino.* Madrid: FCE, 1993.

Zulaika, Joseba. *Basque Violence: Metaphor and Sacrament.* Reno: University of Nevada Press, 1988.

———. *Del Cromagnon al carnaval.* Donostia-San Sebastián: Erein, 1996.

———. *Tratado estético-ritual vasco.* Donostia-San Sebastián: Baroja, 1987.

Filmography

Allen, Charles. *Jai-alai: The Fastest Game.* 1984.

Hualde, Joaquín. *Frontones y pelotaris.* 1950.

Leth, Jørgen. *Pelota.* 1983.

Medem, Julio. *Vacas.* 1992.

———. *La pelota vasca: la piel contra la piedra.* 2003.

Welles, Orson. *Around the world with Orson Welles: Basque Pelota.* 1955.

Index

aberri eguna ("day of the Basque fatherland"), 47
abertzales (left-wing nationalists), 195
aekeguna (pro-Basque culture festival), 189
Abrego, Jesús, 231
agon ("split"), 7, 49, 67, 76, 95, 98, 269, 278, 287. *See also joko, jolas, partido*
agora, 198–99, 201, 205, 269. *See also* plaza
"Agur Jaunak" (song), 166–67
ahala (ingenuity), 122n69, 153, 275–76
aizkolaris (wood choppers), 188
aizkolaritza (woodchopping), 49
alarde (military-style parade), 18, 81, 81n8
Alberdi, Francisco, see Baltasar
Albixuri, 223
Alpargatas ("espadrilles," hemp sandals), 121
Alustiza, Martin, 119, 177
Anasagasti, Iñaki, 273
antagonism (confrontation), 7, 43, 101, 148
Arana, Sabino, 74, 259
Aranzadi, Juan, 18, 42, 44, 47
Archetti, Eduardo P., 272
Aresti, Gabriel, 37
Argentina, 11, 104, 224, 295
Ariznabarreta, Karmelo, 179

arkupes (church atrium), 56
Arpal I, Jesús, 45, 48
Arramendy, Jean, 163
Arretxe I, Fernando, 155, 216
Arriaga, Emiliano, 115, 197
Arriaran I, Felíx, 87
Arriaran II, Joxe, 87
Arroyo II, 90
artekariak (bookmakers), 30, 110
Asegarce (professional pelota company), 12, 68, 92, 94, 288
Aspe (professional pelota company), 12, 68, 94
Atano II (Luciano Juaristi), 87
Atano III (Mariano Juaristi), 12, 81, 84, 87–88, 98, 105
Atano X (Luciano Juaristi), 67, 84–85, 98
Atanos (family), 84, 87, 91
atxiki (fault committed by grabbing the ball), 89, 90, 152, 163, 221–25, 223n27, 286, 291, 298
auzolan (communal work), 38
Azantza (Jean-Pierre Sorhainde), 62, 216
Azkarate, Hilario, 67, 83–84, 91, 98, 151
Azpiroz I, Dionisio, 231

Balandier, Georges, 80
Baltasar, (Francisco Alberdi), 99

Barberito I (Abel San Martín), 81, 119, 158, 161
Baroja, Julio Caro, 74, 101, 196, 213, 267
Baroja, Pío, 15, 156
Baroja, Serafín, 60, 295
Barriola, Abel, 98, 133, 147, 225, 234–35, 285, 287–89
baseball, 76
basketball, 11, 53n7
baserri ("farmstead"), 36–39, 36n2, 46, 49
Basque Country: Christianity in, 43–45; culture, 7, 21, 35–36, 38, 42, 46–47, 49, 53, 61n26, 134, 169, 189, 192, 196, 200, 203, 211, 215; egalitarianism in, 42, 46–47, 73; emigration, 66; history, 43, 53, 267; identity, 74, 180; medieval factions (Oñacinos and Gamboínos) in, 40, 43; mythology, 7, 13, 42, 45, 52–53, 73 75, 216; pelota in, 11, 15; violence in, 74, 79–80, 193, 195; women in, 18, 37, 46–47, 80, 215–17, 262, 274, 276
Basque nationalism: pelota and, 43, 43n19, 49, 49n44, 273
Basque Nationalist Party, 12, 74, 259, 273
Basque pelota. *See* pelota
Bateson, Gregory, 13
Bautista Azcárate, Juan. See Mondragonés
Benveniste, Émile, 79
Beloki, Ruben, 98, 101, 147–48, 151–57, 177, 215, 235, 275, 287–89
Berasaluzes (family), 87
Bergara I (Marcelino Bergara), 82
Berger, John, 276
bertsolaritza (improvised oral Basque poetry), 16, 18, 61, 166, 215

besagain ("arm in the air"), 85
betting: *hordago* (betting everything), 112n53, 296; *momio* (odds), 108–12, 115, 136, 147, 174, 178–79, 197, 292
bettors: *cátedra* (group of strong bettors), 93, 109–110, 115, 117, 136, 147n33, 197, 249, 252, 292; *momistas* (odds takers), 109, 110, 253, 292; *puntos* (odds givers), 93, 109–11, 115, 250, 251, 287, 292. *See also pelotazales*
Blanchard, Kendall, 76
blé (indirect style pelota games), 26–28, 33, 63, 239–40, 245, 291–92
body, the, 50, 79, 95, 172–73, 187, 191, 201, 217–18, 220, 224–26, 238–39, 256, 274
Bombín, 62
bookmakers. *See artekariak*
Bote luzea (long style game), 54
botivolea ("with faint-hearted arms"), 240, 291
Bourdieu, Pierre, 123, 255
Bouzas, Rodolfo, 62
Brau Mayor, Juanito, 118
Brau Menor, Eustaquio, 118
Brecht, Bertold, 180
Bryant, Alfred T., 217
Buytendijk, F. J. J., 267
bullfighting, 62, 186, 225

caceo ("ladle" hit), 222
Caillois, Roger, 173, 199, 204, 218–19, 237, 244, 252
Camus, Albert, 272
Canetti, Elias, 189, 221
Capone, Al, 67
Carballo, Rof, 167
cartón (score count), 28
Cassirer, Ernst, 127, 200, 241
Cavafy, Constantine P., 67

Index

cestaño (basket), 140, 142, 292
cesta-punta, 27, 32, 60, 163, 225. *See* jai-alai
championships, 12, 31–33, 56, 65–66, 69,81, 84–94, 98–99, 105–6, 119–21, 127–28, 131–33, 137, 147–48, 145, 159, 161, 177, 215, 217, 242, 282, 287–90, 266. *See also* manomanista
chance, 226–27, 245, 249, 289, 296
chapa (iron panel on the *frontis*), 26, 28, 113, 154–55, 292–93. *See also* fronton
chaza (type of line in long modality games), 245, 293
Cheska, Alyce Taylor, 76
Chillida, Eduardo, 7
Chiquito de Eibar (Indalecio Sarasqueta), 99, 107, 118
Clastres, Pierre, 201, 213
Coello, Francisco, 50
collective behavior, 49, 293
colors, significance of, 12, 26n2, 43, 49, 75, 110, 114, 124, 130, 134–35, 140, 144–45, 147, 150, 164, 175, 197, 269, 285
community, 16, 17, 19–20, 36, 39, 40, 44, 48, 50–51, 58, 61, 76–78, 81, 102, 103, 106, 125, 158, 160–62, 166, 172, 175–76, 181–82, 185–88, 191, 195, 197–99, 201–2, 204–5, 215, 244, 255, 260–62, 265, 268, 271–72, 275–77, 279, 282
conflict, 7, 40, 41, 43, 68, 76, 78, 81, 88, 149, 175, 183, 193, 195–97, 199–200, 231, 267–71, 288, 293
confrontation, 26, 40–41, 43, 76, 100, 127, 133, 148, 171, 197, 200, 218, 233, 293
conjunction, 97, 122, 172–73, 175–76, 181–82, 204, 237–38, 244, 254, 260, 264–65, 293

cuadrilla (peer group), 48–49, 128, 292
cuadros alegres ("happy squares" or frontcourt squares), 83n13, 222, 292. *See also* fronton
cult: negative, 217–20; positive, 219, 271–73

d'Elbeé, Christian, 60
de Aralar, José, 73
de Arriage, Emiliano, 59
de Monzón, Vicente, 128, 248
de Saussure, Ferdinand, 211
de Soraluce, Inocencio, 63
de Velasco, Pedro, 73
del Valle, Teresa, 46
Delgado, Manuel, 35, 48, 203
devanado ("winding"), 138
Diogenes, 214, 266
Dionysus, 181, 183
disjunction, 134, 175–76, 182, 233, 268, 271, 292
Douglas, Mary, 14, 261
Dunning, Eric, 179
Durkheim, Emile, 14, 16, 19, 78–79, 179–80, 201, 266, 272

Eagle, Sonia Jacqueline, 49
Eceiza, Juan José. *See* Mardura
Ecenarro, Luis, 223
Echevarría, Javier, 148
Eguskitze, Xabier, 152, 275
Eifermann, Rivka, 127
Elicegui, Vicente, 112
Elosegi, Joseba, 194
epaileak (referees), 30. *See* referee
erdalduna (non-Basque speaker), 214
erdera (not Basque), 215
Erijisi, Boesoou, 13
Errandonea, Inaxio, 119, 253n23
Errasti, Jokin, 179
Erratxun Jean. *See* Gaskonia

eskualdun (Basque speaker, variant), 214–15, 262
eskudunak ("possessor of the hand"), 213, 263
eskukoa ("he of the hand"): as free person and slave alike, 214, 266
Estornés Lasa, Bernardo, 244
Ezkurra, José, 82
Ezkurra, Koteto, 94
Ezkurra, Martín, 83–86, 88–90, 92–93, 275
Eugi, Patxi, 94, 101, 121
emic perspective, 13–14, 170n5
eskas (fault lines), 25, 30, 129, 145–46, 245, 260, 264, 292, 293. See *also* fronton
ETA (Euskadi ta Askatasuna, the Basque Country and Freedom), 193, 195
ETB (Euskal Telebista, Basque public television network), 12. See *also* television
etic perspective, 13–14
etxe ("house" or "home"), 36–38, 42, 45–46, 49–50, 101
etxekoandre ("woman or mistress of the house"), 37
euskaldun (Basque speaker, variant), 35, 214–15, 262
Euskara (the Basque language), 29, 37, 45, 53, 60, 79, 124, 130, 148, 189, 191

falta ("fail" or low-off area in a pelota court), 26, 29. See *also* fronton
fans, *see* pelotazales
Ferrándiz, Francisco, 13
Fossier, Robert, 59, 198
France 56, 58, 74, 86, 161, 187, 192–93
four-and-a-half (pelota game), 92, 293. See *also jaula*, pelota

four-and-a-half (pelota game) mark final: 1997, 10; 1999, 177, 216–17; 2002, 133, 234, 285; as principal contest, 32
frontis (front wall of a pelota court), 16, 25–26, 28–32, 34n10, 69, 96n33, 136, 140–1, 143, 146–48, 151–52, 156, 179, 193–94, 220, 223n27, 227, 231–32, 234–35, 246, 248, 257, 292–94, 296, 299 see *also* fronton
fronton (pelota court): around the world, 27–31, 53, 57, 60, 65–68, 104, 224; bar, 31, 32; countercourt, 27, 30; description of, 7, 16, 26, 28, 31–32, 129–30, 139, 141, 174, 186, 216–17, 220, 222, 246; iconography of, 16, 191–94, 255; industrial, 27–29, 34, 60, 65, 67, 188; in Hegoalde, 53, 56, 58–59, 66, 68, 192–94, 197, 273; in Iparralde, 59, 75, 192–93; public in, 11–12, 16, 25, 32, 34n11, 68, 80, 82, 100, 103, 108, 113–19, 122, 124–25, 129, 131, 149, 176–77, 179–81, 187–88, 194–95, 205, 247–49, 281–83, 286–87, 290–300; socialization in, 20, 25, 33, 49, 58, 64, 69, 88, 102, 108, 115, 120, 124–27, 232, 244–46, 253–55; symbolic value of, 7–8, 17, 20, 67, 75, 85, 95, 97, 100, 123, 150–51, 157–58, 160, 187–91, 194, 204–5, 241–42, 247, 250, 261–62, 264, 266, 270, 273, 278. See *also chapa*; *cuadros alegres*; *eskas*; *falta*; *frontis*; *pasa*; *rebote*
fueros, 42–43, 259

Gadamer, Hans Georg, 77, 177, 180, 182, 190, 202, 204, 232, 236, 238, 240, 253–54, 272, 277
Galarza III, Ladis, 81–82, 88, 98, 101, 119, 132
Gallastegi, Miguel, 81–82, 88, 95, 98, 106, 121
Gallop, Rodney, 44
Galván, Tierno, 16, 225, 268
Gamboas, 40
games. *See* sports
Garay, Jesús, 161
Garcés, Fortún, 290
García Ariño I, Jesús, 84, 87, 102, 161, 290
García Ariño II, Ángel, 87
Garcia Ariño IV, Roberto, 89, 92
García Ariños (family), 84, 87
Gardner, Ava 67
Gaskonia (Jean Erratxun), 186
Geertz, Clifford, 10, 14, 17, 108, 122, 212
gerrikoak (sashes: *gerriko*, sing.), 75, 134, 147, 269, 293
Gheusi, Pierre-Barthélemy, 216
Gil Calvo, Enrique, 47, 62
Girard, René, 18, 40, 47, 73, 75–76, 79, 148, 175, 197
Giraudoux, Jean, 75
Goethe, 255
Goñi I, Oscar, 134
Goñi II, Mikel, 11, 98, 123, 134
Goldarazena, Miguel. *See* Saralegi 68
Gorostiza, Iñaki, 85
gorriak ala urdiñak (red or blue): as representative of clan wars, 39–43. *See also* colors
Guardini, Romano, 271
Guignebert, Charles, 44
Guttmann, Allen, 127, 307

hand, the: ambidextrousness, 216–17, 220; as competence, 215; as norm, 214; as power, 143–44, 160, 212–13, 215 218–21, closure and, 160, 217, 221–23; left-handedness, 83, 153, 215–20, protection of in pelota, 58, 130, 135, 140, 217–18, 244, 281 299; right-handedness, 83–84, 87, 151, 216, 220n23; symbolic use of in pelota, 212, 215, 217–18, 221
hand modality. *See* hand pelota
hand pelota (pelota modality), 7, 9–13, 27–30, 32–33, 65–66, 68–69, 81, 83–85, 87, 89, 92, 96–97, 103, 105, 119–21, 125, 131n7, 136, 139n23, 147–48, 157, 163, 215, 242, 281, 283, 287, 289; *jaula* (four-and-a-half), 29.
hand trinquet (pelota modality), 27, 56
hauts (ash); *hautsi* (broken), 318
Heers, Jacques, 75
Hemingway, Ernest, 67
Henry IV, 74
Heraclitus, 175
Hegoalde, 53, 56, 58–59, 66, 68, 192–94, 197, 273
hermandad ("brotherhood" or "fraternity"), 196
herri ("village" or "people"), 36, 38–39, 42, 45, 102
Hori da ahala, hori! ("that's it, that is power!"): phrase to denote player's strength, 122n69, 153, 275
Hualde, Joaquín, 143
Hubert, Henri, 156
Huizinga, Johan, 145, 149, 158, 169, 178, 199, 237, 244, 267
Humboldt, Wilhelm von, 15, 25

hunting, 7, 150, 154–55, 204
huts ("void" or "error"), 7–8, 204, 275
Hölderlin, Friedrich, 181, 195

Ibáñez, Jesús, 145
Ibáñez Sacristán, Augusto. *See* Titín III
Inda, Juan Martin. *See* Perkain
indarra ("strength" or "force"), 18–19, 45, 79–81, 121–25, 141, 160, 187, 222, 275–76
individual behavior, 45, 49
Iparralde: Basque and French identity in, 58–59, 61, 66, 75, 85, 192–94
Irigoyen, José, 99–100, 197, 290
Ithurria, Victor, 257
Iturain, Juan, 231
Iturri (Juan Manuel Martínez Iturri), 67–68

jai-alai (pelota modality), 7–8, 10–11, 27, 29–31, 33, 58, 60, 65–66, 68, 105, 121, 131n6, 163, 217, 223–225, 291–95, 299–300
jaula (four-and-a-half). *See under* hand pelota
Jaungoikoa eta lege zaharrak ("God and the Old Laws"), 259
jentilak (pre-Christian mythical personae): as originators of the game of pelota, 52–53
jo (Basque prefix implying play and struggle), 237, 276
joko (competitive play or formal game), 7, 19, 109, 169–75, 183, 233, 244, 269–71; definition of, 19n11, 170n5, 233n5, 269, 269n48, 295. *See also* agon; jolas; play
joko-garbi (pelota modality), 58, 163, 224, 291

jolas (noncompetitive play), 19, 169–73, 175–76, 181, 183, 232–33, 239, 270–71, 278, 295: and 170–75. *See also* agon; joko; play
Jovellanos, Gaspar Melchor de, 58–59, 256
Juaristi, Luciano. *See* Atano X
Juaristi, Luciano. *See* AtanoII
Juaristi, Mariano. *See* Atano III
juego de palma (palm game): Middle Ages precursor to pelota, 56
Jung, Carl Gustav, 212

kiski, *see potro*
konsejupe (atrium of city council building), 56, 59, 30
kontatzaile (traditional scorekeeper), 156, 295; as embodiment of historical memory, 189–90

La Rioja, 67, 81, 93, 102, 119, 138, 161, 194, 247
Lange, Johannes, 52
Lajos, Julián, 86, 88, 90, 119
Lanceros, Patxi, 148
Larrañaga, Chucho (Jesús Larrañaga), 68, 220
Larrañaga, Jesús. *See* Larrañaga, Chucho
Lasa, Oskar, 179
laxoa (pelota modality), 53–56, 163, 268, 293–94
Le Goff, Jacques, 185
Leach, Edmund, 134, 165
Leenhardt, Maurice, 13
Lefebvre, 162, 165
Letamendia, Ander, 243
Lévi-Strauss, Claude, 175, 179, 182, 201, 203, 244
Liga de Empresas de Pelota Mano (LEPM, League of Hand Pelota companies), 13

Liminality, 133, 176
Lizarralde, Daniel, 282, 284
Loroño, Jesús, 161
Louis XI, 74

Maffesoli, Michel, 176, 181, 201–2, 204, 236, 239–41
Maiz II, Antxon, 89
Mallarmé, Stéphane, 8
Manco de Villabona (Pedro Yarza), 118
manomanista (singles championship), 84, 87, 92, 97, 103, 154, 225, 296
Mardura (Juan José Eceiza), 99
Marecq, 75
Mari (principal must of Basque mythology), 42, 46, 84
Martínez de Irujo, Juan, 94, 275
Martínez de Oñaz, 39–40
Martínez Iturri, Juan Manuel. *See* Iturri
Martínez Montoya, Josetxu, 14
Martirikorena, 86
masculinity, 80, 171n9, 220
Mauss, Marcel, 156, 238, 277
Medem, Julio, 7, 101, 195
Melchor de Jovellanos, Gaspar, 58
Mendiola, Ignacio, 165
memory: collective, 42, 77, 119, 120, 195; historical, 190
Mina I (Martin Olloquiegui), 231
Moles, Abraham A., 243
momio, *see* betting
momista, *see* bettor
Mondragonés (Juan Bautista Azcárate), 98, 105
Montesinos, Lidia, 13
monuments, 11, 20, 185, 187
Monzón, Telesforo, 195
Muchona, 13

Nagore, Jorge, 179
negation, 180, 182, 219

Nietzsche, 180, 183, 185, 198, 202, 211, 241, 261
Norbert, Elias, 179
Novia de Salcedo, Pedro, 213, 214n5

Ogueta (Jose Mari Palacios), 84–86, 89, 93, 98, 103, 119
Olaizola II, Aimar, 98, 100, 131n7, 147, 151–57, 234, 275, 285, 287–89
Olloquiegui, Martin. *See* Mina I
Orbea, Fernando, 68
Ortega y Gasset, José, 116, 150, 257
Ortiz-Osés, Andrés, 46, 133, 154, 162
Otazu y Llena, Alfonso, 18, 42n15, 46, 267
Oteiza, Jorge, 7, 150, 155, 166, 205–6, 217, 220, 228
Ott, Sandra, 79, 244

pala (pelota modality), 10, 12, 27, 30, 32–33, 33n9, 65–68, 105, 113, 163, 173, 217, 291, 294, 296, 299, 300
pala (wooden instrument used to play pelota), 27, 217, 296
Palacios, Jose Mari. *See* Orgueta
Pareto, Vilfredo, 98
parientes mayores (senior lineage heads), 53
partido (game or split) 18–19, 135, 148, 161; as rupture, 183; as synonym for "encounter," 269; logic of, 269. *See also* agon
pasa (pass or high-off area), 26, 29. *See also* fronton
Paysandú (Pedro Zabaleta), 65n32, 107
Pelay Orozco, Miguel, 223, 269
pelota: amateur, 16, 69, 83, 85–86, 103, 127, 285, 294, 297; appeal

of, 9, 34, 63, 66, 69, 80, 85, 117, 125, 160, 262, 215, 268, 290; as cultural manifestation, 15, 17–18, 53, 125, 161, 189, 247, 260; as performance, 16, 50, 116, 118–20, 123–24, 137, 187–88 ; as source of social status, 62–63, 132–33, 250; Basque emigration and, 64, 66; Basque identity and, 13, 34, 49; betting on, 67, 106, 108–10, 112–16, 124, 127–28, 135–36, 159–60, 169, 178, 197, 249, 252, 270, 283, 287, 296; championships, 12, 31–33, 56, 65–66, 69, 81, 84–94, 98–99, 105–6, 119–21, 127–28, 131–33, 137, 147–48, 145, 159, 161, 177, 215, 217, 242, 282, 287–90, 266; changes in, 34, 37, 109, 196, 242; Church and, 16, 36–37, 51–52, 54, 56n13, 59–60, 82, 185–86, 198–99, 291; colors in, 12, 43, 49, 75, 110, 114, 124, 130, 134–35, 140, 144–45, 147, 150, 164, 175, 197, 269, 285; crowd, 20, 28, 32, 48, 56, 63, 94, 103–4, 108, 111, 113–25, 129–30, 137, 142, 149, 156–60, 162, 176, 179, 186–88, 190, 194, 221, 228, 239–40, 242, 247–49, 253, 264, 210, 274, 276–79, 283–86; direct style games, 26, 28, 53; doubles, 26, 32–33, 66, 69, 82, 84, 86–88, 92, 95–98, 127–28, 130, 136, 223, 269; history of, 10, 52–53, 60, 99, 159, 215, 228; hunting metaphor of, 7, 150, 154–55, 204; imaginary of, 11, 13, 17–18, 34, 37, 39, 47, 55, 61, 69, 73, 101, 215, 259, 266–67, 273; indirect style games, *see blé*; long style games, 53–54, 59;

masculinity of, 80, 171, 220; outside the Basque Country, 27–31, 53, 57, 60, 65–68, 104, 224; professional, 9–11, 13, 16, 18, 27, 32–33, 64–66, 68–69, 80–82, 88–89, 103, 105–6, 123, 128, 134, 137, 156, 174, 194, 215, 291–92, 294, 296, 298; rankings in, 131, 139; rhythm of, *see* rhythm; ritual of, 7–8, 14, 18–20, 34, 36, 38, 73–78, 80–81, 113, 122, 125, 128, 133–34, 138, 141, 146, 160–66, 174–77, 180–82, 187–90, 196, 198–99, 201–5, 212, 217–18, 221, 232, 236, 241–42, 261–63, 265, 268–73, 275–78; rural character of, 34; short style games, 56; singles, 12, 26, 32, 66, 69, 95–98, 296; socialization in, *see* fonton, socialization; symbolic nature of, *see* ritual, *see* symbolic nature of hand; television and, 9, 12, 31, 69, 93, 122, 128–29, 134, 136–37, 141, 156, 194, 248, 275; women and, 18, 37, 46–47, 80, 215–17, 262, 274, 276

pelota (ball): materials used in making, 227–29, 231–32; selection of, 227, 234; types of, 228–29, 234

pelotaris (pelota players): backcourt, 83, 84, 86, 89, 90, 96–98, 101, 103, 128, 147, 164, 222, 234–35; character, 20, 234, 23–239, 242, 246, 250, 264, 273; clothing of, 12, 49, 134–35; consecration of, 119–21, 123–25, 160–61; coronation of, 159–60; families of, 62–63, 84, 86–88, 95, 102, 108, 134, 160, 171n9; "foxes," 95, 98–99, 151, 222, 234, 257, 260–61, 276; frontcourt, 54–55,

83–84, 90, 96–98, 101, 103, 123, 128, 147; "lions," 95, 98, 151, 234, 257; personalities of, 20, 74, 101, 230, 232–33, 236, 243–44, 258, 261, 263; strategies of, 110, 132, 136, 146, 149–51, 174, 231, 246, 263
pelotazales (pelota fans): imaginary, 259; impartiality of, 117–18, 248, 254, 270, 284, 286; role in games, 11, 103, 115–16, 121–25, 128, 147, 159–60, 248, 253. *See also* bettors
Peña y Goñi, Antonio, 114, 250
Perkain (Juan Martin Inda), 60–62, 216, 259
performance, 16, 50, 116, 118–20, 123–24, 137, 187–89, 199, 205, 272
Perrault, Charles, 120
Piaget, Jean, 244
pido (request for a fault), 152, 297
pie quieto (heavy-footed), 116
pilotari zintzoa (noble pelotari), 257. *See also* Ithurria, Victor; pelotari
play, 49–62, 69, 80, 88. *See also jolas, joko*
plaza (square), 16, 297; as communal space, 32, 49–50, 62, 189, 215; as embodiment of society, 20, 199, 243–79; as physical representation of community, 50, 187, 192, 199, 201; as ritual symbol, 17, 143, 171, 191; as synonym for fronton, 58–60; as venue for playing pelota, 18, 27, 50, 80, 88, 174, 220, 296; in history of pelota, 62, 65. *See also* agora
plaza-gizon (public man), 121–22, 255–56, 258–61, 265
play: "deep play," 7, 10
positive cults, 183, 203

potro (ball's bounce or vigor), 138–39, 142, 229, 234, 297. *See also* pelota (ball)
proto-agonism, 100
Pujol, Jordi, 122
pueblo ("village," "people"), 39, 75, 182, 304, 310, 315
punta-volea (pelota modality), 223–24, 292
puntista (jai alai player), 224
punto (odds-giver), 82, 93, 109-11, 115, 250–51, 291–92, 298

quinzes(fifteens), 56

Raimon, 122
raya (line), 54, 252, 268, 298
rebote (rebound wall of a pelota court), 16, 53–56, 105, 163, 189–90, 194, 224, 245, 248, 268, 291, 293–94. *See also* fronton
rebound (a play in pelota), 16, 28–32, 34n10, 69, 96, 186, 231, 240, 293
"redressive action," 17, 74, 76–77, 197, 201
referee: and rules, 245–46, 255; as representation of elements of the game, 27, 145–46; authority of, 161, 222, 227, 252–53, 262, 264, 284; changing role of, 284–87; conduct of, 90–91, 129, 137, 140n25, 142–44, 148; female, 80; relationship to ball, 228, 231, 242; relationship to crowd, 13, 114, 117–19, 199, 248, 253, 264, 282; space of, 30, 32
remonte (pelota modality), 10, 12, 27, 29–30, 33n9, 66, 68, 94, 105, 127, 163, 217, 231, 291, 298–99

remonte (long wicker basket used to play pelota), 27, 30, 32, 58, 163 294
representation, 16, 34, 37, 42, 46, 53, 61, 78, 81, 100, 125, 146, 161, 164, 197–99, 201–3, 213, 264–65, 268–69, 271–72, 286
Retegi I, Juan Ignacio, 82–84, 86–88, 90–91, 98, 142, 151
Retegi II, Julián, 10, 81–82, 85–95, 97–98, 121, 132, 157, 225, 235–36, 242, 260, 262, 289n8
Retegi IV, José María, 87
rhythm, 45, 162–66, 172–74, 203, 251, 278, 283
ritual, 7, 8,8 14, 16–20, 34, 36, 38–39, 44–46, 48, 62, 73–78, 80–81, 113, 122, 125, 128, 133–34, 138, 141, 146, 160–66, 174–77, 180–82, 187–90, 196, 198–99, 201–5, 212, 217–18, 221, 232, 236, 241–42, 261–63, 265, 268–73, 275–78
rivalry, 18, 75, 88, 95, 99–101, 108–9, 124, 125, 157, 172, 198–99, 270
Ruiz, Maite, 215
Ruiz, Patxi, 119, 147, 288, 289
rural sports, 49

sabelgorriak (red bellies), 75
sabeltxuriak (white bellies), 75
sacrifice, 18, 47, 62, 76, 81, 87, 91, 95, 120–21, 127, 150, 156–58, 161–62, 187, 196, 203, 268, 282
Salaberri, Yves. *See* Xala
Salaverría, José María, 95, 257
Salsamendi III, Jose María, 231
San Martín, Abe. *See* Barberito I
San Martín, Alejandro, 63
saque y remate (serve and return), 153
Saralegi (Miguel Goldarazena), 68

Sarasqueta, Indalecio (Chiquito de Eibar), 99
Schutz, Alfred, 230, 236, 244
semifinals, 91, 128, 147, 288
Serres, Michel, 215, 266
Simmel, Georg, 187, 267, 269
Sir Egge, 180
soccer, 11, 161, 187, 281
socialization, 20, 48, 190, 263
Sorhainde, Jean-Pierre. *See* Arantza
sotamano (to hit the ball from below), 174, 254, 299
Spain, 56, 107, 193, 294
Spanish Civil War, 43n19, 194
Spanish Federation, 12, 105
sports: betting on, 129, 131; conflict and, 49, 75–76, 269; equality in, 12, 125, 127, 229
Subirats, Eduard, 180, 200–1
symbolism, 143, 195

tacos (small protective pads), 130, 135, 140, 299
tantear/tanteo ("sizing up"), 151, 154, 161, 299
Tapia I, Fernando, 87
Tapia II, Juan Ramón, 87
television, 9, 12, 31, 69, 93, 122, 128–29, 134, 136–37, 141, 156, 194, 248, 275. *See also* ETB
tener mano izquierda ("to have left hand"), 219
tennis, 30n8, 53n7, 55–56, 110, 134, 228, 283
tension, 19, 49, 62, 73, 77, 112–13, 131, 143–146, 149, 150, 153, 156, 158–59, 163–64, 173–79, 181, 183, 202, 247, 252, 260, 275
tercer cojón ("third ball"), 171
Tierno Galván, Enrique, 16, 225, 268
Titín III (Augusto Ibáñez Sacristán), 10, 12, 93, 102, 119, 235

Tolosa, Joxean, 11, 31, 33, 85, 89, 91–92, 131, 246
tomar postura (take a posture), 125
tongo (the game having been fixed), 249
Trías, Eugenio, 271
trinquet (a space closed at four sides), 11, 27, 34, 56–58, 66, 189, 215, 294, 297, 299–300
Turner, Victor, 76, 133, 146, 182, 201, 104, 212, 236, 238, 269, 272
time, 15, 19, 20, 26, 33, 52–53, 58, 61, 73, 74–75, 94, 108, 119, 128, 154, 162–66, 172, 180, 182, 185, 190, 291
tragedy, 175, 197–98
trinquet (closed pelota court), 27, 34n10, 56–58, 66, 189, 215, 294, 297, 299–300
txalos (applause), 281
txapela ("beret," maximum trophy a pelotari may aspire for), 84–86, 89, 91, 92, 119, 131, 135, 137, 158–61, 230, 289, 299
txik-txak (jai alai move), 29, 299
txoko (corner), 18, 48, 93, 154, 155, 174, 300
txula (jai alai move), 29, 299, 300

Unamuno, Miguel de, 99, 107–8, 112, 116, 164, 182, 197, 206, 213, 215n7, 228, 261, 266, 274
Unanue, Mikel, 119, 155, 216–17
Uribarri, Ignacio, 9
Urrestarazu, Polonio, 123
Urtasun, 281
United States, 7, 11, 49, 65, 68, 76, 224

van Gennep, Arnold, 182
Vega, Roberto, 99–100, 118
Verjat, 196
Virgin of Begoña, 161
villas (boroughs or towns with foundational characters), 39, 52–53, 73, 198, 268
violence: control of, 74, 76–77, 200, 268; ritual and, 76, 78; sacred, 79–80
void, the, 7–8, 121, 133, 172, 188, 202, 204–6, 277–78

war, 43, 74, 76–77, 79, 124, 158, 193–94, 197, 256, 267–68
Welles, Orson, 7, 67

Xala (Yves Salaberri), 85, 288n7
xare (pelota modality), 27, 58, 246, 291, 294, 299–300
xare kiski (or potro, the center of the pelota), 138, 139, 142, 229, 234, 295, 297
xistera (wicker instrument used to play pelota), 27, 33, 54, 58, 65, 105, 121, 163, 217, 223–24, 293–95, 298–300

Zabaleta, Pedro. *See* Paysandú
Zambrano, María, 203
Zarathustra, 172, 174, 180, 185, 211, 241
zimitorio ("place of burial"), 59, 199
zintzoa (being loyal to oath, law, and common norms), 257, 266
Zulaika, Joseba, 3, 8, 14, 38, 47, 80, 169, 170n5, 173, 175, 180, 204, 221, 260, 275–76

Made in the USA
Charleston, SC
30 January 2013